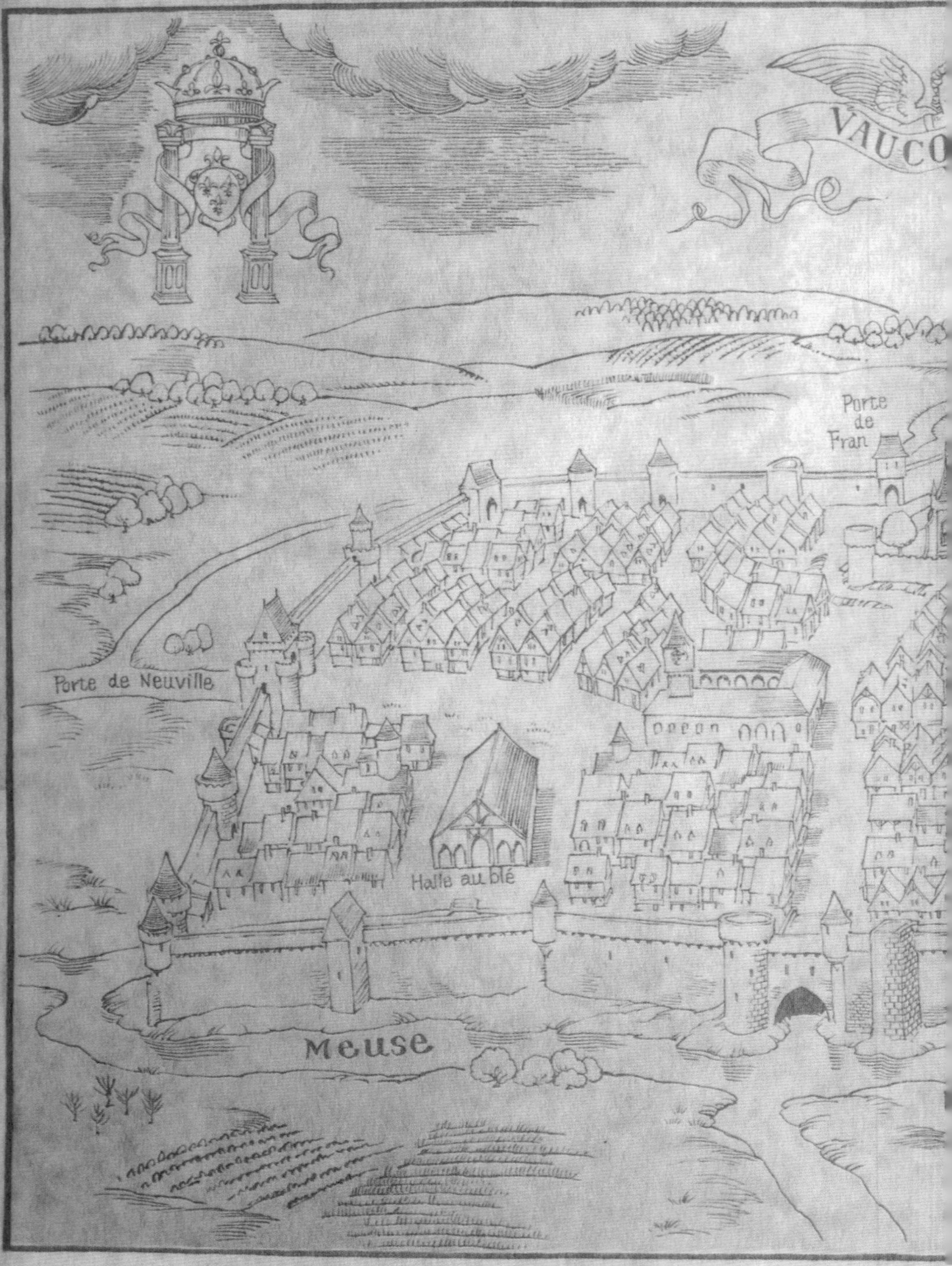

VAUCO
Porte de Fran
Porte de Neuville
Halle au blé
Meuse

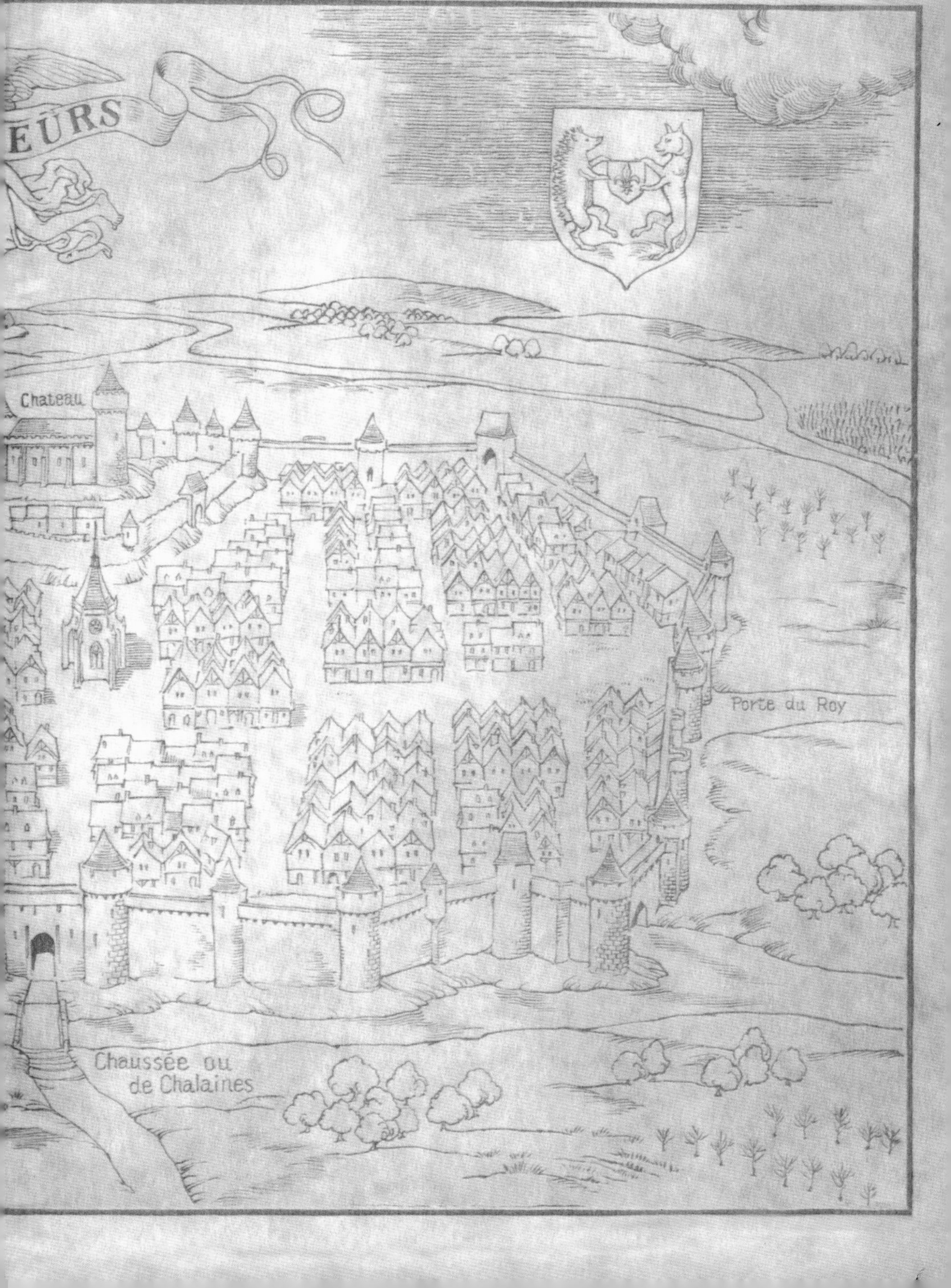
EURS
Chateau
Porte du Roy
Chaussée ou
de Chalaines

Translators
Reiko Terui
Kate Bundy

Editor
Darren W. Jenkins

Production Artists
Anthony Shumskas
Yuki Chung
Atsuko Hattori

US Cover Design
Yuki Chung

Lettering Fonts
Comicraft
Comicbookfonts.com

President
Robin Kuo

Jeanne I by Yoshikazu Yasuhiko
© 1995 Yoshikazu Yasuhiko
Originally published in Japan in October 15, 1995
by Japan Broadcasting Co., Ltd.
English translation rights arranged through
Japan Broadcasting Co., Ltd.

Joan I
English translation © 2000
ComicsOne, Corp.
All rights reserved.

Publisher
ComicsOne Corporation
47257 Fremont Blvd.
Fremont, CA 94538
www.ComicsOne.com

First Edition: August 2001
ISBN 1-58899-090-7

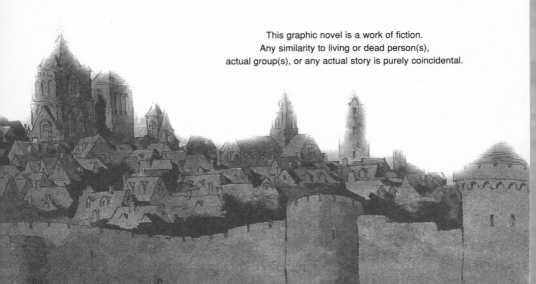

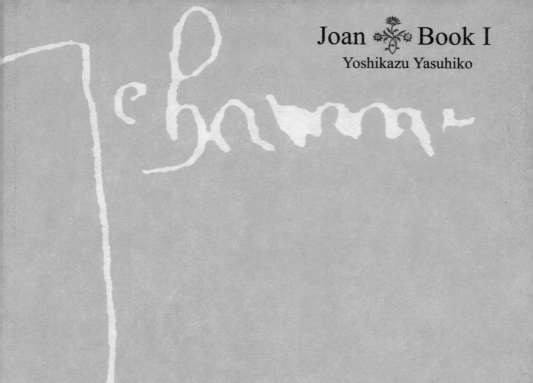

# Joan ❀ Book I

### Yoshikazu Yasuhiko

# Joan - Book 1

# PROLOGUE

# Joan - Book I

Yoshikazu Yasuhiko

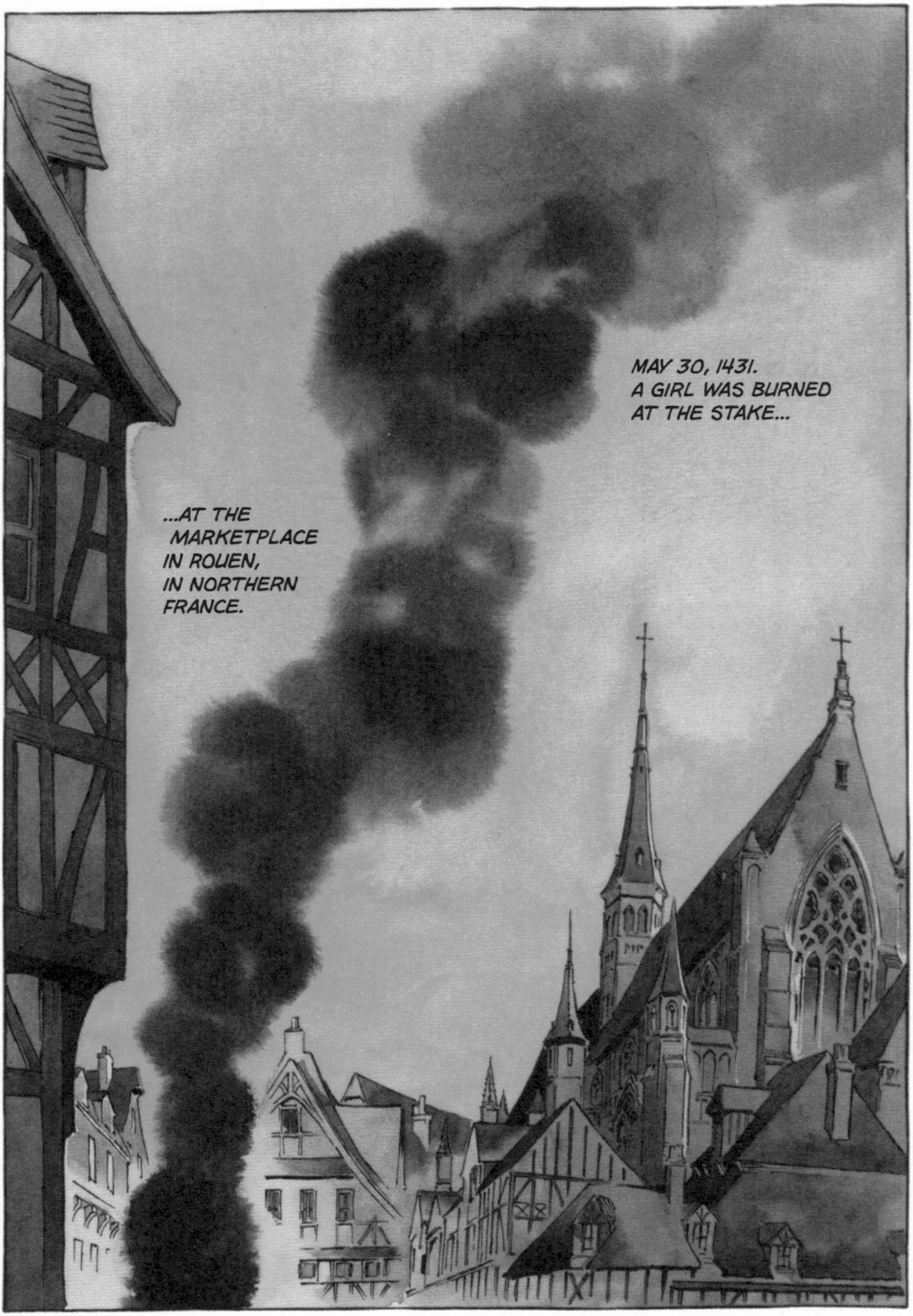
MAY 30, 1431.
A GIRL WAS BURNED
AT THE STAKE...
...AT THE
MARKETPLACE
IN ROUEN,
IN NORTHERN
FRANCE.

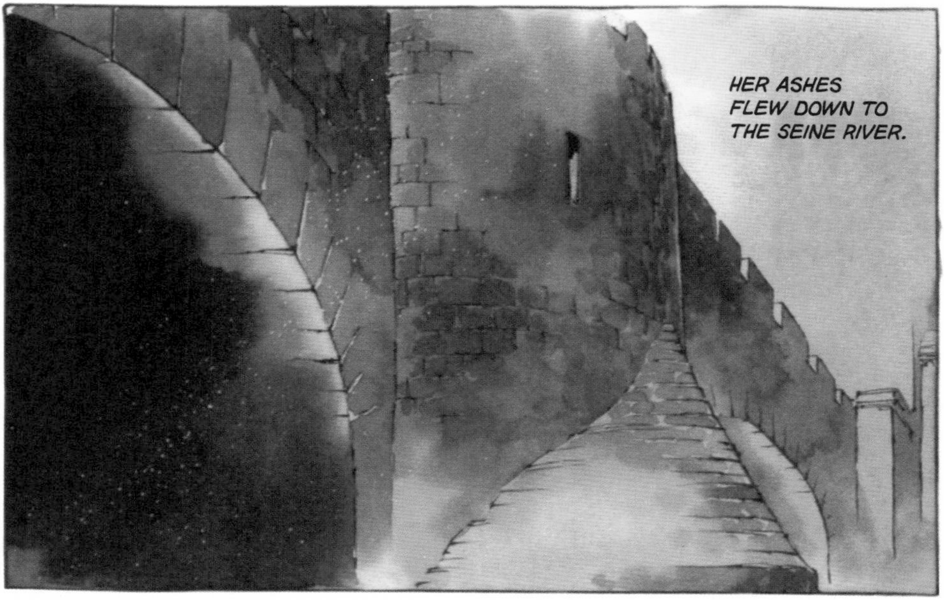
HER ASHES FLEW DOWN TO THE SEINE RIVER.

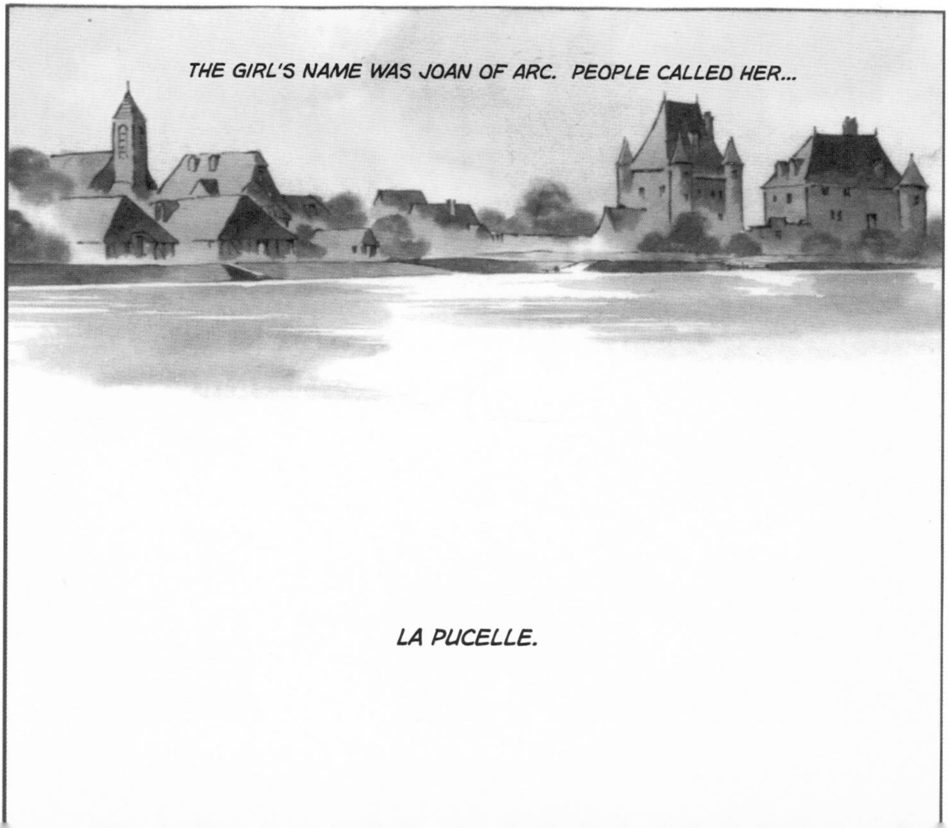
THE GIRL'S NAME WAS JOAN OF ARC. PEOPLE CALLED HER...
LA PUCELLE.

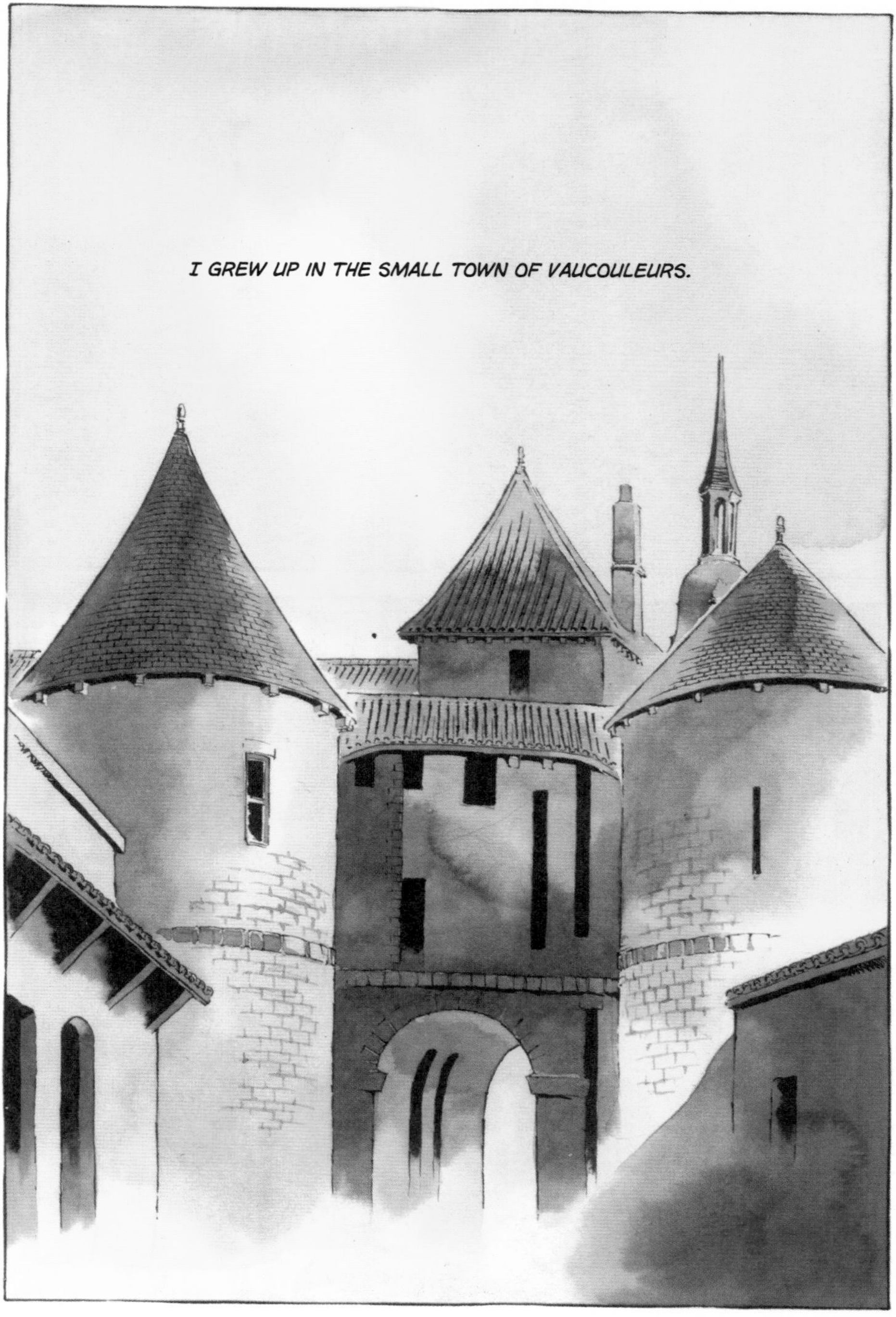
I GREW UP IN THE SMALL TOWN OF VAUCOULEURS.

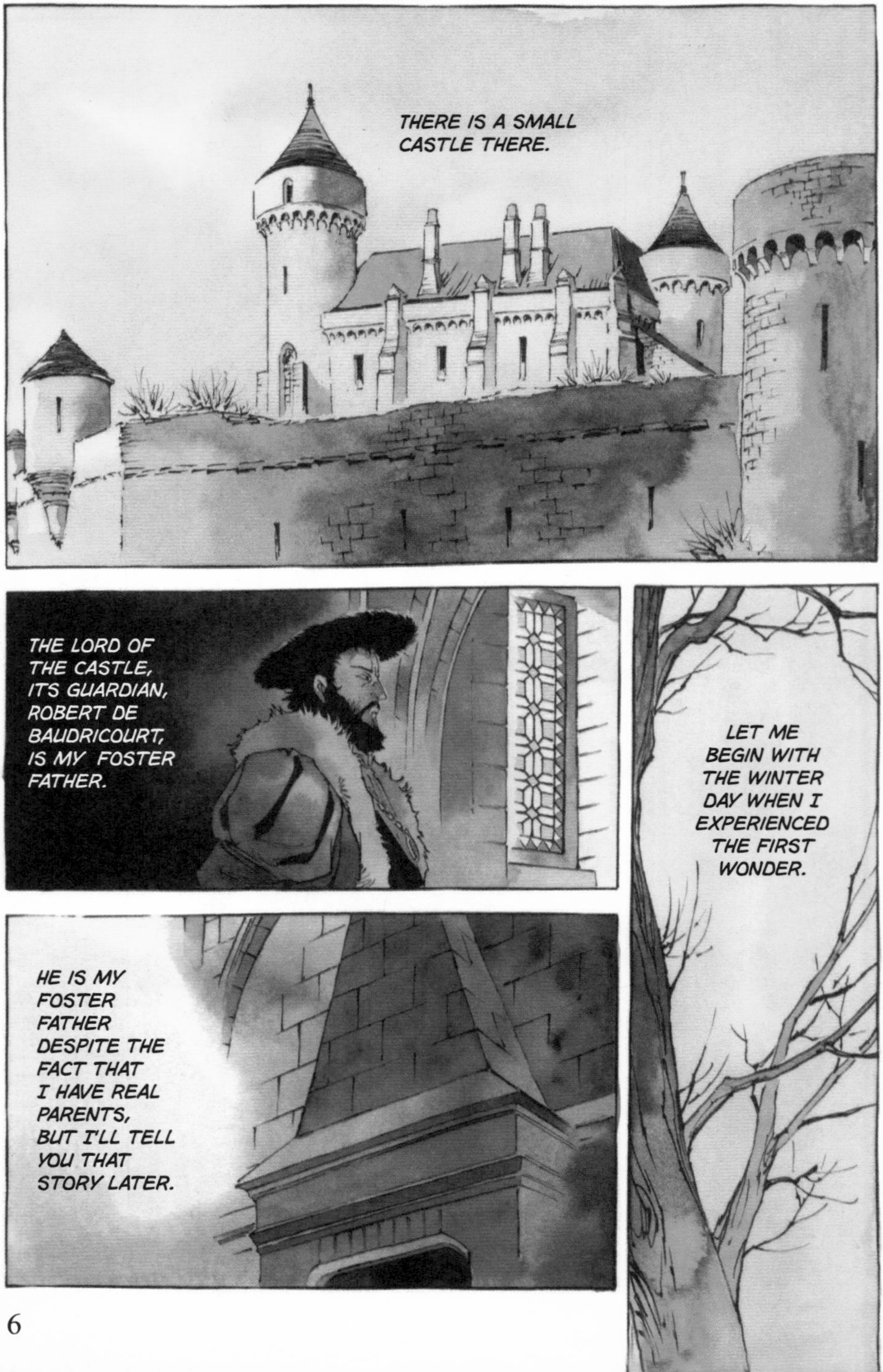
THERE IS A SMALL CASTLE THERE.
THE LORD OF THE CASTLE, ITS GUARDIAN, ROBERT DE BAUDRICOURT, IS MY FOSTER FATHER.
LET ME BEGIN WITH THE WINTER DAY WHEN I EXPERIENCED THE FIRST WONDER.
HE IS MY FOSTER FATHER DESPITE THE FACT THAT I HAVE REAL PARENTS, BUT I'LL TELL YOU THAT STORY LATER.

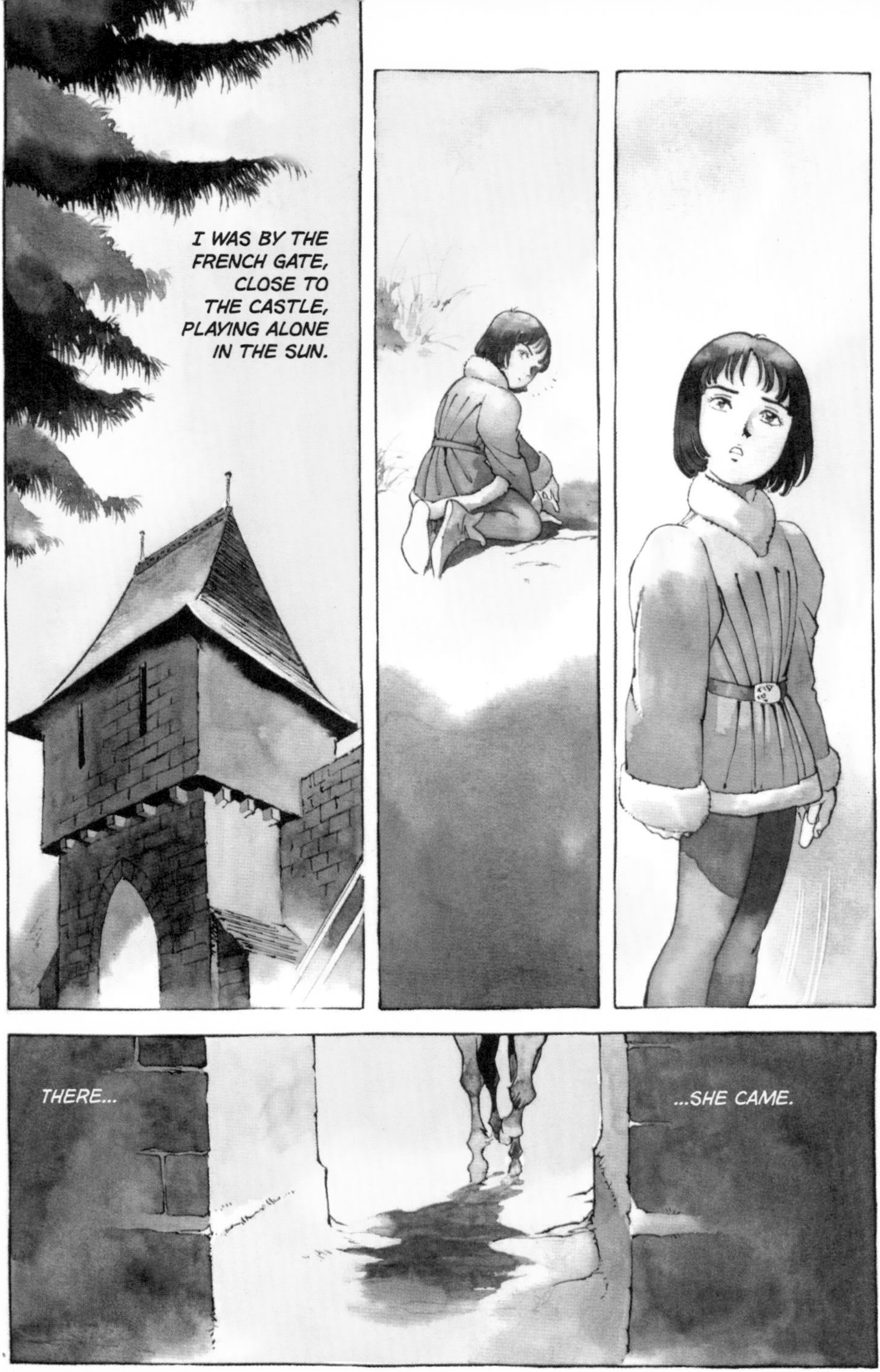
I WAS BY THE FRENCH GATE, CLOSE TO THE CASTLE, PLAYING ALONE IN THE SUN.
THERE...
...SHE CAME.

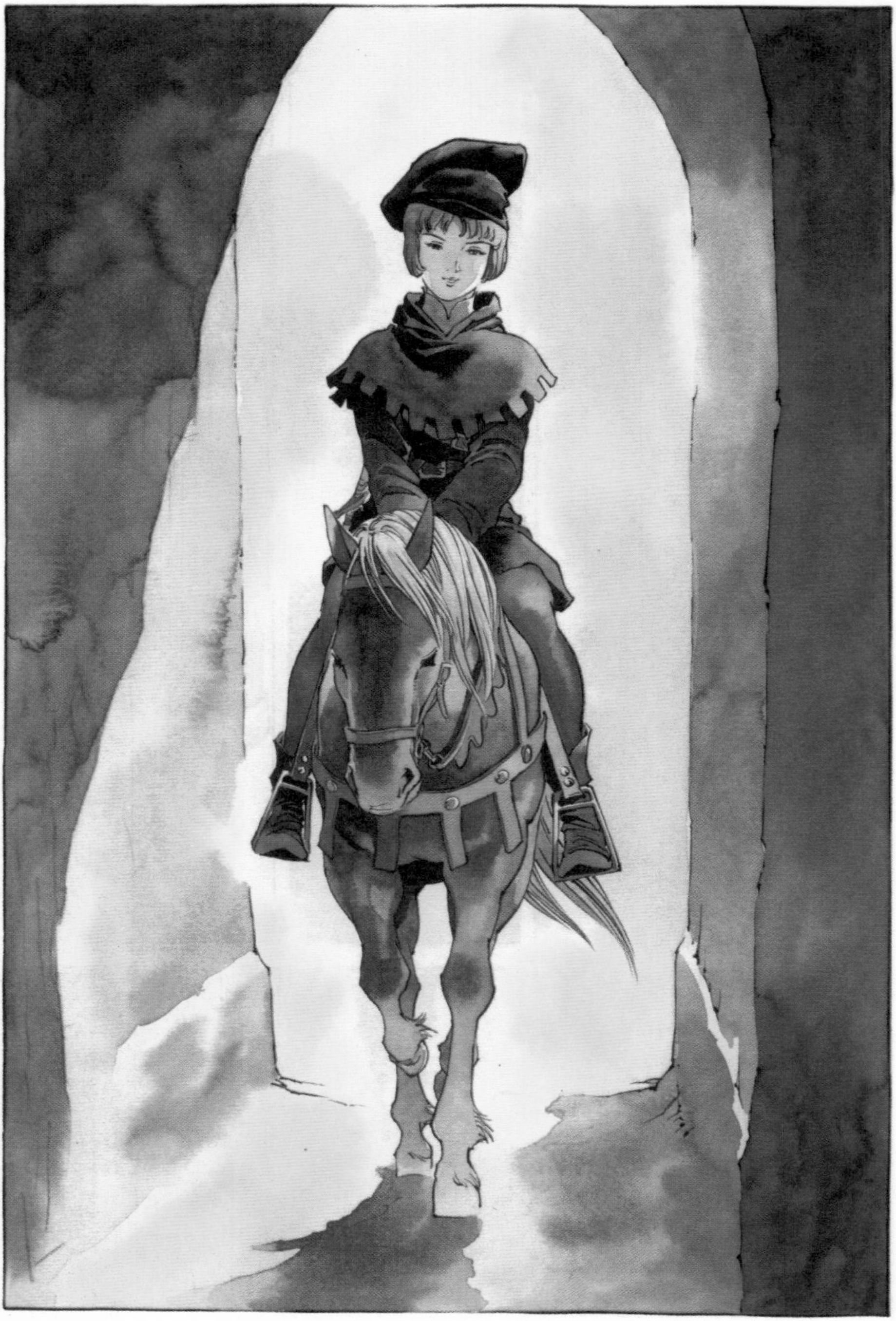

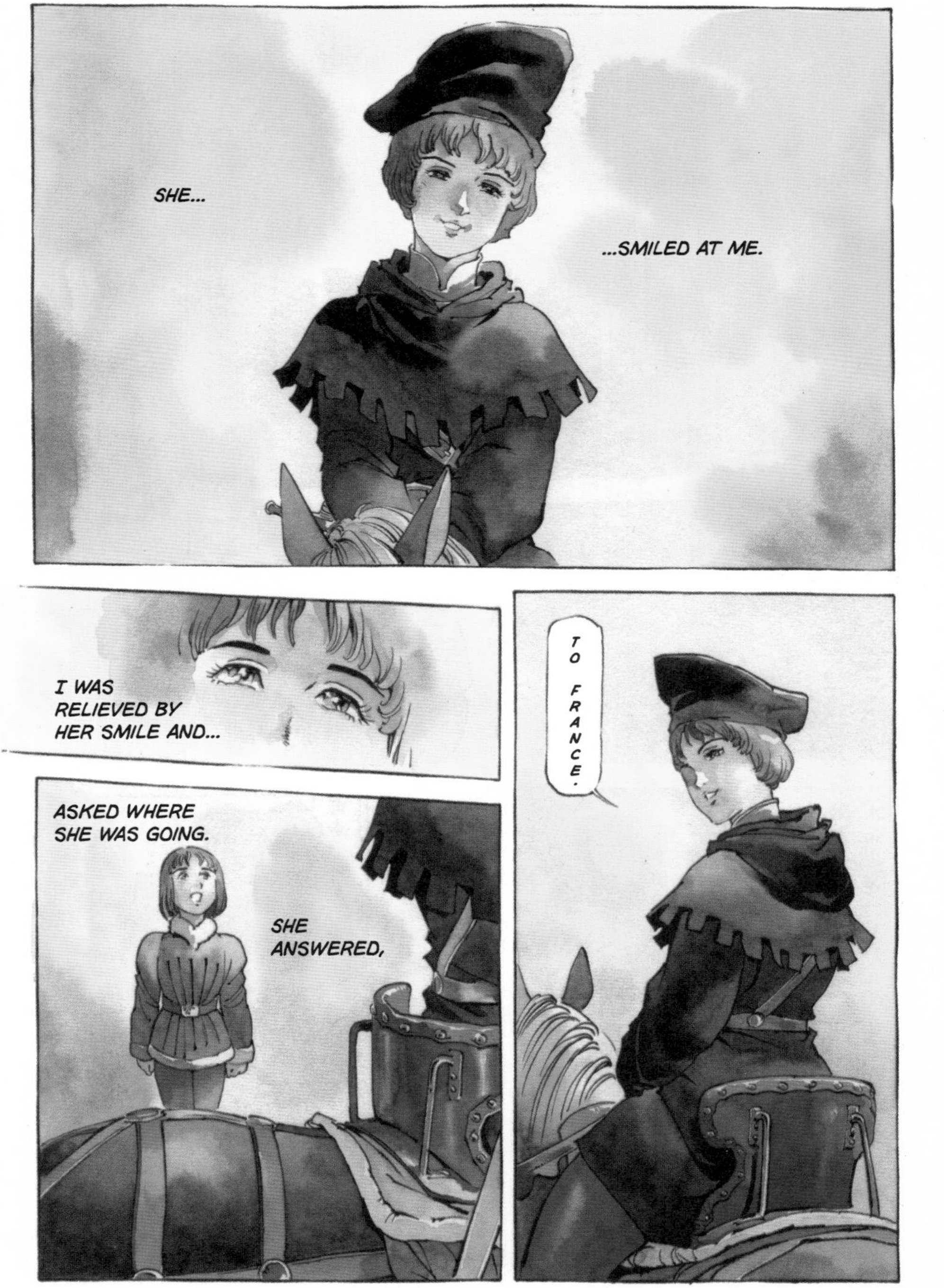
SHE...
...SMILED AT ME.
I WAS RELIEVED BY HER SMILE AND...
ASKED WHERE SHE WAS GOING.
SHE ANSWERED,
TO FRANCE.

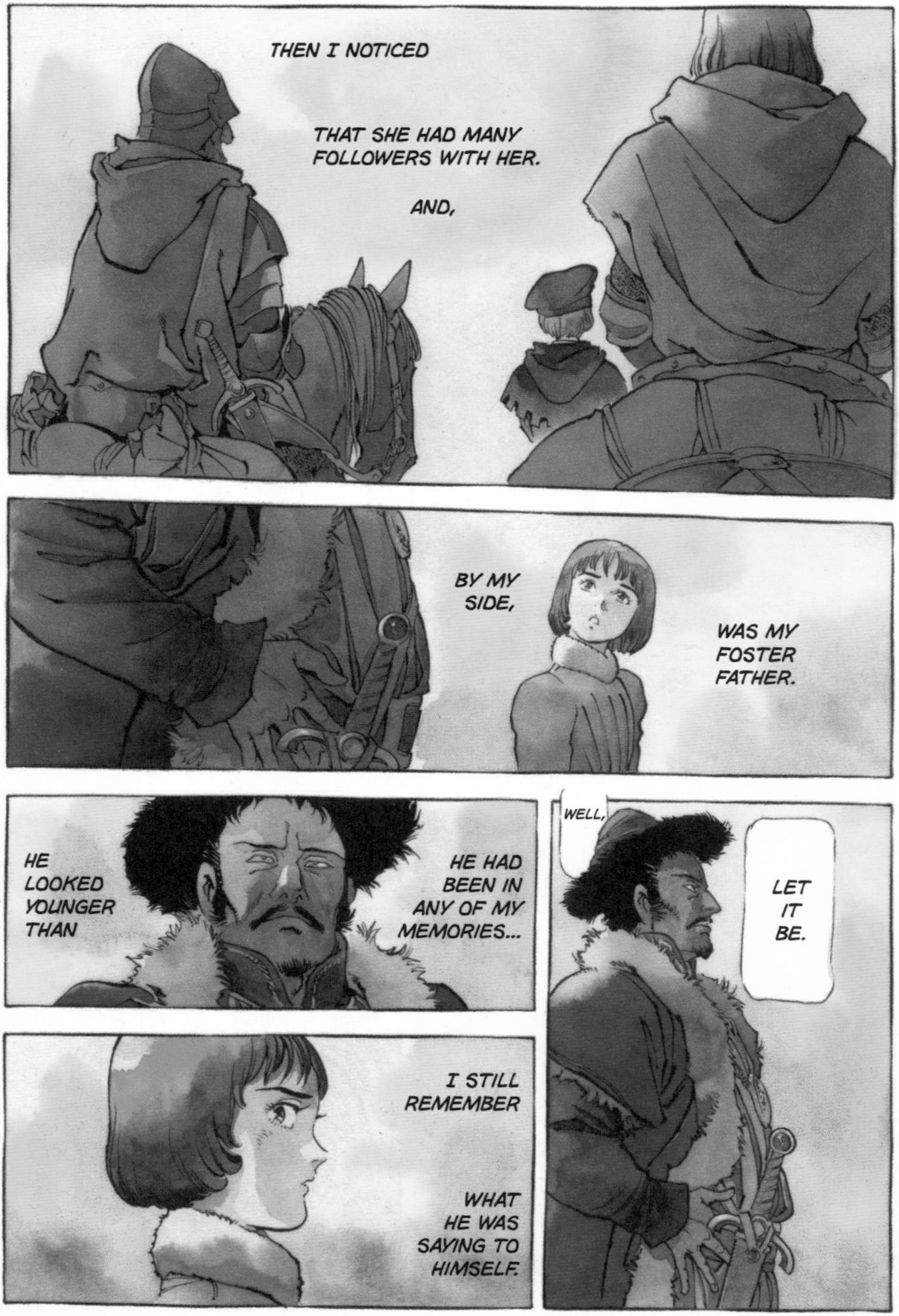
THEN I NOTICED
THAT SHE HAD MANY FOLLOWERS WITH HER.
AND,
BY MY SIDE,
WAS MY FOSTER FATHER.
HE LOOKED YOUNGER THAN
HE HAD BEEN IN ANY OF MY MEMORIES...
WELL,
LET IT BE.
I STILL REMEMBER
WHAT HE WAS SAYING TO HIMSELF.

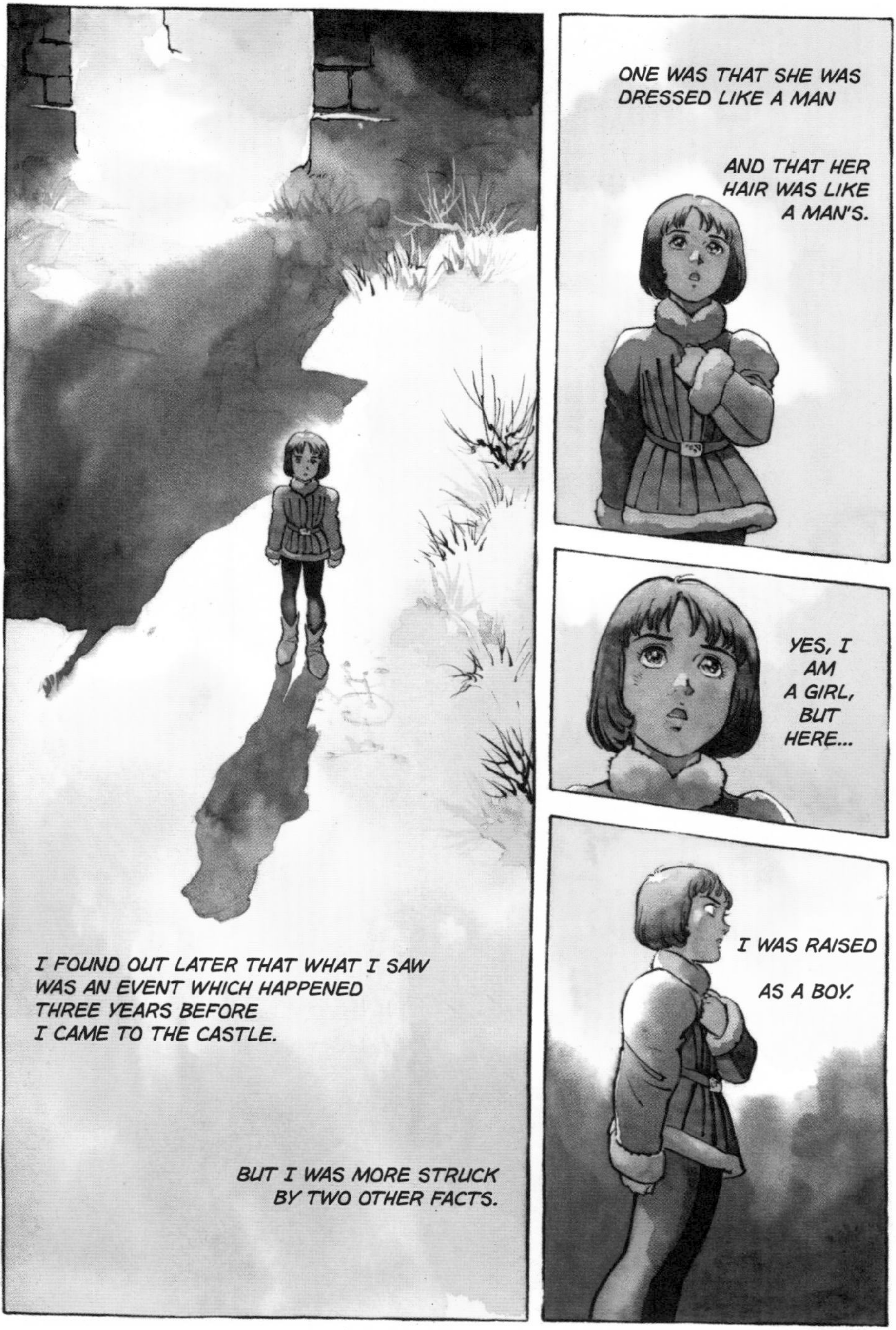
I FOUND OUT LATER THAT WHAT I SAW WAS AN EVENT WHICH HAPPENED THREE YEARS BEFORE I CAME TO THE CASTLE.
BUT I WAS MORE STRUCK BY TWO OTHER FACTS.
ONE WAS THAT SHE WAS DRESSED LIKE A MAN
AND THAT HER HAIR WAS LIKE A MAN'S.
YES, I AM A GIRL, BUT HERE...
I WAS RAISED
AS A BOY.

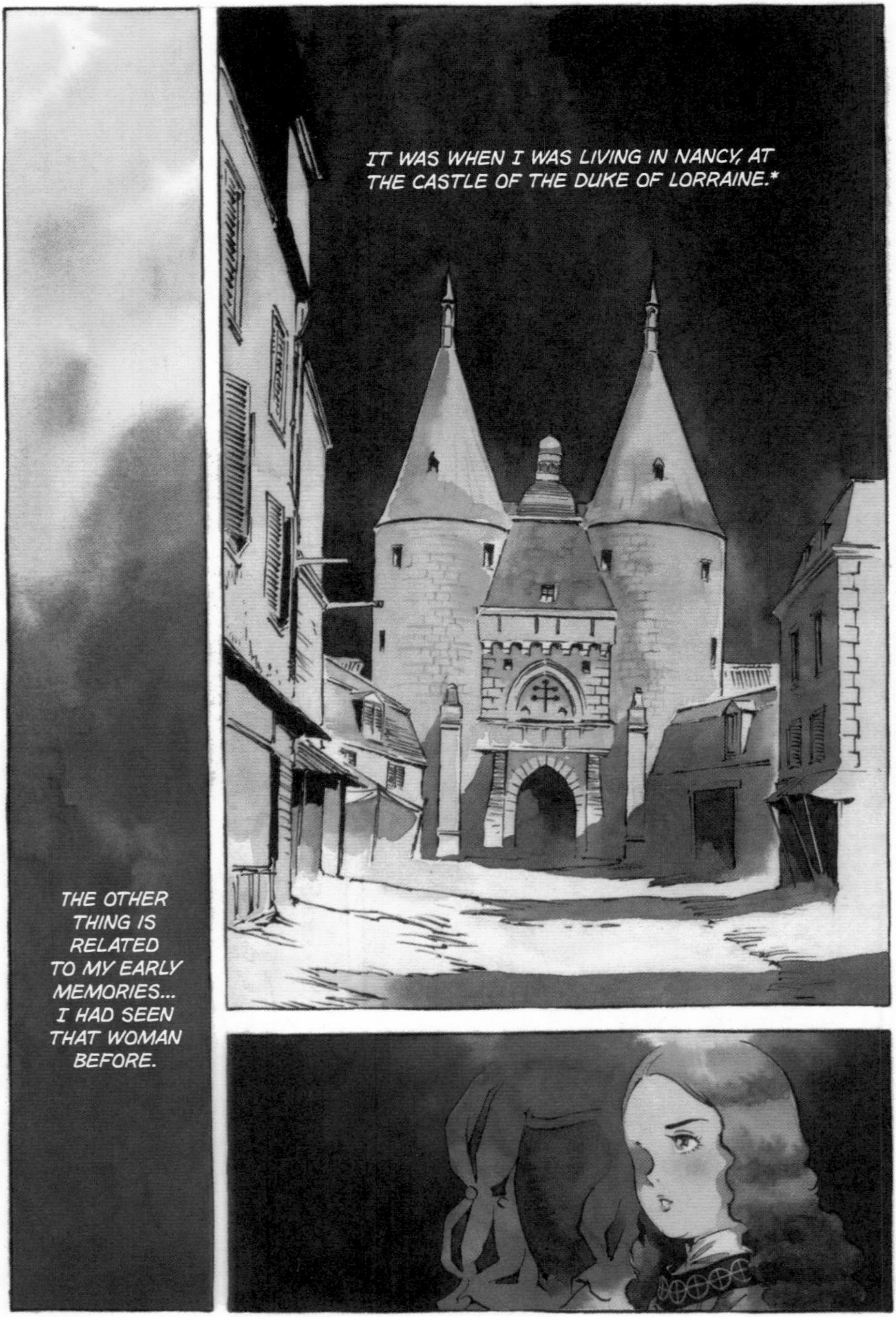
IT WAS WHEN I WAS LIVING IN NANCY, AT THE CASTLE OF THE DUKE OF LORRAINE.*
THE OTHER THING IS RELATED TO MY EARLY MEMORIES... I HAD SEEN THAT WOMAN BEFORE.

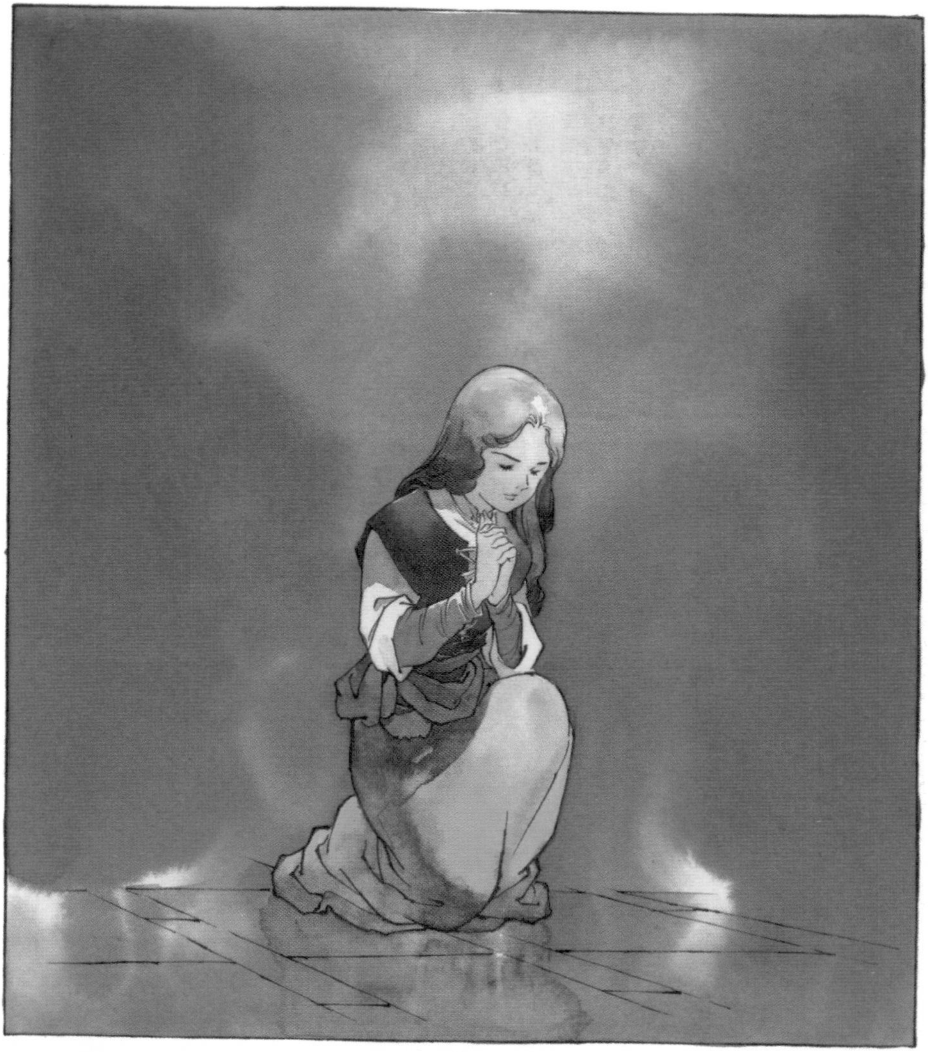

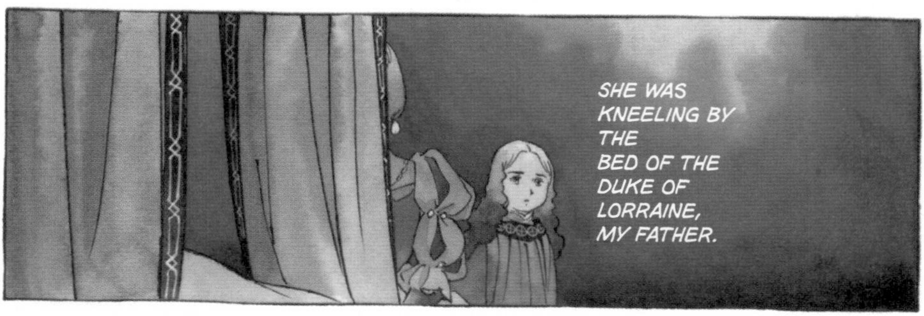
SHE WAS KNEELING BY THE BED OF THE DUKE OF LORRAINE, MY FATHER.

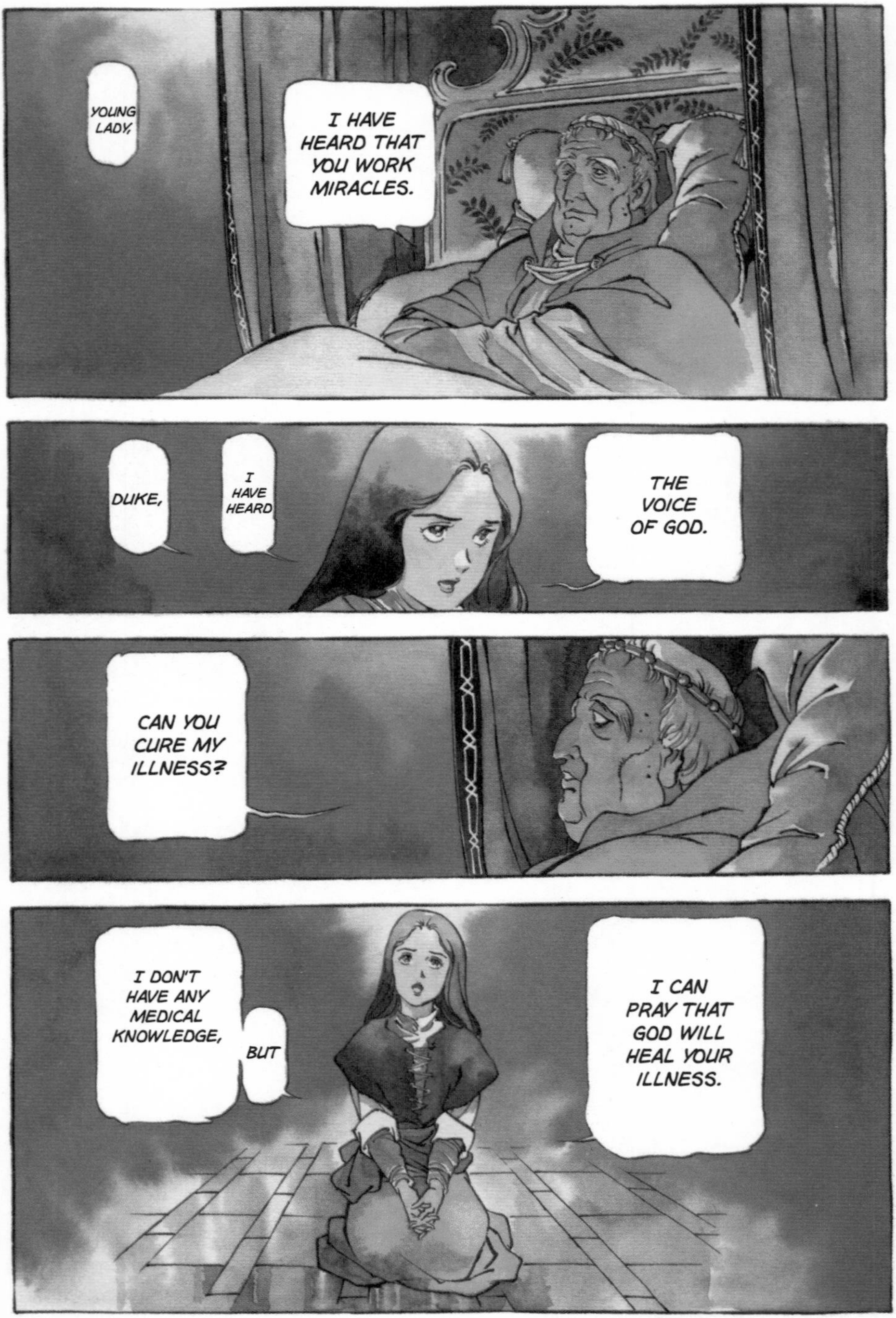
YOUNG LADY,
I HAVE HEARD THAT YOU WORK MIRACLES.
DUKE,
I HAVE HEARD
THE VOICE OF GOD.
CAN YOU CURE MY ILLNESS?
I DON'T HAVE ANY MEDICAL KNOWLEDGE,
BUT
I CAN PRAY THAT GOD WILL HEAL YOUR ILLNESS.

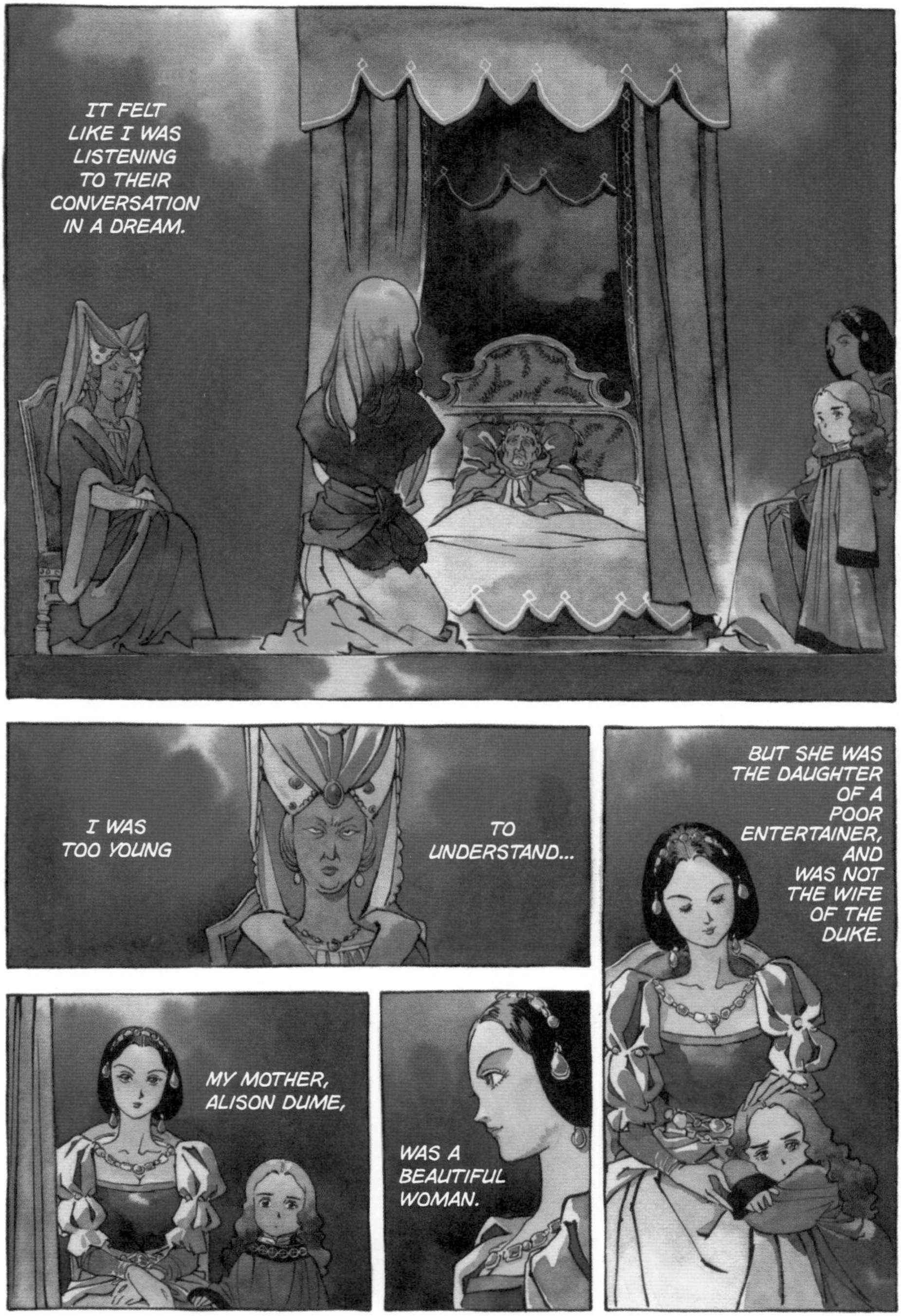
IT FELT LIKE I WAS LISTENING TO THEIR CONVERSATION IN A DREAM.
I WAS TOO YOUNG
TO UNDERSTAND...
MY MOTHER, ALISON DUME,
WAS A BEAUTIFUL WOMAN.
BUT SHE WAS THE DAUGHTER OF A POOR ENTERTAINER, AND WAS NOT THE WIFE OF THE DUKE.

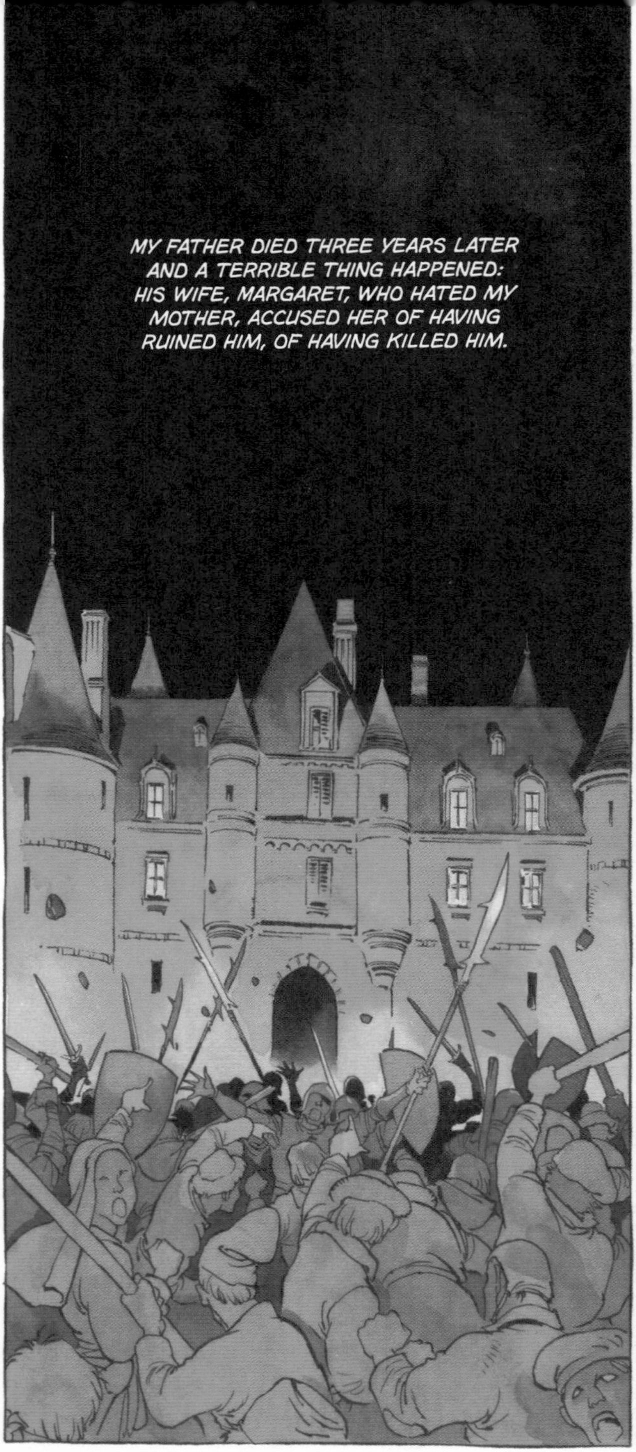
MY FATHER DIED THREE YEARS LATER AND A TERRIBLE THING HAPPENED: HIS WIFE, MARGARET, WHO HATED MY MOTHER, ACCUSED HER OF HAVING RUINED HIM, OF HAVING KILLED HIM.

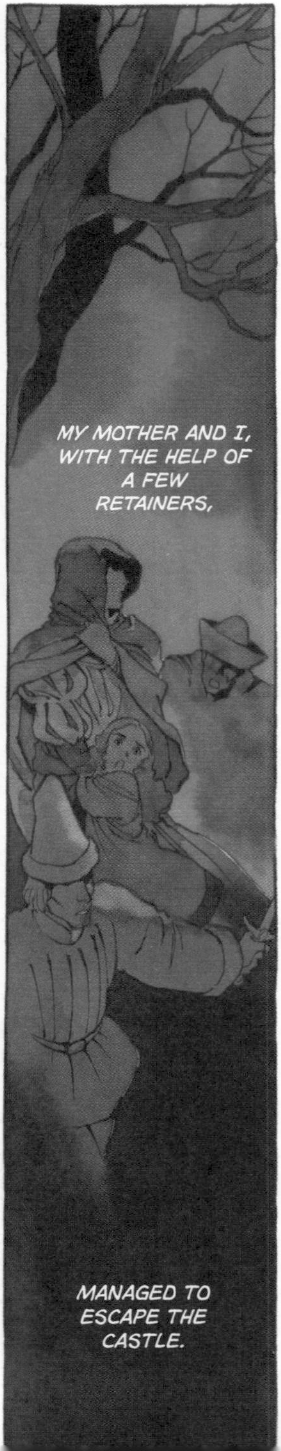
MY MOTHER AND I, WITH THE HELP OF A FEW RETAINERS,
MANAGED TO ESCAPE THE CASTLE.

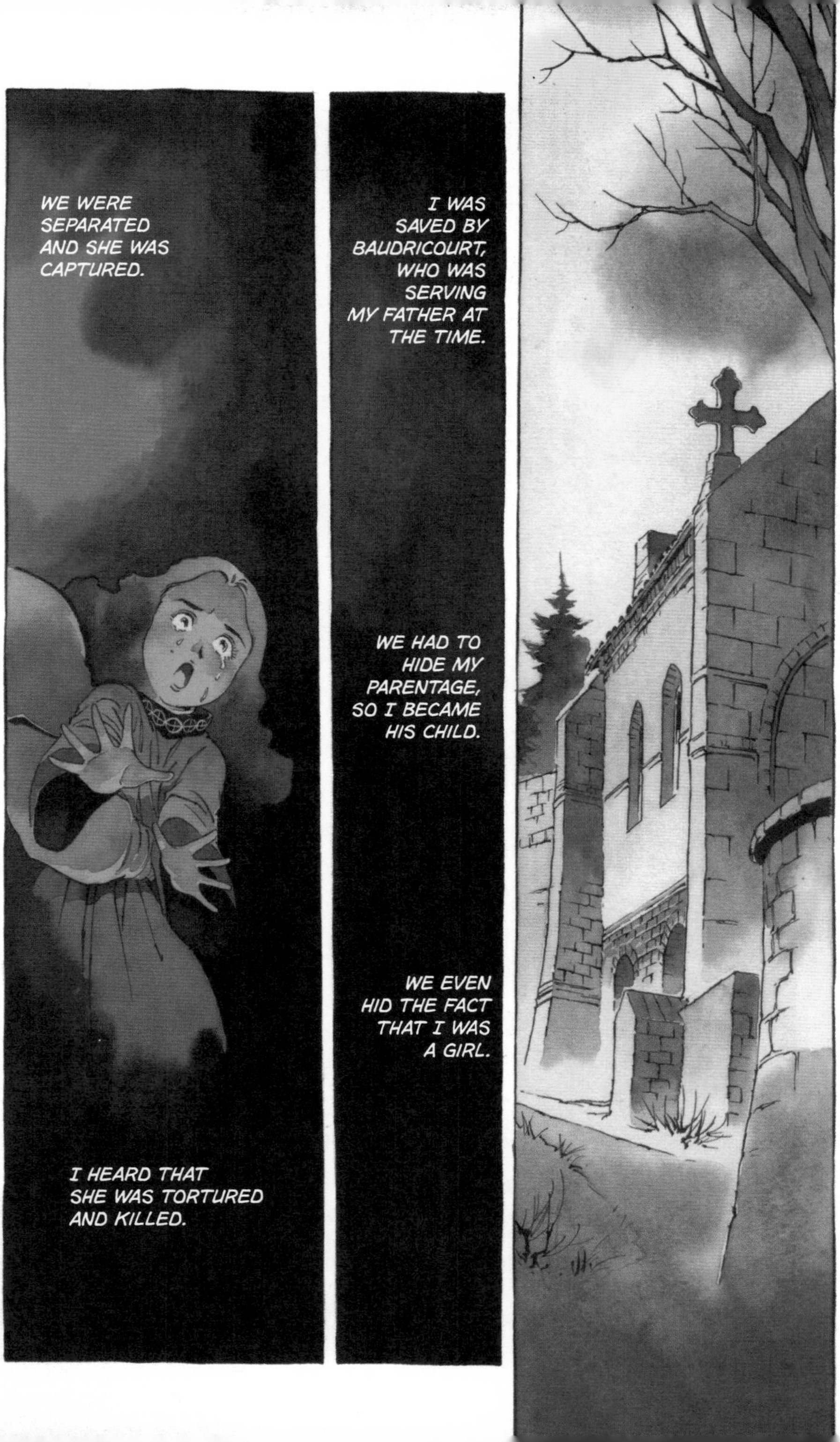
WE WERE SEPARATED AND SHE WAS CAPTURED.
I HEARD THAT SHE WAS TORTURED AND KILLED.
I WAS SAVED BY BAUDRICOURT, WHO WAS SERVING MY FATHER AT THE TIME.
WE HAD TO HIDE MY PARENTAGE, SO I BECAME HIS CHILD.
WE EVEN HID THE FACT THAT I WAS A GIRL.

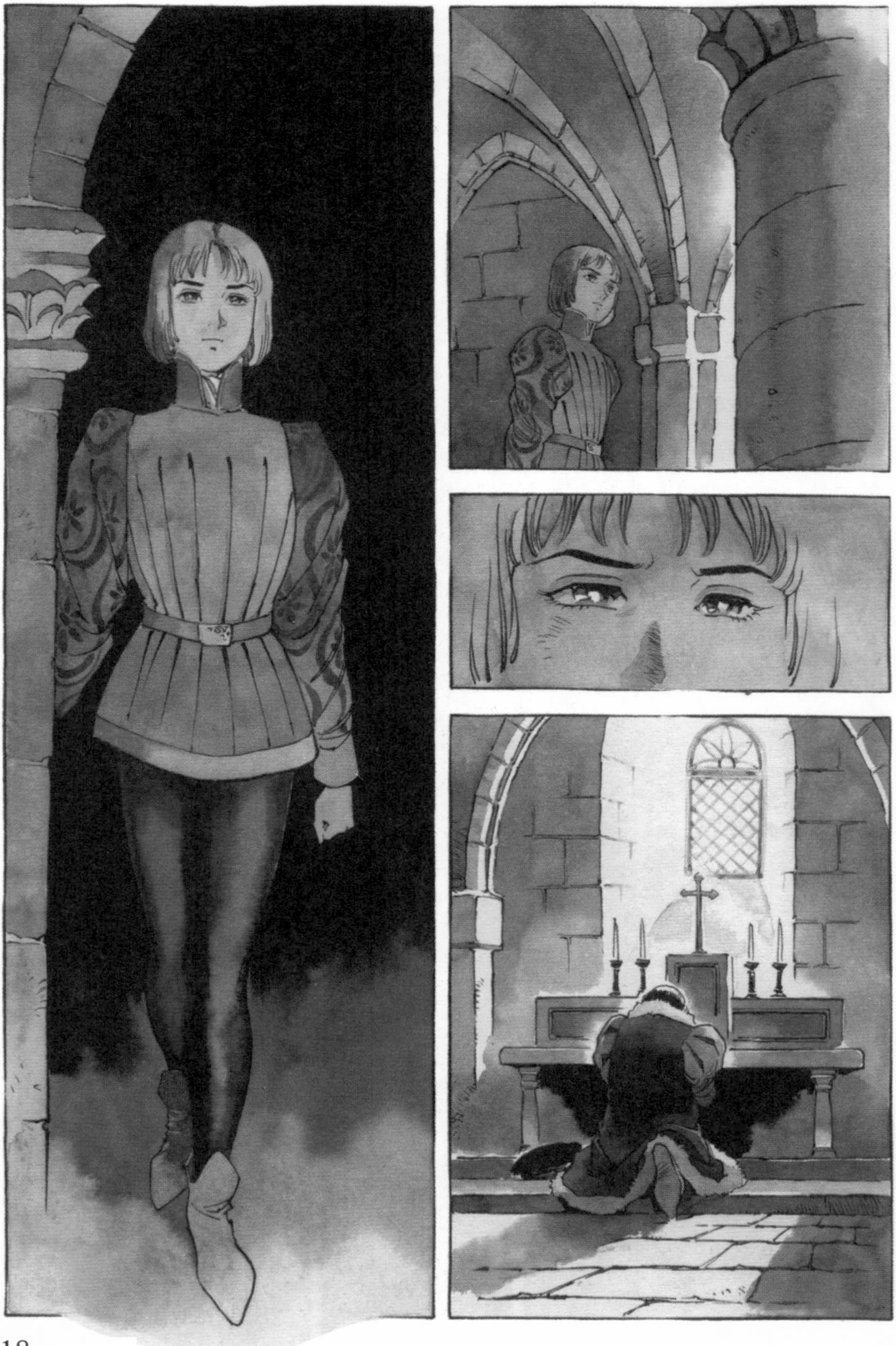

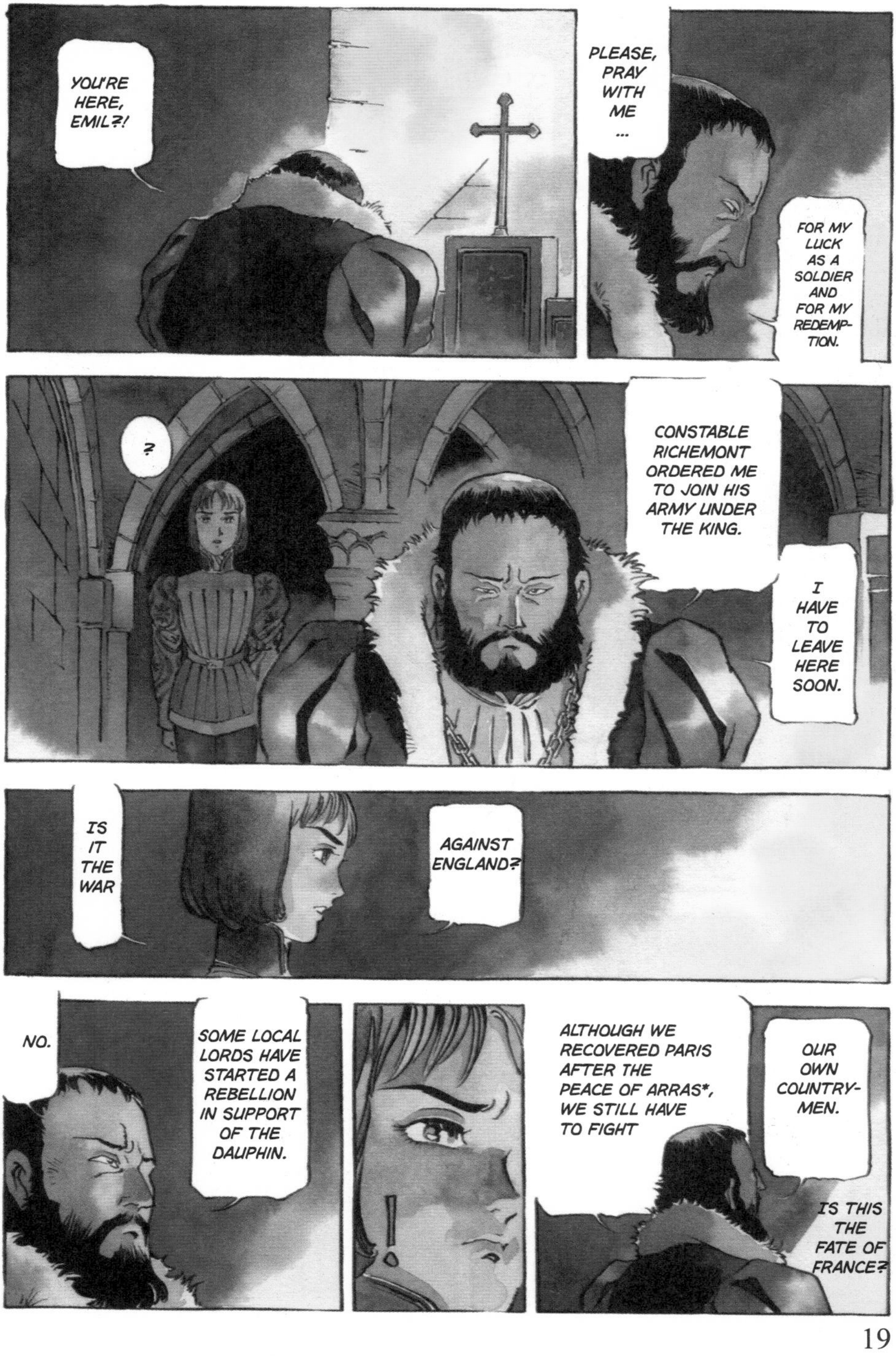
YOU'RE HERE, EMIL?!
PLEASE, PRAY WITH ME ...
FOR MY LUCK AS A SOLDIER AND FOR MY REDEMP-TION.
?
CONSTABLE RICHEMONT ORDERED ME TO JOIN HIS ARMY UNDER THE KING.
I HAVE TO LEAVE HERE SOON.
IS IT THE WAR
AGAINST ENGLAND?
NO.
SOME LOCAL LORDS HAVE STARTED A REBELLION IN SUPPORT OF THE DAUPHIN.
!
ALTHOUGH WE RECOVERED PARIS AFTER THE PEACE OF ARRAS*, WE STILL HAVE TO FIGHT
OUR OWN COUNTRY-MEN.
IS THIS THE FATE OF FRANCE?

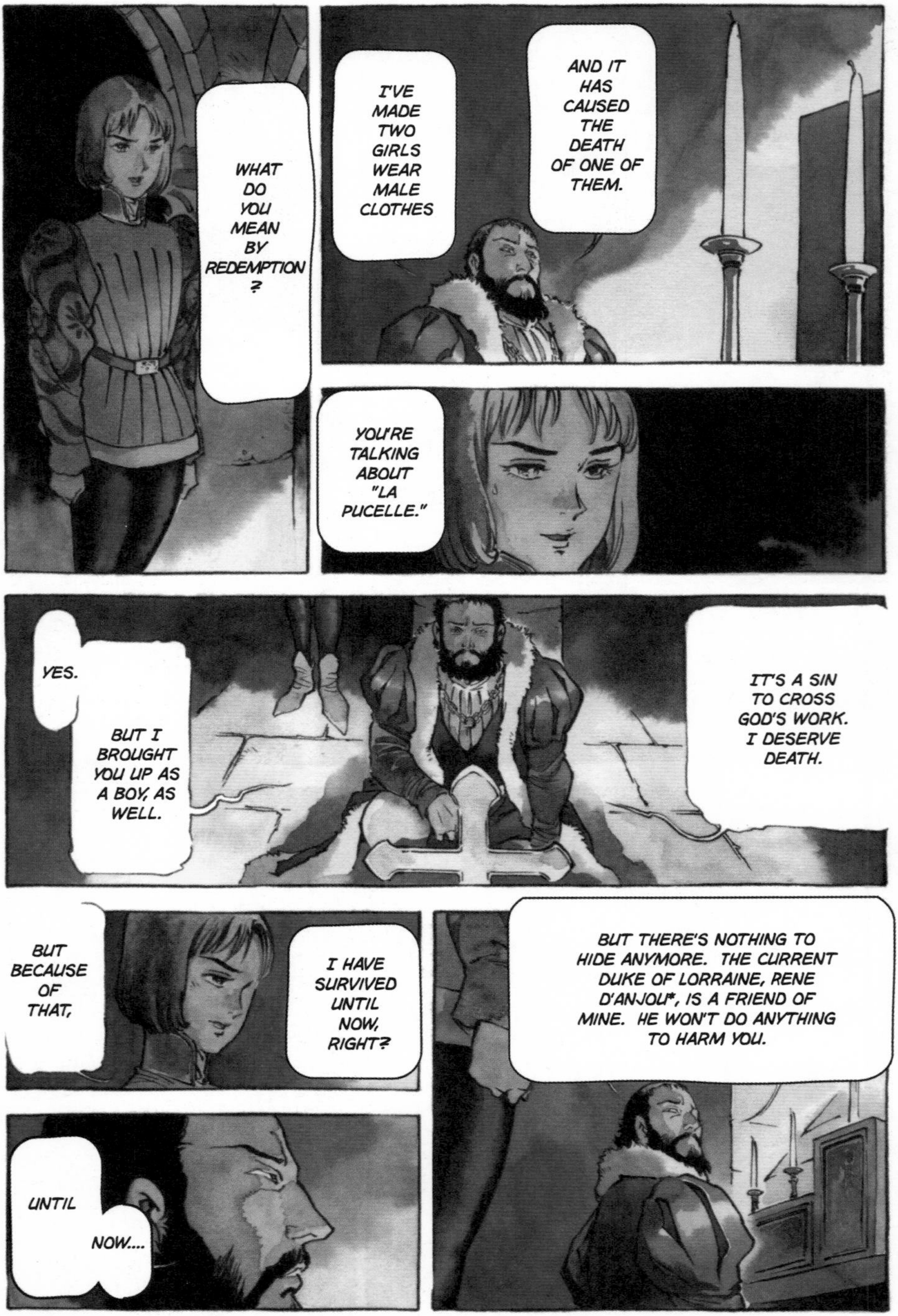

WHAT DO YOU MEAN BY REDEMPTION?
I'VE MADE TWO GIRLS WEAR MALE CLOTHES
AND IT HAS CAUSED THE DEATH OF ONE OF THEM.
YOU'RE TALKING ABOUT "LA PUCELLE."
IT'S A SIN TO CROSS GOD'S WORK. I DESERVE DEATH.
YES.
BUT I BROUGHT YOU UP AS A BOY, AS WELL.
I HAVE SURVIVED UNTIL NOW, RIGHT?
BUT BECAUSE OF THAT,
UNTIL
NOW....
BUT THERE'S NOTHING TO HIDE ANYMORE. THE CURRENT DUKE OF LORRAINE, RENE D'ANJOU*, IS A FRIEND OF MINE. HE WON'T DO ANYTHING TO HARM YOU.

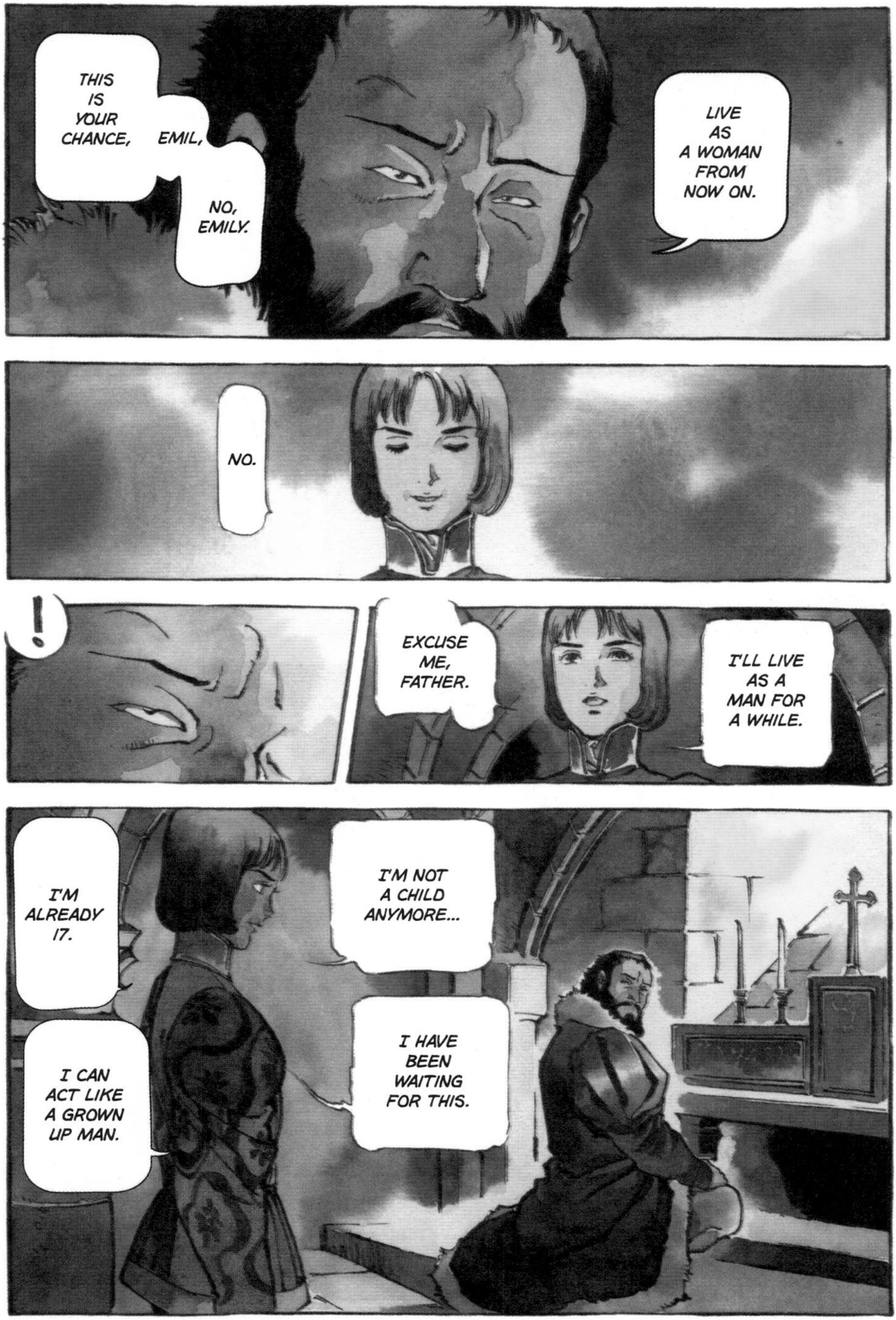
THIS IS YOUR CHANCE,
EMIL,
NO, EMILY.
LIVE AS A WOMAN FROM NOW ON.
NO.
!
EXCUSE ME, FATHER.
I'LL LIVE AS A MAN FOR A WHILE.
I'M ALREADY 17.
I'M NOT A CHILD ANYMORE...
I CAN ACT LIKE A GROWN UP MAN.
I HAVE BEEN WAITING FOR THIS.

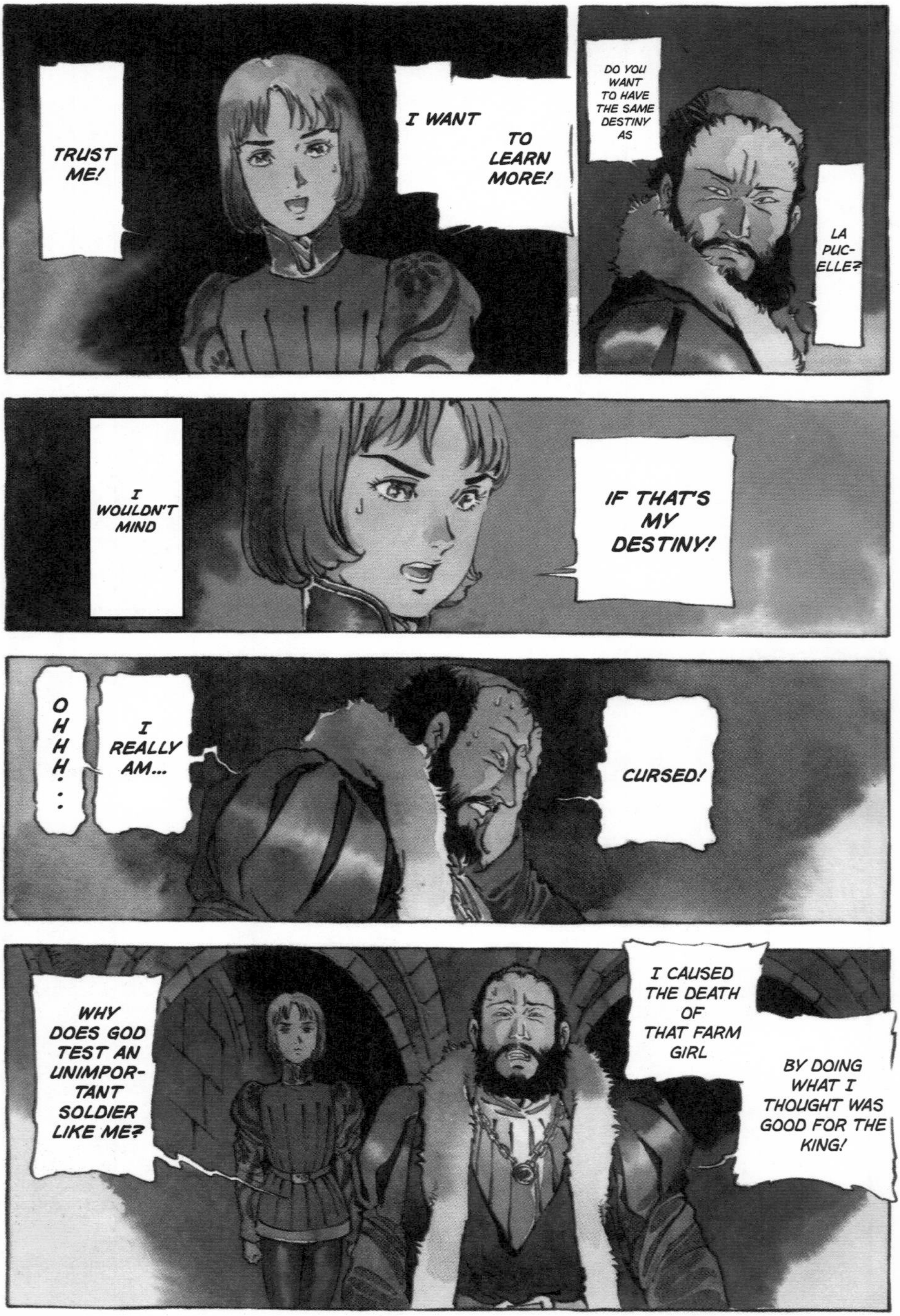
TRUST ME!
I WANT TO LEARN MORE!
DO YOU WANT TO HAVE THE SAME DESTINY AS
LA PUC-ELLE?
I WOULDN'T MIND
IF THAT'S MY DESTINY!
OHHH...
I REALLY AM...
CURSED!
WHY DOES GOD TEST AN UNIMPOR-TANT SOLDIER LIKE ME?
I CAUSED THE DEATH OF THAT FARM GIRL
BY DOING WHAT I THOUGHT WAS GOOD FOR THE KING!

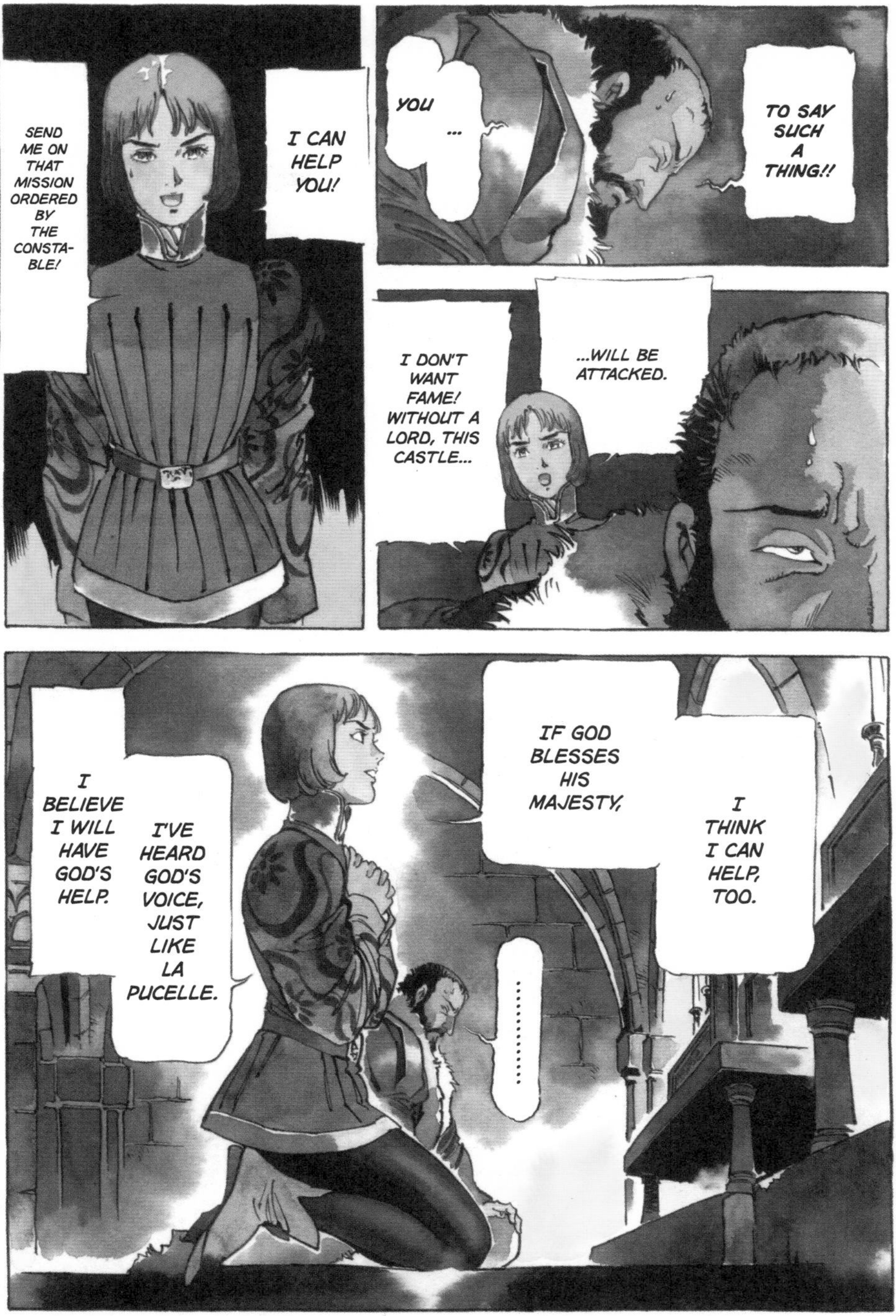

SEND ME ON THAT MISSION ORDERED BY THE CONSTA-BLE!
I CAN HELP YOU!
YOU ...
TO SAY SUCH A THING!!
I DON'T WANT FAME! WITHOUT A LORD, THIS CASTLE...
...WILL BE ATTACKED.
I BELIEVE I WILL HAVE GOD'S HELP.
I'VE HEARD GOD'S VOICE, JUST LIKE LA PUCELLE.
IF GOD BLESSES HIS MAJESTY,
I THINK I CAN HELP, TOO.
.........

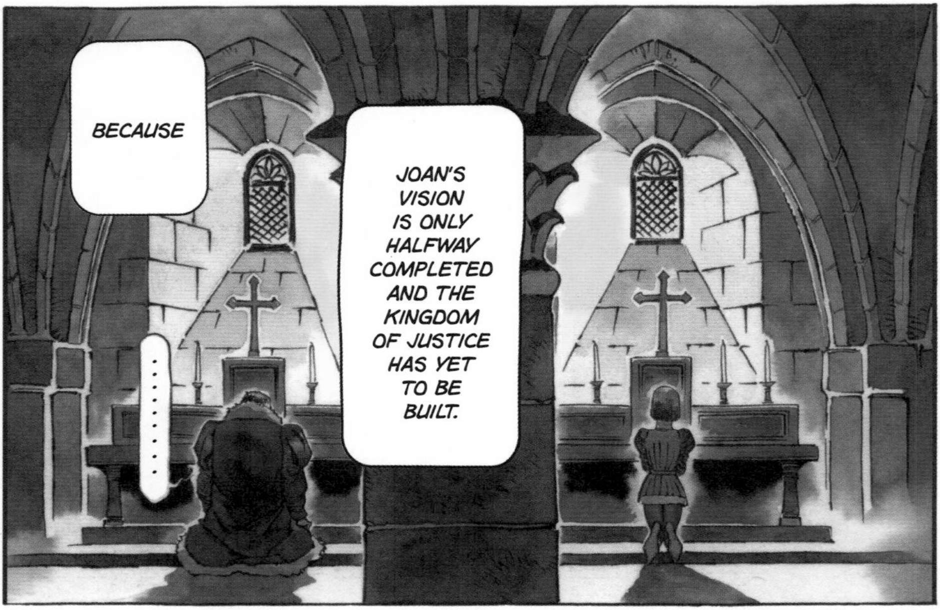
BECAUSE
JOAN'S VISION IS ONLY HALFWAY COMPLETED AND THE KINGDOM OF JUSTICE HAS YET TO BE BUILT.
........

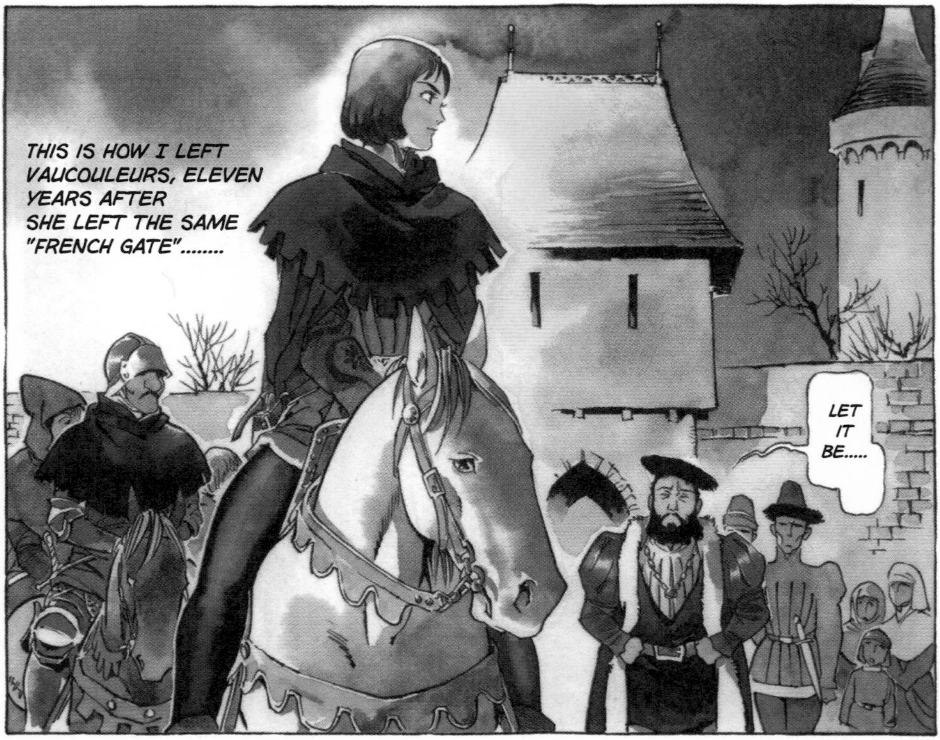
THIS IS HOW I LEFT VAUCOULEURS, ELEVEN YEARS AFTER SHE LEFT THE SAME "FRENCH GATE"........
LET IT BE.....

# Chapter 1

# DOMREMY

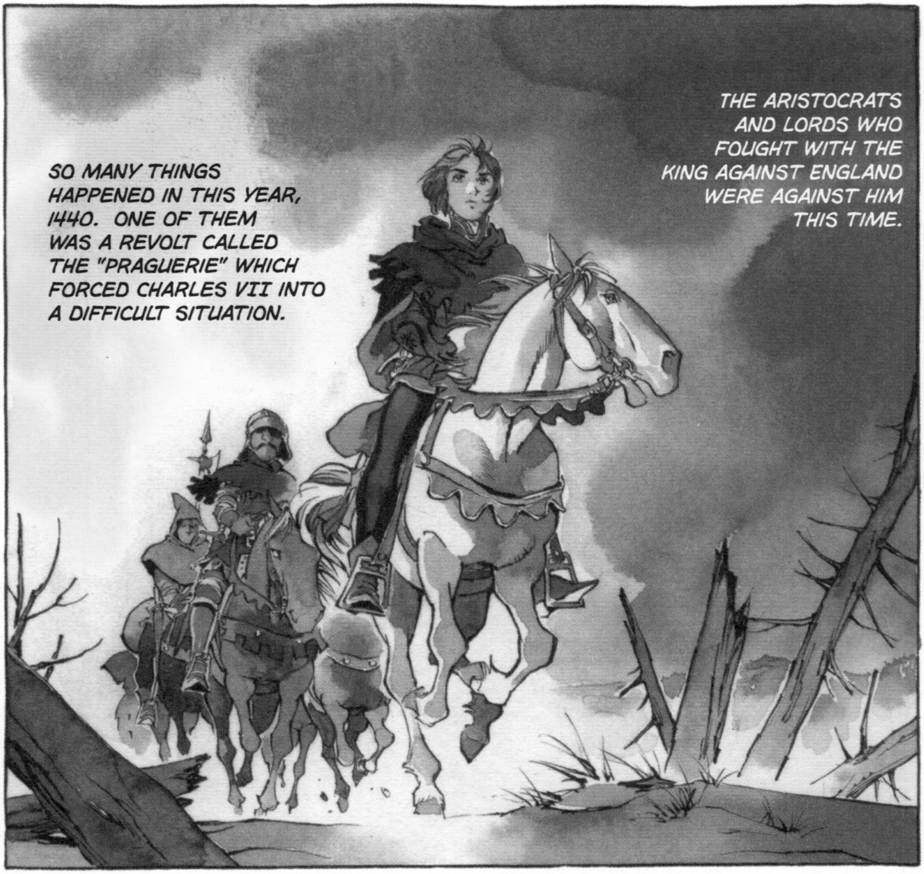
SO MANY THINGS HAPPENED IN THIS YEAR, 1440. ONE OF THEM WAS A REVOLT CALLED THE "PRAGUERIE" WHICH FORCED CHARLES VII INTO A DIFFICULT SITUATION.
THE ARISTOCRATS AND LORDS WHO FOUGHT WITH THE KING AGAINST ENGLAND WERE AGAINST HIM THIS TIME.

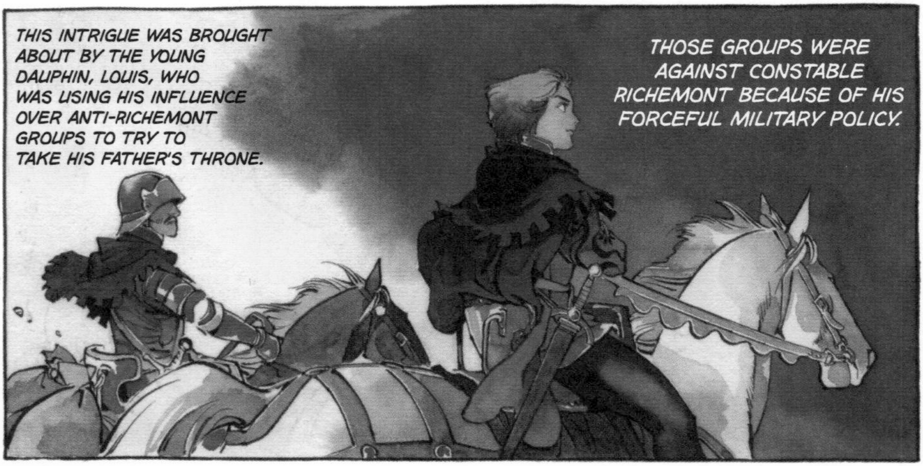
THIS INTRIGUE WAS BROUGHT ABOUT BY THE YOUNG DAUPHIN, LOUIS, WHO WAS USING HIS INFLUENCE OVER ANTI-RICHEMONT GROUPS TO TRY TO TAKE HIS FATHER'S THRONE.
THOSE GROUPS WERE AGAINST CONSTABLE RICHEMONT BECAUSE OF HIS FORCEFUL MILITARY POLICY.

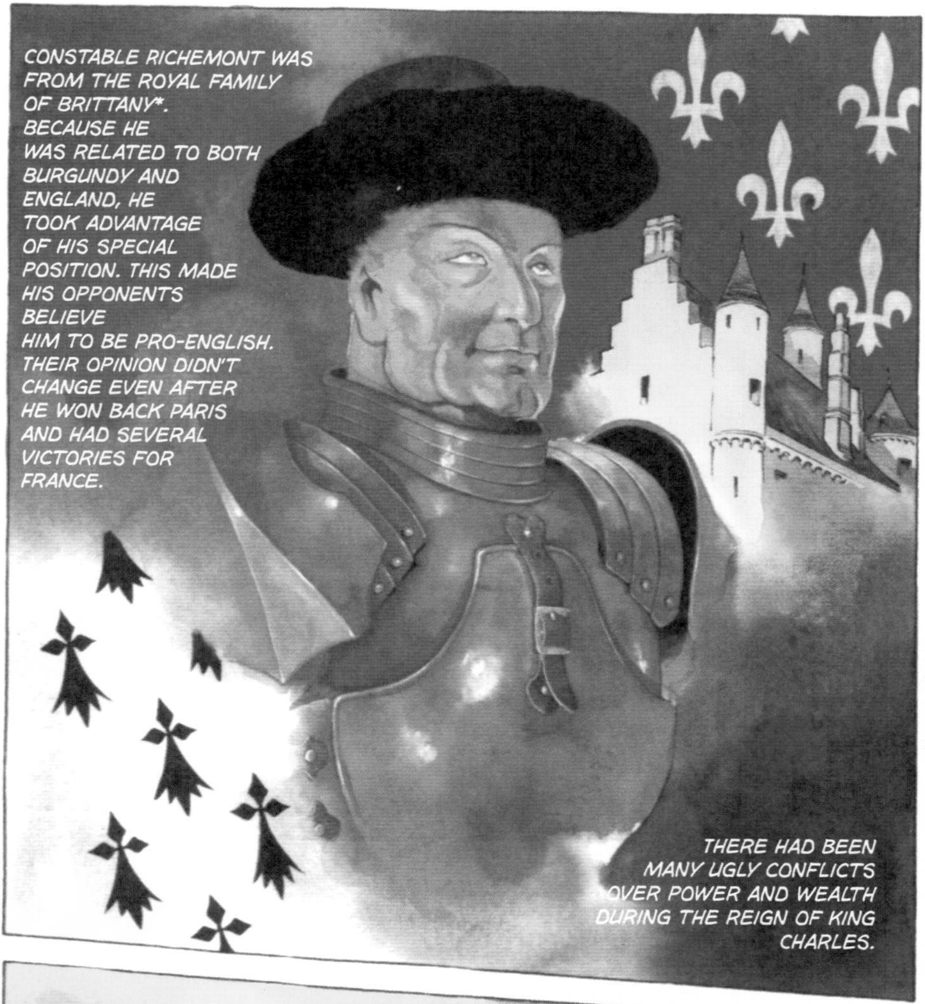
CONSTABLE RICHEMONT WAS FROM THE ROYAL FAMILY OF BRITTANY*. BECAUSE HE WAS RELATED TO BOTH BURGUNDY AND ENGLAND, HE TOOK ADVANTAGE OF HIS SPECIAL POSITION. THIS MADE HIS OPPONENTS BELIEVE HIM TO BE PRO-ENGLISH. THEIR OPINION DIDN'T CHANGE EVEN AFTER HE WON BACK PARIS AND HAD SEVERAL VICTORIES FOR FRANCE.
THERE HAD BEEN MANY UGLY CONFLICTS OVER POWER AND WEALTH DURING THE REIGN OF KING CHARLES.

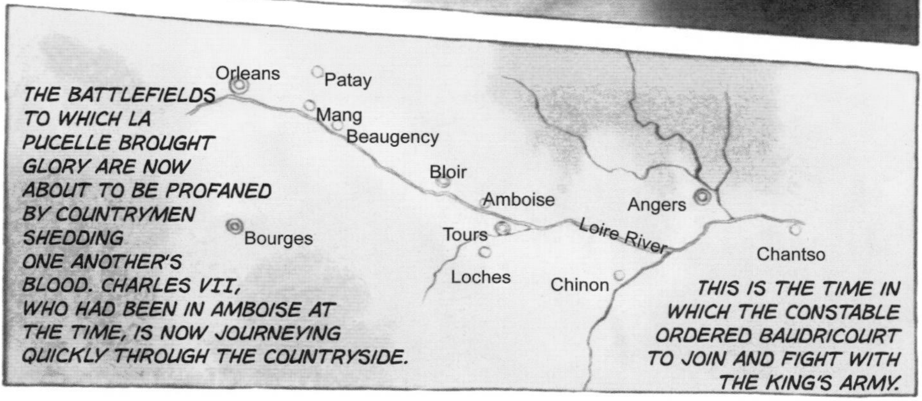
THE BATTLEFIELDS TO WHICH LA PUCELLE BROUGHT GLORY ARE NOW ABOUT TO BE PROFANED BY COUNTRYMEN SHEDDING ONE ANOTHER'S BLOOD. CHARLES VII, WHO HAD BEEN IN AMBOISE AT THE TIME, IS NOW JOURNEYING QUICKLY THROUGH THE COUNTRYSIDE.
Orleans
Patay
Mang
Beaugency
Bloir
Amboise
Angers
Tours
Loire River
Bourges
Chantso
Loches
Chinon
THIS IS THE TIME IN WHICH THE CONSTABLE ORDERED BAUDRICOURT TO JOIN AND FIGHT WITH THE KING'S ARMY.

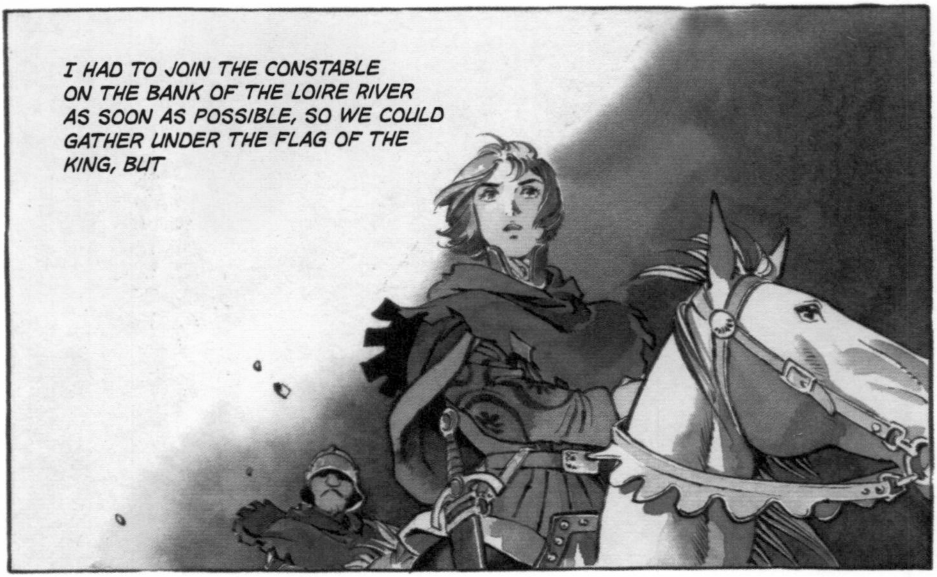
I HAD TO JOIN THE CONSTABLE ON THE BANK OF THE LOIRE RIVER AS SOON AS POSSIBLE, SO WE COULD GATHER UNDER THE FLAG OF THE KING, BUT

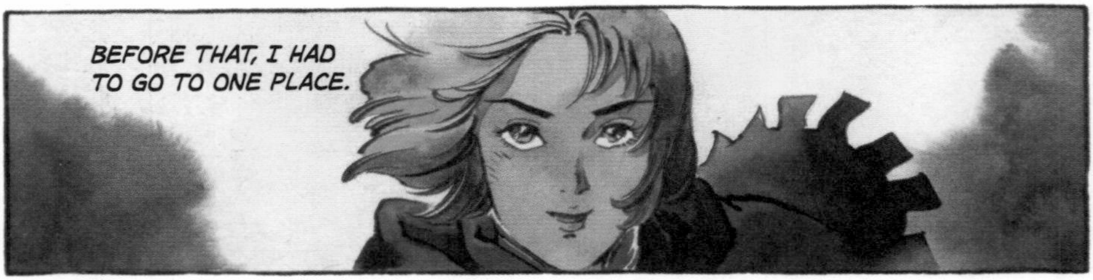
BEFORE THAT, I HAD TO GO TO ONE PLACE.

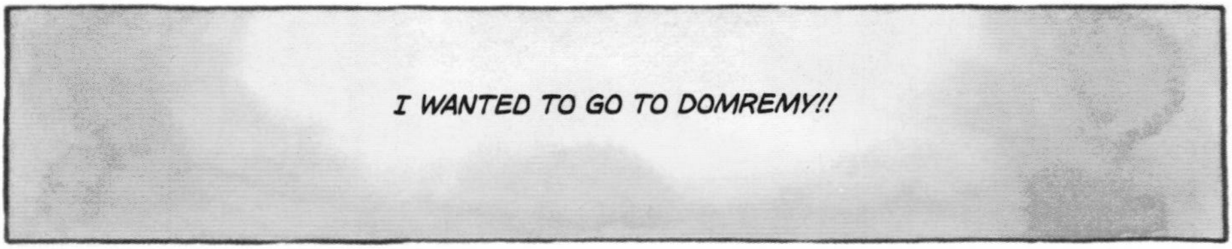
I WANTED TO GO TO DOMREMY!!

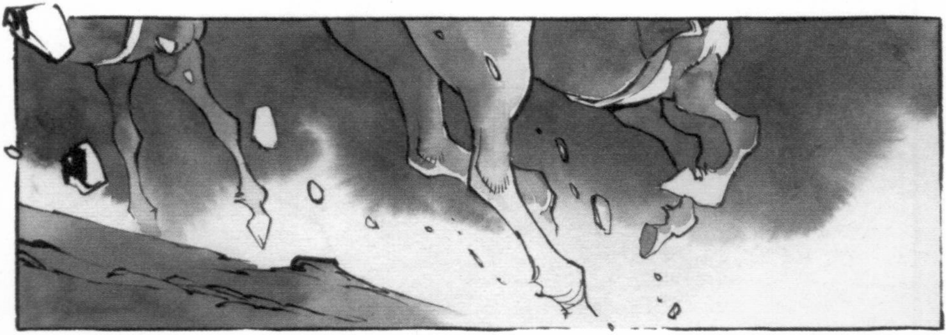

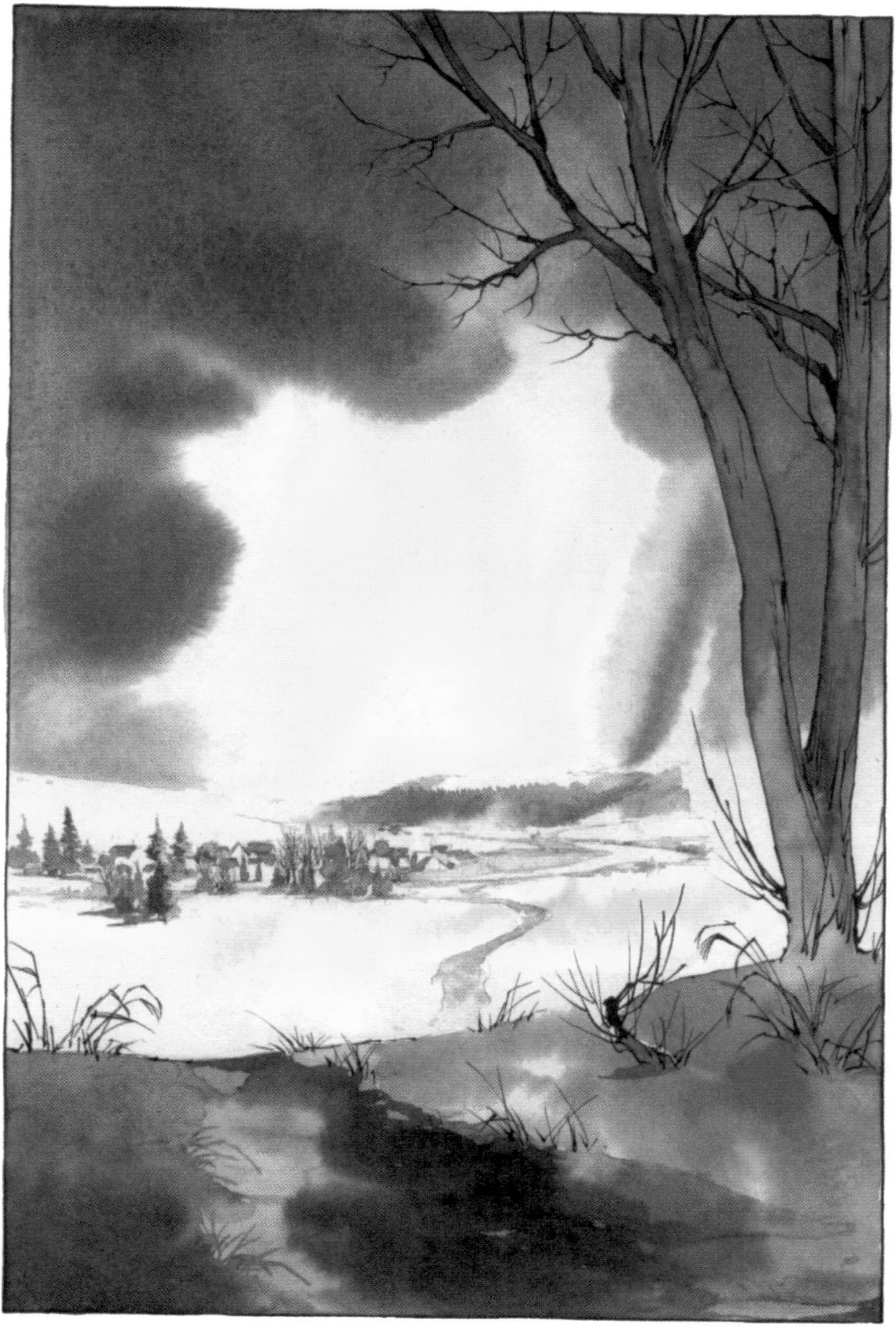

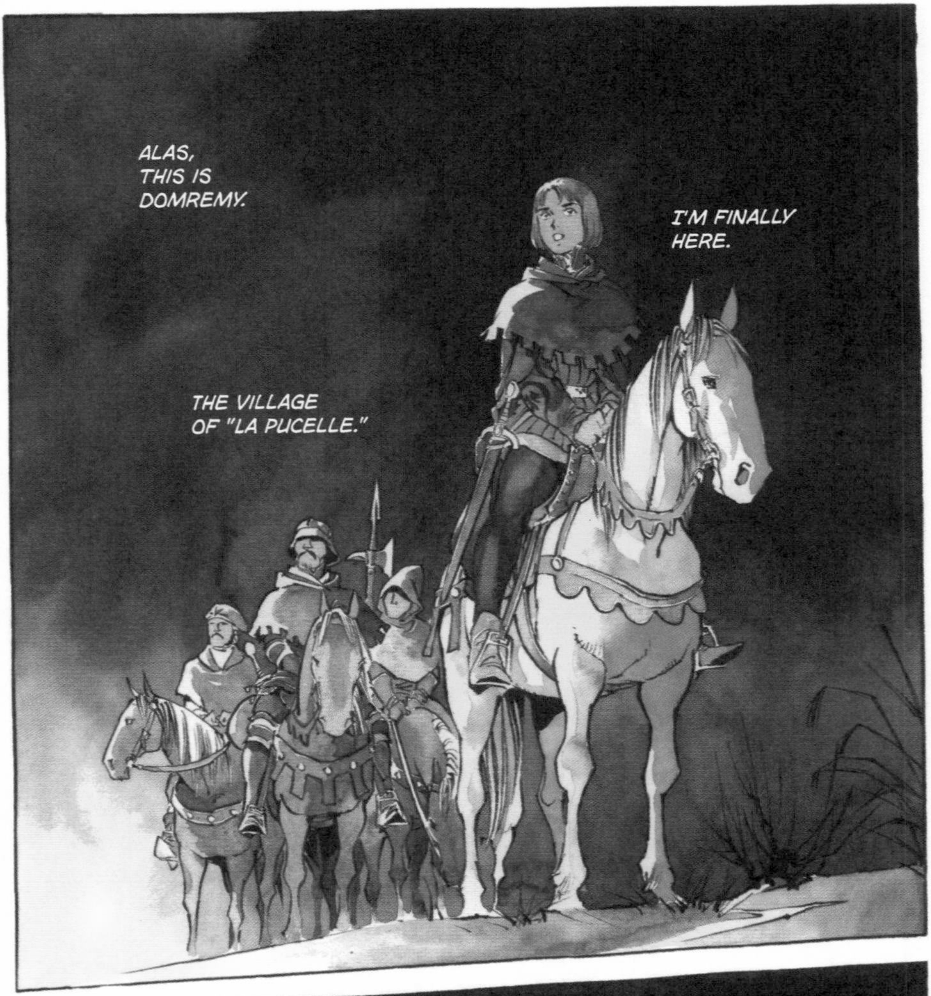
ALAS, THIS IS DOMREMY.
I'M FINALLY HERE.
THE VILLAGE OF "LA PUCELLE."

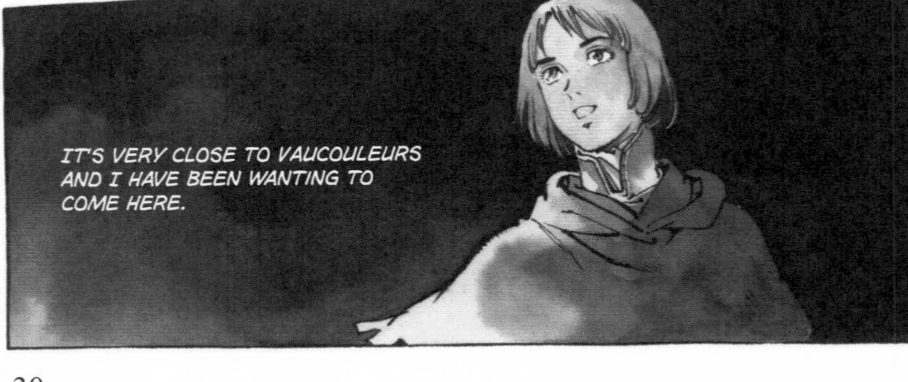
IT'S VERY CLOSE TO VAUCOULEURS AND I HAVE BEEN WANTING TO COME HERE.

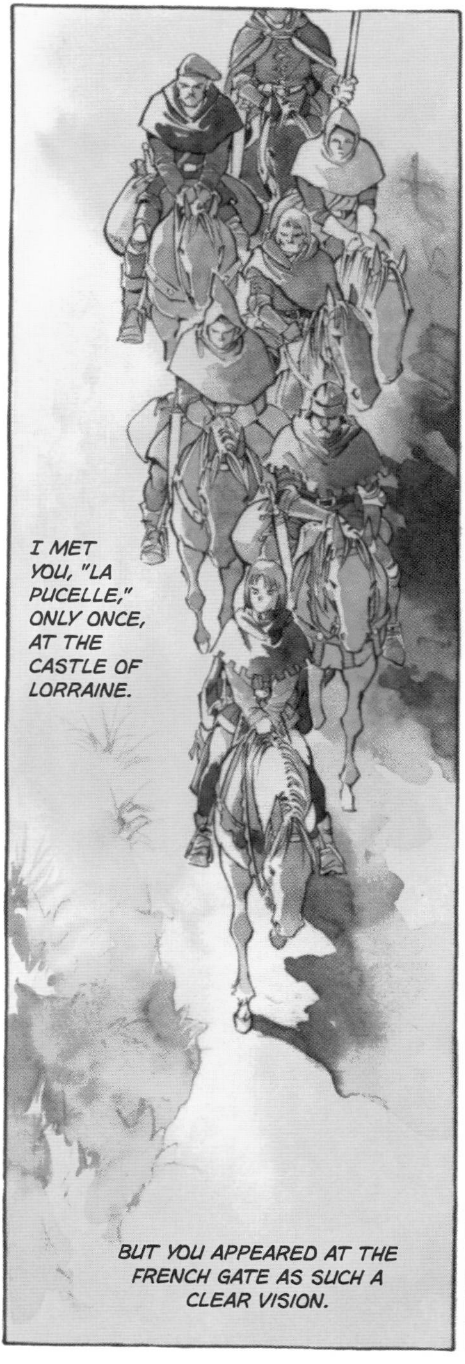
I MET YOU, "LA PUCELLE," ONLY ONCE, AT THE CASTLE OF LORRAINE.
BUT YOU APPEARED AT THE FRENCH GATE AS SUCH A CLEAR VISION.

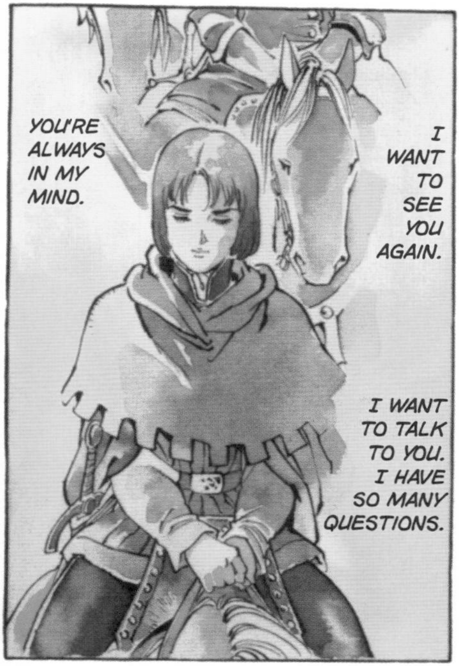
I WANT TO SEE YOU AGAIN.
YOU'RE ALWAYS IN MY MIND.
I WANT TO TALK TO YOU. I HAVE SO MANY QUESTIONS.

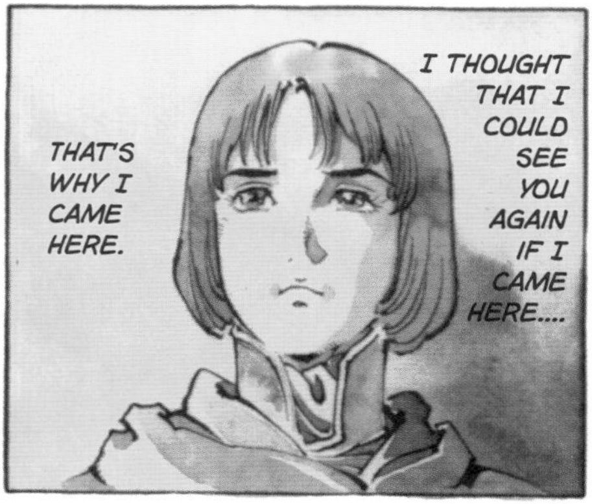
I THOUGHT THAT I COULD SEE YOU AGAIN IF I CAME HERE....
THAT'S WHY I CAME HERE.

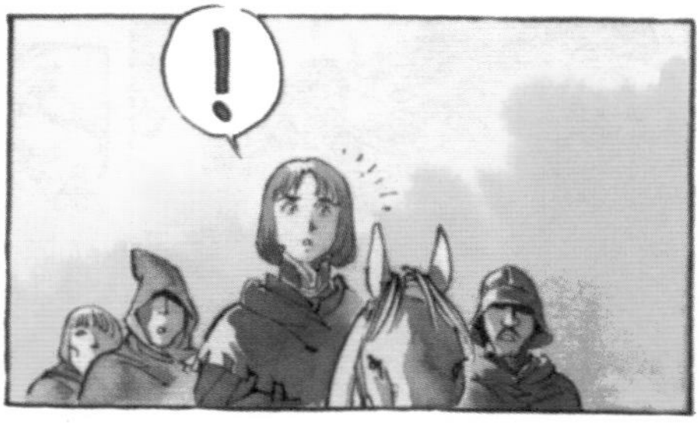
!

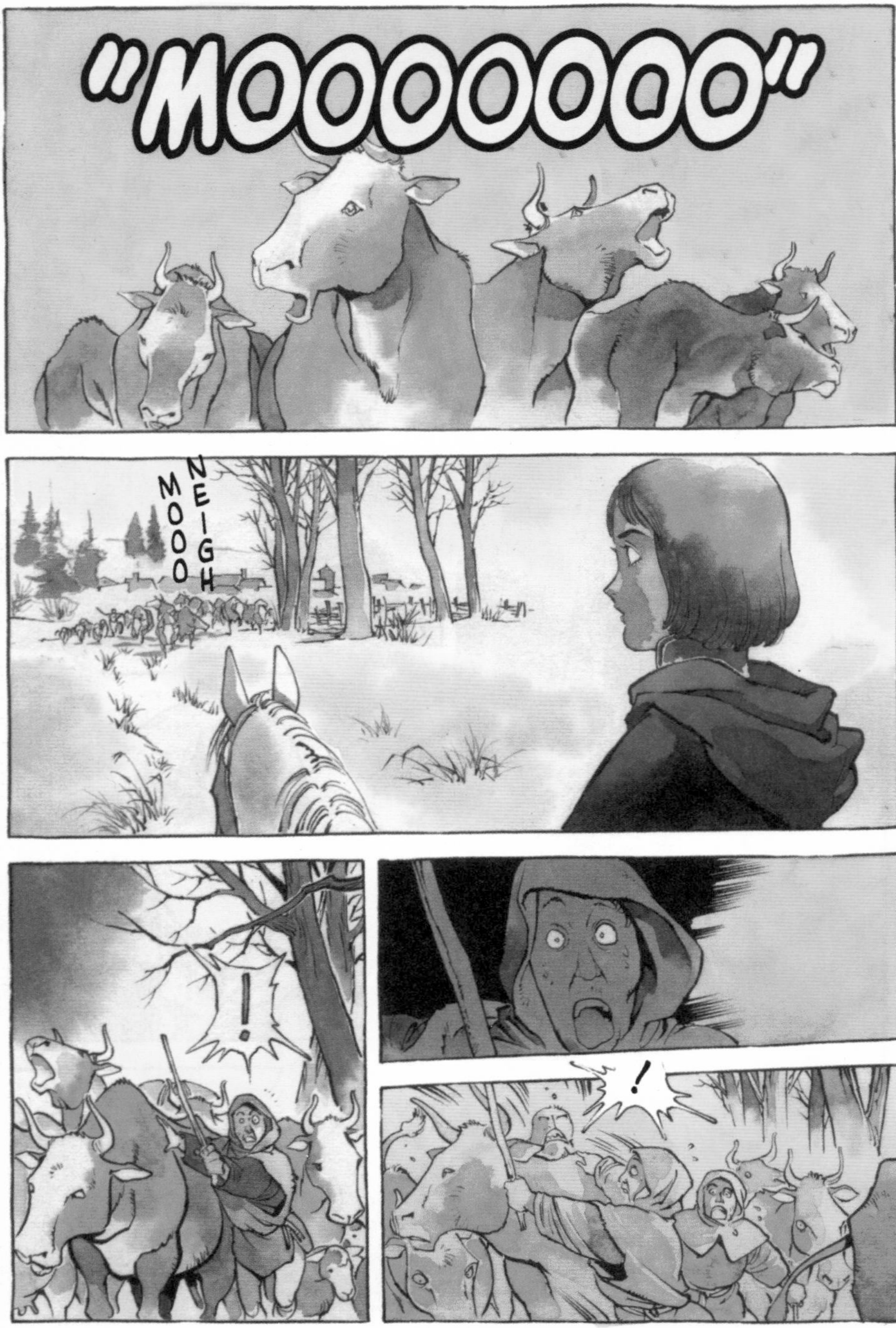
"MOOOOOOO"
MOOO
NEIGH
!
!

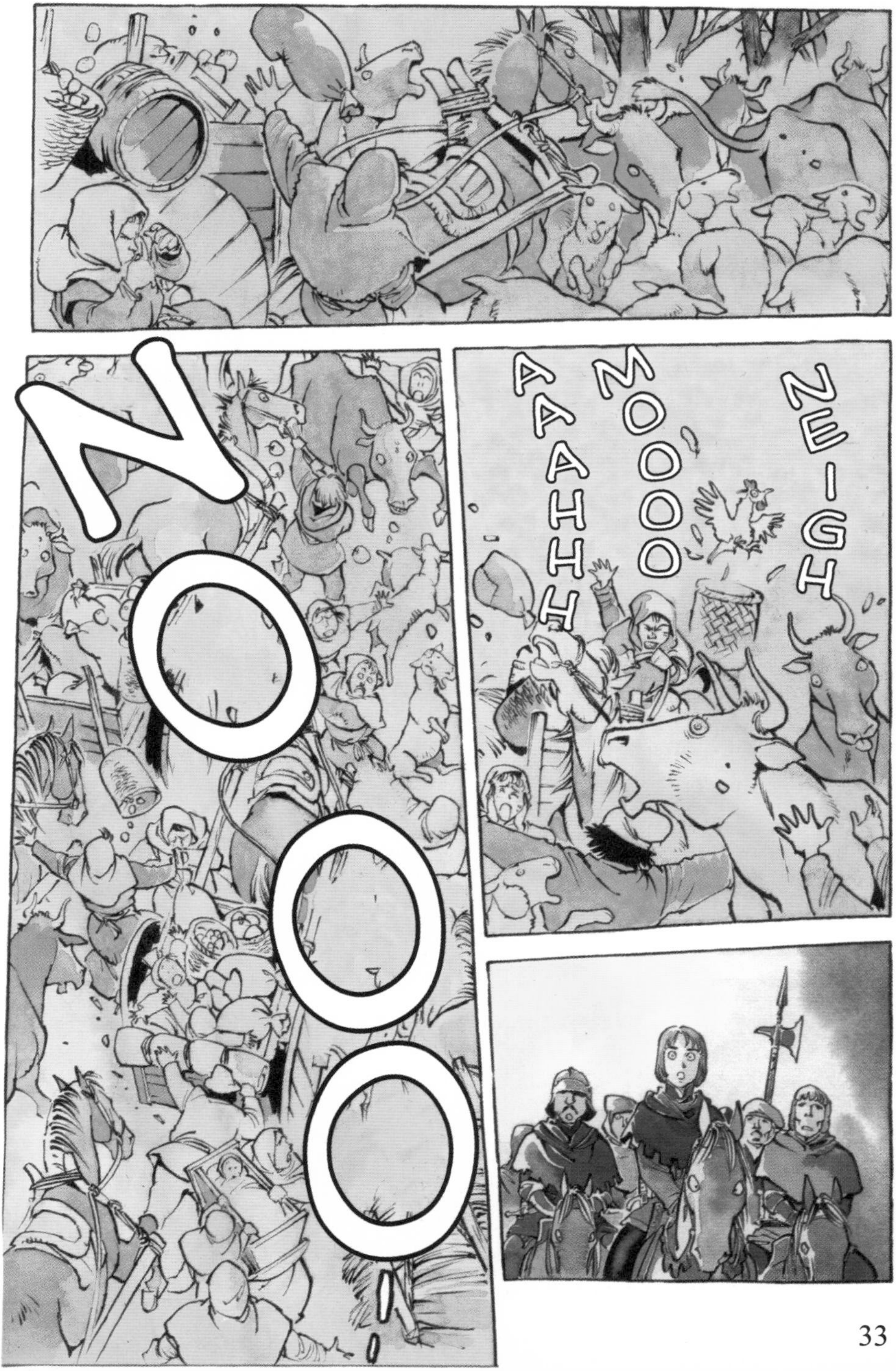
NOOOO!
AAAHHH
MOOOOO
NEIGH

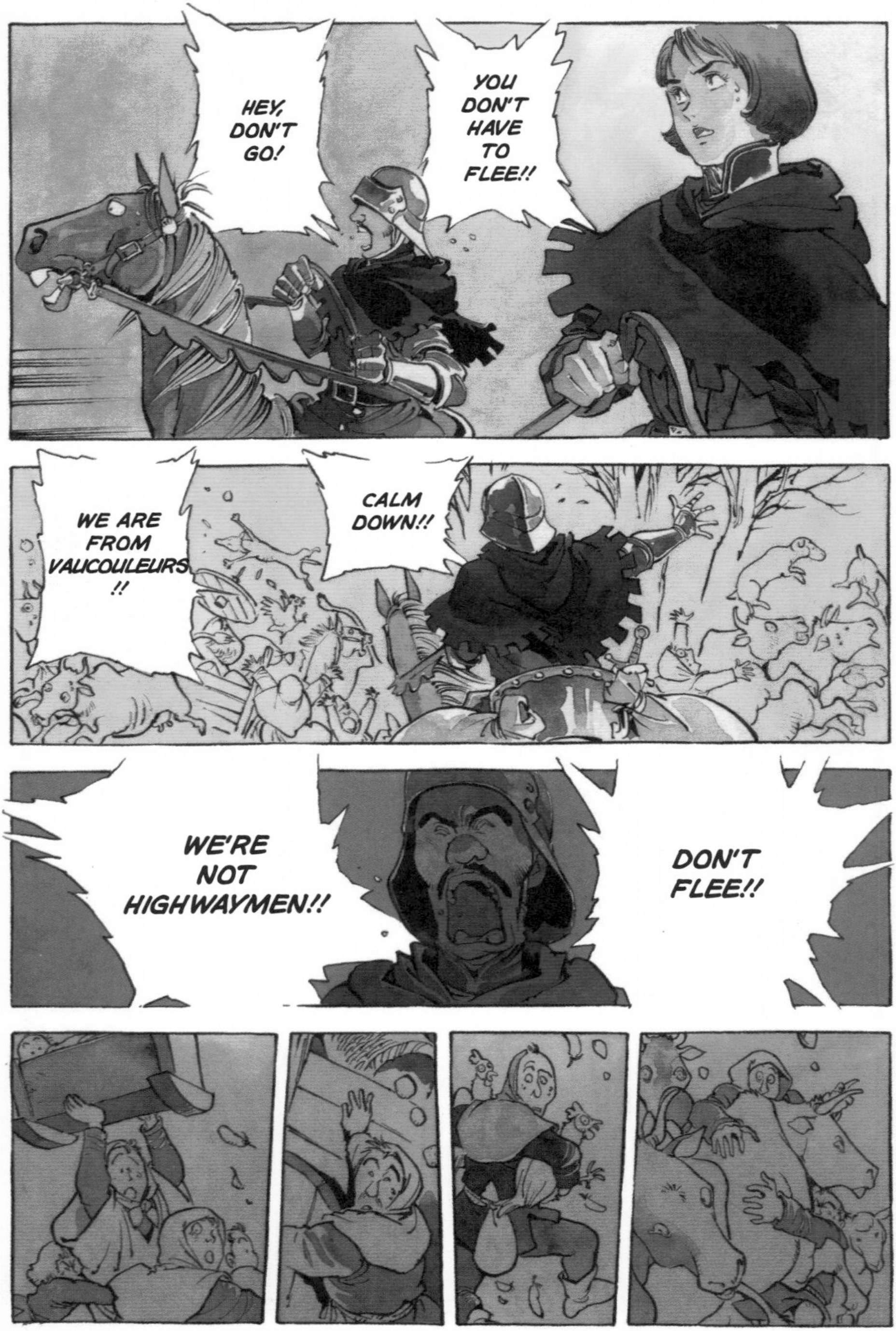
HEY, DON'T GO!
YOU DON'T HAVE TO FLEE!!
WE ARE FROM VAUCOULEURS!!
CALM DOWN!!
WE'RE NOT HIGHWAYMEN!!
DON'T FLEE!!

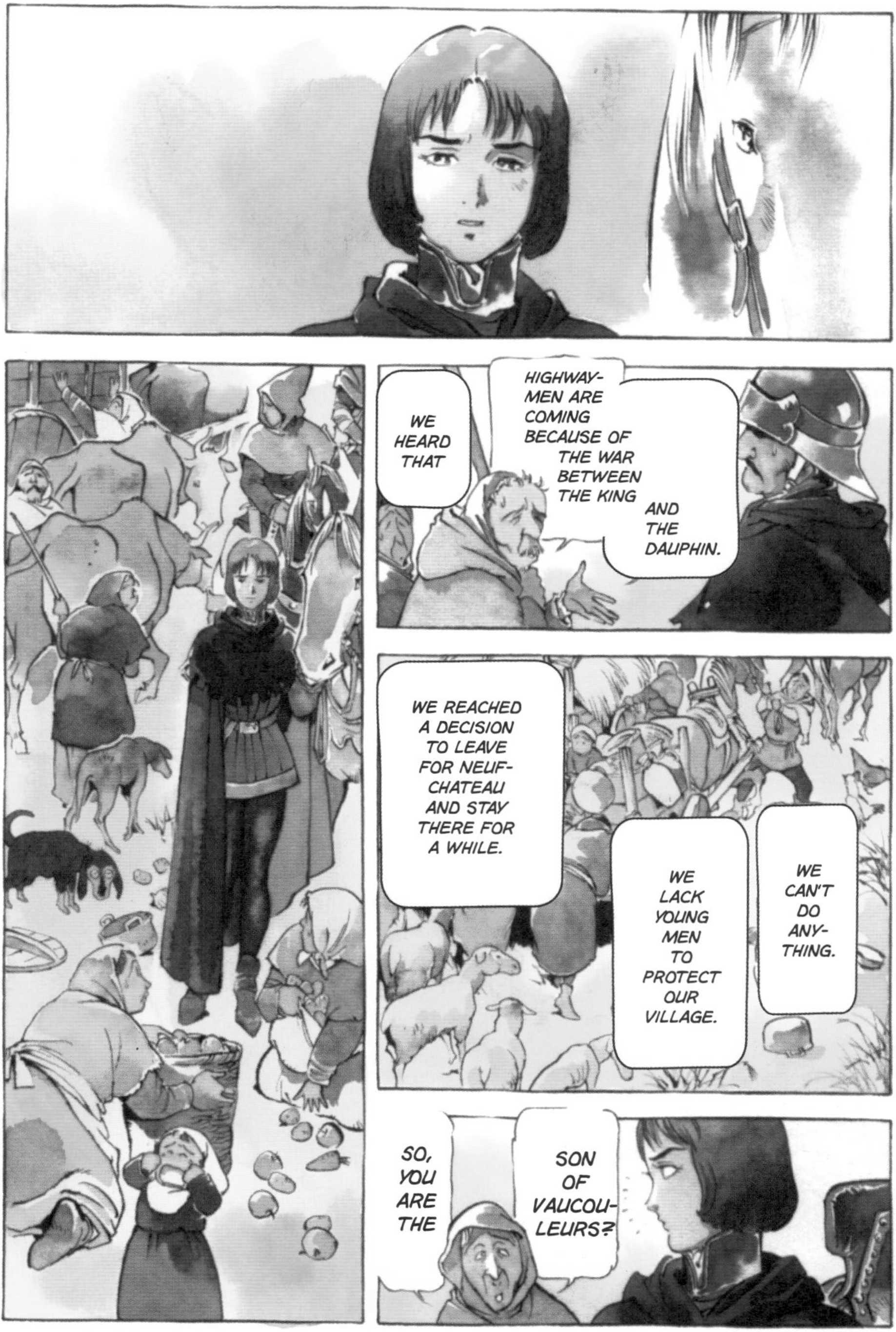
WE HEARD THAT
HIGHWAY-MEN ARE COMING BECAUSE OF THE WAR BETWEEN THE KING
AND THE DAUPHIN.
WE REACHED A DECISION TO LEAVE FOR NEUF-CHATEAU AND STAY THERE FOR A WHILE.
WE CAN'T DO ANY-THING.
WE LACK YOUNG MEN TO PROTECT OUR VILLAGE.
SO, YOU ARE THE
SON OF VAUCOU-LEURS?

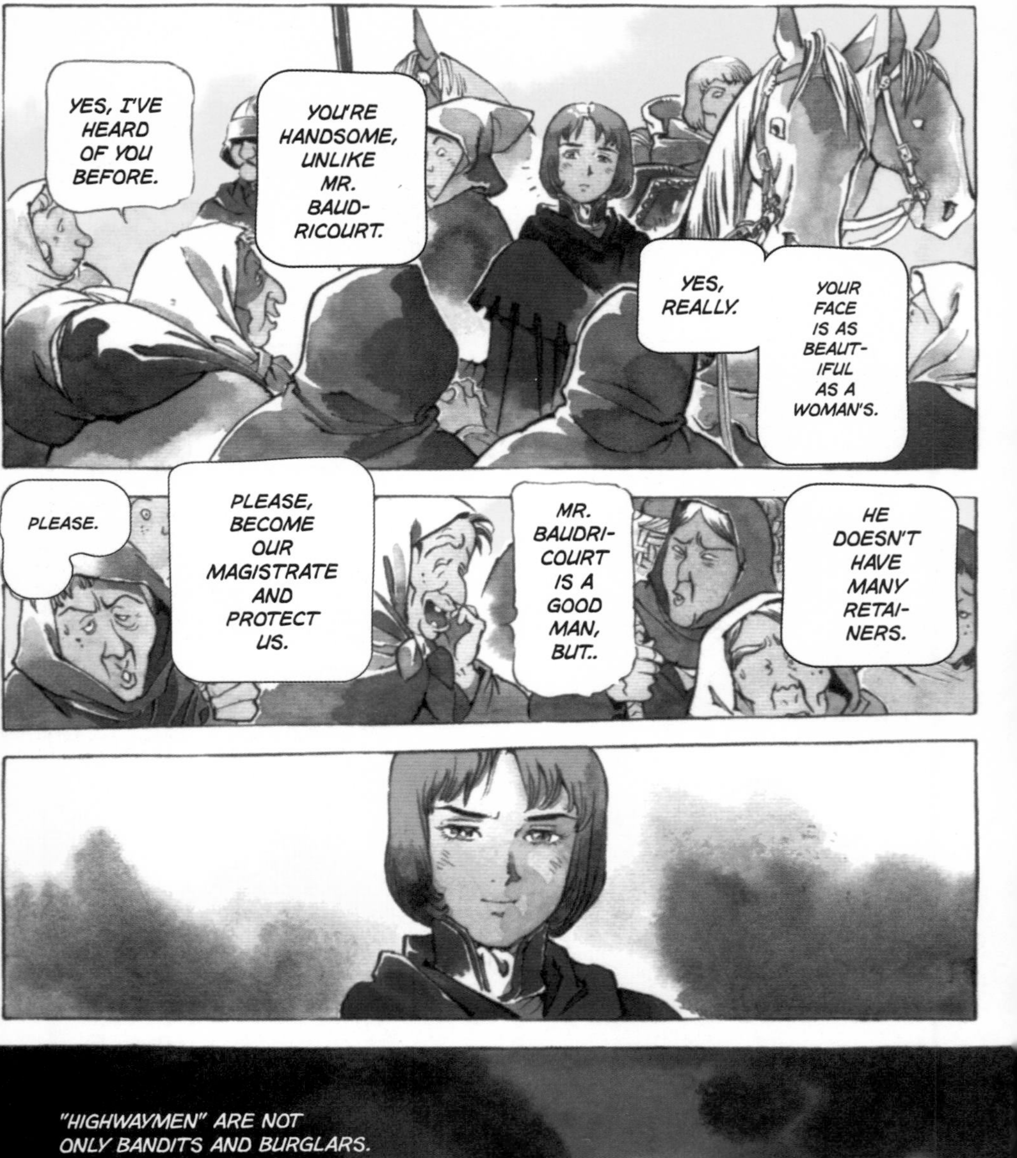
YES, I'VE HEARD OF YOU BEFORE.
YOU'RE HANDSOME, UNLIKE MR. BAUD-RICOURT.
YES, REALLY.
YOUR FACE IS AS BEAUT-IFUL AS A WOMAN'S.
PLEASE.
PLEASE, BECOME OUR MAGISTRATE AND PROTECT US.
MR. BAUDRI-COURT IS A GOOD MAN, BUT..
HE DOESN'T HAVE MANY RETAI-NERS.
"HIGHWAYMEN" ARE NOT ONLY BANDITS AND BURGLARS.

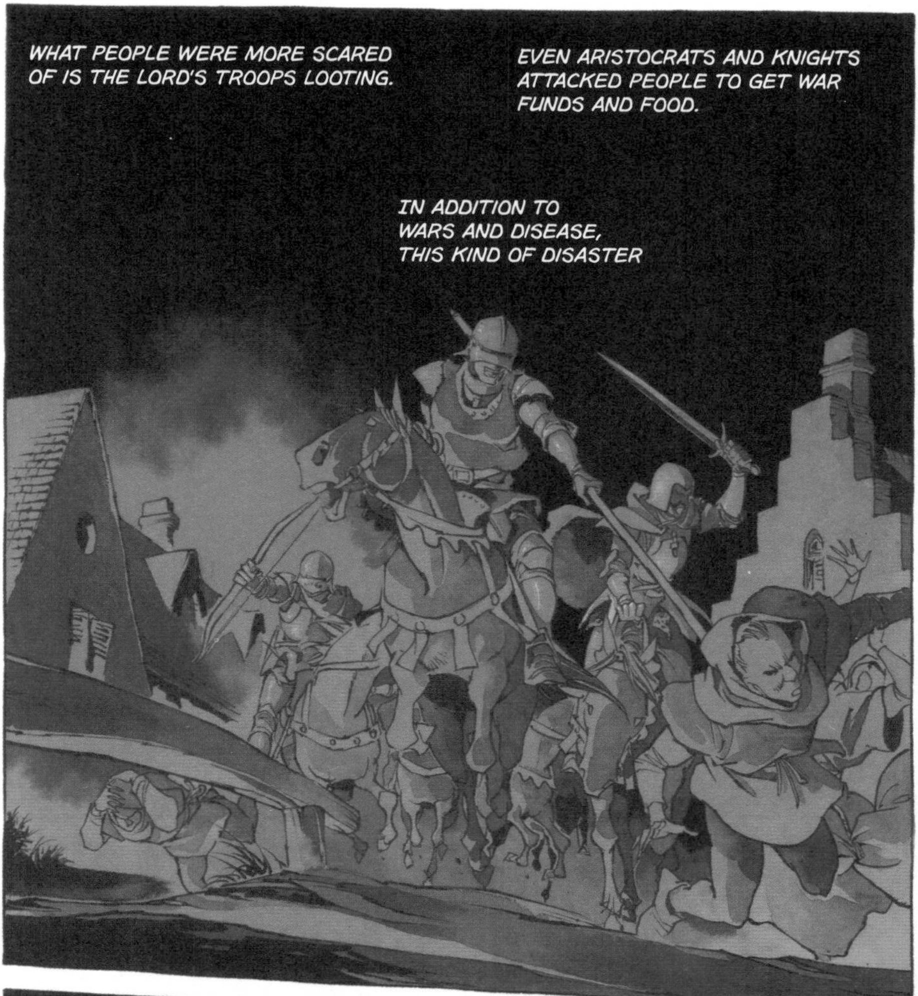
WHAT PEOPLE WERE MORE SCARED OF IS THE LORD'S TROOPS LOOTING.
EVEN ARISTOCRATS AND KNIGHTS ATTACKED PEOPLE TO GET WAR FUNDS AND FOOD.
IN ADDITION TO WARS AND DISEASE, THIS KIND OF DISASTER

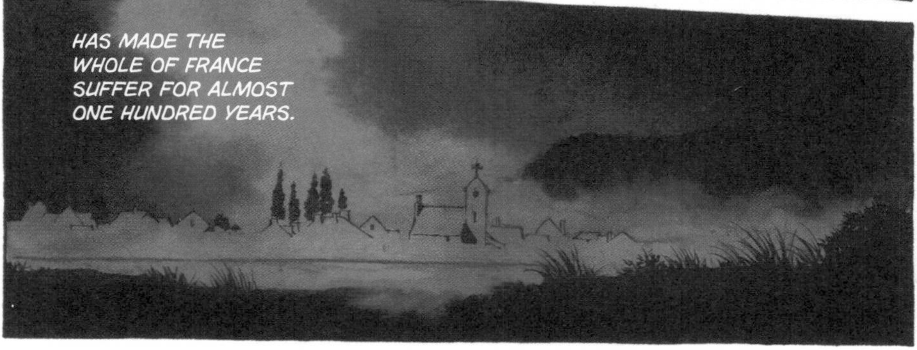
HAS MADE THE WHOLE OF FRANCE SUFFER FOR ALMOST ONE HUNDRED YEARS.

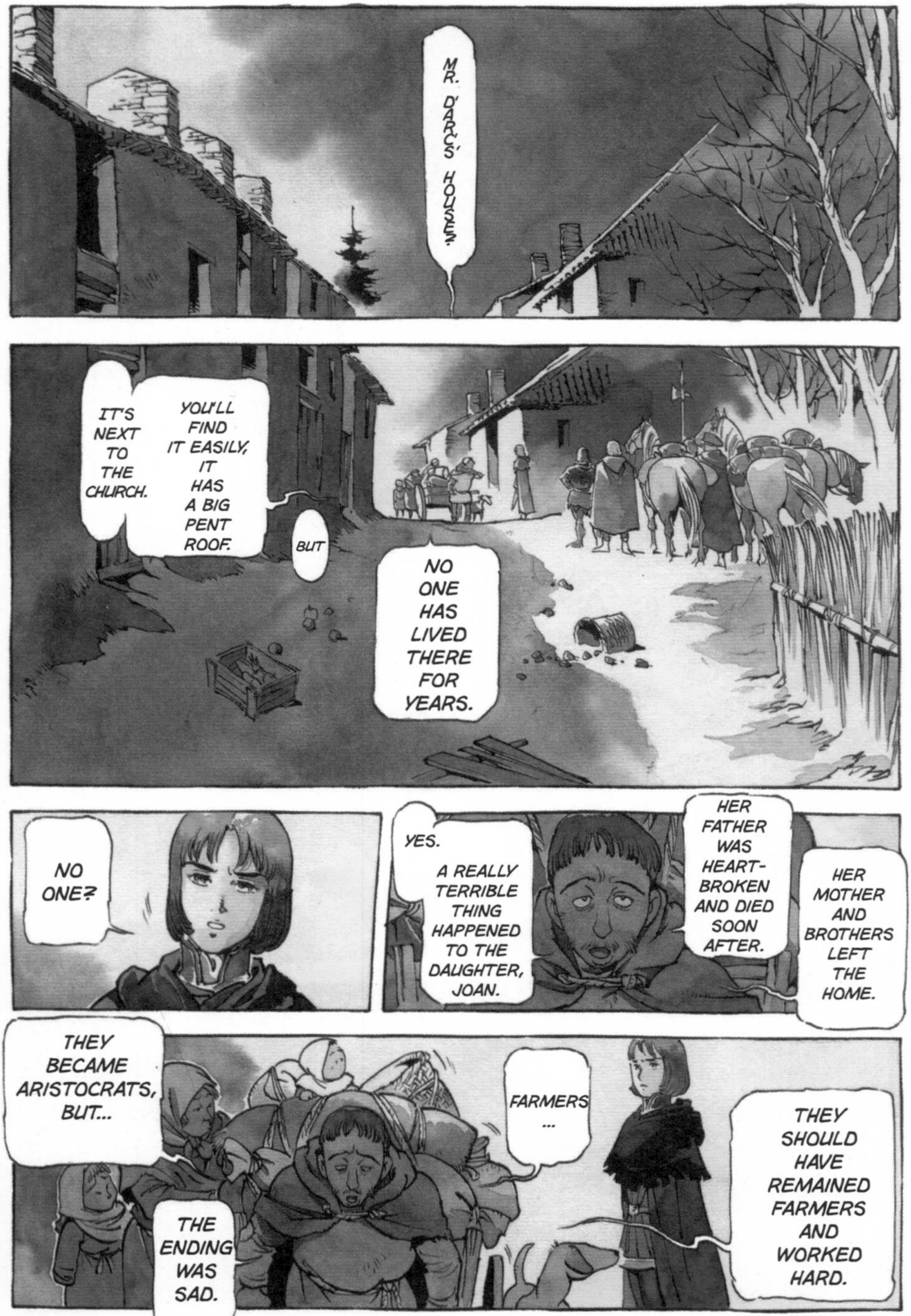
MR. D'ARC'S HOUSE?
IT'S NEXT TO THE CHURCH.
YOU'LL FIND IT EASILY, IT HAS A BIG PENT ROOF.
BUT
NO ONE HAS LIVED THERE FOR YEARS.
NO ONE?
YES.
A REALLY TERRIBLE THING HAPPENED TO THE DAUGHTER, JOAN.
HER FATHER WAS HEART-BROKEN AND DIED SOON AFTER.
HER MOTHER AND BROTHERS LEFT THE HOME.
THEY BECAME ARISTOCRATS, BUT...
THE ENDING WAS SAD.
FARMERS ...
THEY SHOULD HAVE REMAINED FARMERS AND WORKED HARD.

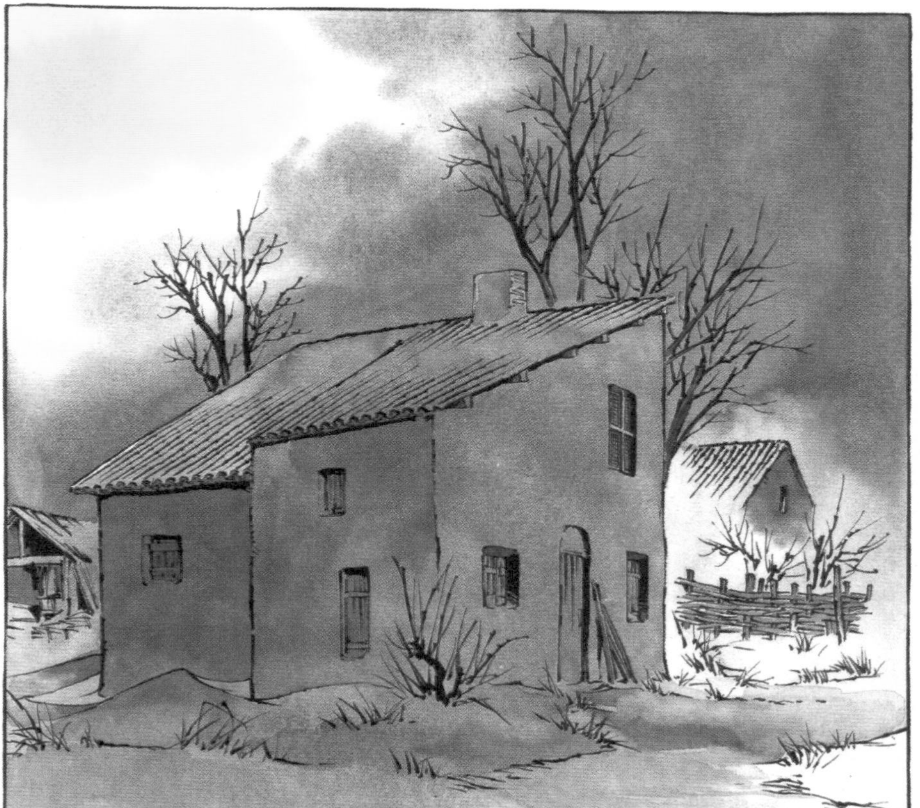

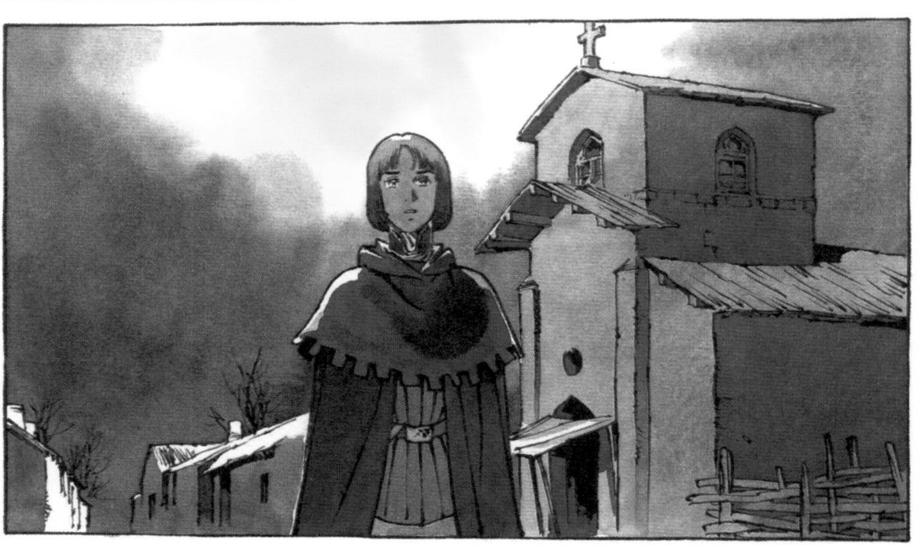

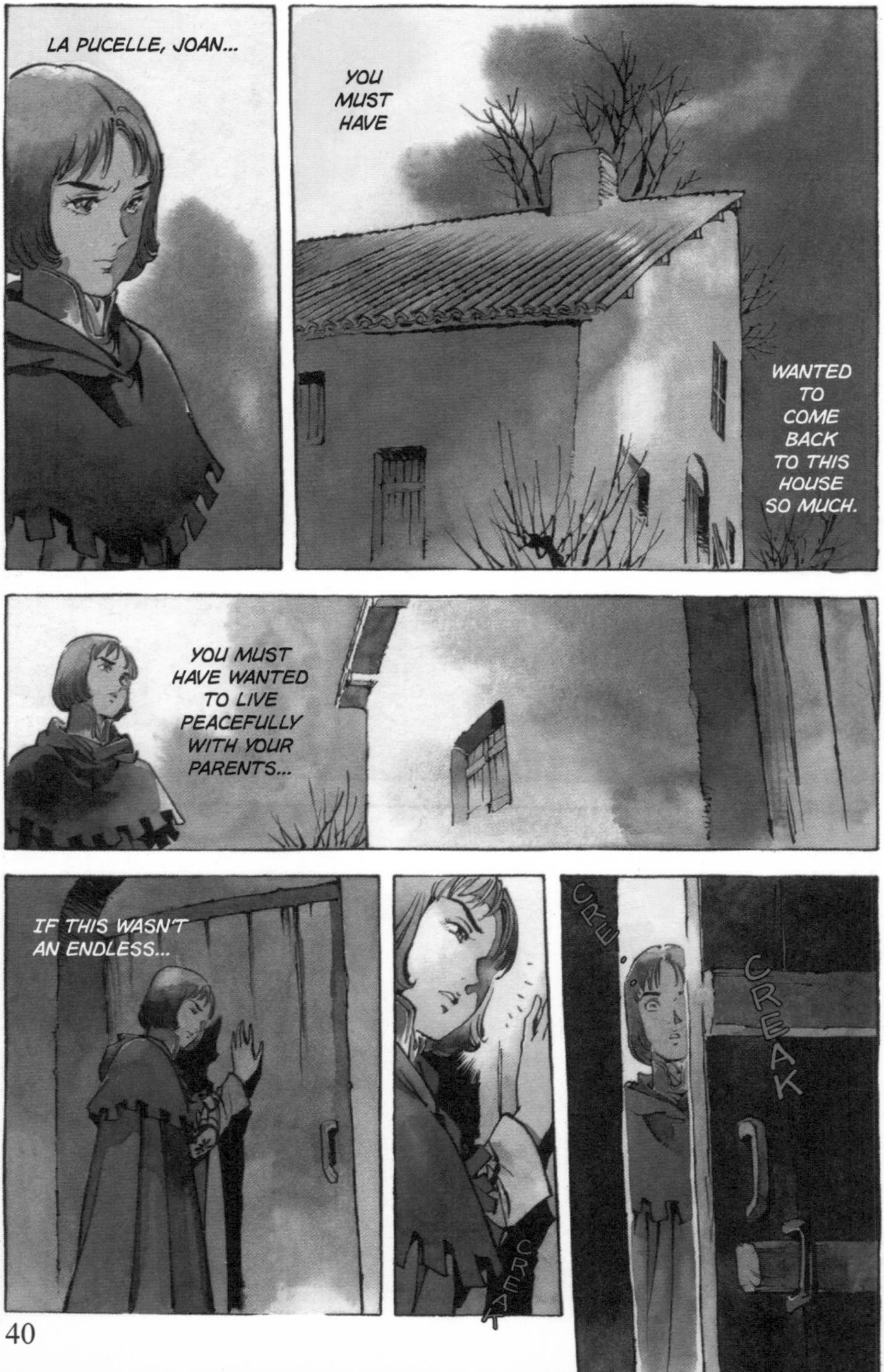
LA PUCELLE, JOAN...
YOU MUST HAVE
WANTED TO COME BACK TO THIS HOUSE SO MUCH.
YOU MUST HAVE WANTED TO LIVE PEACEFULLY WITH YOUR PARENTS...
IF THIS WASN'T AN ENDLESS...
CREAK
CREU
CREAK

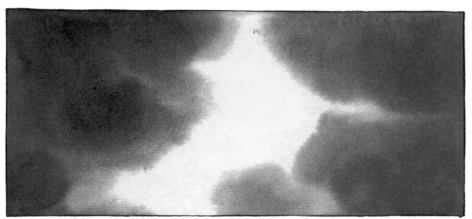

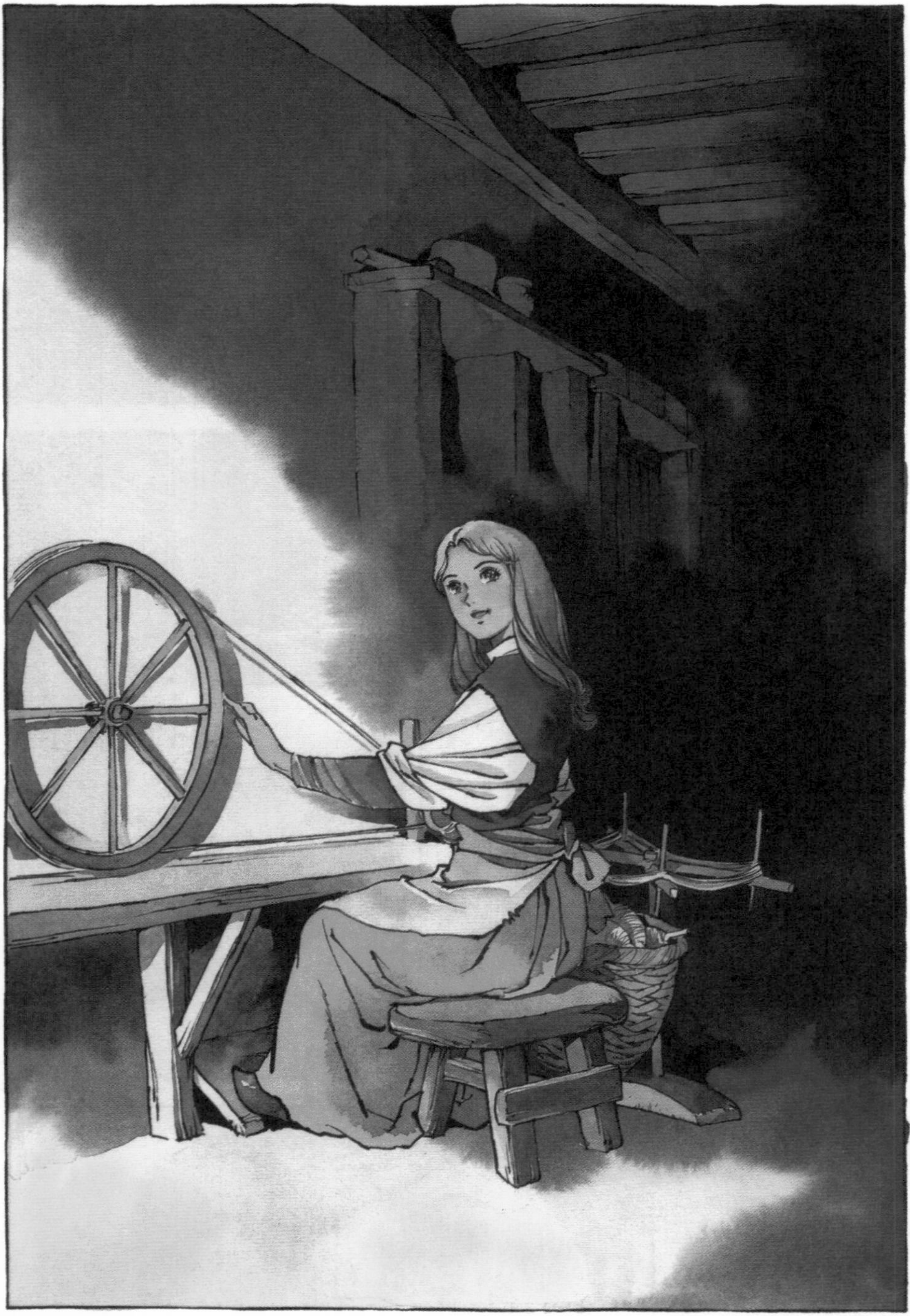

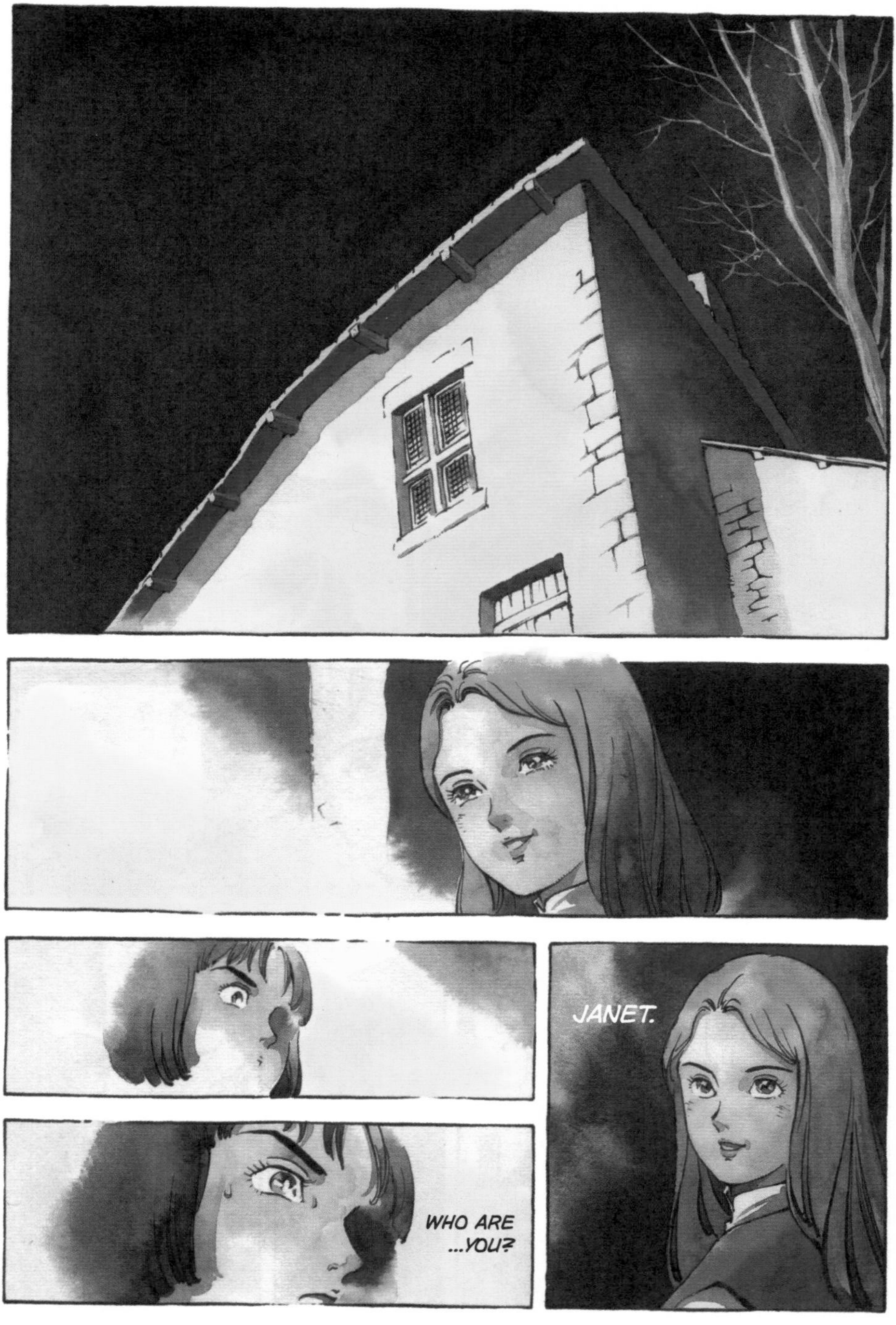
JANET.
WHO ARE
...YOU?

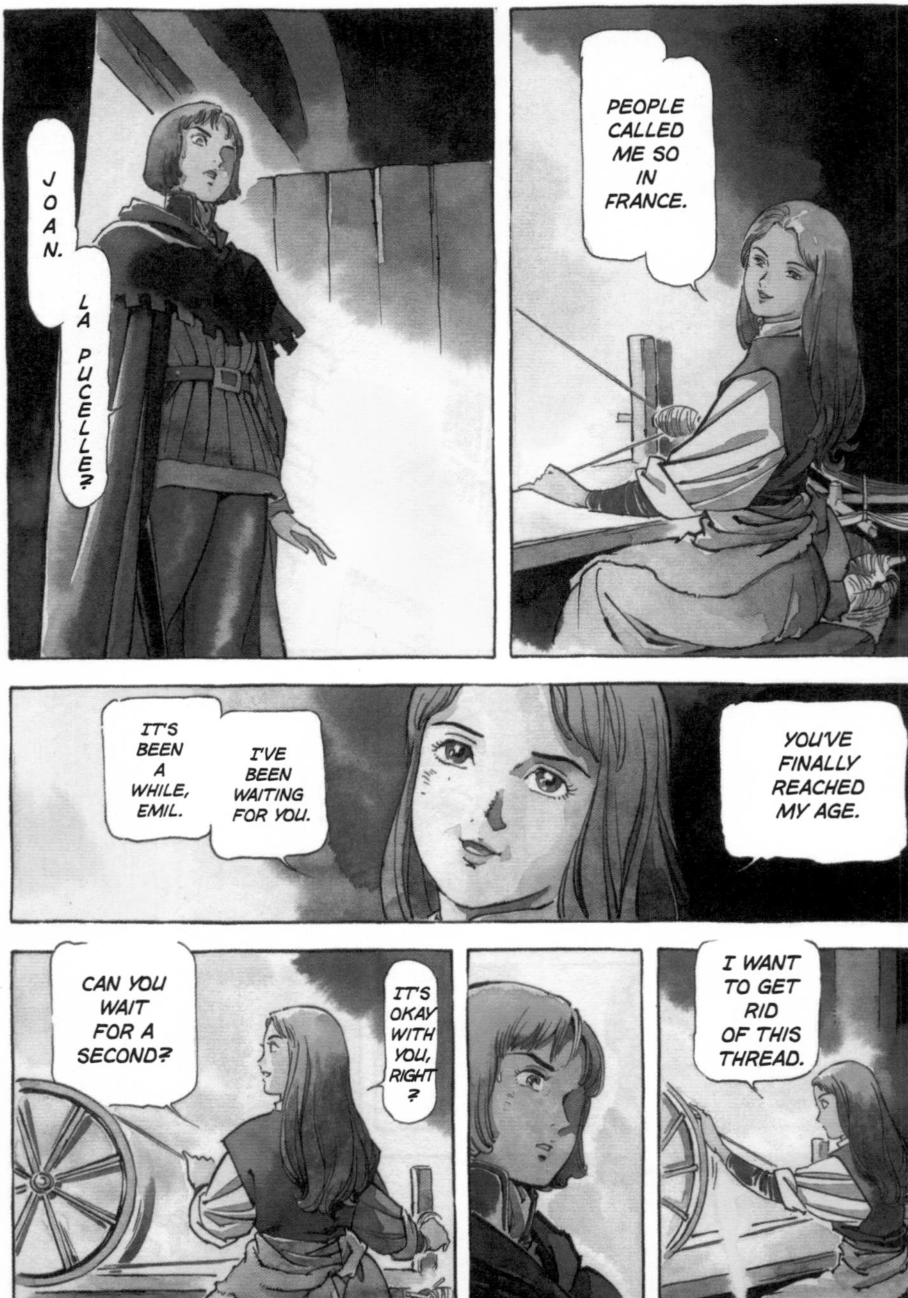
JOAN.
LA PUCELLE?
PEOPLE CALLED ME SO IN FRANCE.
IT'S BEEN A WHILE, EMIL.
I'VE BEEN WAITING FOR YOU.
YOU'VE FINALLY REACHED MY AGE.
CAN YOU WAIT FOR A SECOND?
IT'S OKAY WITH YOU, RIGHT?
I WANT TO GET RID OF THIS THREAD.

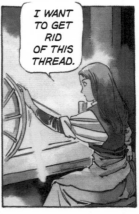

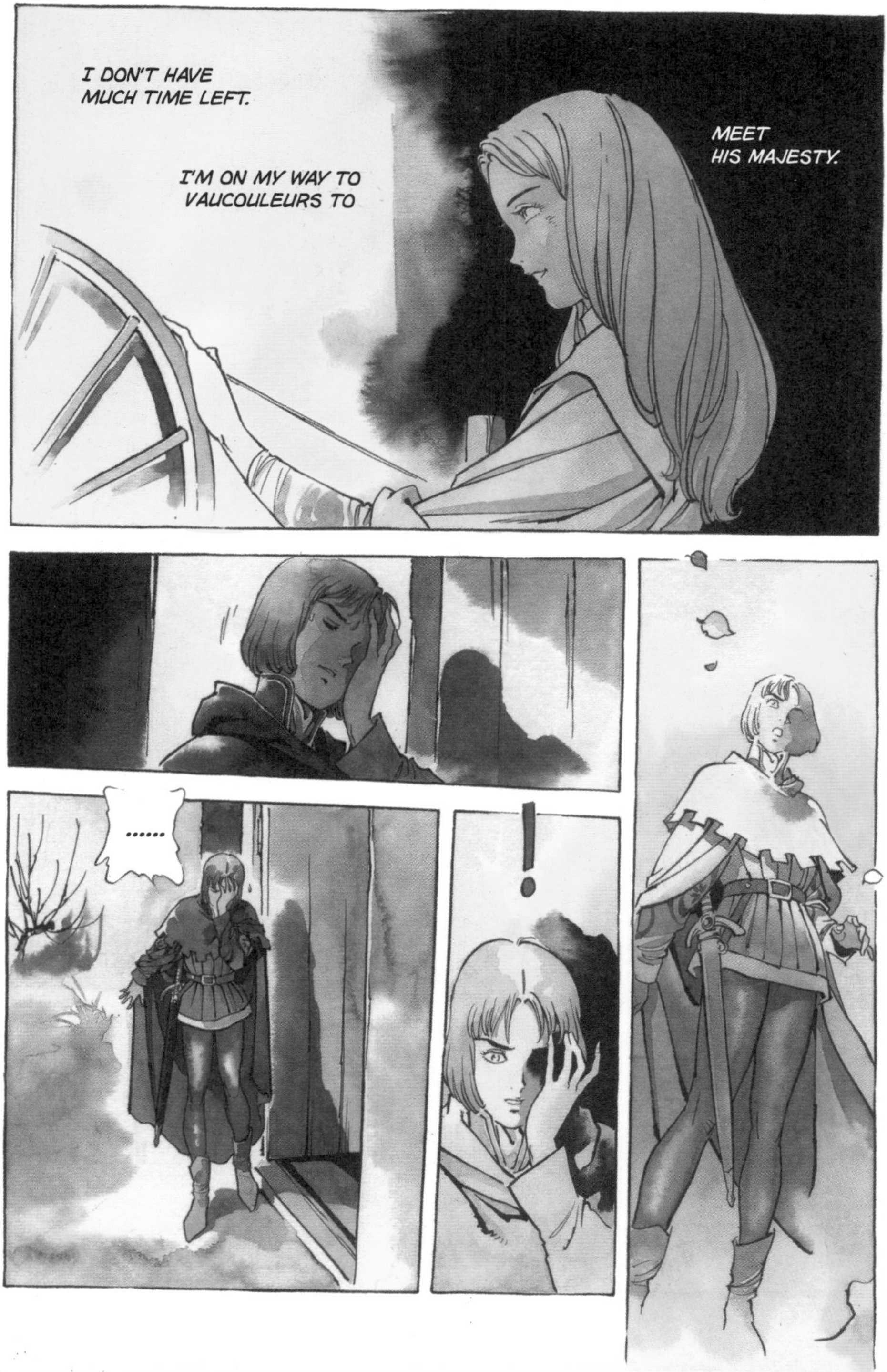

I DON'T HAVE MUCH TIME LEFT.
I'M ON MY WAY TO VAUCOULEURS TO
MEET HIS MAJESTY.
......
!

FALL?!    IS IT FALL NOW?

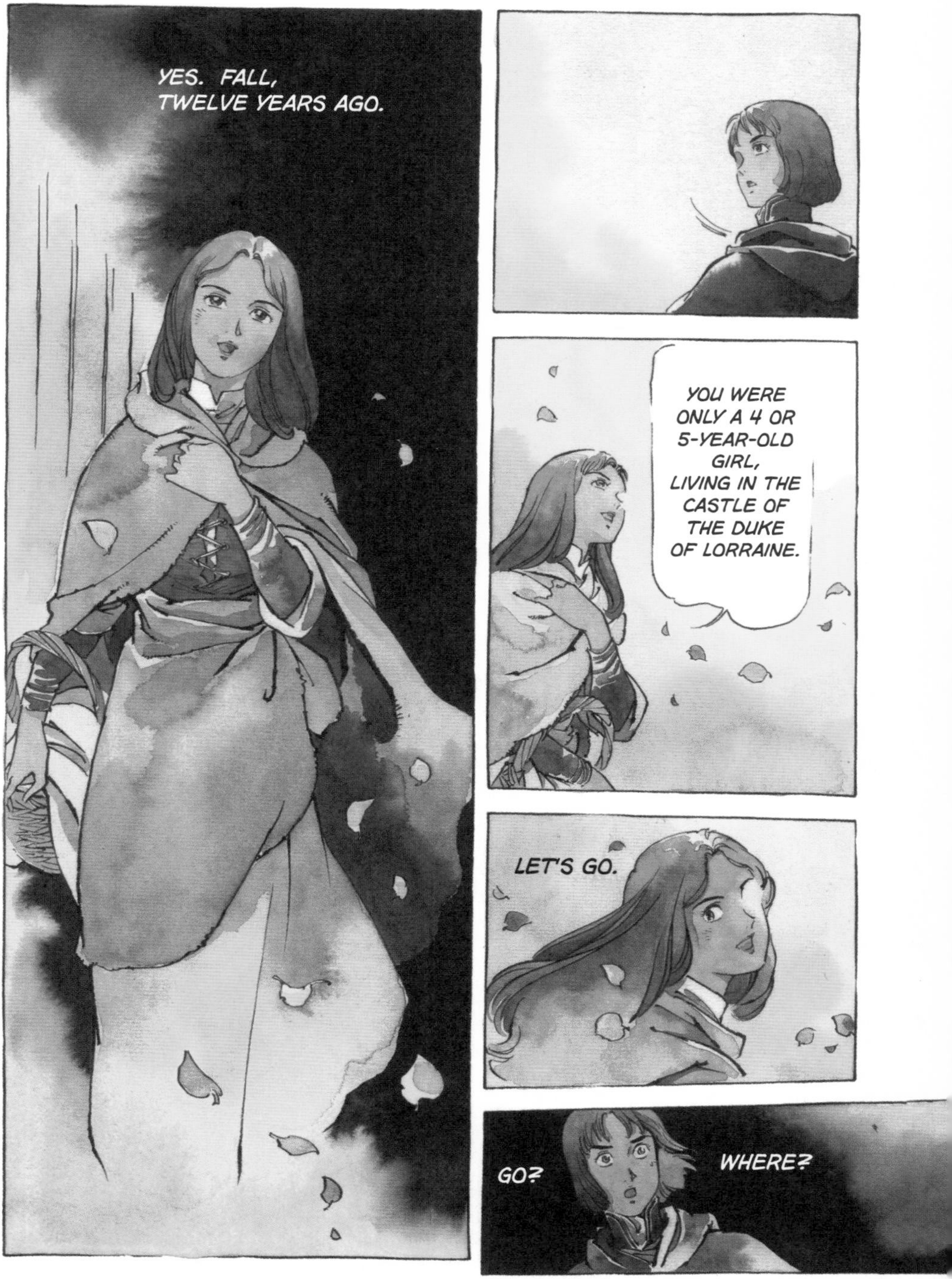
YES. FALL, TWELVE YEARS AGO.
YOU WERE ONLY A 4 OR 5-YEAR-OLD GIRL, LIVING IN THE CASTLE OF THE DUKE OF LORRAINE.
LET'S GO.
GO?
WHERE?

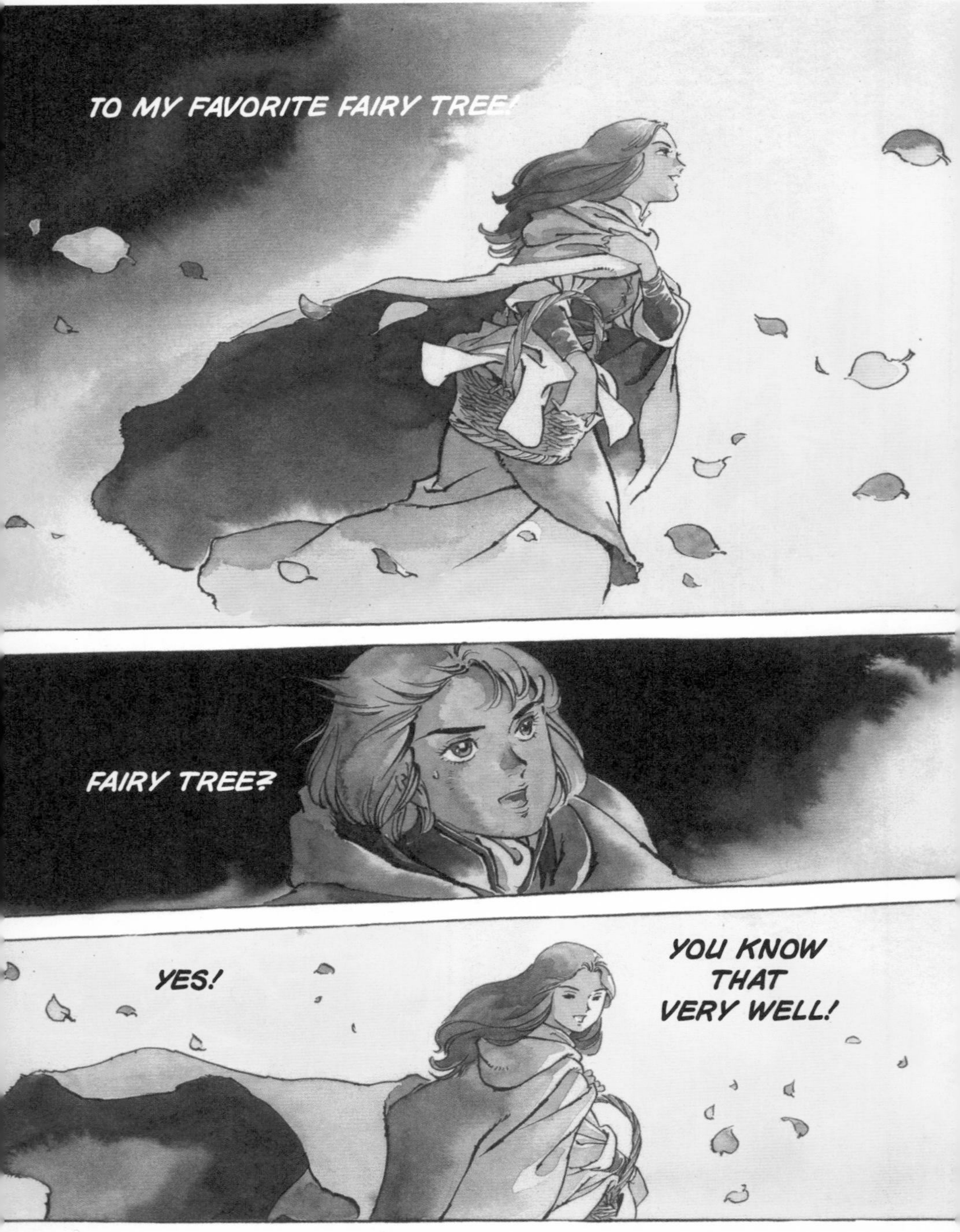
TO MY FAVORITE FAIRY TREE!
FAIRY TREE?
YES!
YOU KNOW THAT VERY WELL!

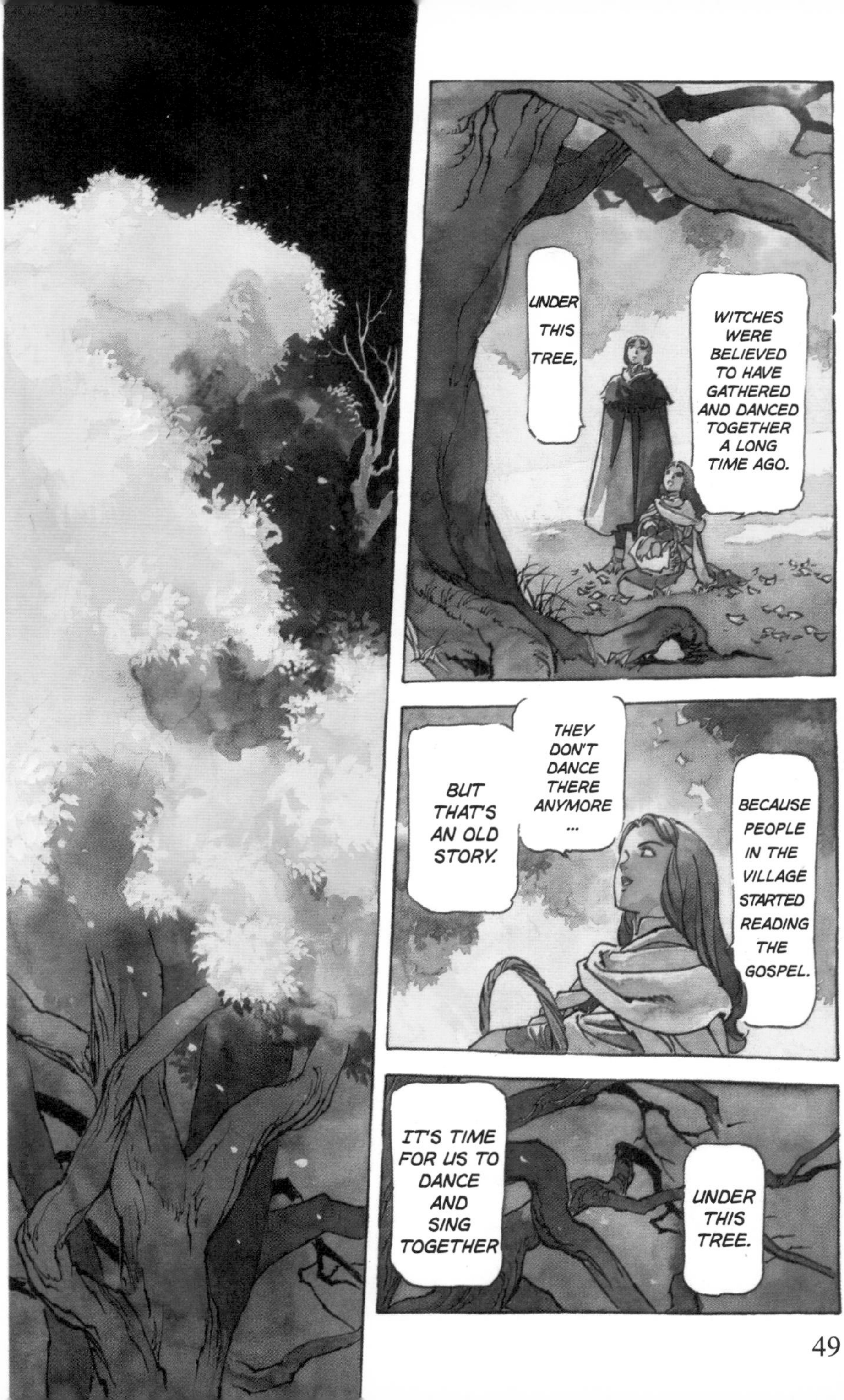
UNDER THIS TREE,
WITCHES WERE BELIEVED TO HAVE GATHERED AND DANCED TOGETHER A LONG TIME AGO.
BUT THAT'S AN OLD STORY.
THEY DON'T DANCE THERE ANYMORE ...
BECAUSE PEOPLE IN THE VILLAGE STARTED READING THE GOSPEL.
IT'S TIME FOR US TO DANCE AND SING TOGETHER
UNDER THIS TREE.

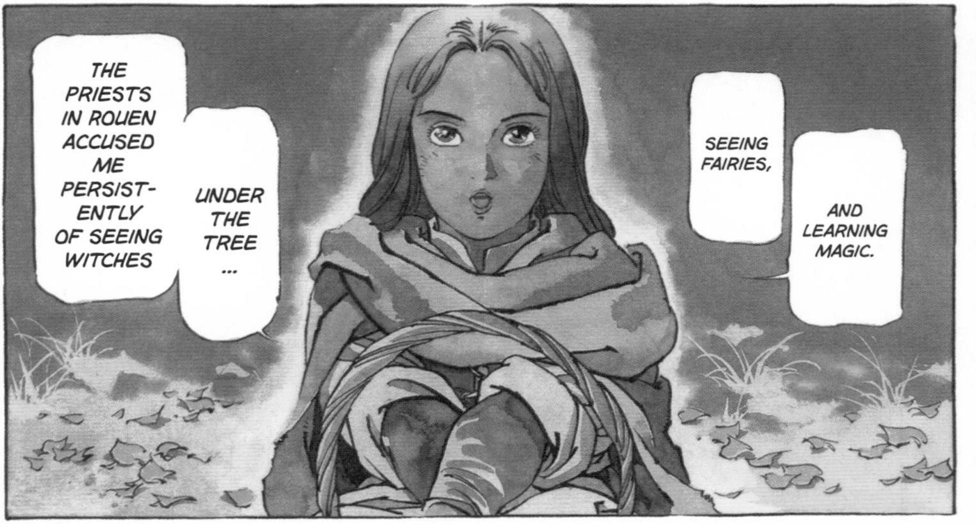
THE PRIESTS IN ROUEN ACCUSED ME PERSIST-ENTLY OF SEEING WITCHES
UNDER THE TREE ...
SEEING FAIRIES,
AND LEARNING MAGIC.

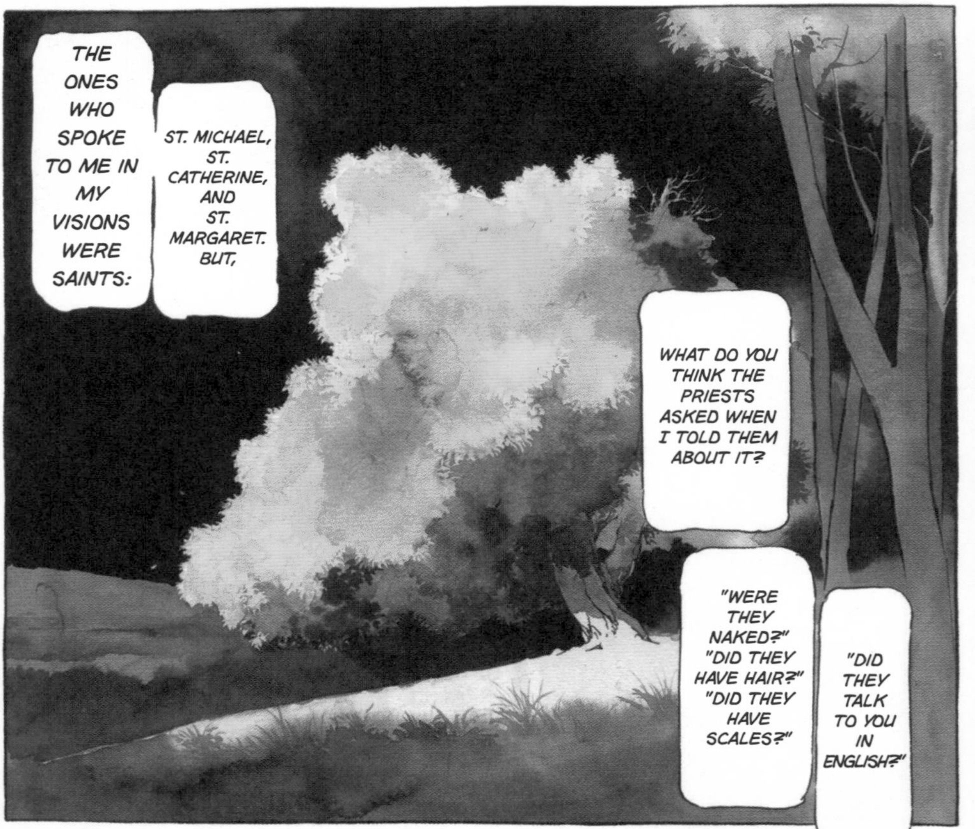
THE ONES WHO SPOKE TO ME IN MY VISIONS WERE SAINTS:
ST. MICHAEL, ST. CATHERINE, AND ST. MARGARET. BUT,
WHAT DO YOU THINK THE PRIESTS ASKED WHEN I TOLD THEM ABOUT IT?
"WERE THEY NAKED?" "DID THEY HAVE HAIR?" "DID THEY HAVE SCALES?"
"DID THEY TALK TO YOU IN ENGLISH?"

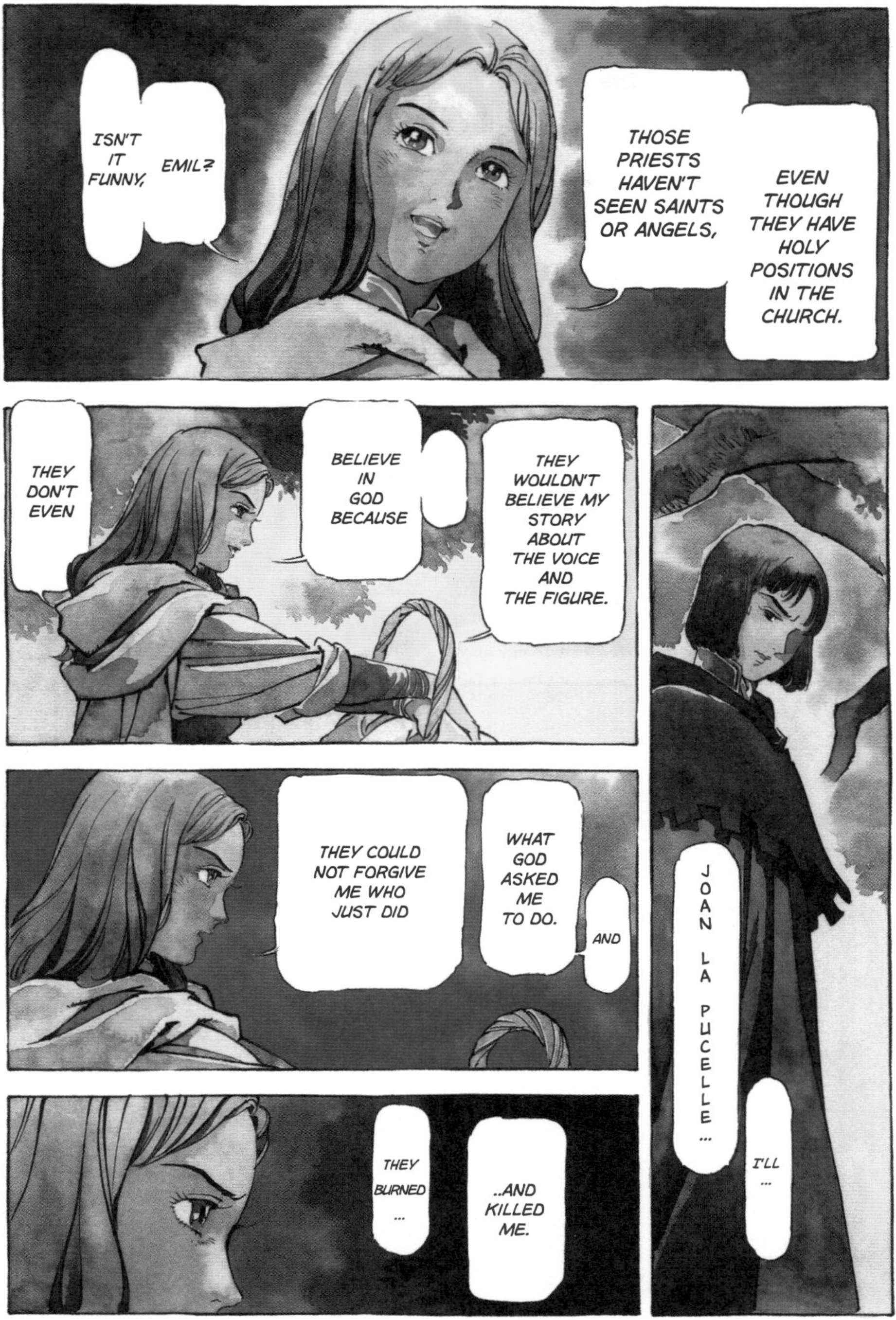

ISN'T IT FUNNY,
EMIL?
THOSE PRIESTS HAVEN'T SEEN SAINTS OR ANGELS,
EVEN THOUGH THEY HAVE HOLY POSITIONS IN THE CHURCH.
THEY DON'T EVEN
BELIEVE IN GOD BECAUSE
THEY WOULDN'T BELIEVE MY STORY ABOUT THE VOICE AND THE FIGURE.
THEY COULD NOT FORGIVE ME WHO JUST DID
WHAT GOD ASKED ME TO DO.
AND
THEY BURNED ...
..AND KILLED ME.
JOAN LA PUCELLE ...
I'LL ...

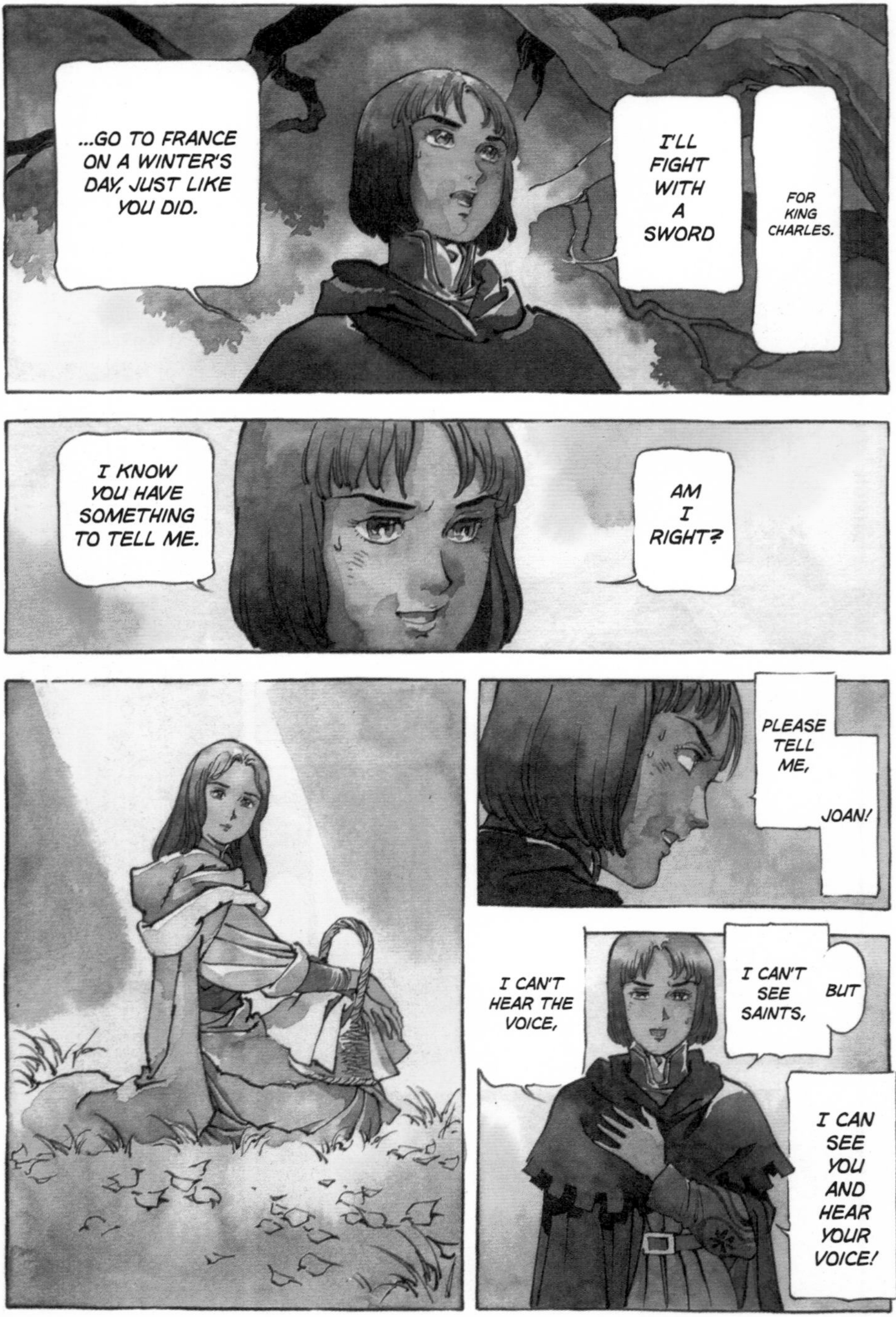
...GO TO FRANCE ON A WINTER'S DAY, JUST LIKE YOU DID.
I'LL FIGHT WITH A SWORD
FOR KING CHARLES.
I KNOW YOU HAVE SOMETHING TO TELL ME.
AM I RIGHT?
PLEASE TELL ME,
JOAN!
I CAN'T SEE SAINTS,
BUT
I CAN'T HEAR THE VOICE,
I CAN SEE YOU AND HEAR YOUR VOICE!

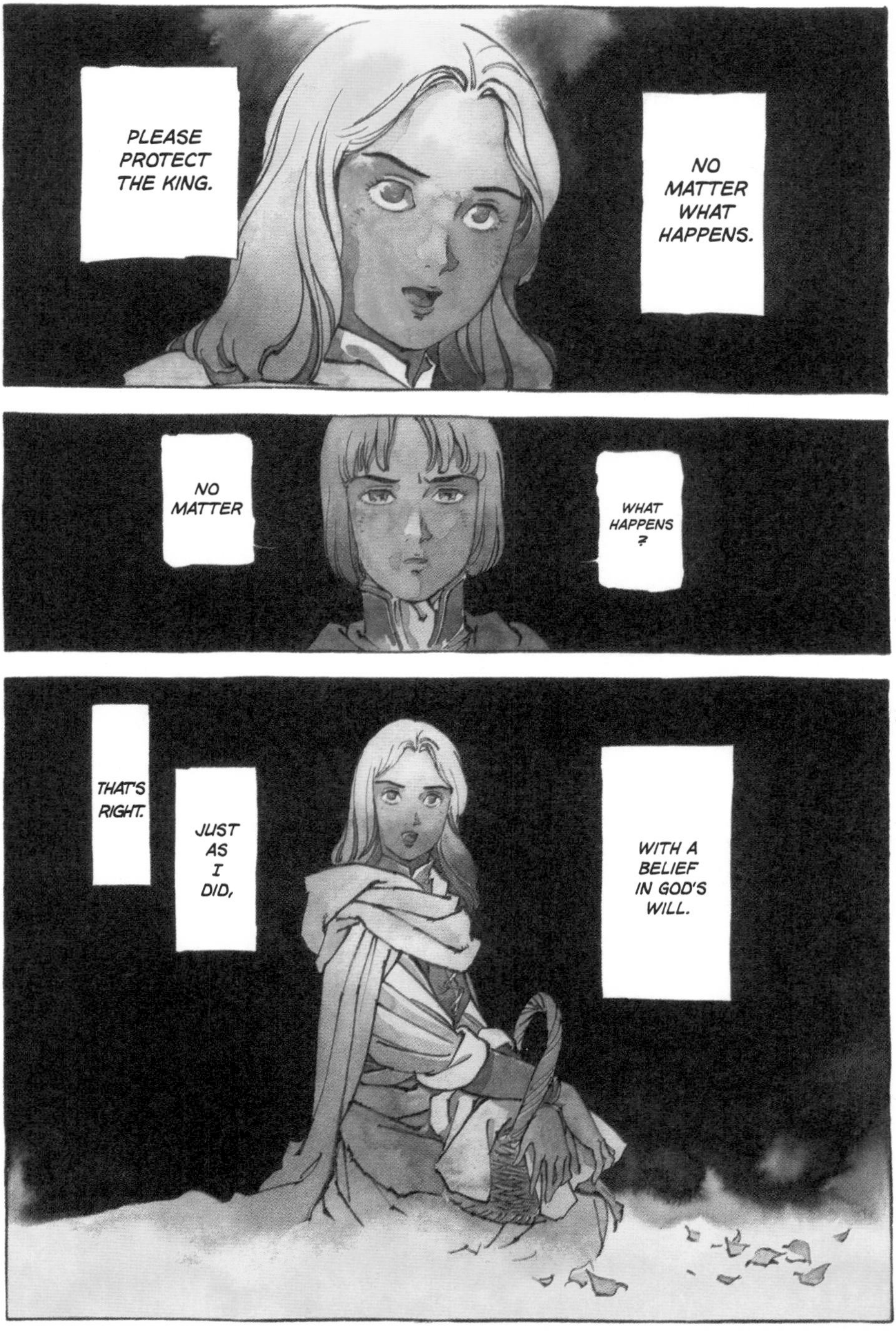
PLEASE PROTECT THE KING.
NO MATTER WHAT HAPPENS.
NO MATTER
WHAT HAPPENS ?
THAT'S RIGHT.
JUST AS I DID,
WITH A BELIEF IN GOD'S WILL.

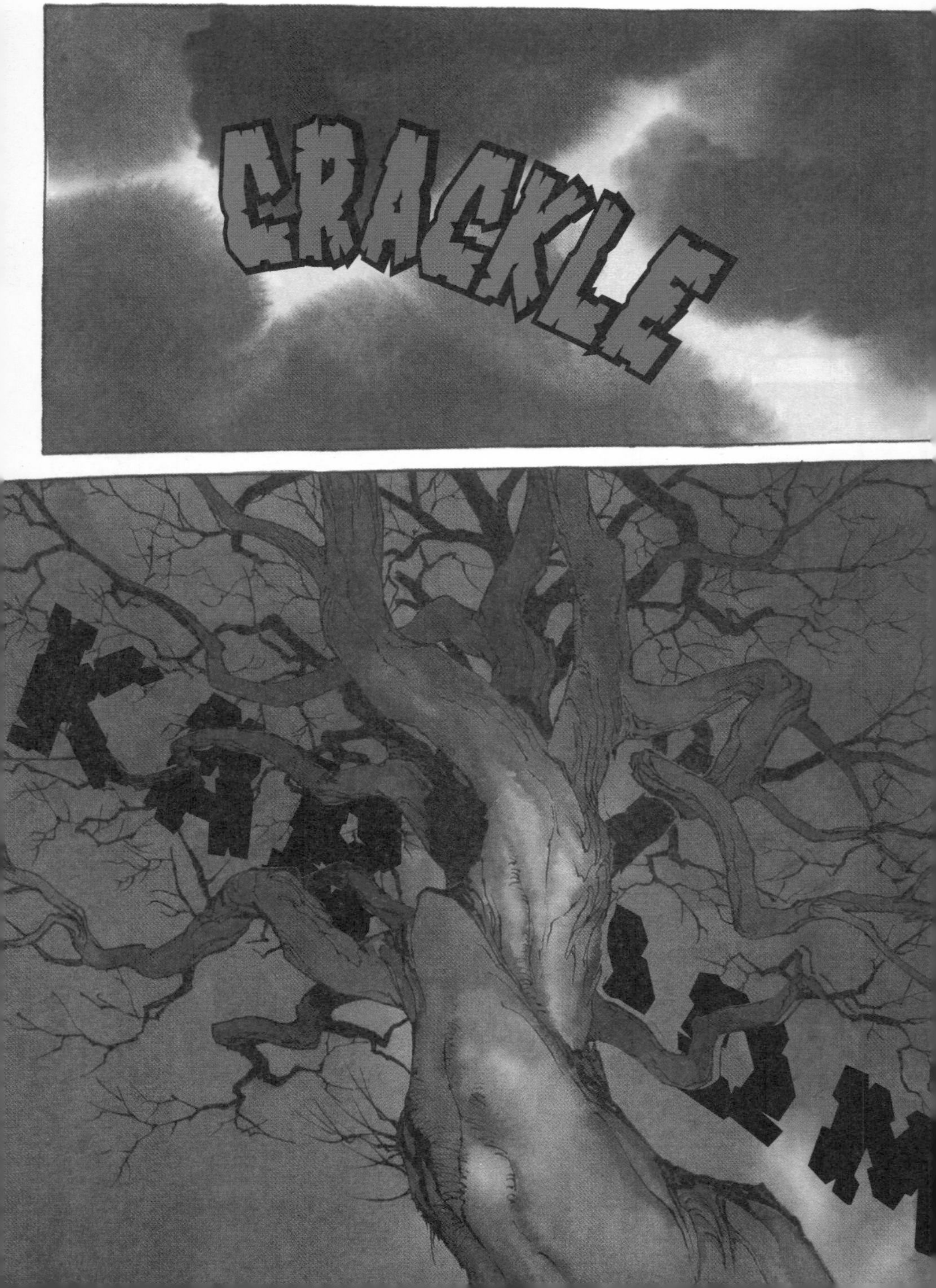
CRACKLE
KABOOM

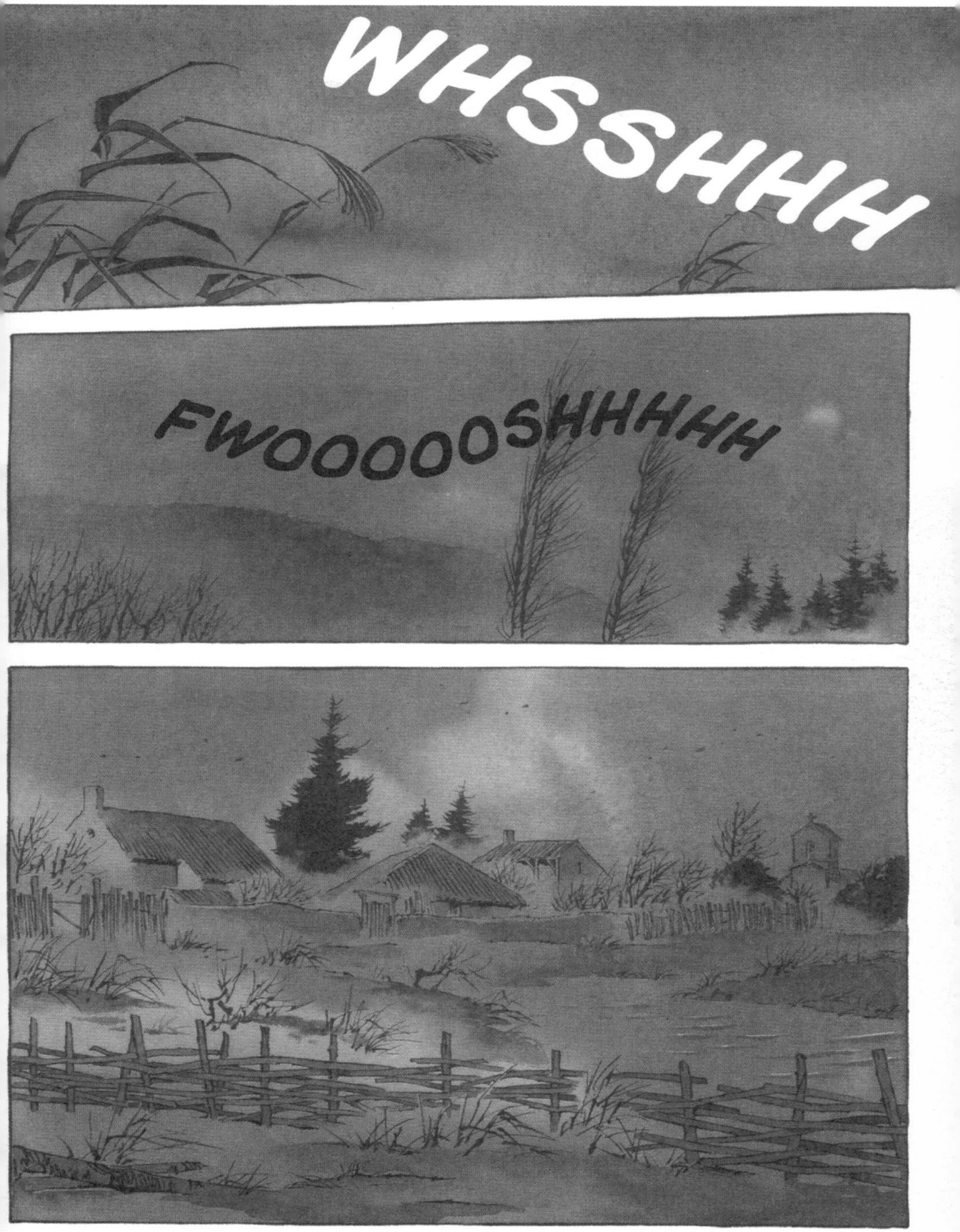
WHSSHHH
FWOOOOOOSHHHHH

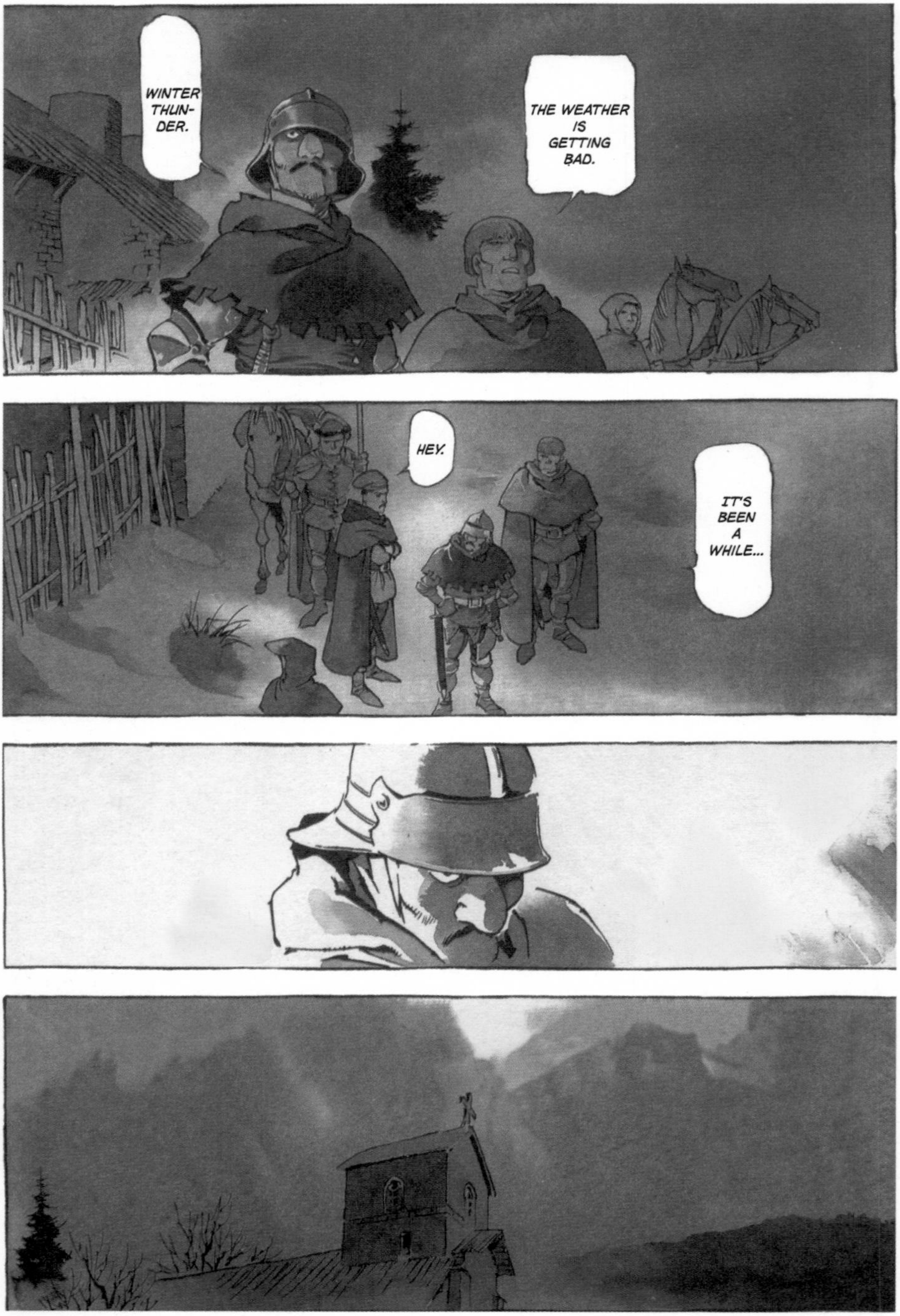

WINTER THUNDER.
THE WEATHER IS GETTING BAD.
HEY.
IT'S BEEN A WHILE...

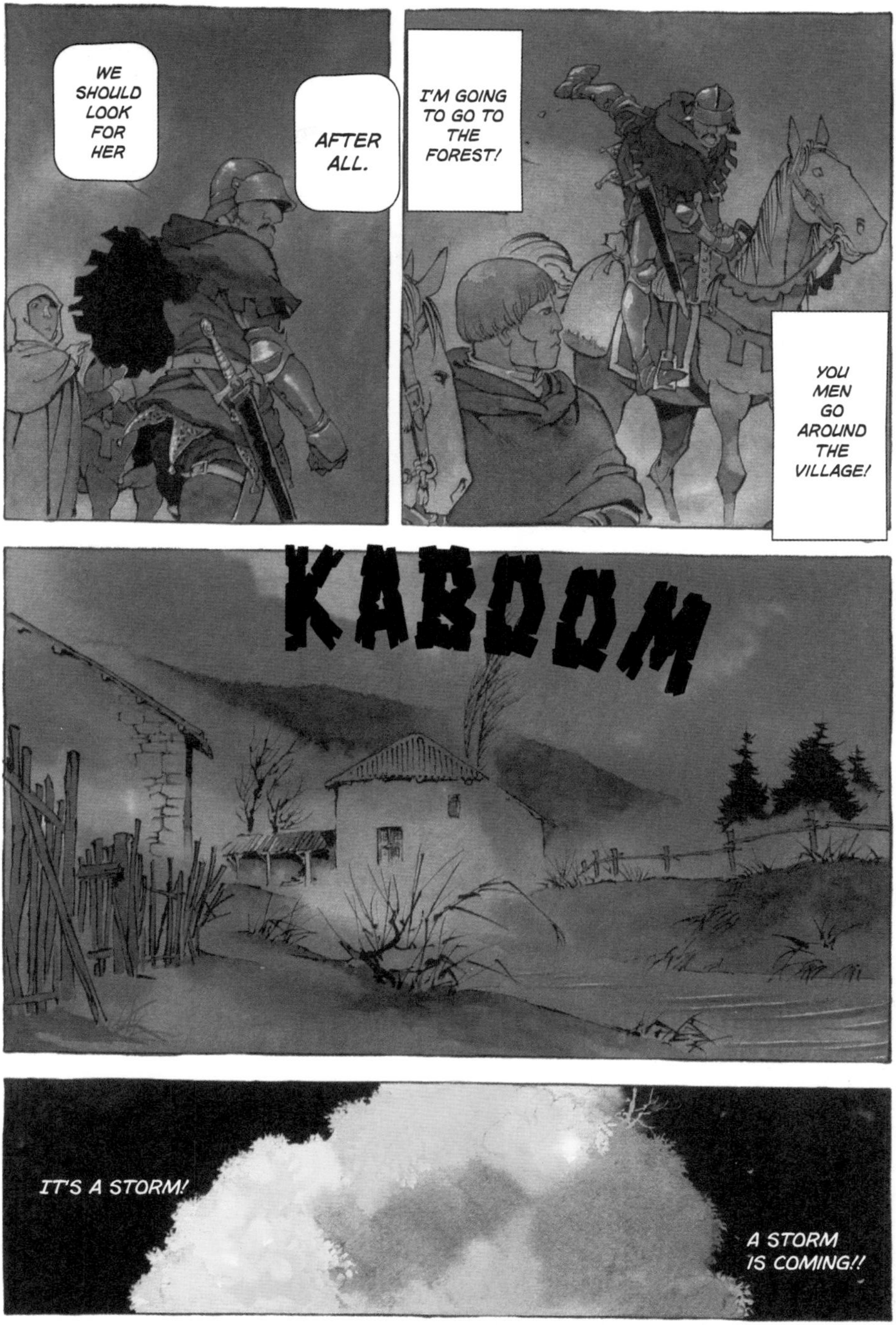
WE SHOULD LOOK FOR HER
AFTER ALL.
I'M GOING TO GO TO THE FOREST!
YOU MEN GO AROUND THE VILLAGE!
KABOOM
IT'S A STORM!
A STORM IS COMING!!

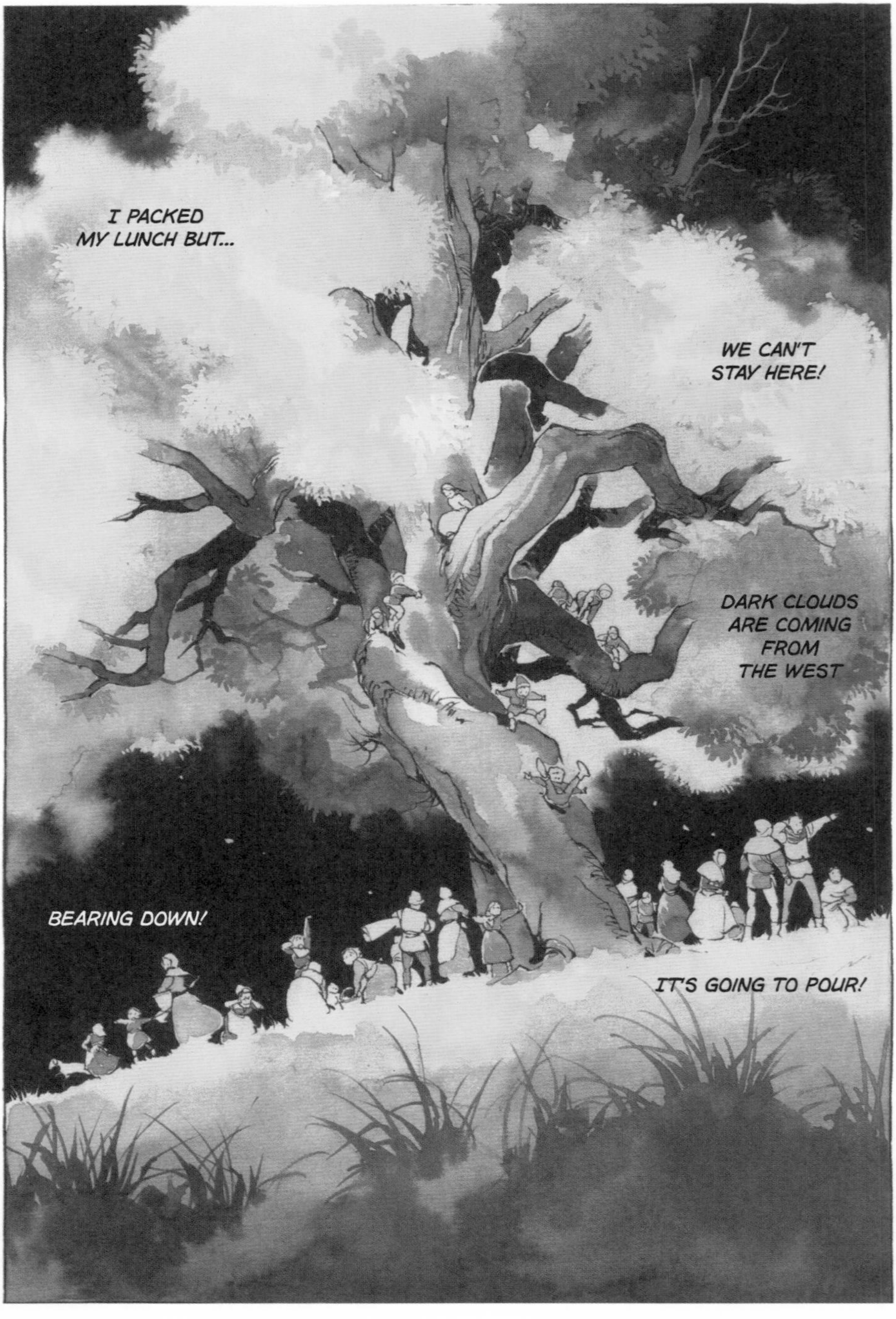
I PACKED
MY LUNCH BUT...
WE CAN'T
STAY HERE!
DARK CLOUDS
ARE COMING
FROM
THE WEST
BEARING DOWN!
IT'S GOING TO POUR!

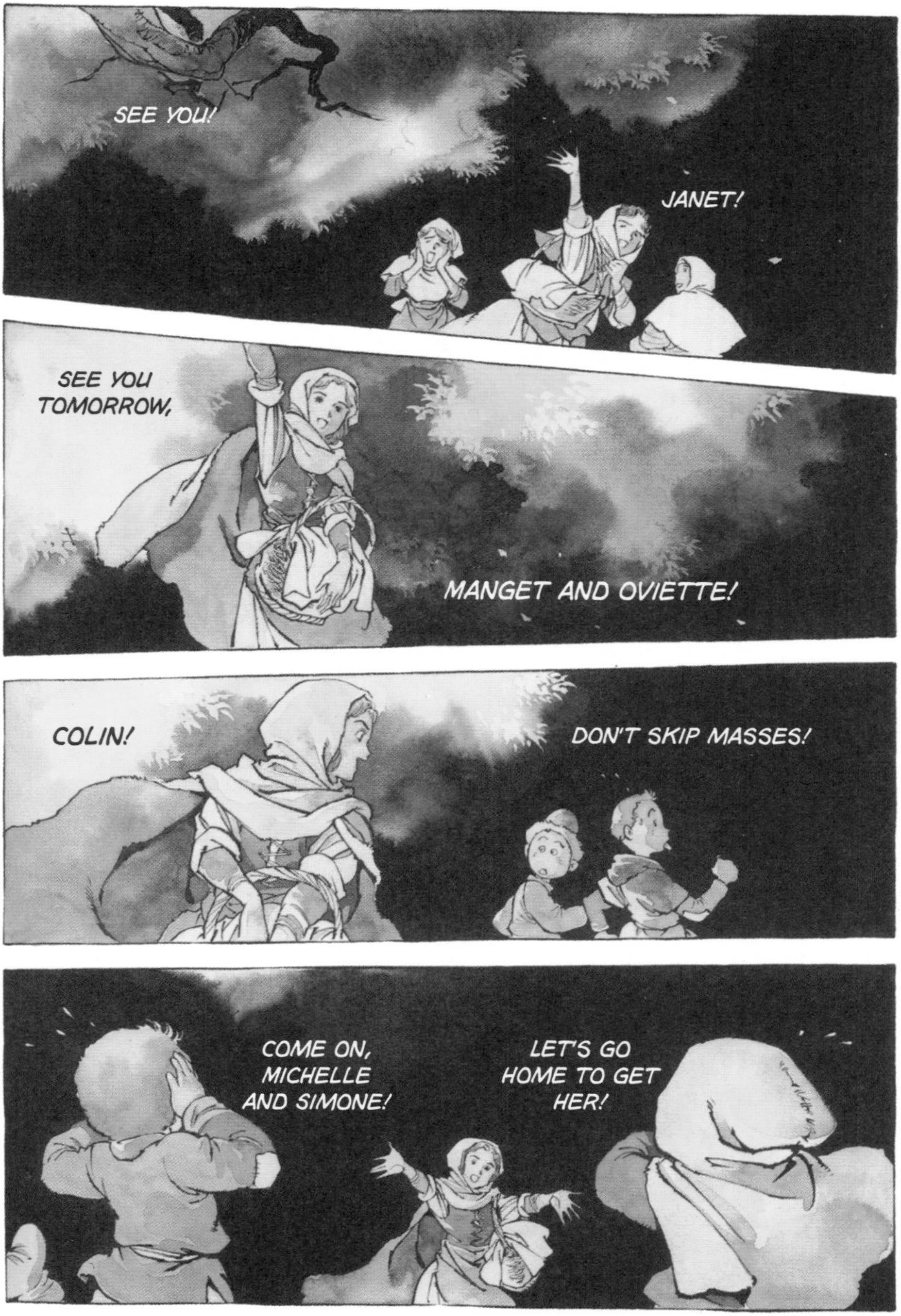
SEE YOU!
JANET!
SEE YOU TOMORROW,
MANGET AND OVIETTE!
COLIN!
DON'T SKIP MASSES!
COME ON, MICHELLE AND SIMONE!
LET'S GO HOME TO GET HER!

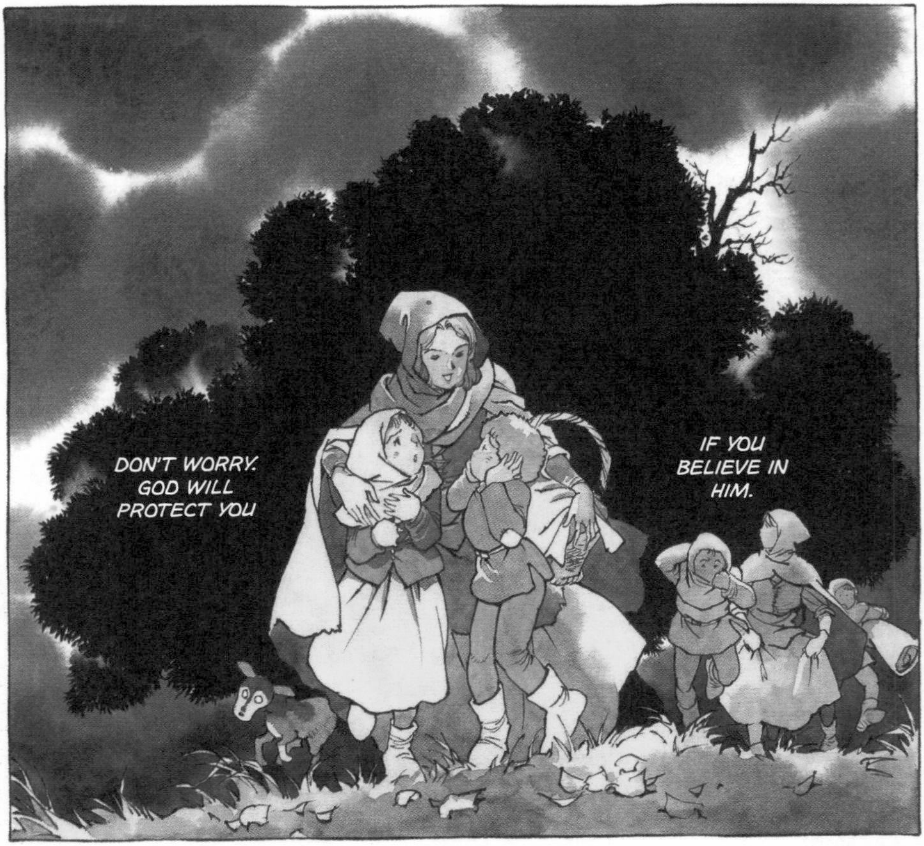
DON'T WORRY. GOD WILL PROTECT YOU
IF YOU BELIEVE IN HIM.

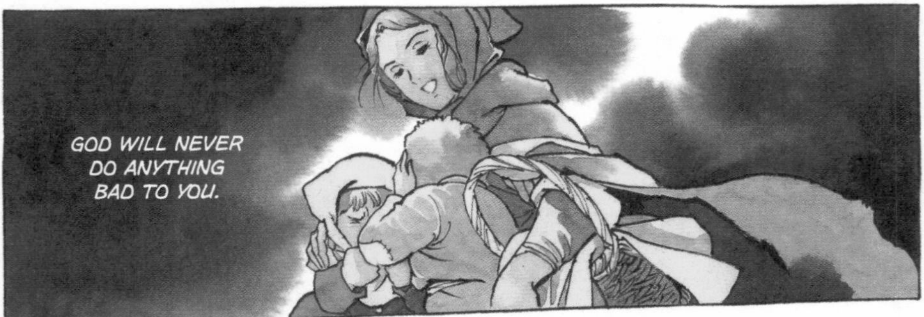
GOD WILL NEVER DO ANYTHING BAD TO YOU.

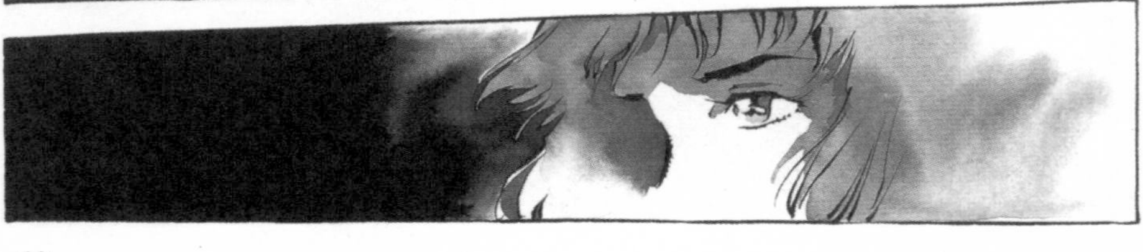

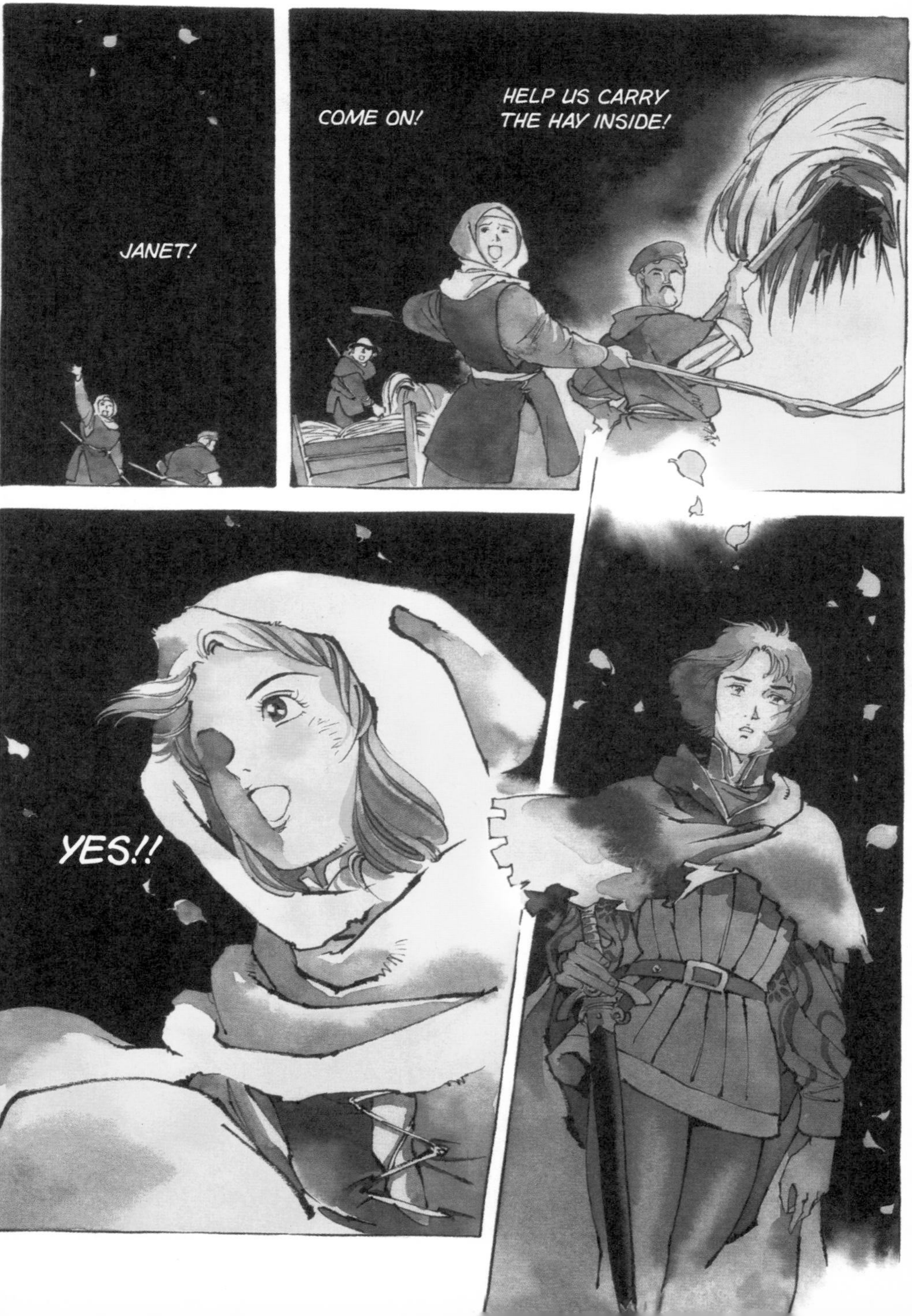
JANET!
COME ON!
HELP US CARRY THE HAY INSIDE!
YES!!

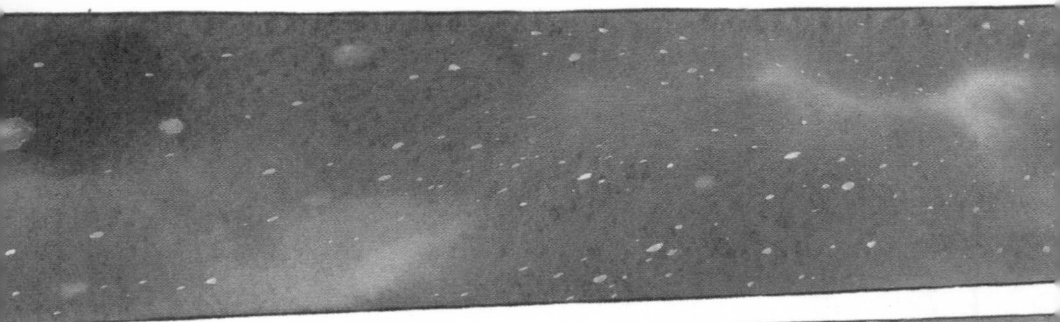
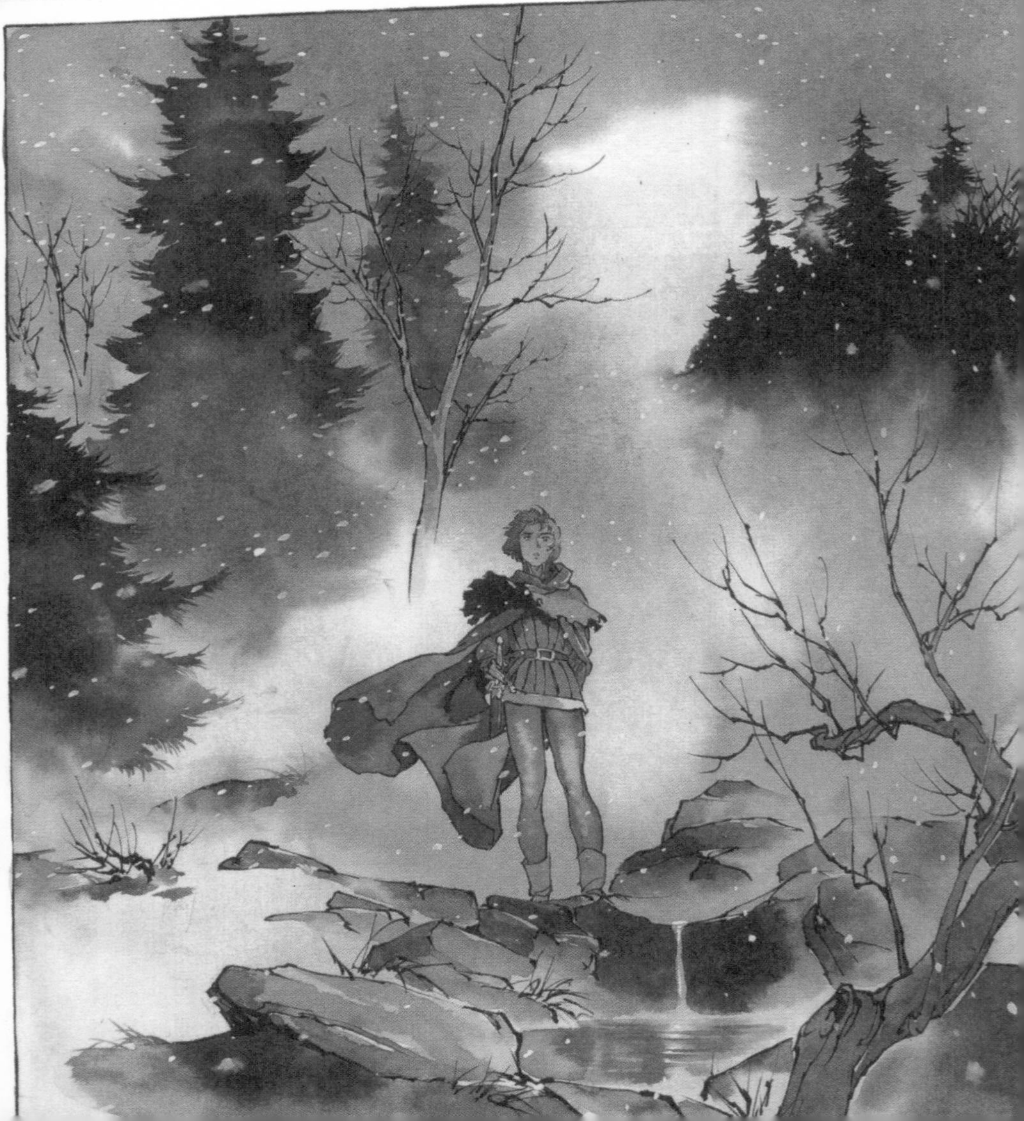

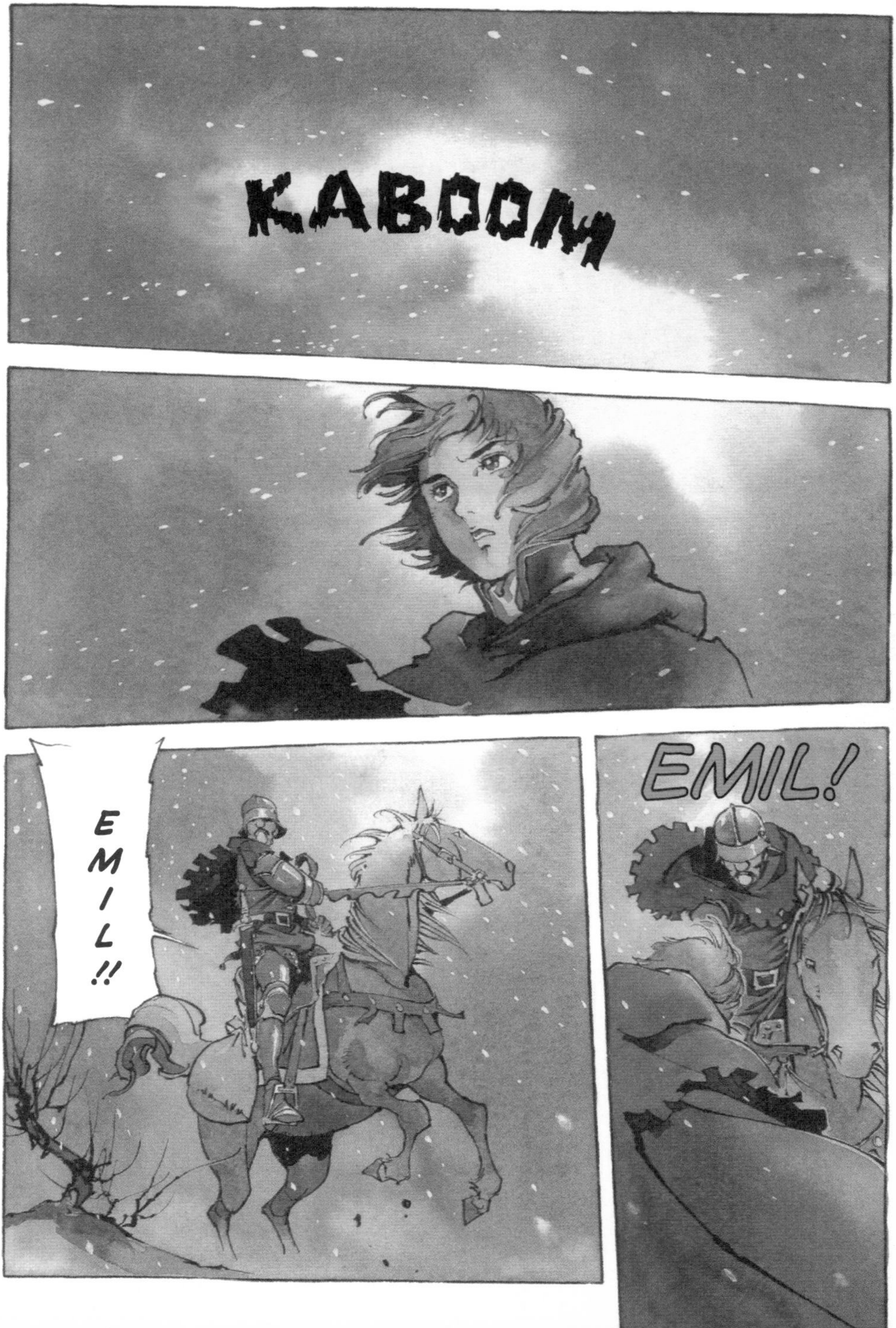
KABOOM
EMIL!!
EMIL!

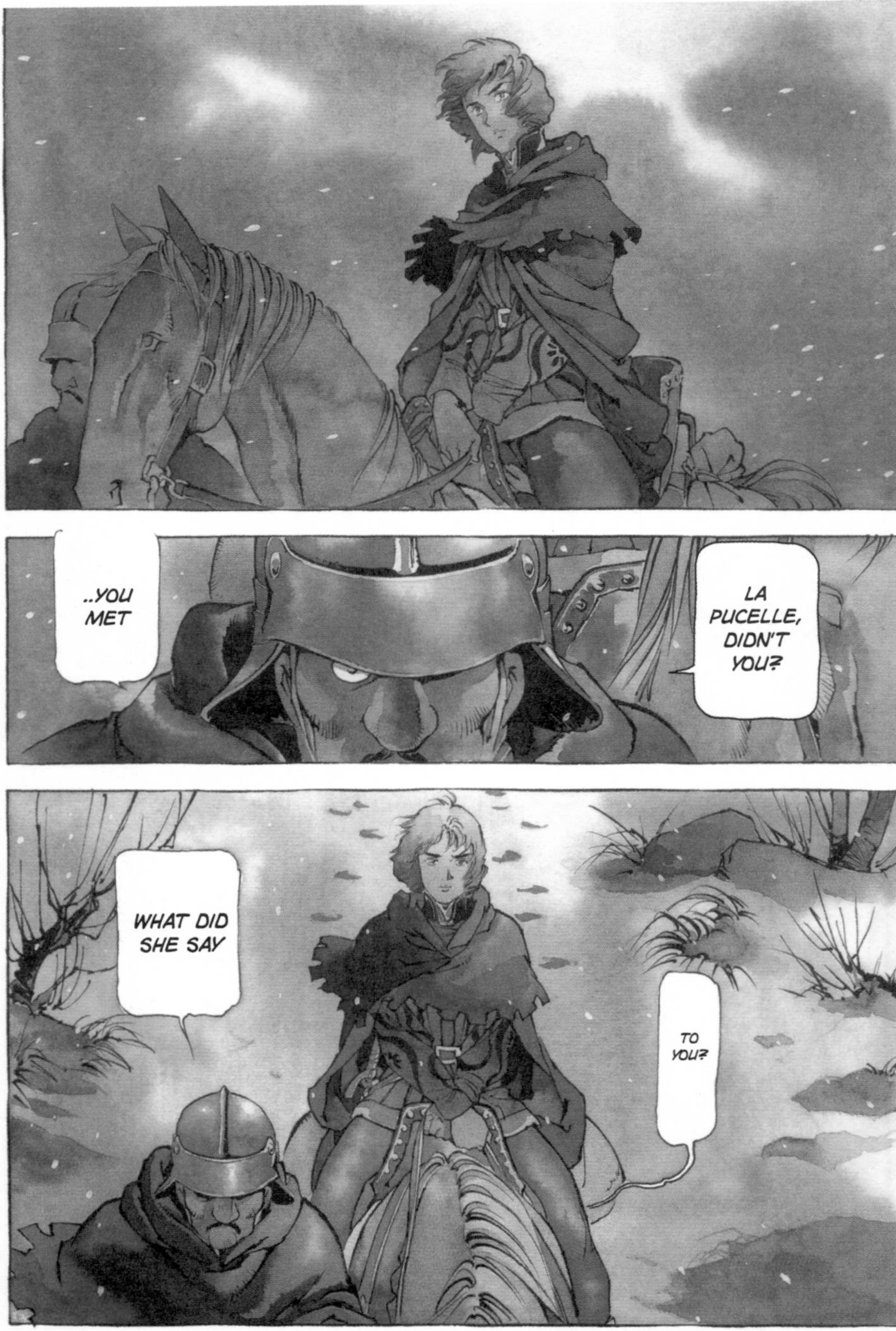
..YOU MET
LA PUCELLE, DIDN'T YOU?
WHAT DID SHE SAY
TO YOU?

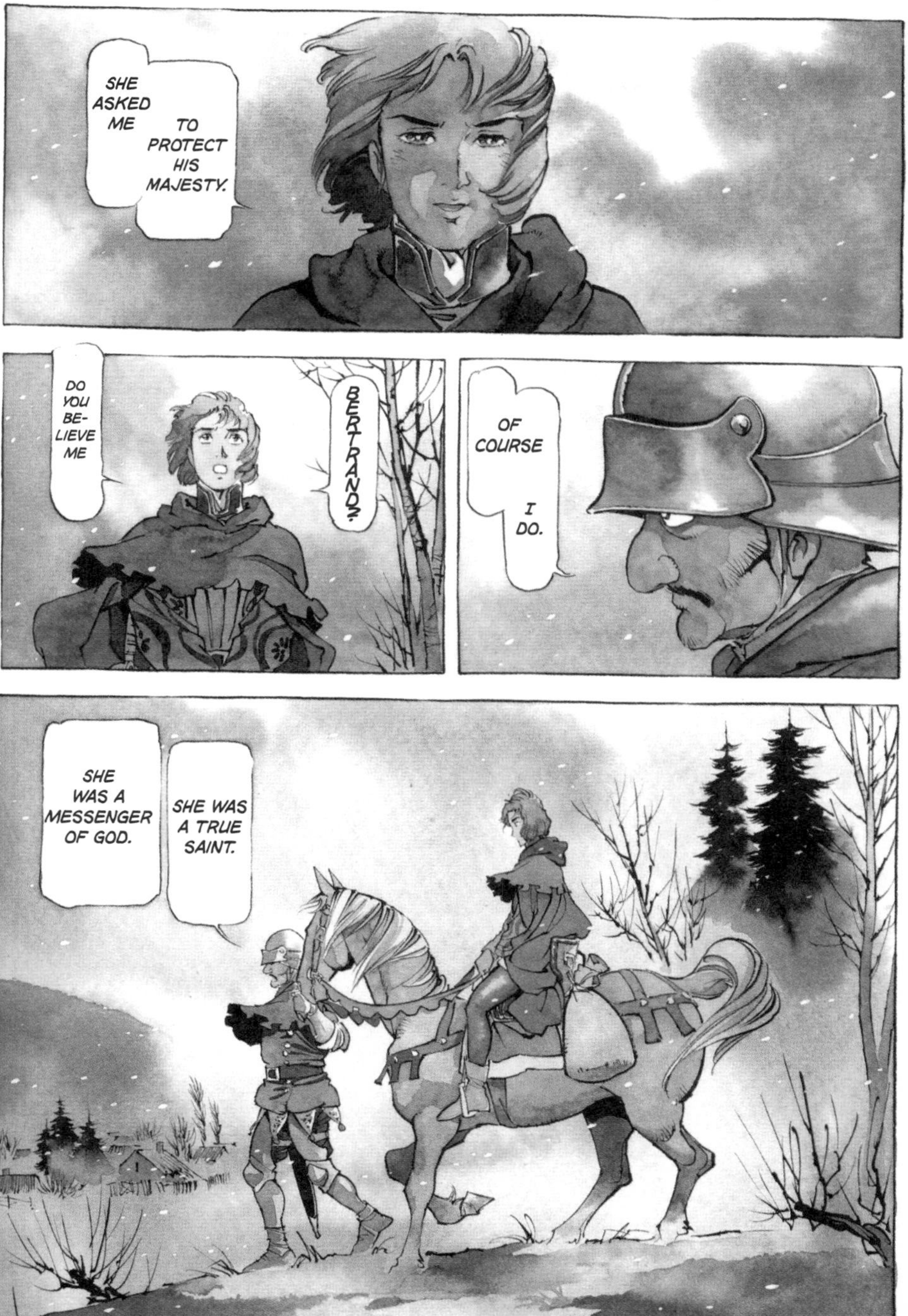
SHE ASKED ME TO PROTECT HIS MAJESTY.
DO YOU BE-LIEVE ME
BERTRAND?
OF COURSE I DO.
SHE WAS A MESSENGER OF GOD.
SHE WAS A TRUE SAINT.

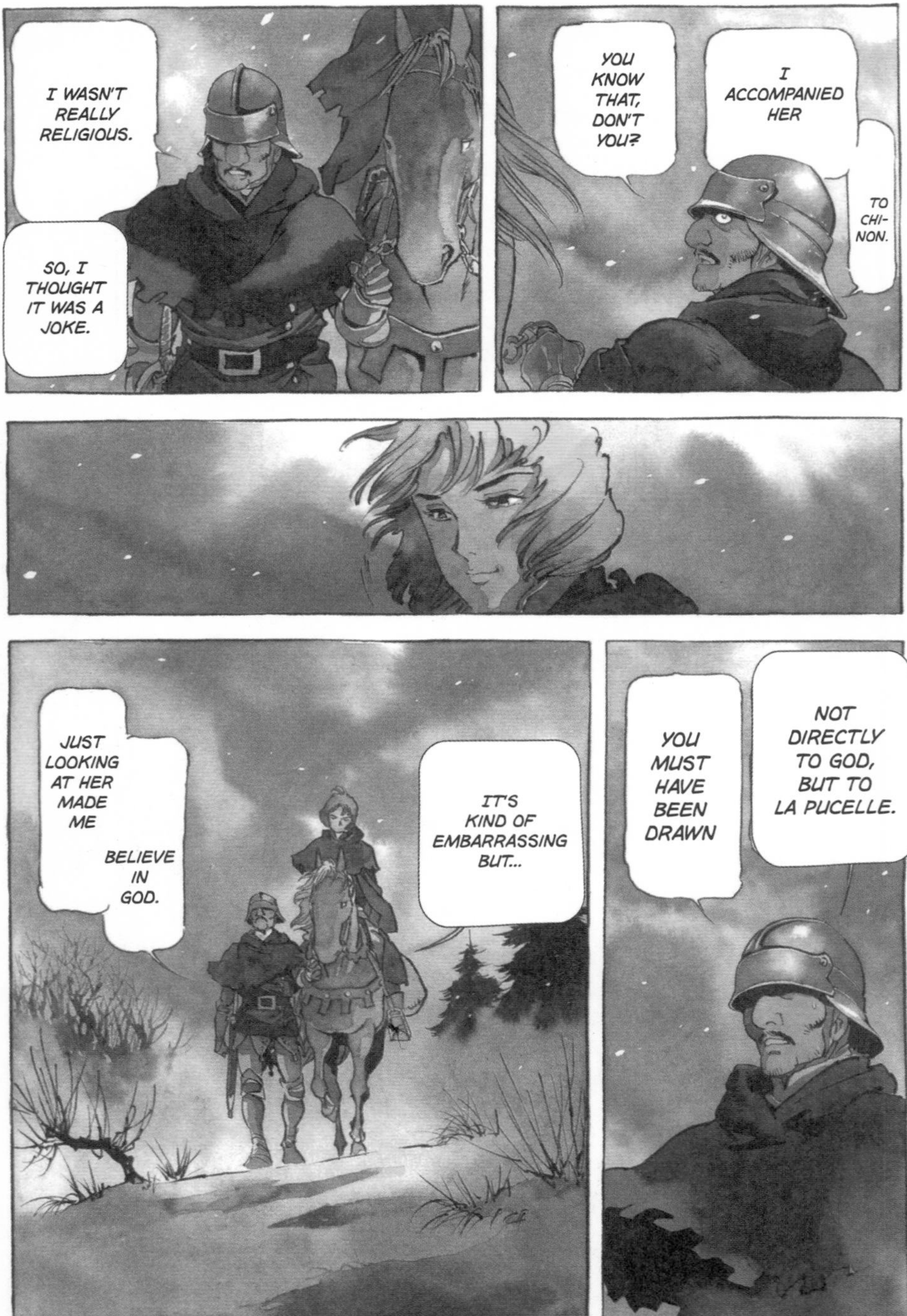
I WASN'T REALLY RELIGIOUS.
SO, I THOUGHT IT WAS A JOKE.
YOU KNOW THAT, DON'T YOU?
I ACCOMPANIED HER
TO CHI-NON.
JUST LOOKING AT HER MADE ME
BELIEVE IN GOD.
IT'S KIND OF EMBARRASSING BUT...
YOU MUST HAVE BEEN DRAWN
NOT DIRECTLY TO GOD, BUT TO LA PUCELLE.

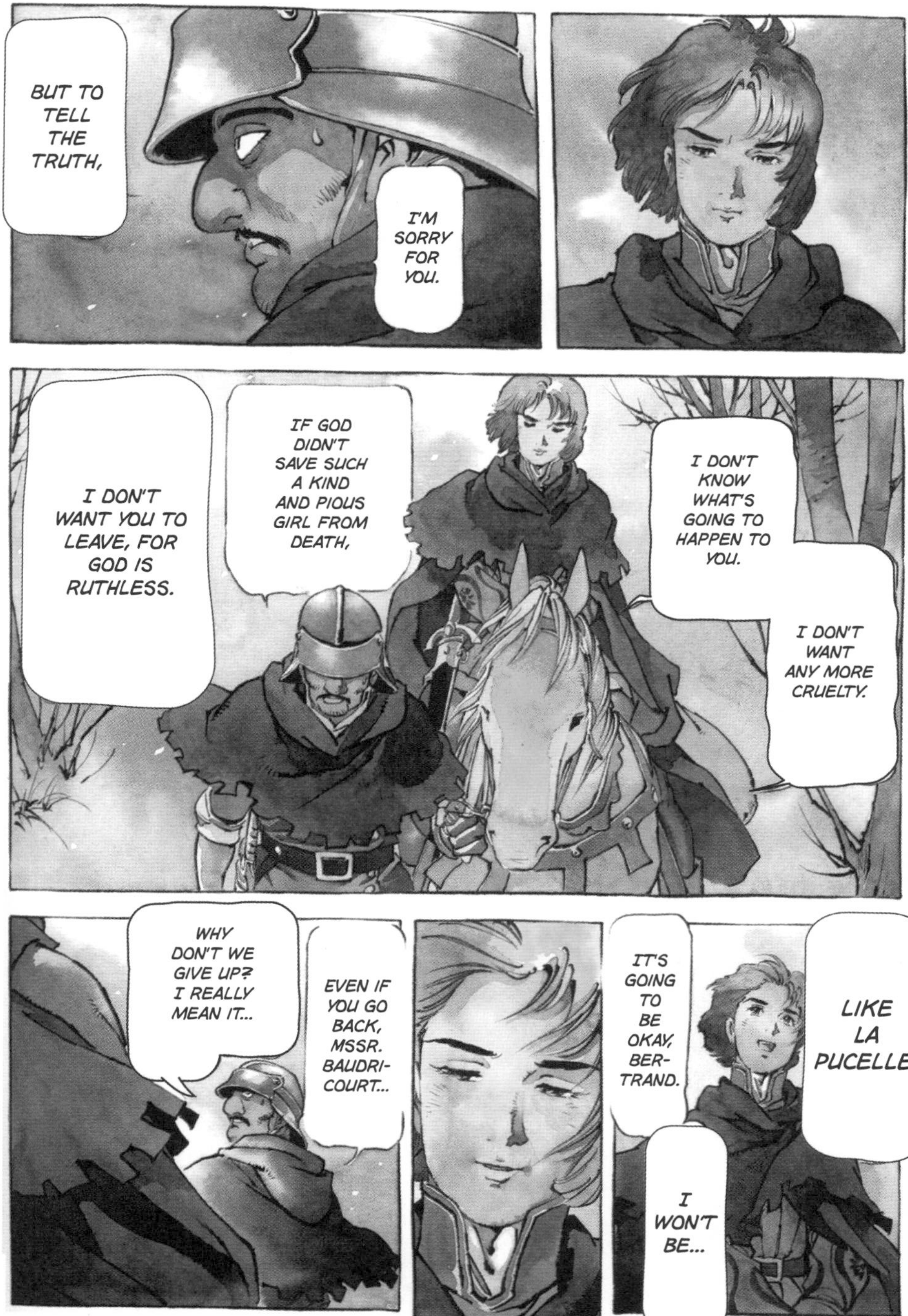
BUT TO TELL THE TRUTH,
I'M SORRY FOR YOU.
I DON'T WANT YOU TO LEAVE, FOR GOD IS RUTHLESS.
IF GOD DIDN'T SAVE SUCH A KIND AND PIOUS GIRL FROM DEATH,
I DON'T KNOW WHAT'S GOING TO HAPPEN TO YOU.
I DON'T WANT ANY MORE CRUELTY.
WHY DON'T WE GIVE UP? I REALLY MEAN IT...
EVEN IF YOU GO BACK, MSSR. BAUDRI-COURT...
IT'S GOING TO BE OKAY, BER-TRAND.
I WON'T BE...
LIKE LA PUCELLE.

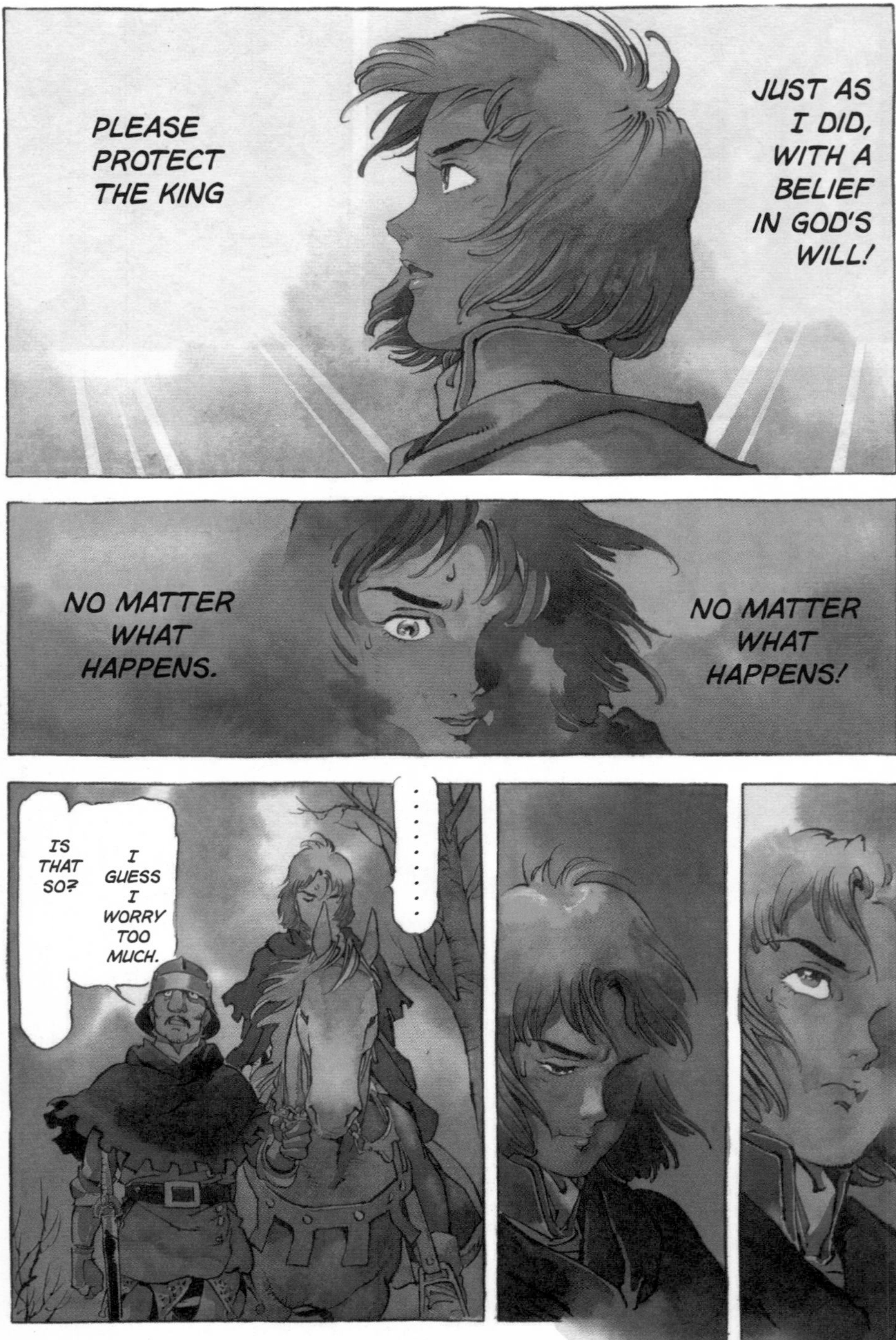
PLEASE PROTECT THE KING
JUST AS I DID, WITH A BELIEF IN GOD'S WILL!
NO MATTER WHAT HAPPENS.
NO MATTER WHAT HAPPENS!
IS THAT SO?
I GUESS I WORRY TOO MUCH.
.......

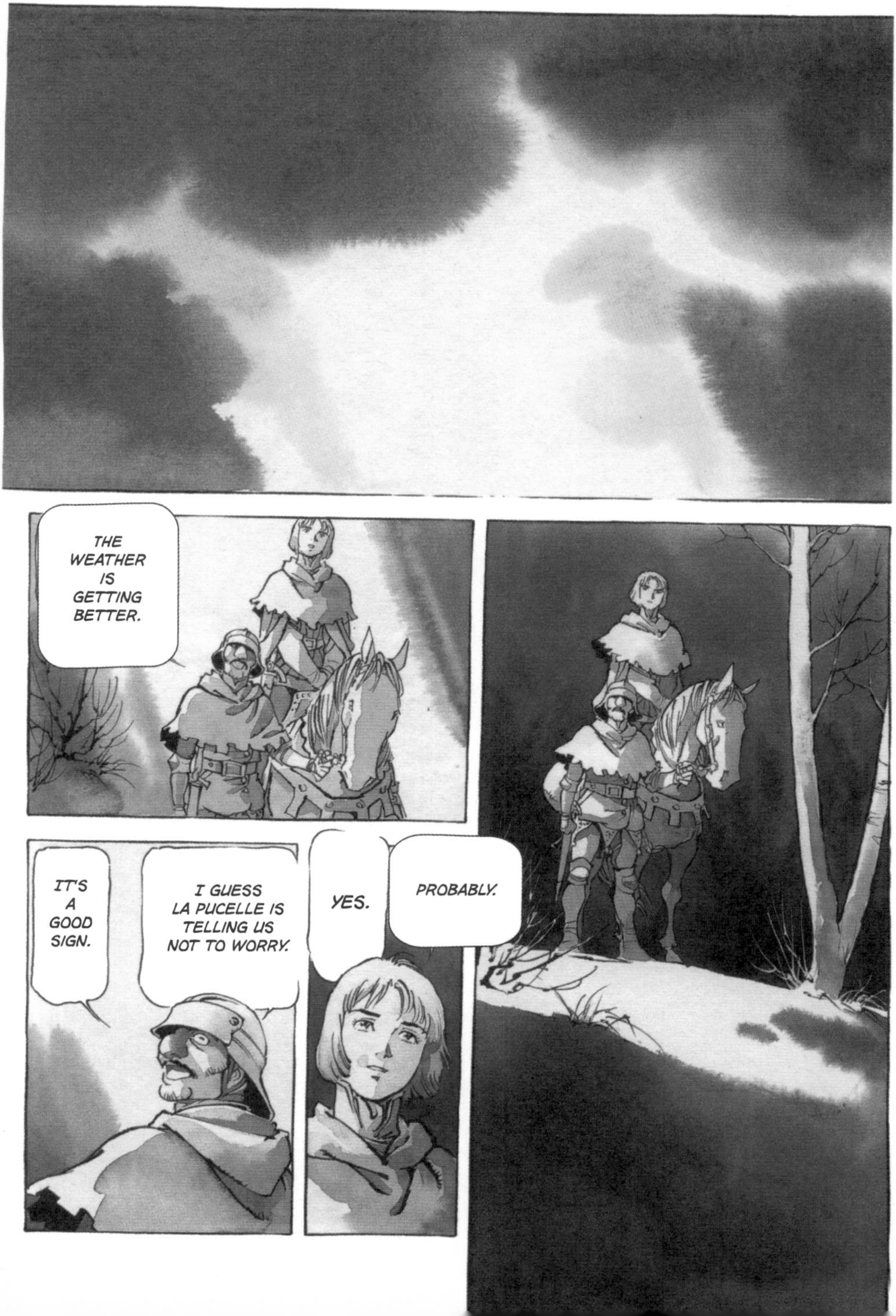
THE WEATHER IS GETTING BETTER.
IT'S A GOOD SIGN.
I GUESS LA PUCELLE IS TELLING US NOT TO WORRY.
YES.
PROBABLY.

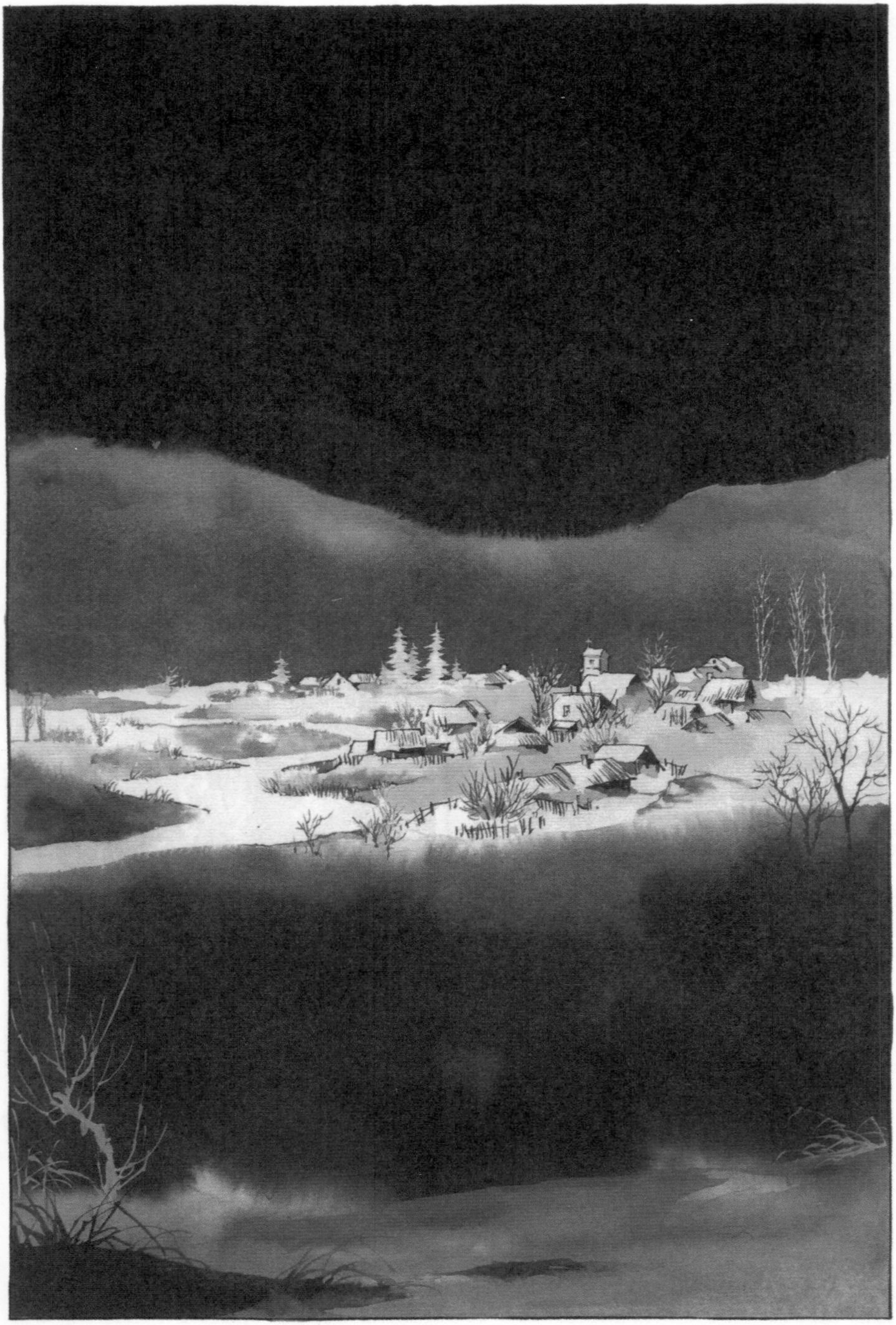

# Chapter 2

# ORLEANS

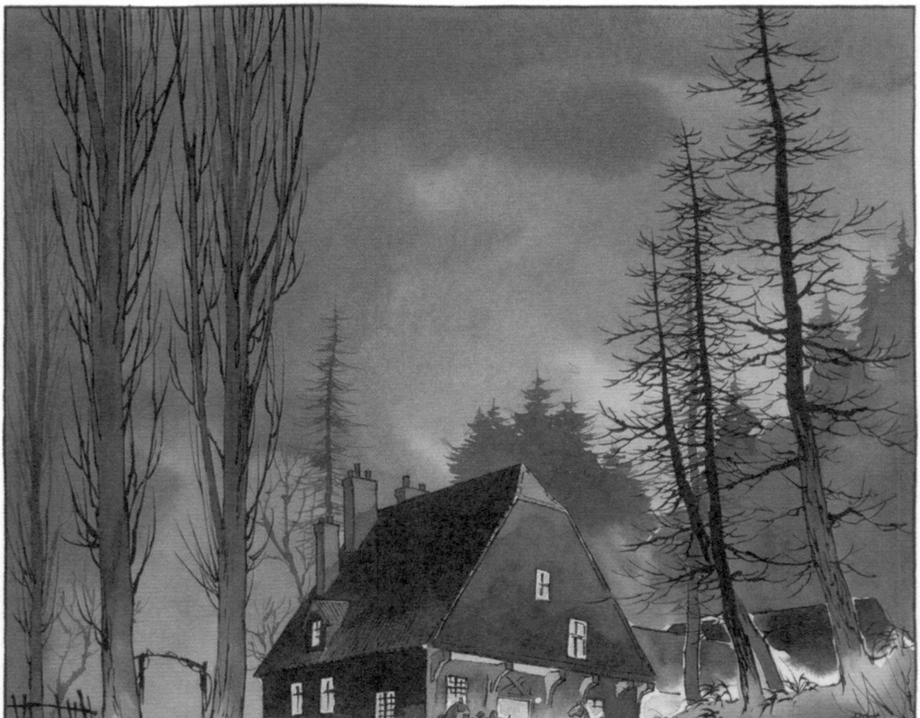

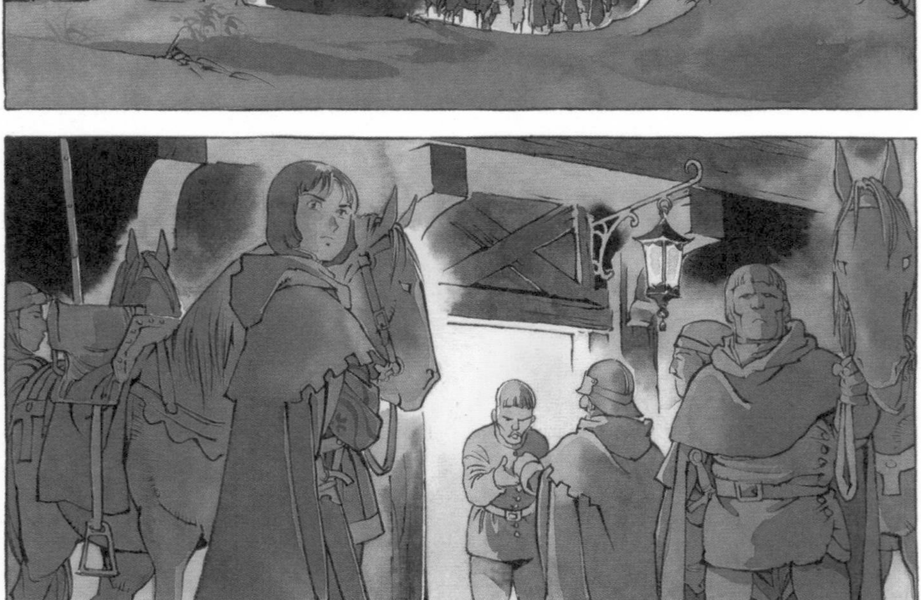

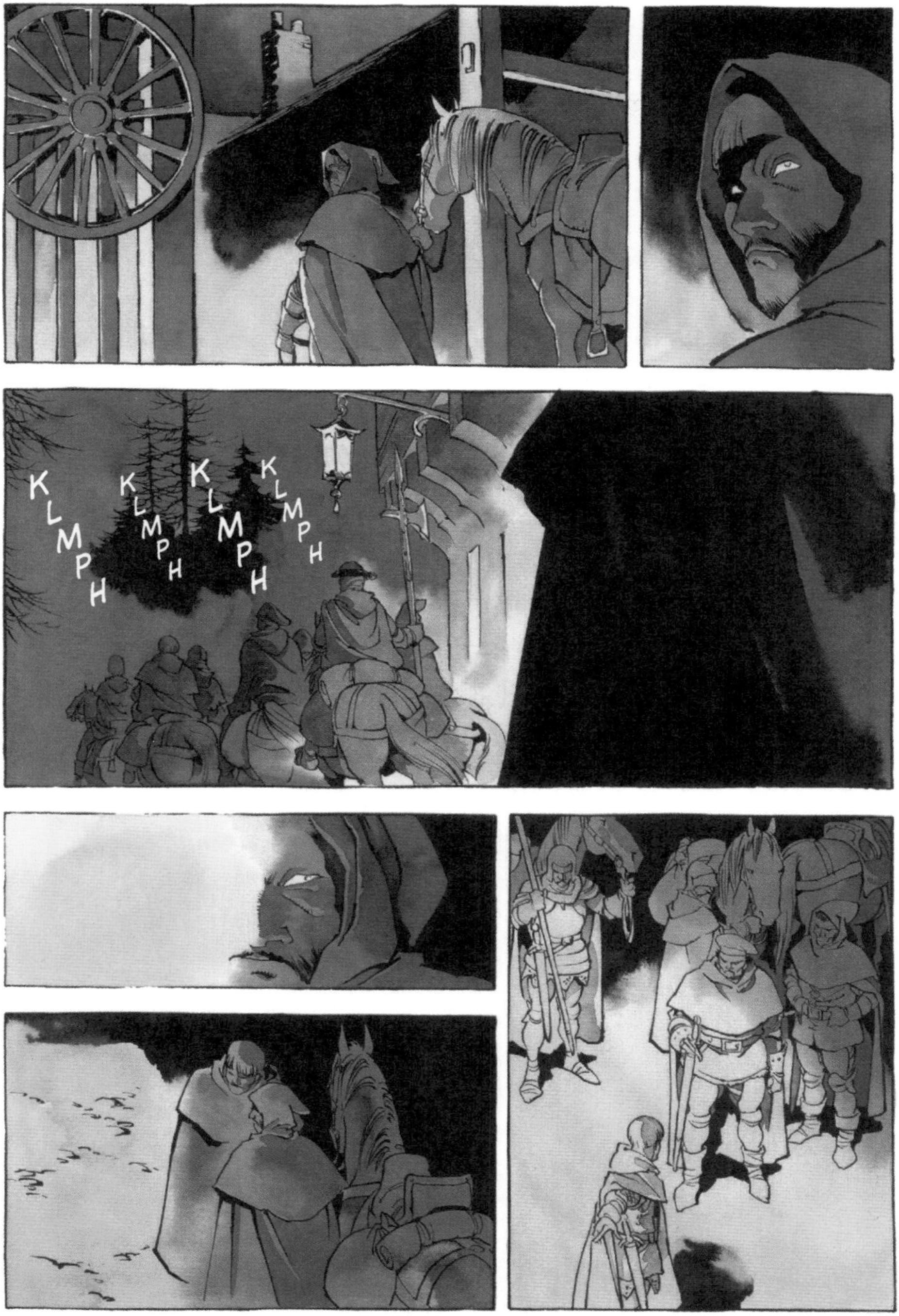
KLMPH
KLMPH
KLMPH
KLMPH

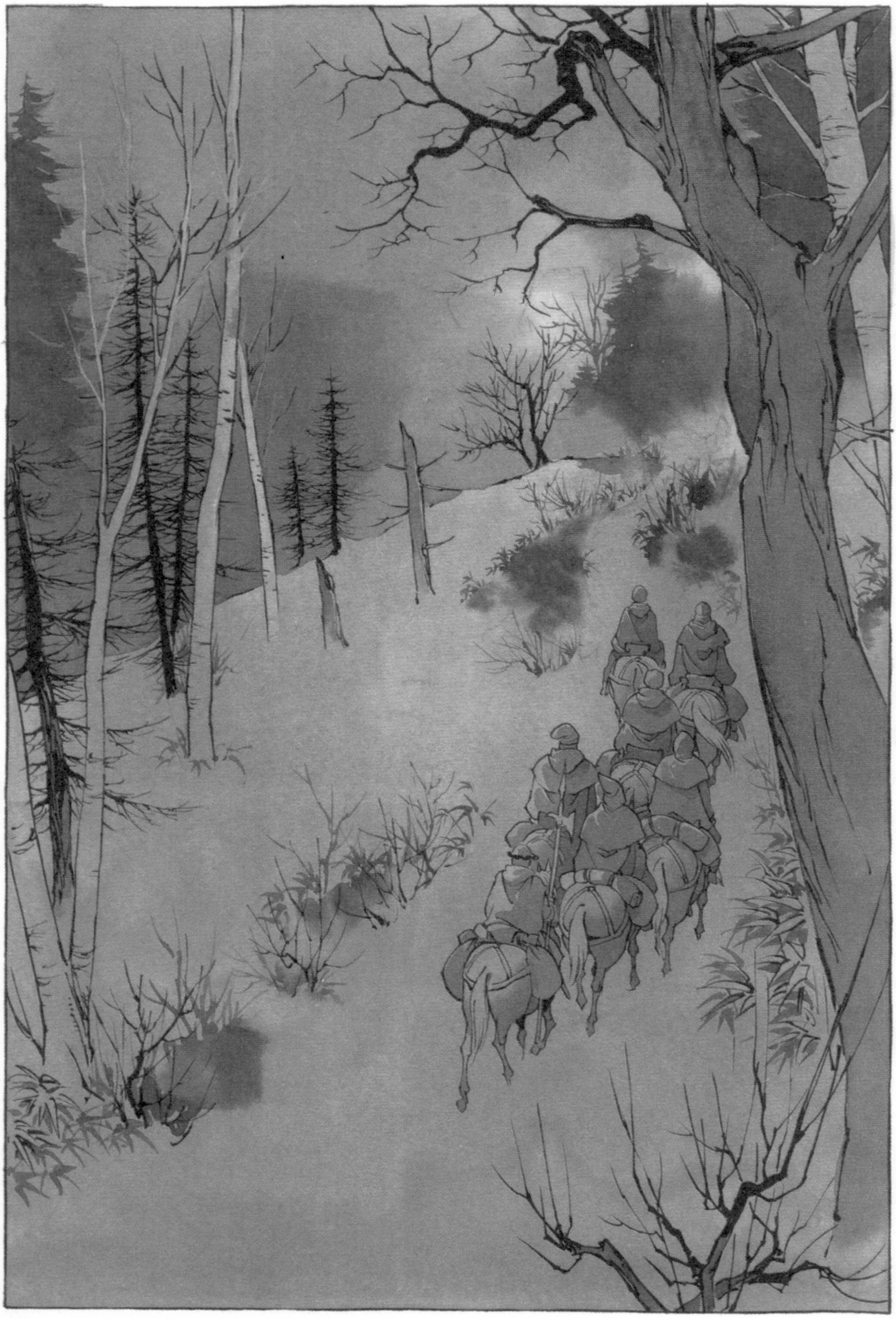

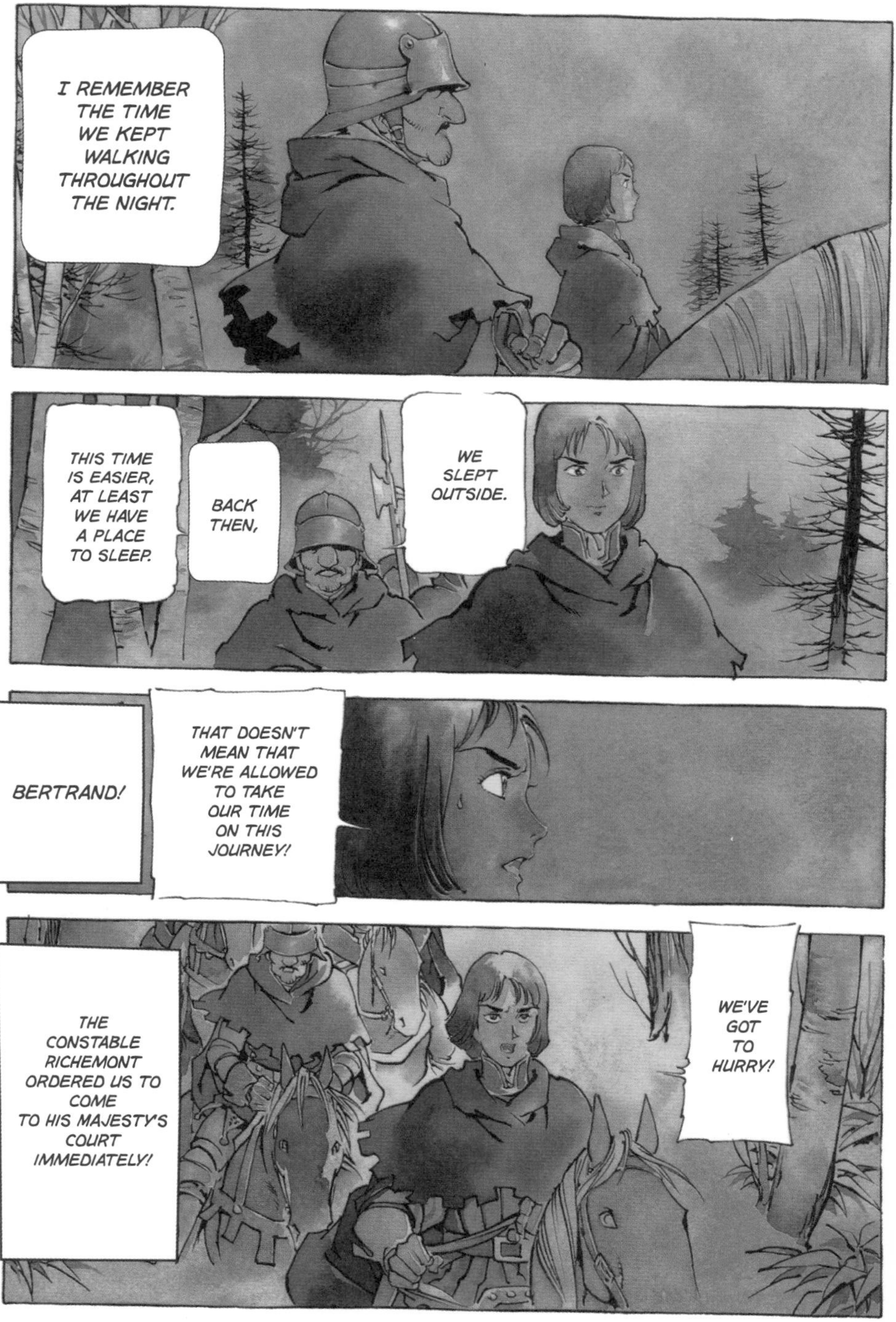
I REMEMBER THE TIME WE KEPT WALKING THROUGHOUT THE NIGHT.
THIS TIME IS EASIER, AT LEAST WE HAVE A PLACE TO SLEEP.
BACK THEN,
WE SLEPT OUTSIDE.
BERTRAND!
THAT DOESN'T MEAN THAT WE'RE ALLOWED TO TAKE OUR TIME ON THIS JOURNEY!
THE CONSTABLE RICHEMONT ORDERED US TO COME TO HIS MAJESTY'S COURT IMMEDIATELY!
WE'VE GOT TO HURRY!

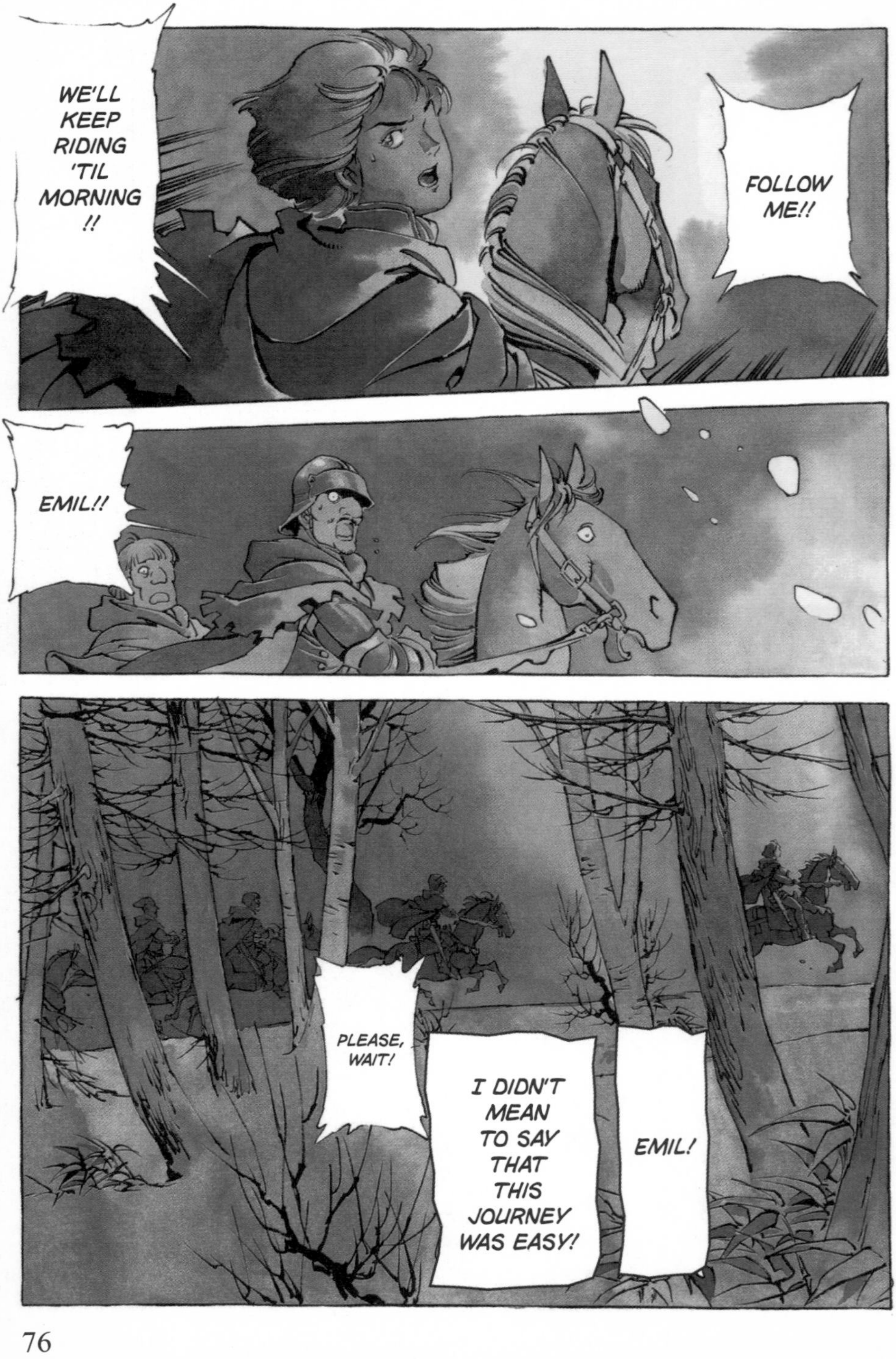
WE'LL KEEP RIDING 'TIL MORNING !!
FOLLOW ME!!
EMIL!!
PLEASE, WAIT!
I DIDN'T MEAN TO SAY THAT THIS JOURNEY WAS EASY!
EMIL!

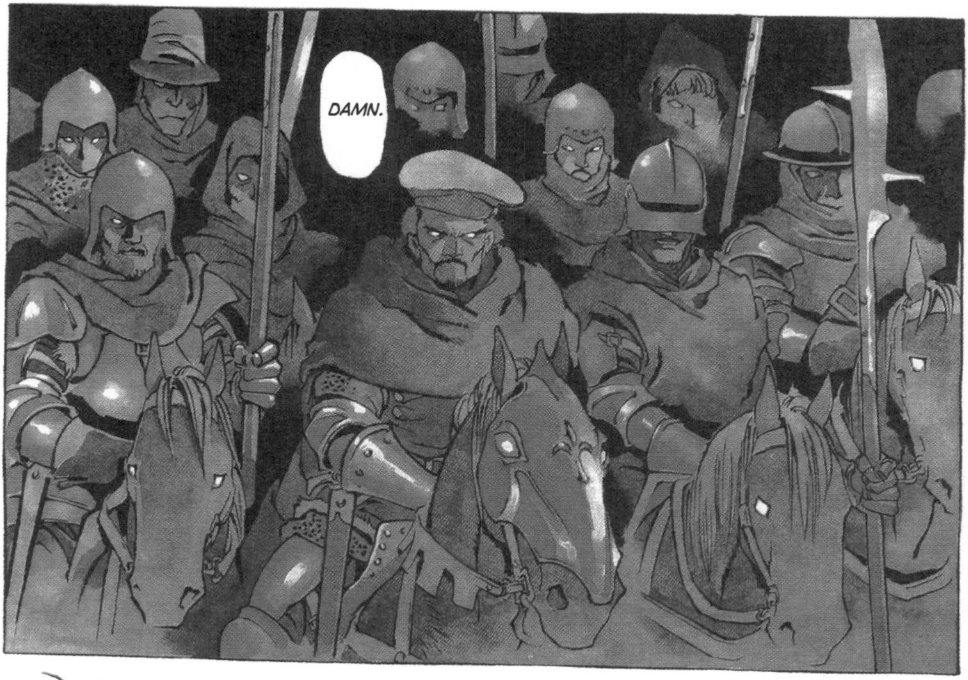
DAMN.

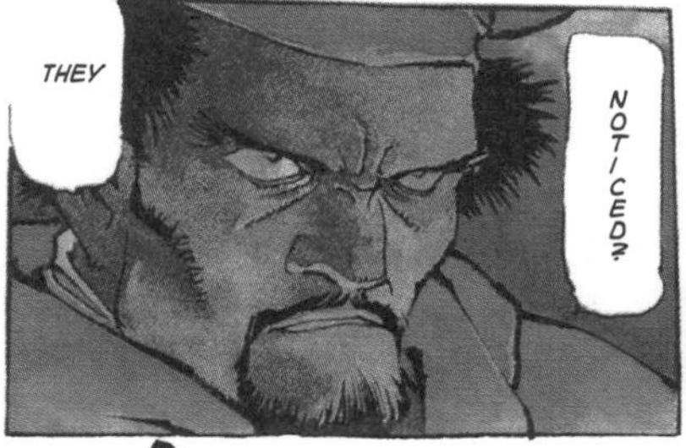
THEY
NOTICED?

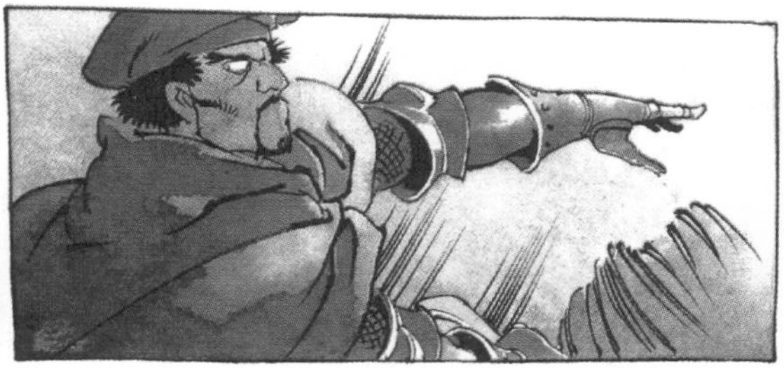

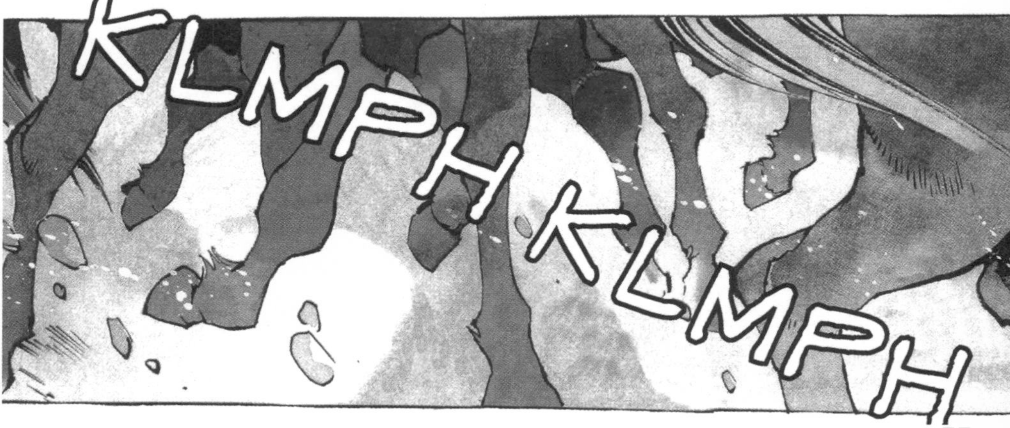
KLMPH KLMPH

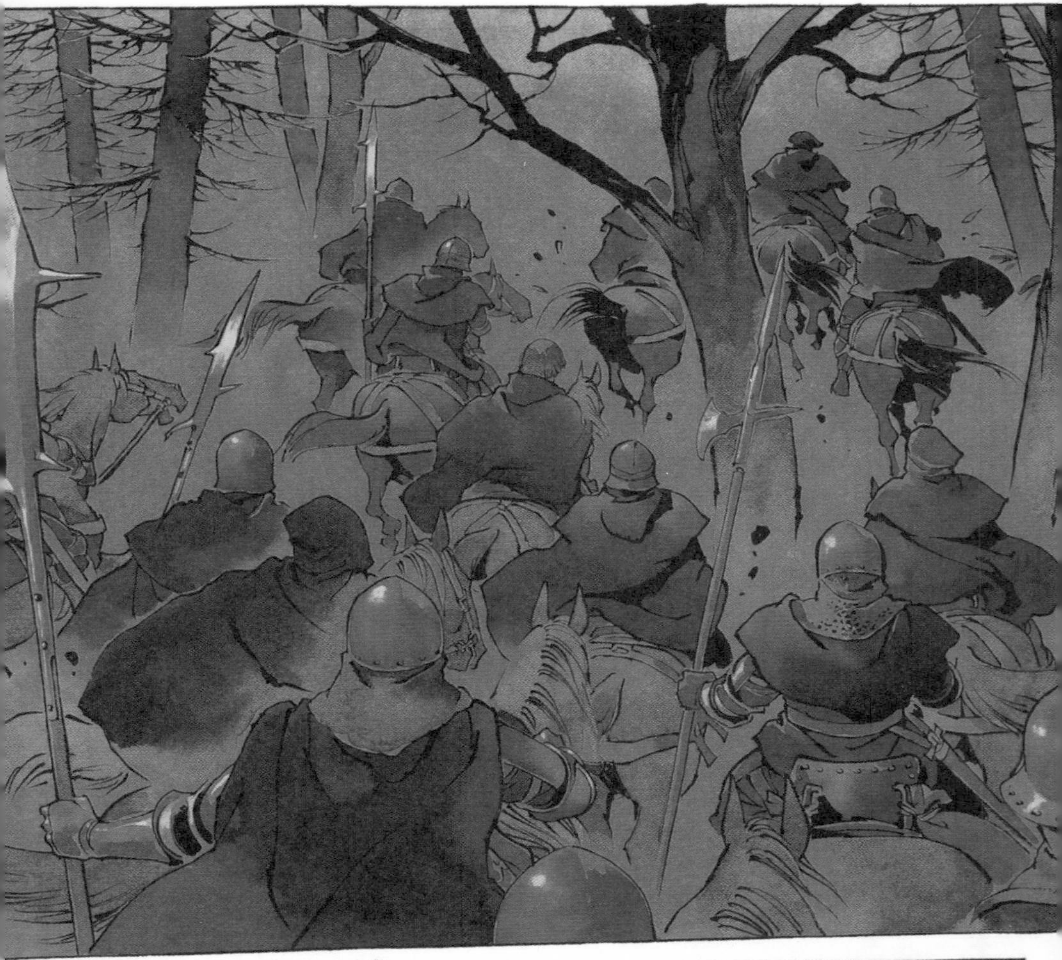

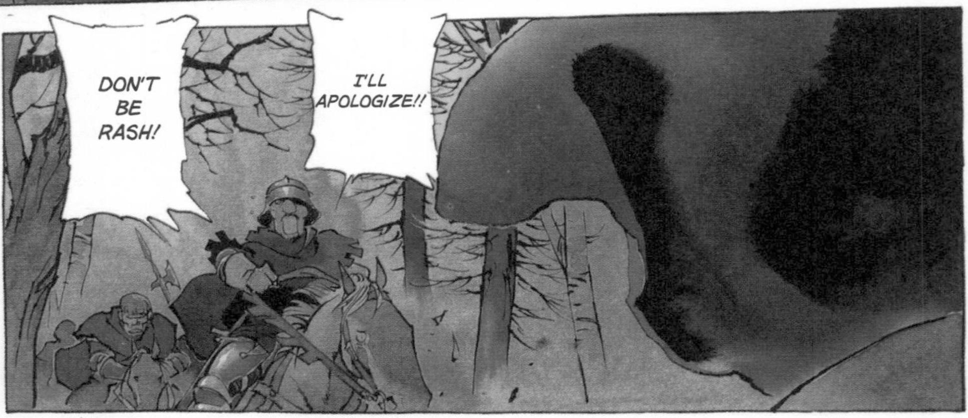
DON'T BE RASH!
I'LL APOLOGIZE!!

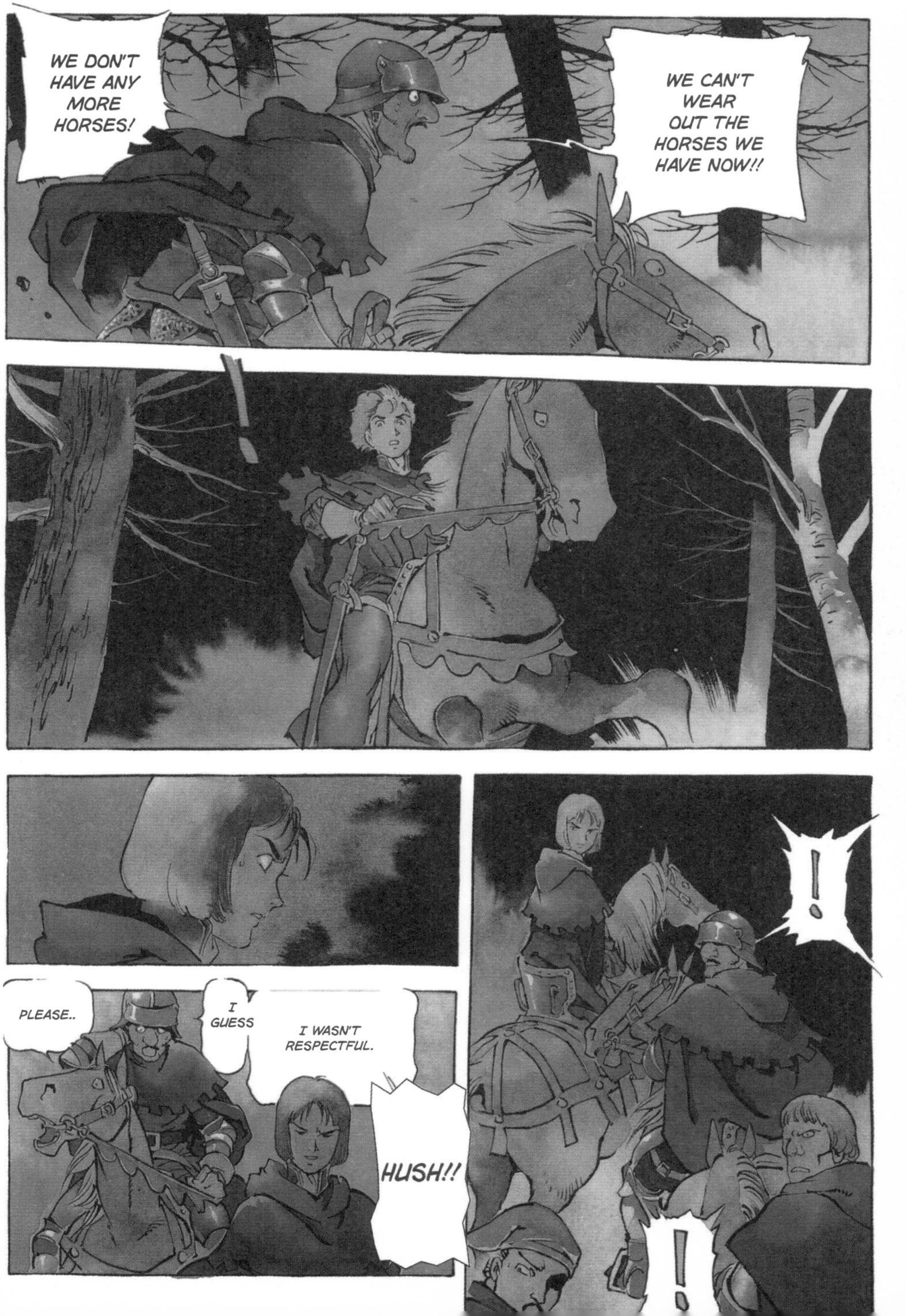

WE DON'T HAVE ANY MORE HORSES!
WE CAN'T WEAR OUT THE HORSES WE HAVE NOW!!
!
!
PLEASE..
I GUESS
I WASN'T RESPECTFUL.
HUSH!!
!

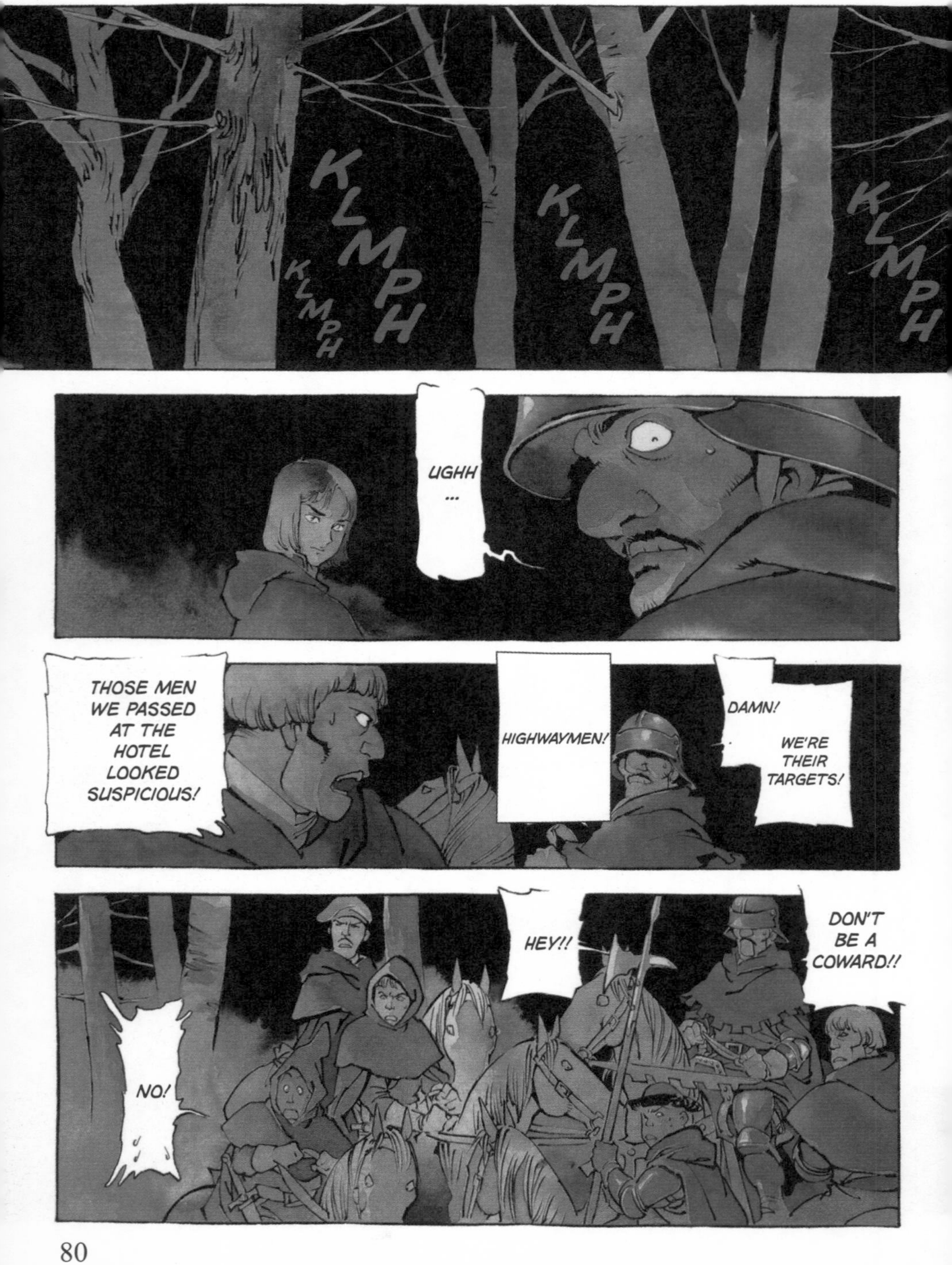
KLMPH
KLMPH
KLMPH
KLMPH
UGHH ...
THOSE MEN WE PASSED AT THE HOTEL LOOKED SUSPICIOUS!
HIGHWAYMEN!
DAMN!
WE'RE THEIR TARGETS!
HEY!!
DON'T BE A COWARD!!
NO!

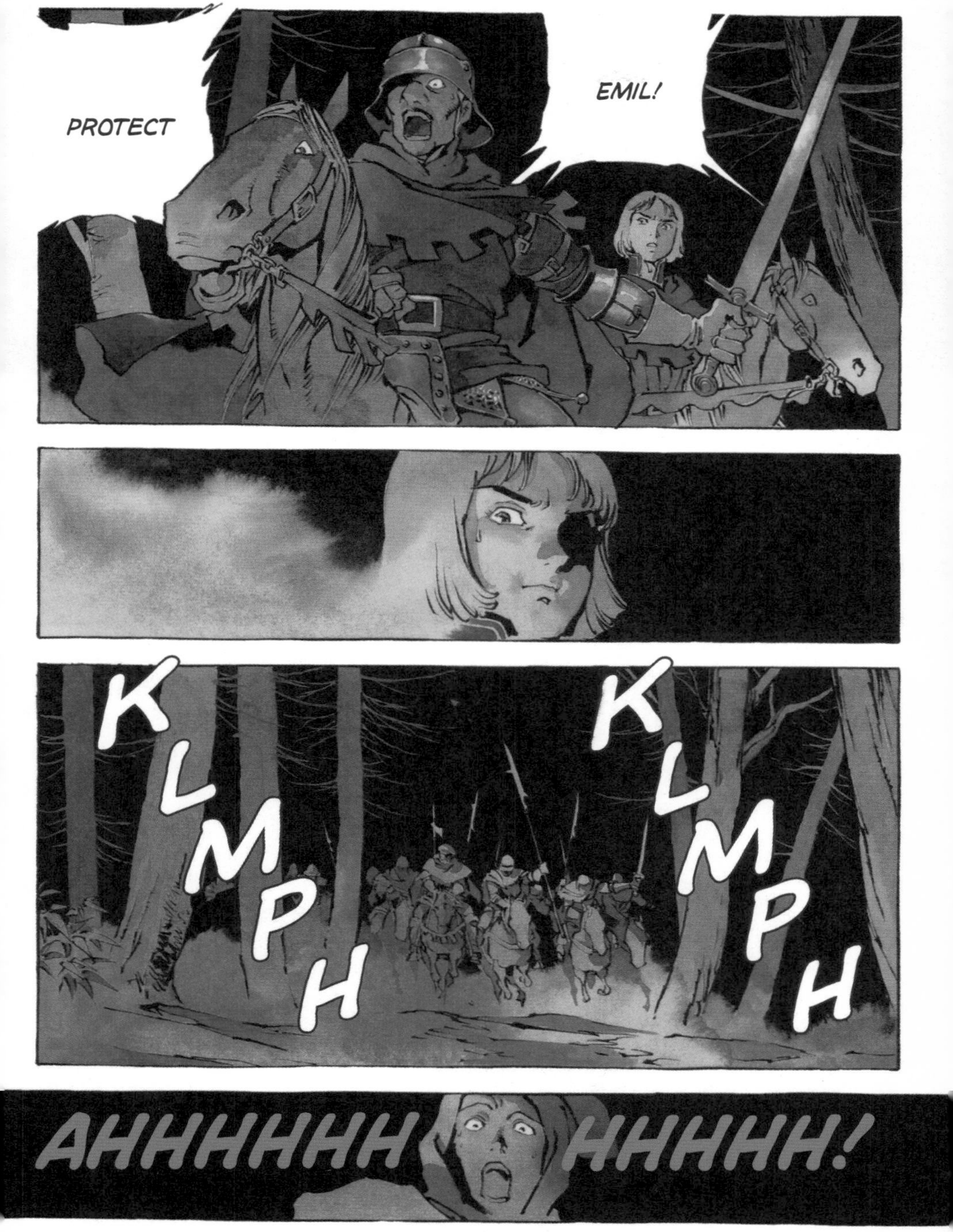
PROTECT
EMIL!
KLMPH
KLMPH
AHHHHHH HHHHH!

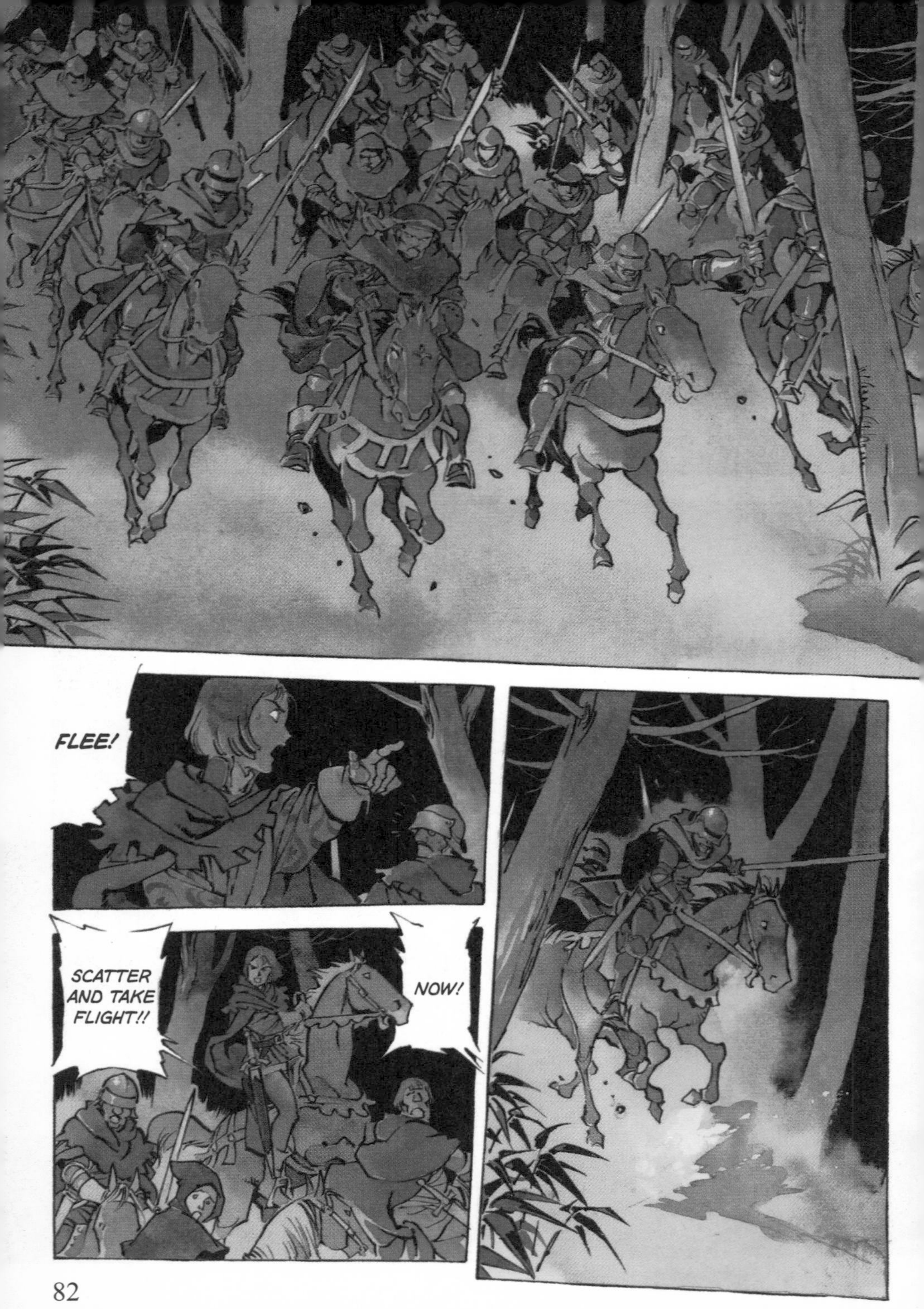
FLEE!
SCATTER AND TAKE FLIGHT!!
NOW!

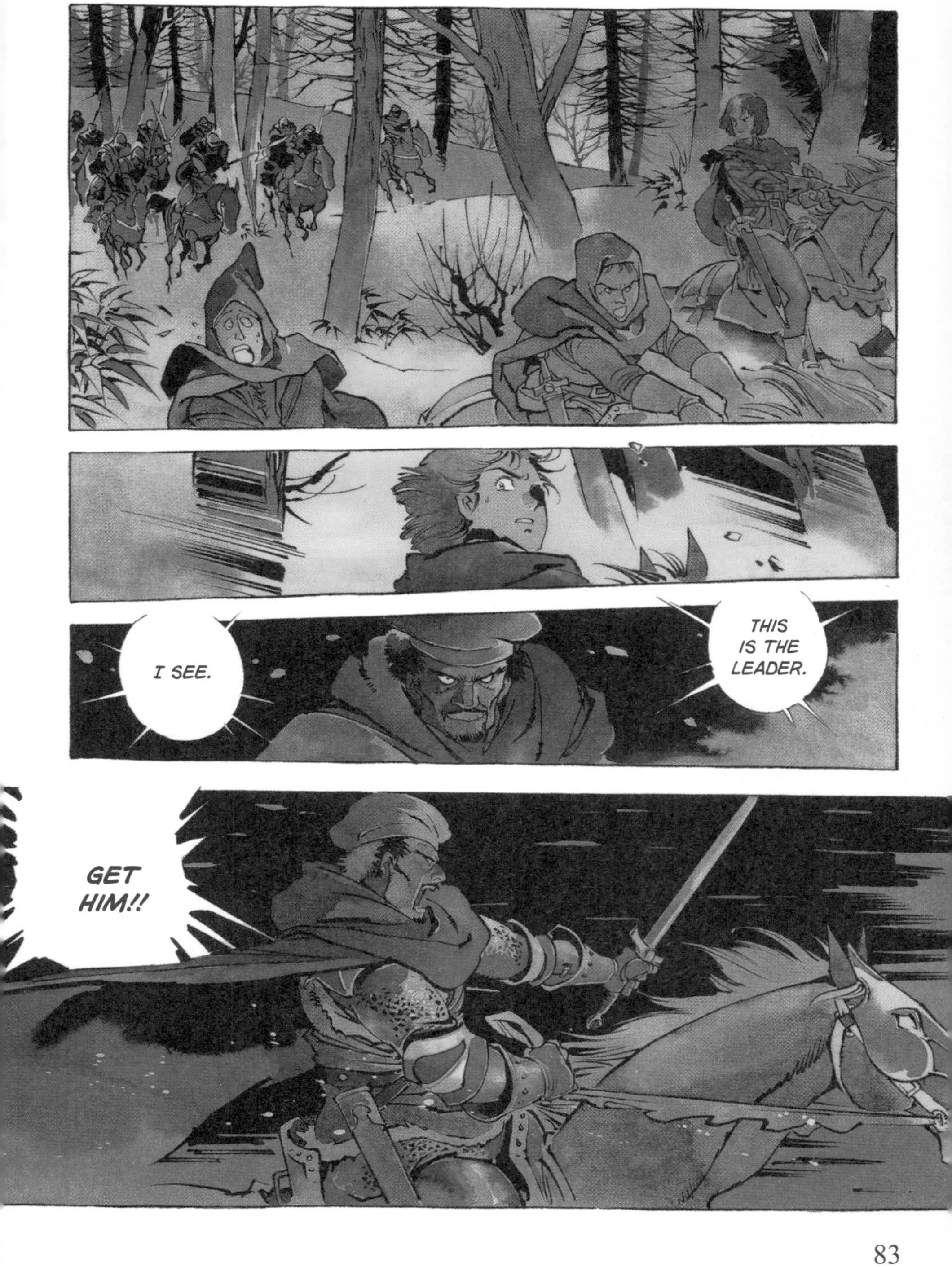
THIS IS THE LEADER.
I SEE.
GET HIM!!

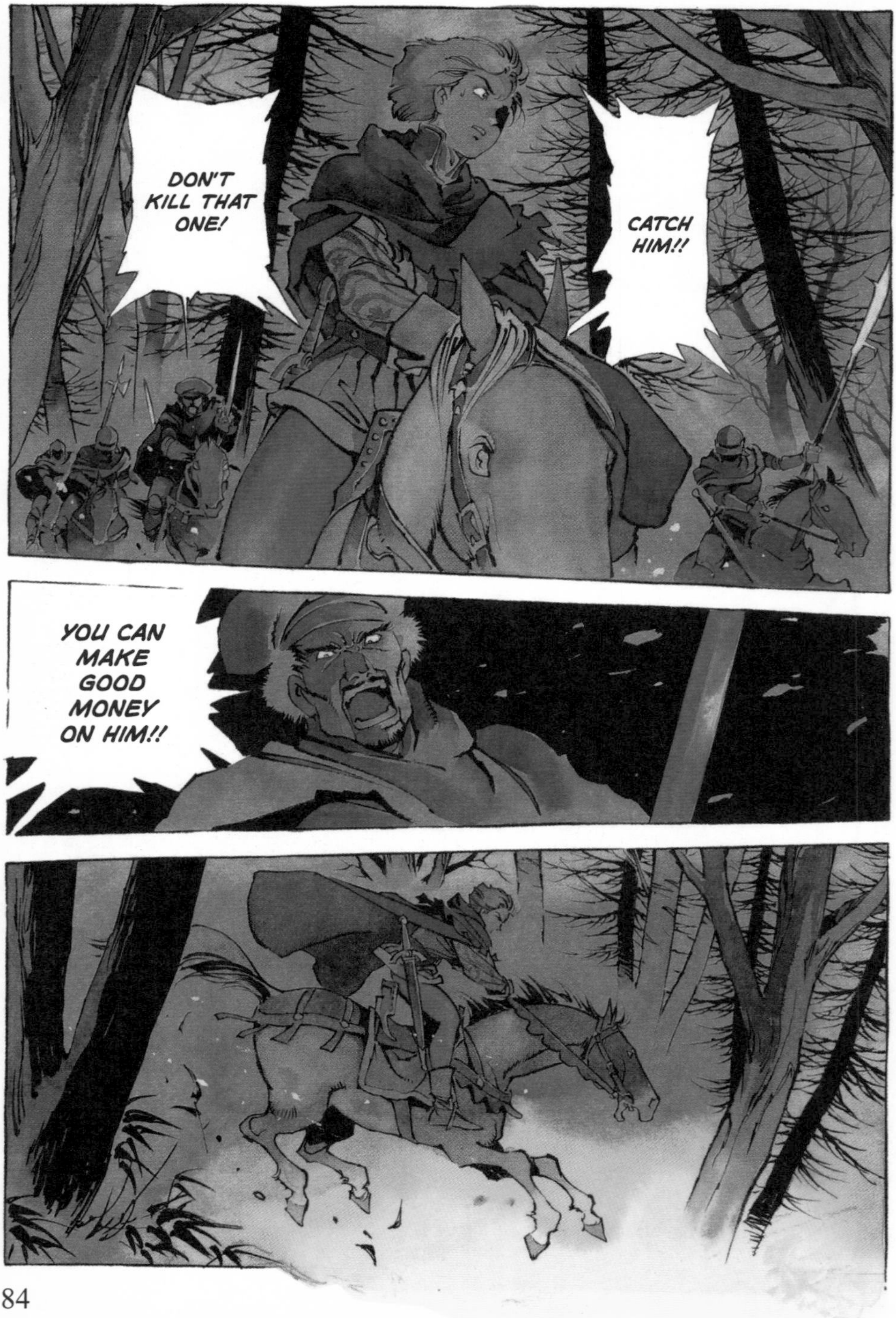
DON'T KILL THAT ONE!
CATCH HIM!!
YOU CAN MAKE GOOD MONEY ON HIM!!

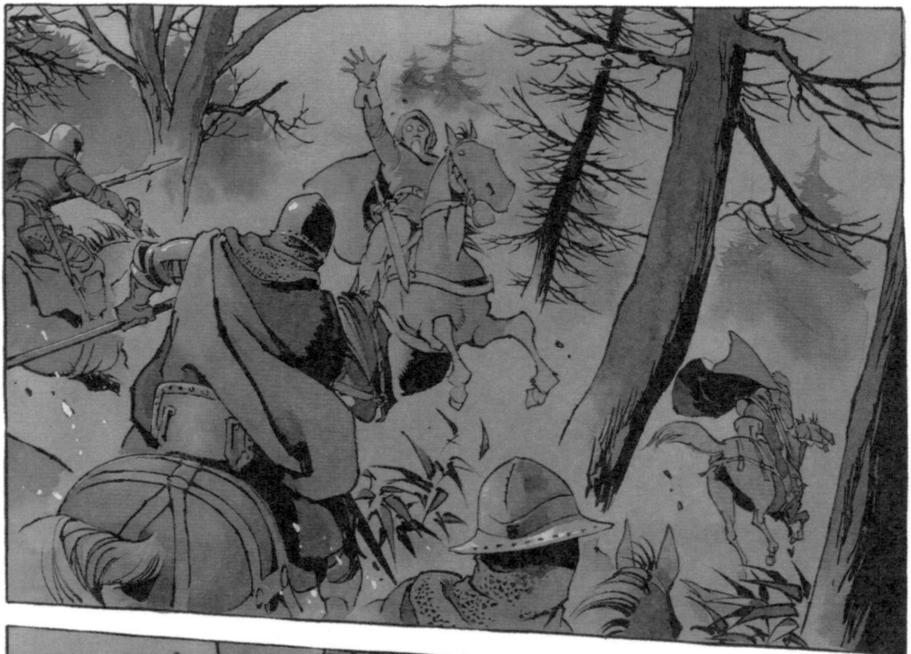
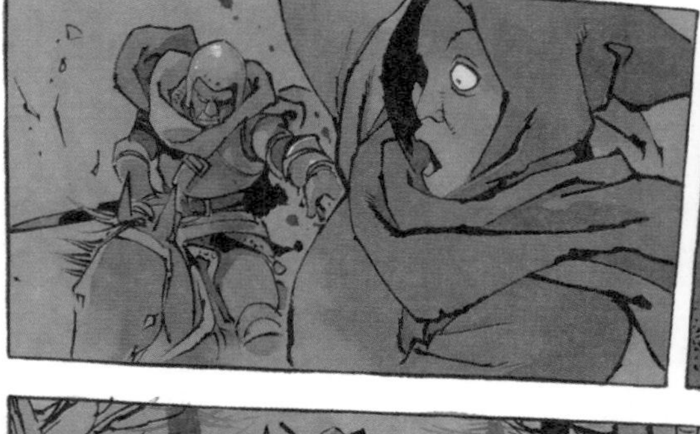
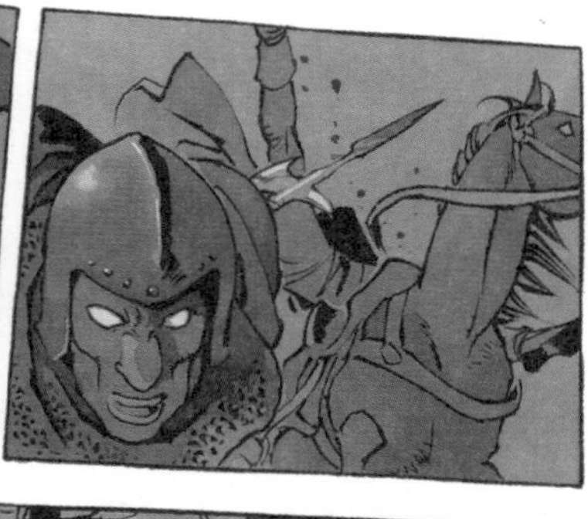
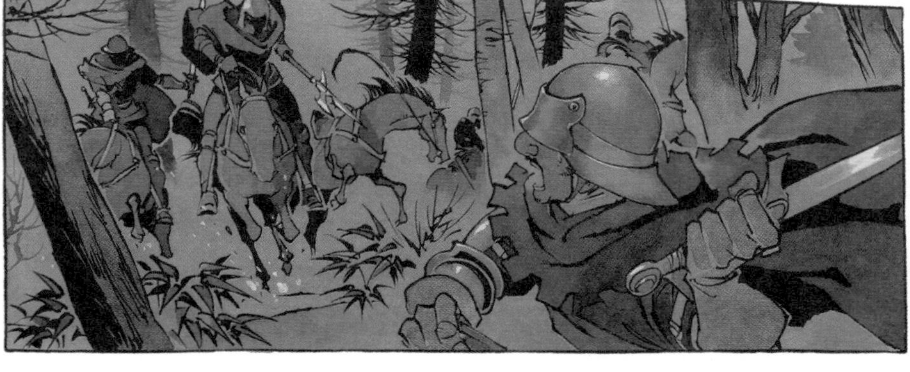

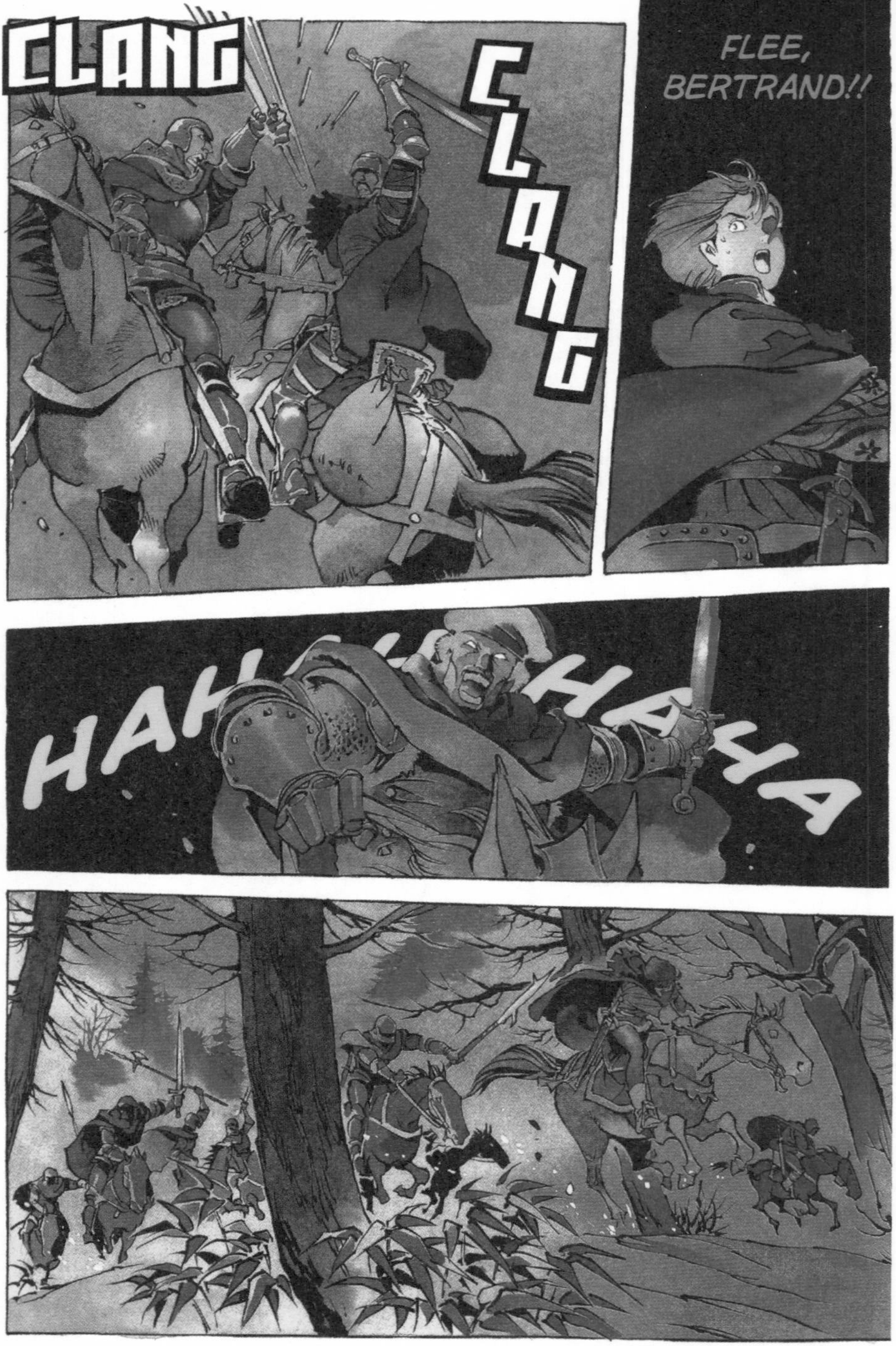
CLANG
CLANG
FLEE, BERTRAND!!
HAH
HAHA

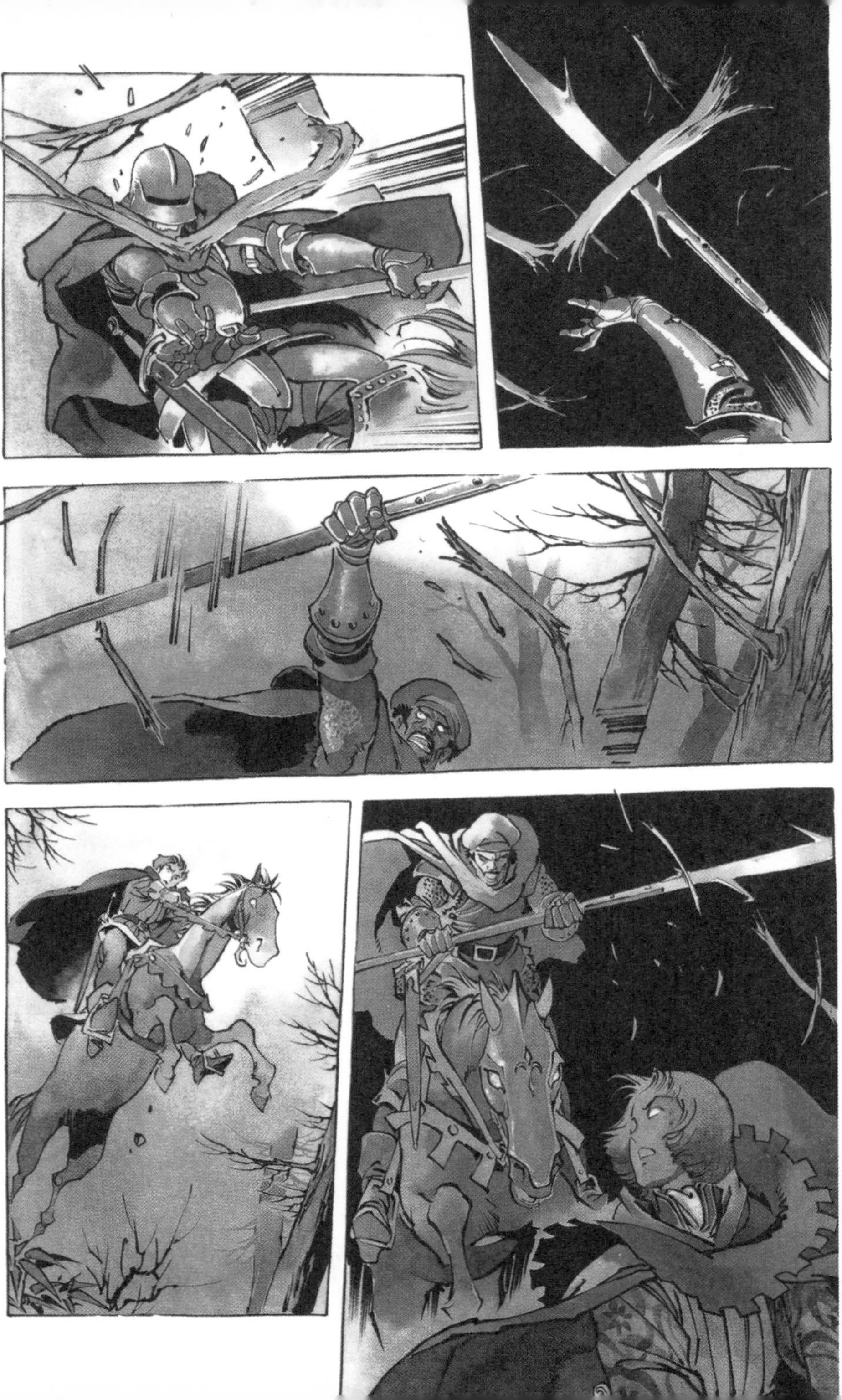

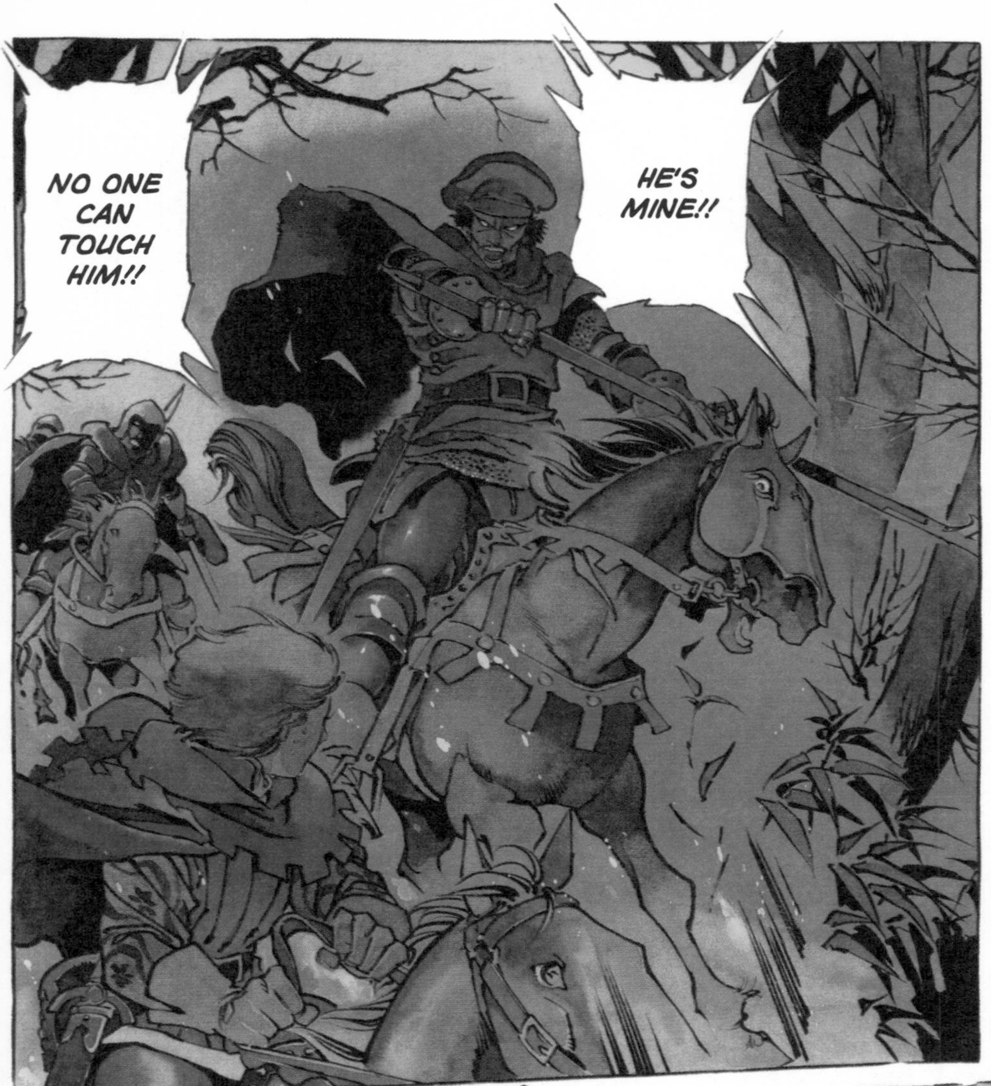
HE'S MINE!!
NO ONE CAN TOUCH HIM!!

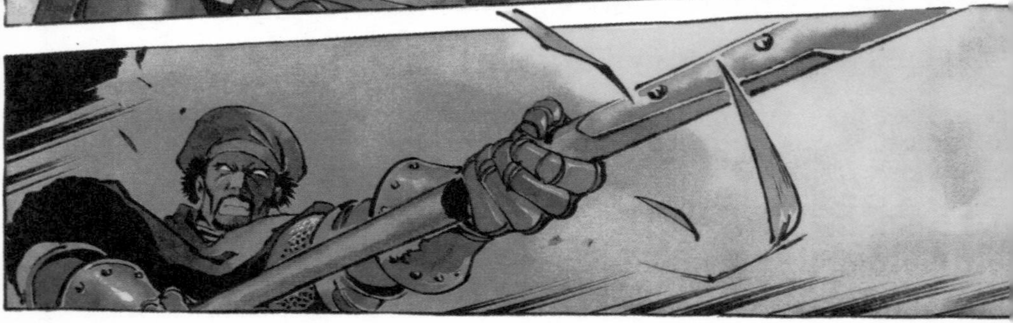

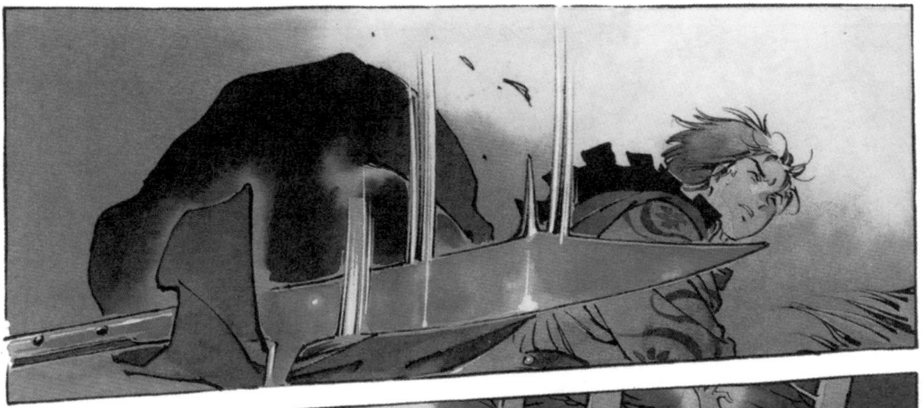
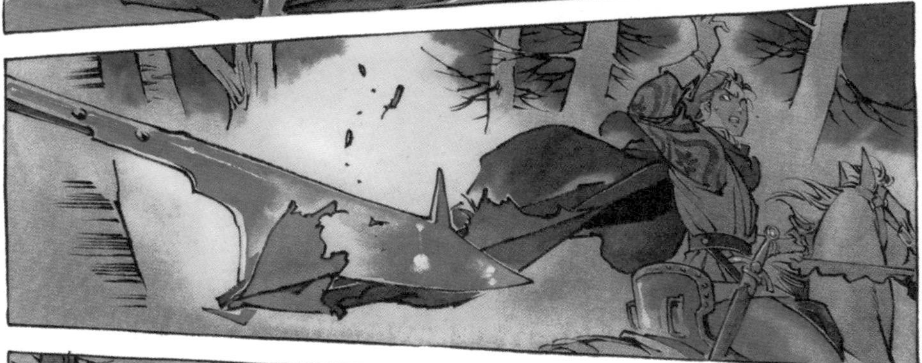
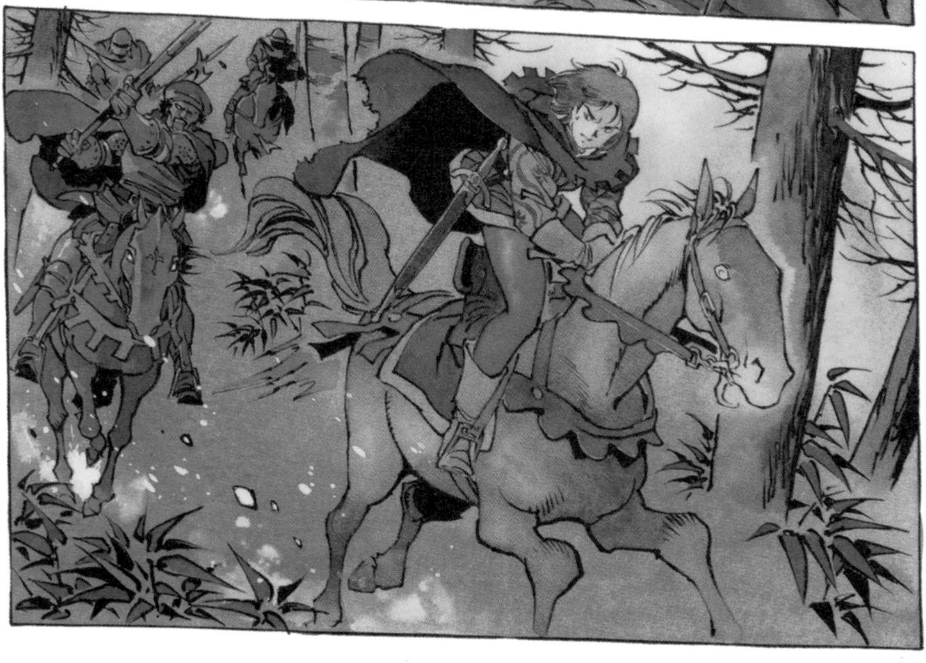

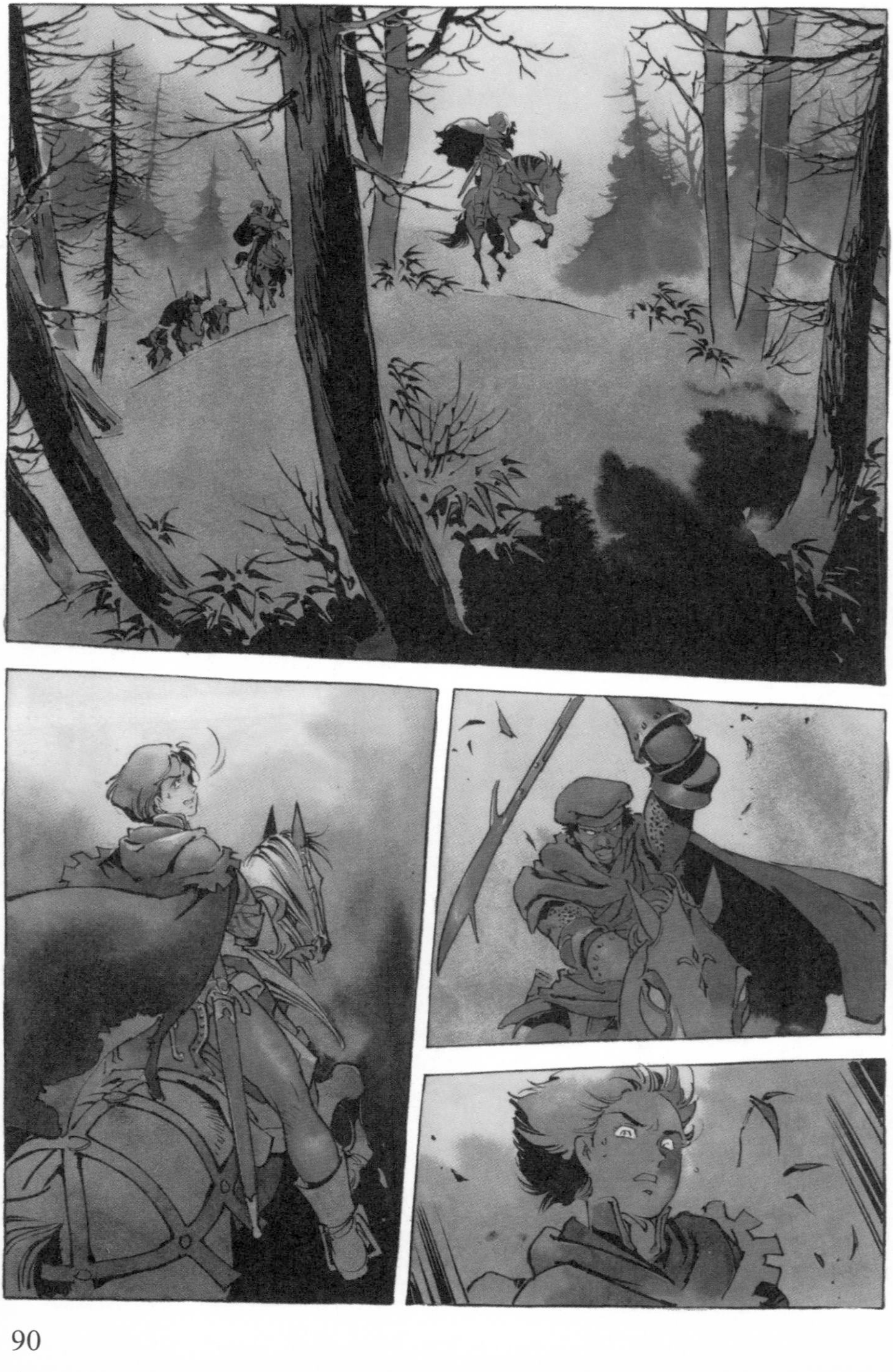

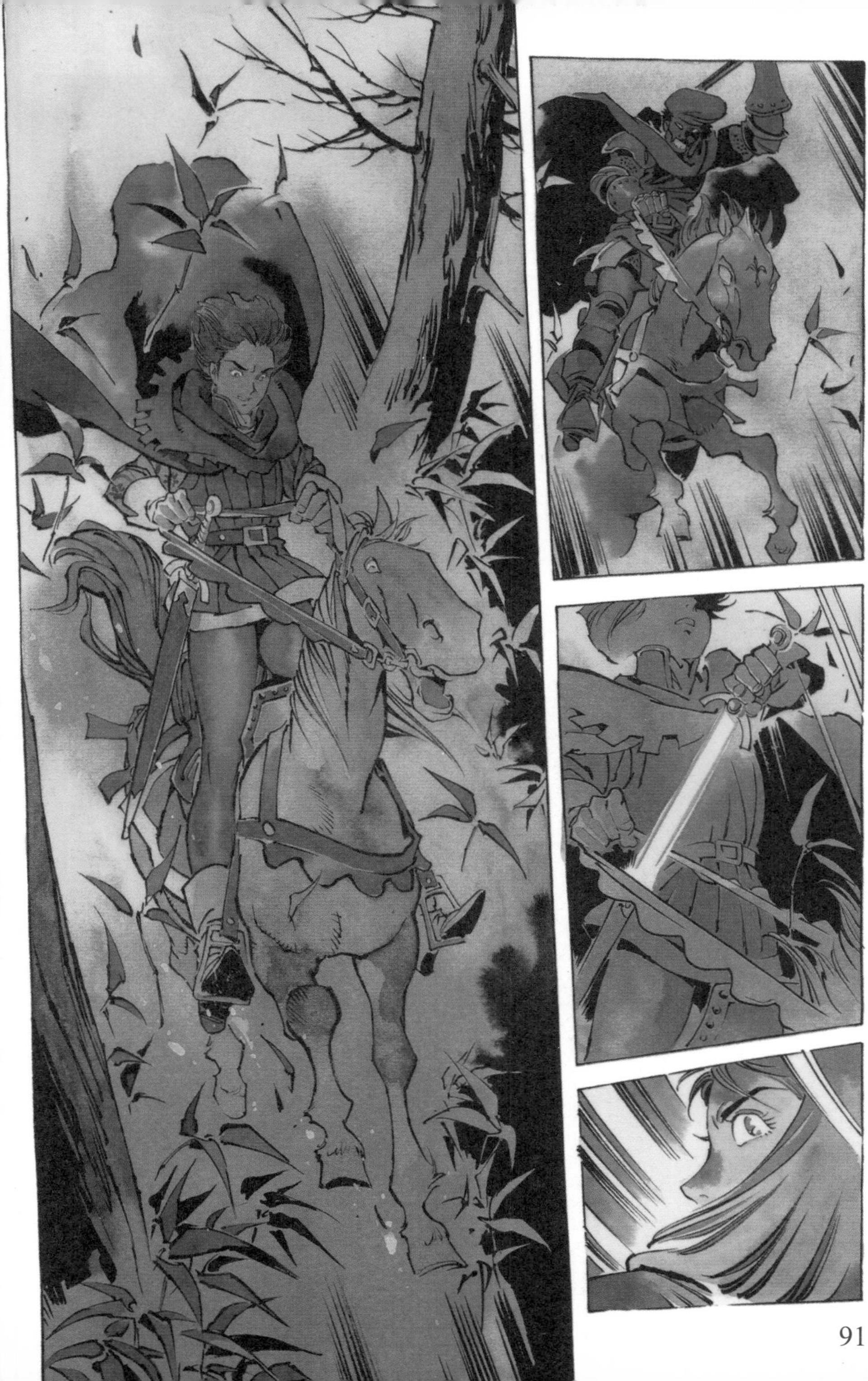

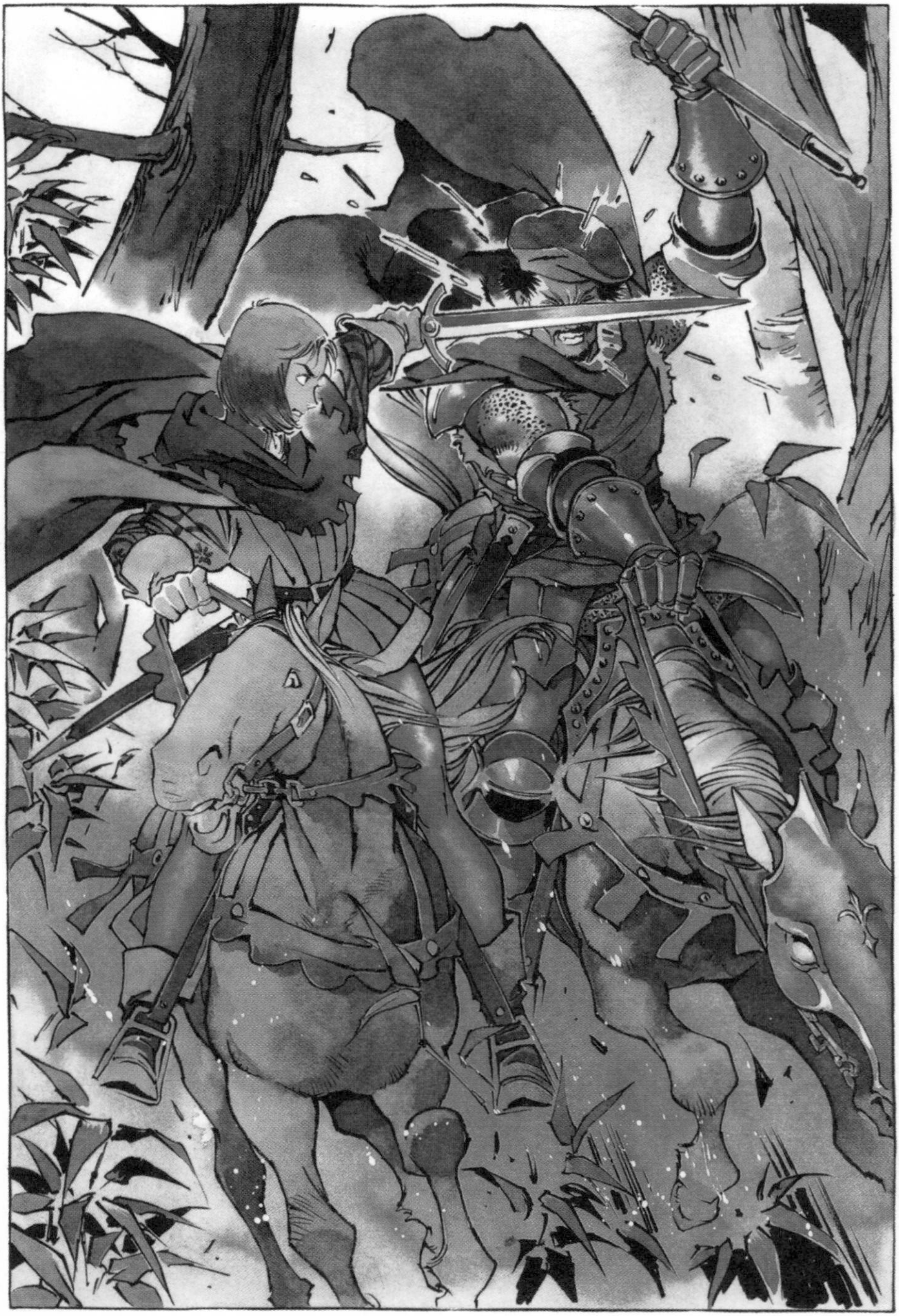

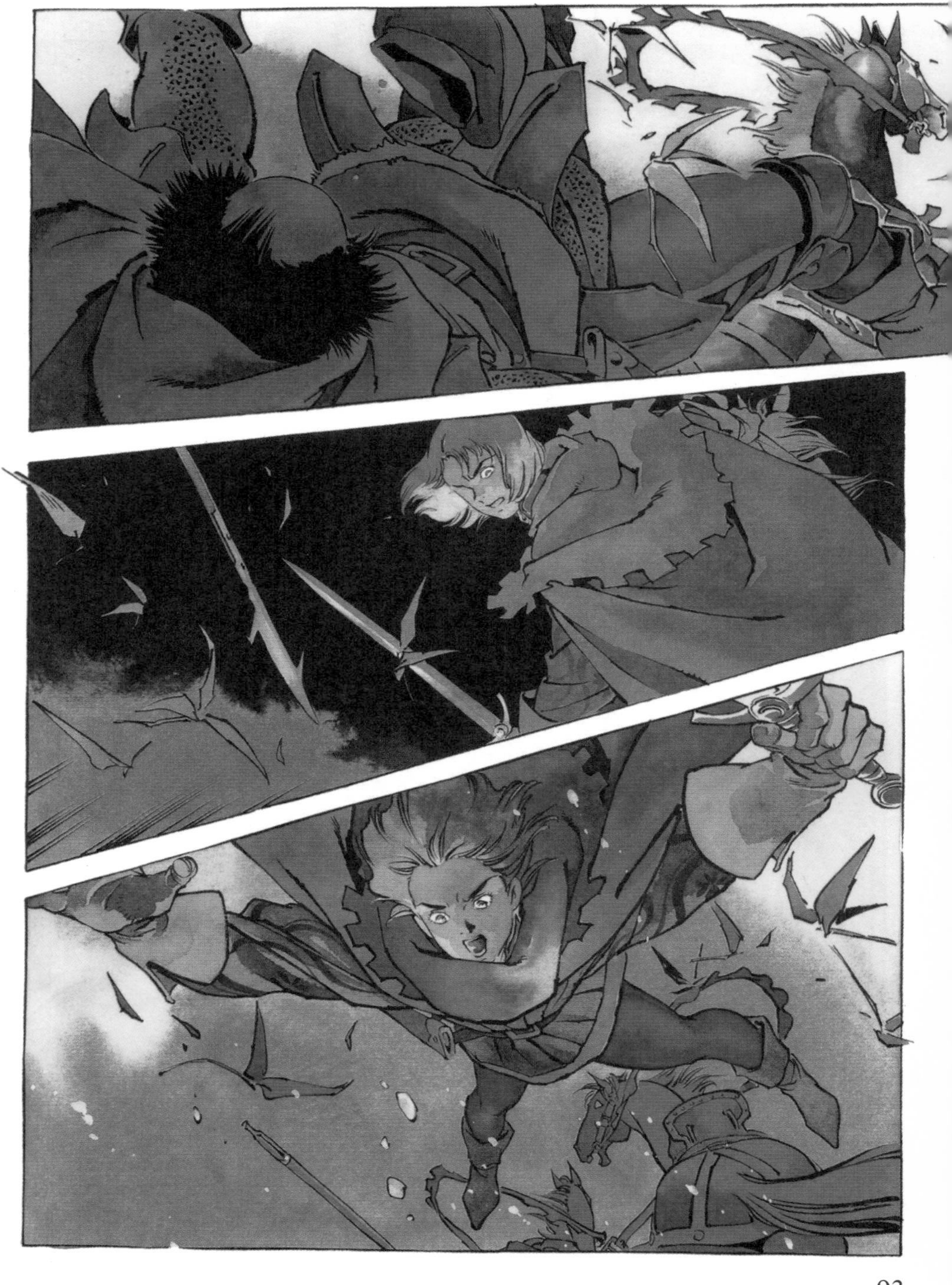

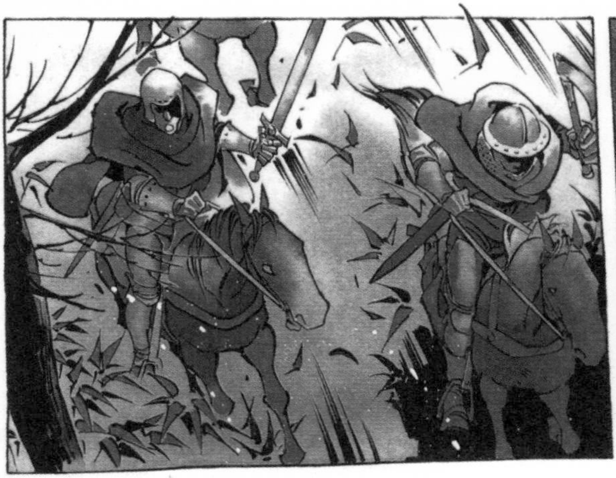
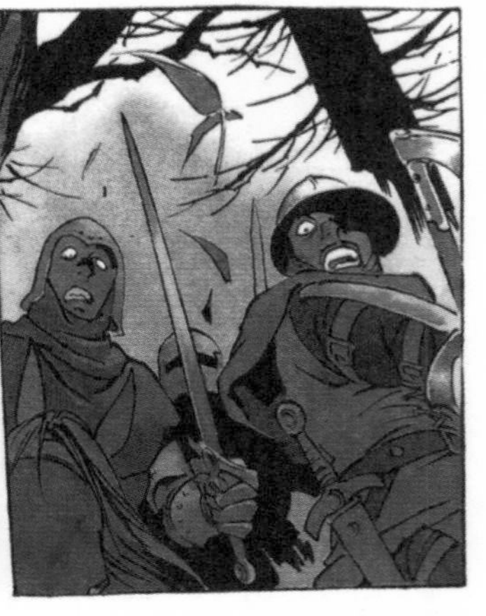
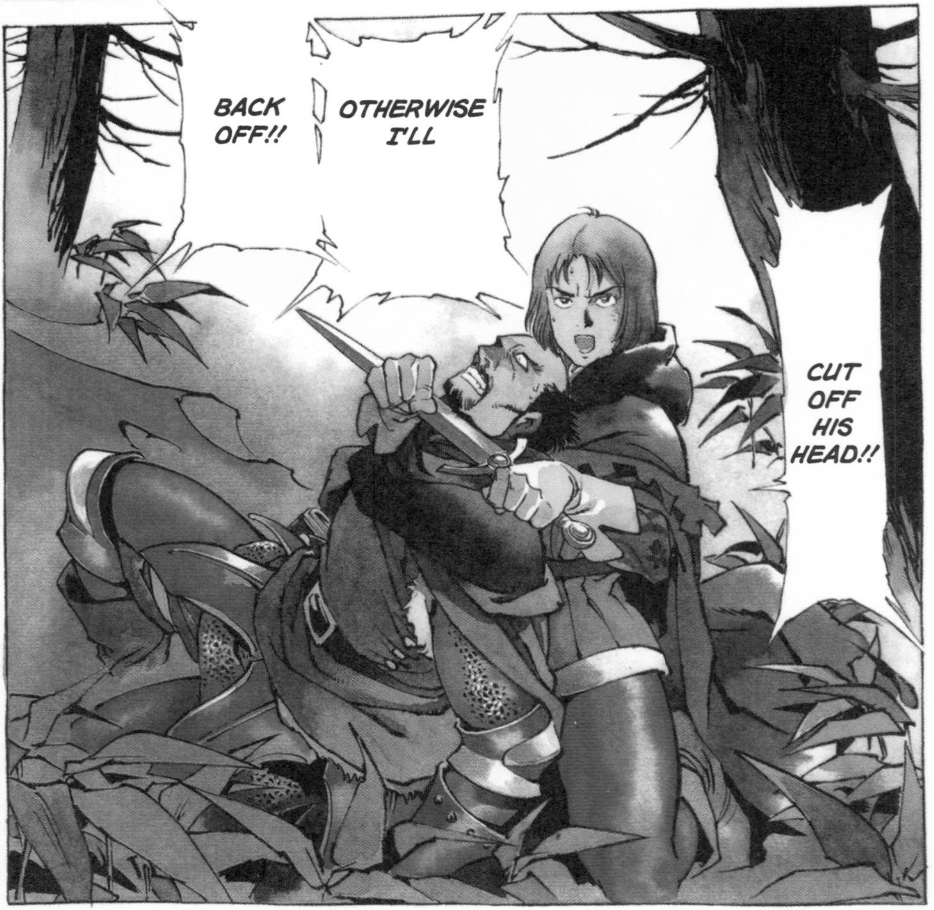
BACK OFF!!
OTHERWISE I'LL
CUT OFF HIS HEAD!!

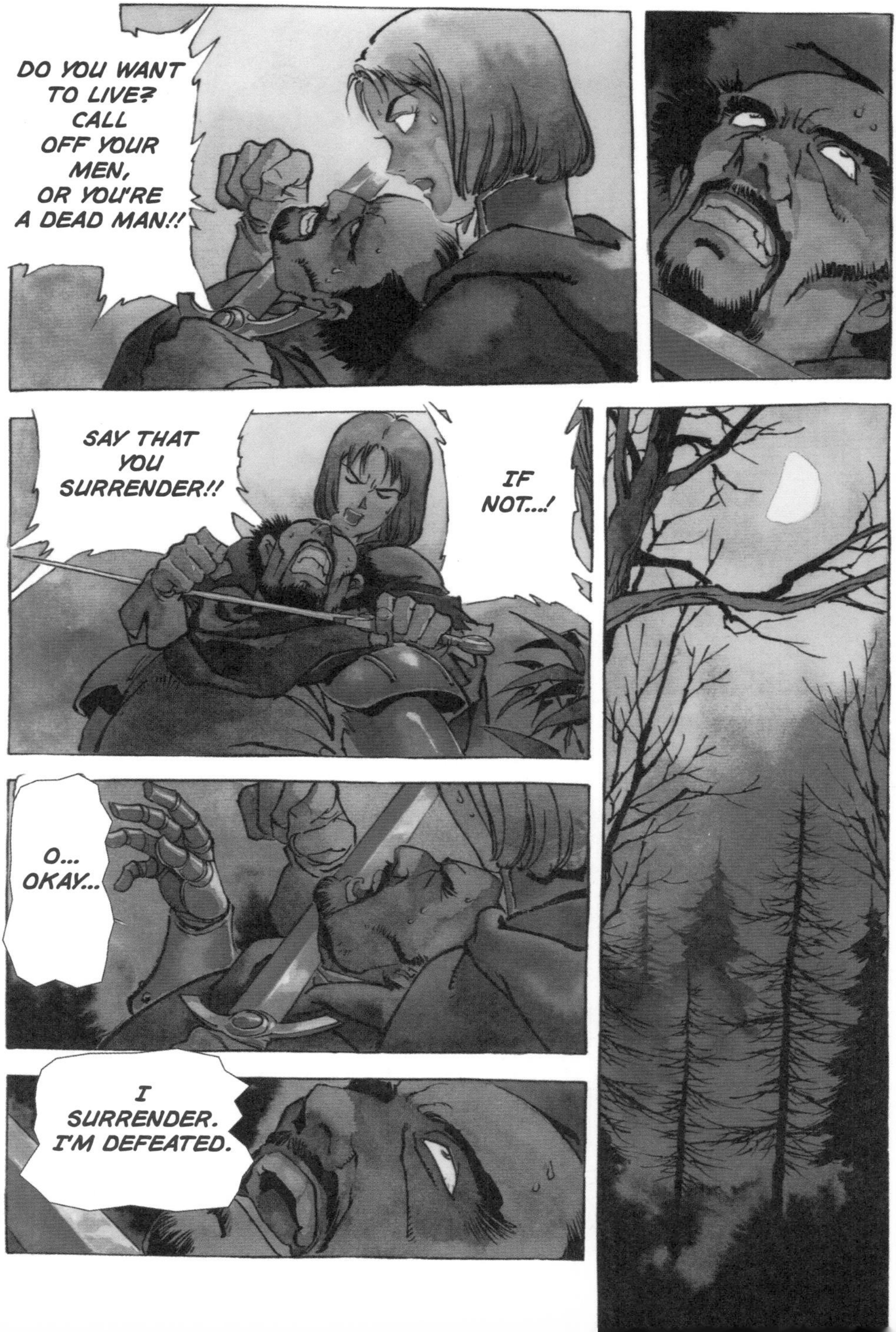
DO YOU WANT TO LIVE? CALL OFF YOUR MEN, OR YOU'RE A DEAD MAN!!
SAY THAT YOU SURRENDER!!
IF NOT...!
O... OKAY...
I SURRENDER. I'M DEFEATED.

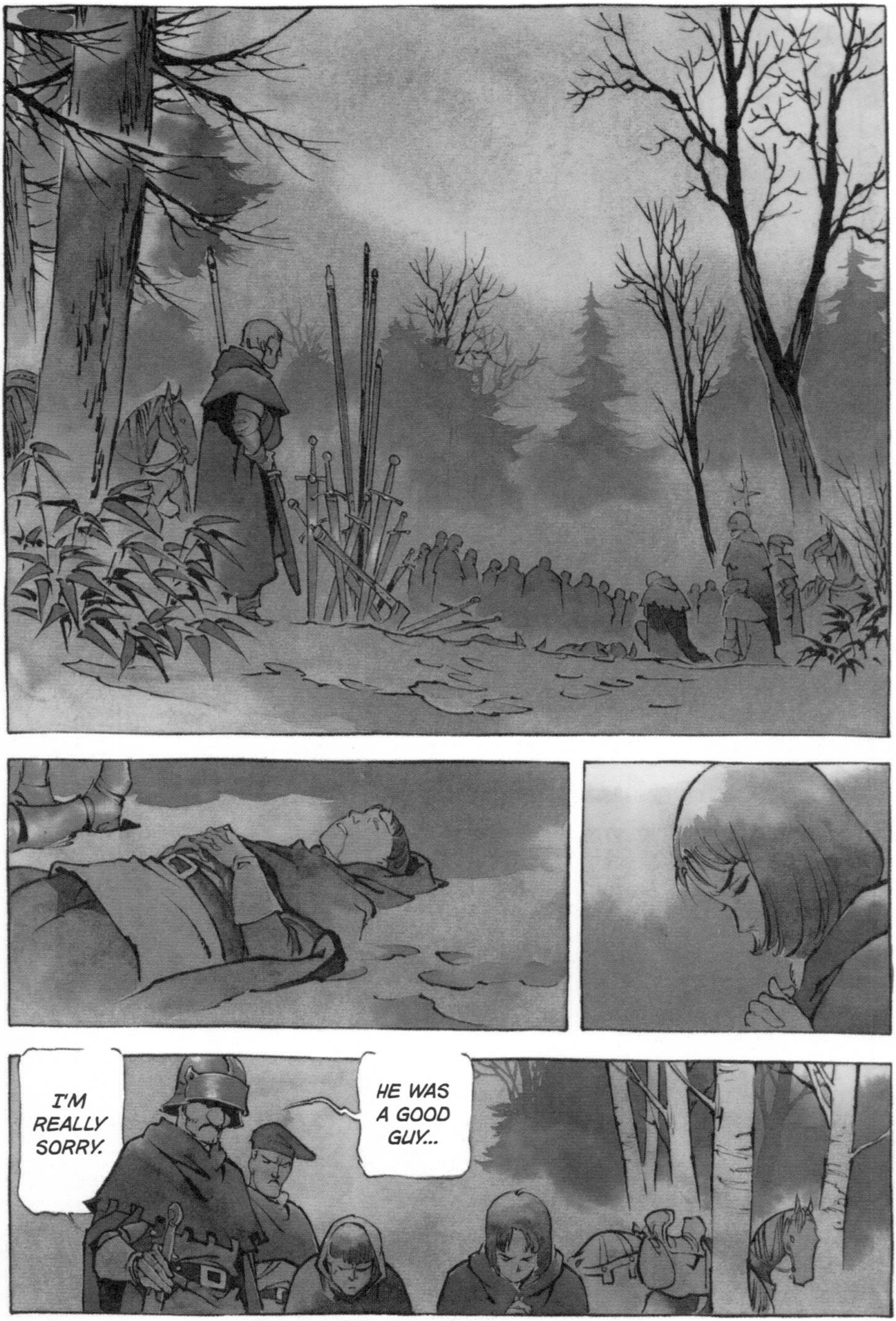
I'M REALLY SORRY.
HE WAS A GOOD GUY...

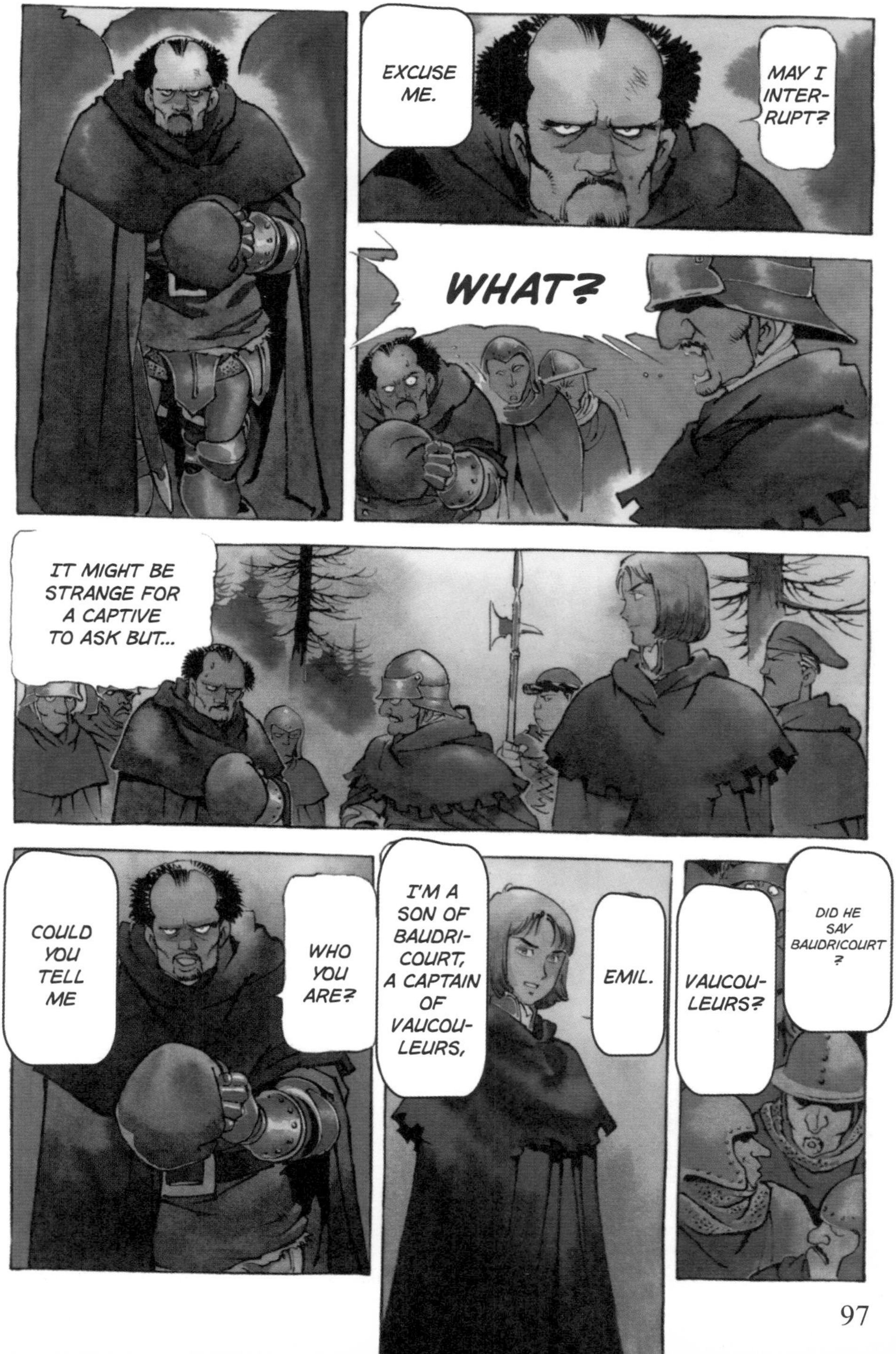
EXCUSE ME.
MAY I INTER-RUPT?
WHAT?
IT MIGHT BE STRANGE FOR A CAPTIVE TO ASK BUT...
COULD YOU TELL ME
WHO YOU ARE?
I'M A SON OF BAUDRI-COURT, A CAPTAIN OF VAUCOU-LEURS,
EMIL.
VAUCOU-LEURS?
DID HE SAY BAUDRICOURT?

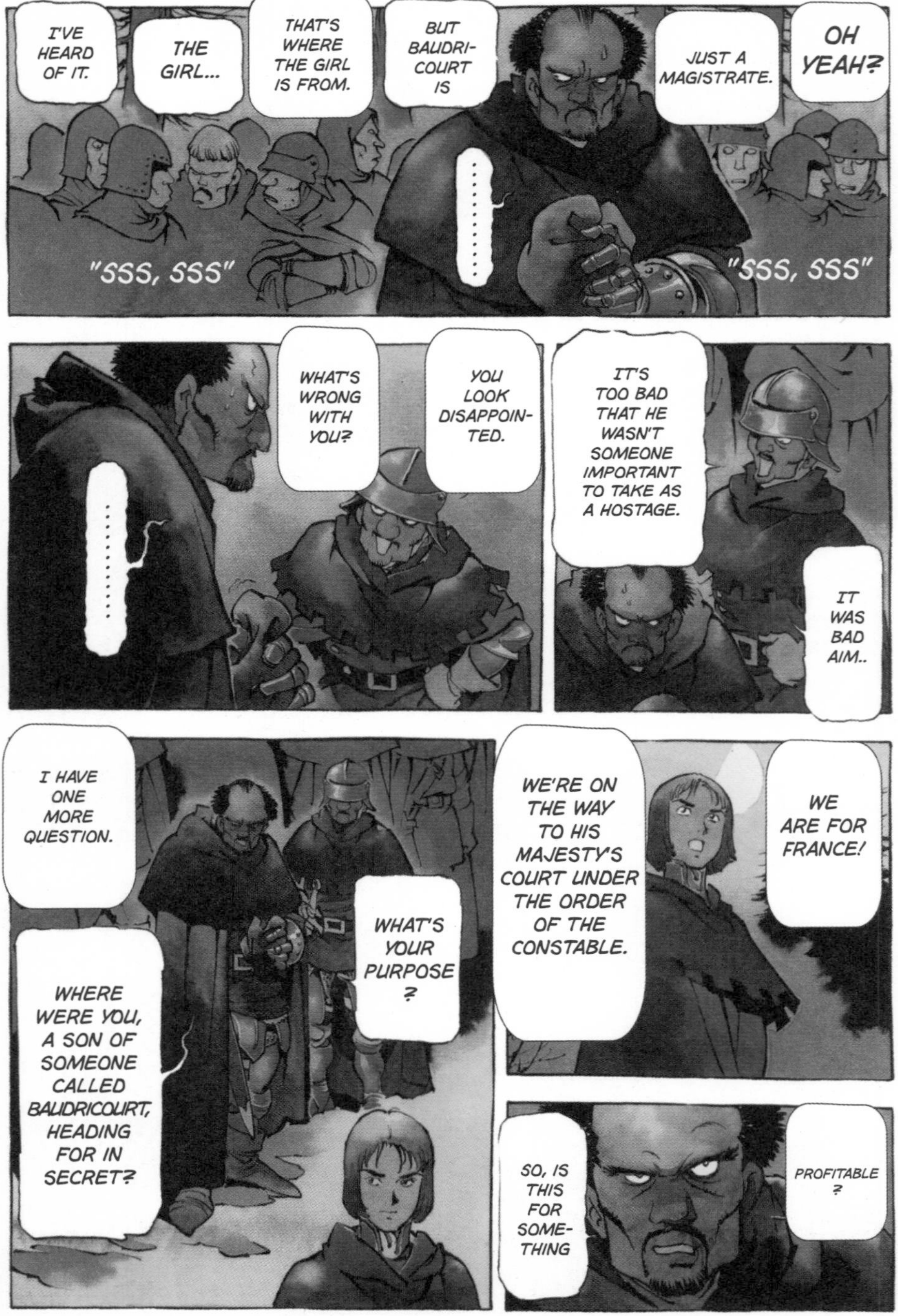
I'VE HEARD OF IT.
THE GIRL...
THAT'S WHERE THE GIRL IS FROM.
BUT BAUDRI-COURT IS
JUST A MAGISTRATE.
OH YEAH?
"SSS, SSS"
"SSS, SSS"
WHAT'S WRONG WITH YOU?
YOU LOOK DISAPPOIN-TED.
IT'S TOO BAD THAT HE WASN'T SOMEONE IMPORTANT TO TAKE AS A HOSTAGE.
IT WAS BAD AIM..
I HAVE ONE MORE QUESTION.
WHERE WERE YOU, A SON OF SOMEONE CALLED BAUDRICOURT, HEADING FOR IN SECRET?
WHAT'S YOUR PURPOSE ?
WE'RE ON THE WAY TO HIS MAJESTY'S COURT UNDER THE ORDER OF THE CONSTABLE.
WE ARE FOR FRANCE!
SO, IS THIS FOR SOME-THING
PROFITABLE ?

SHAME ON YOU!

HOLD ON, BERT-RAND!

IF IT'S PROFITABLE,

DO YOU WANT TO BE ON HIS MAJESTY'S SIDE?

CERTAINLY.

I SURRENDERED TO YOU, SO

I'LL FOLLOW YOU.

BUT ...

I KNOW WHAT YOU WANT. MONEY, RIGHT?

DON'T WORRY ABOUT IT.

FOLLOW ME!

REALLY?

YEAH.

I'LL TALK TO HIS MAJESTY'S FINANCIAL COMMISSIONER!

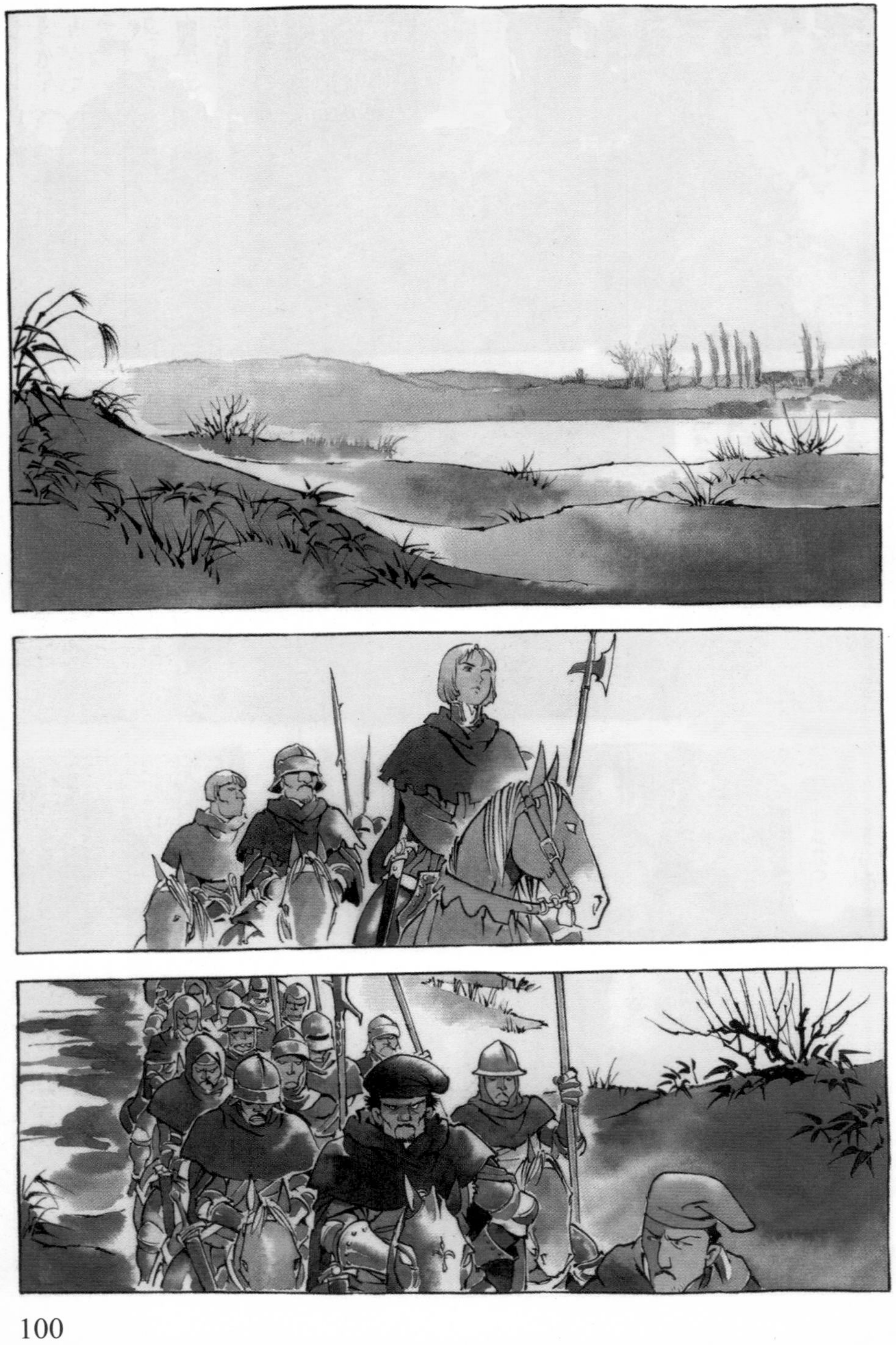

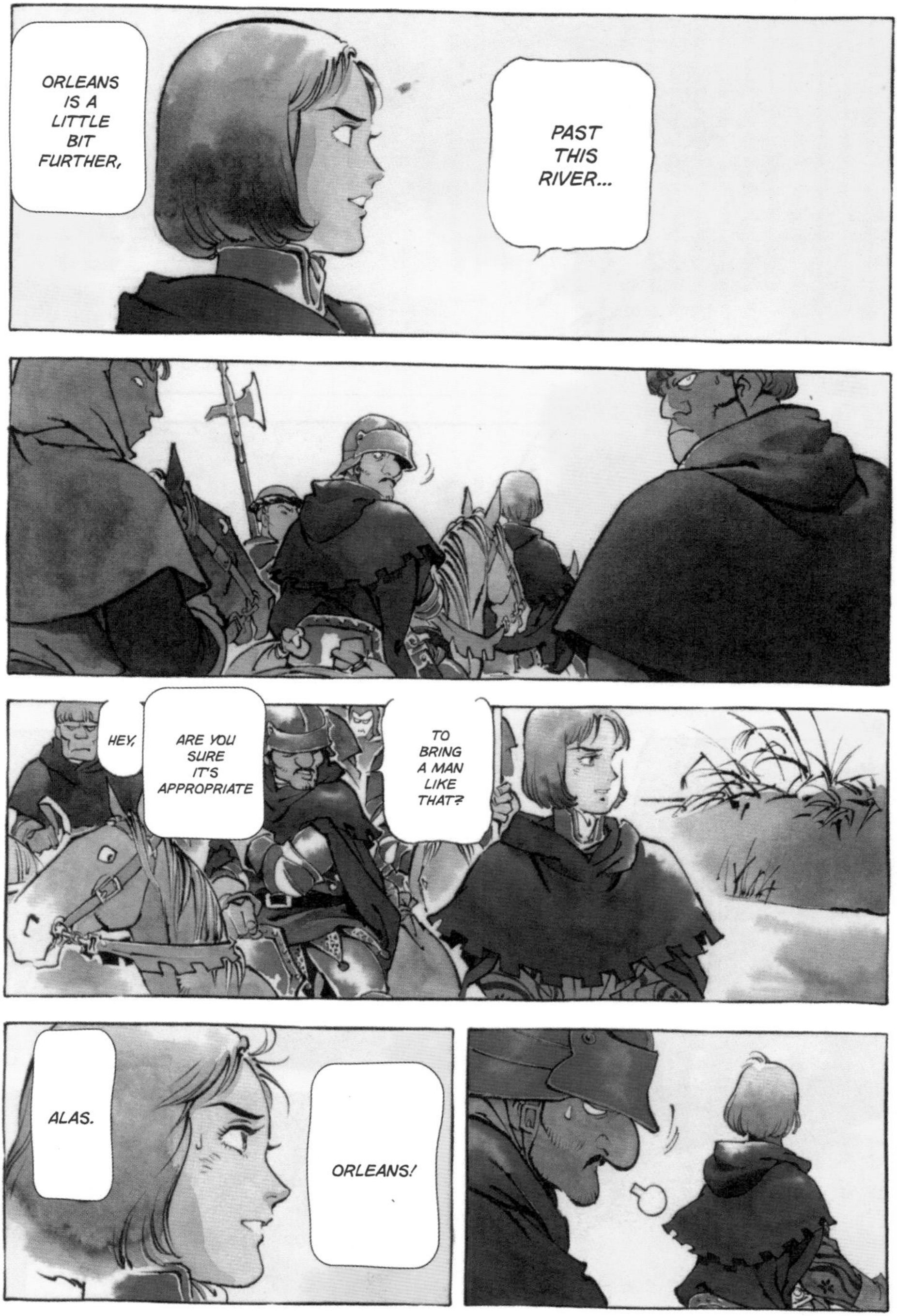
ORLEANS IS A LITTLE BIT FURTHER,
PAST THIS RIVER...
HEY,
ARE YOU SURE IT'S APPROPRIATE
TO BRING A MAN LIKE THAT?
ALAS.
ORLEANS!

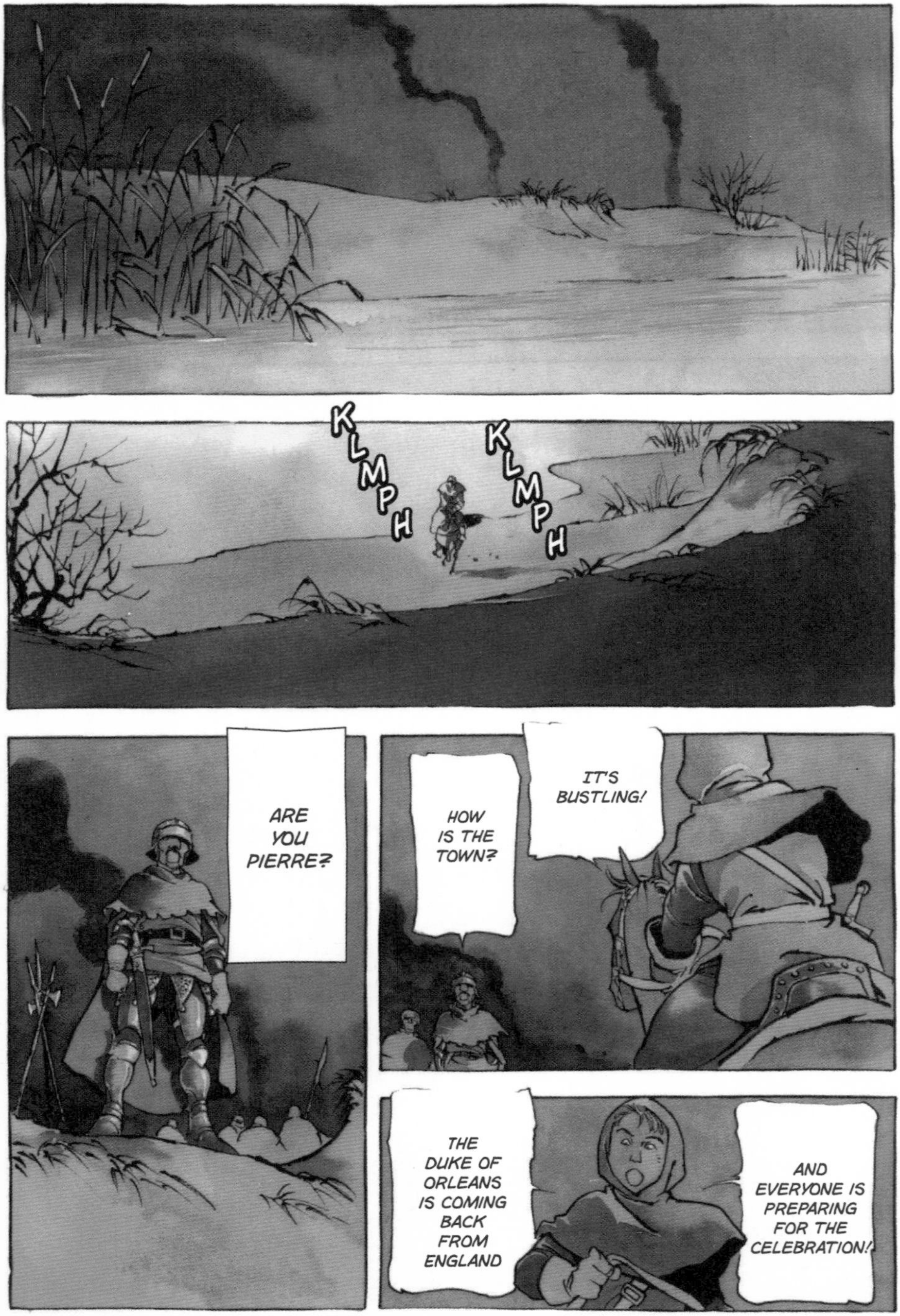

KLMPH
KLMPH
ARE YOU PIERRE?
HOW IS THE TOWN?
IT'S BUSTLING!
THE DUKE OF ORLEANS IS COMING BACK FROM ENGLAND
AND EVERYONE IS PREPARING FOR THE CELEBRATION!

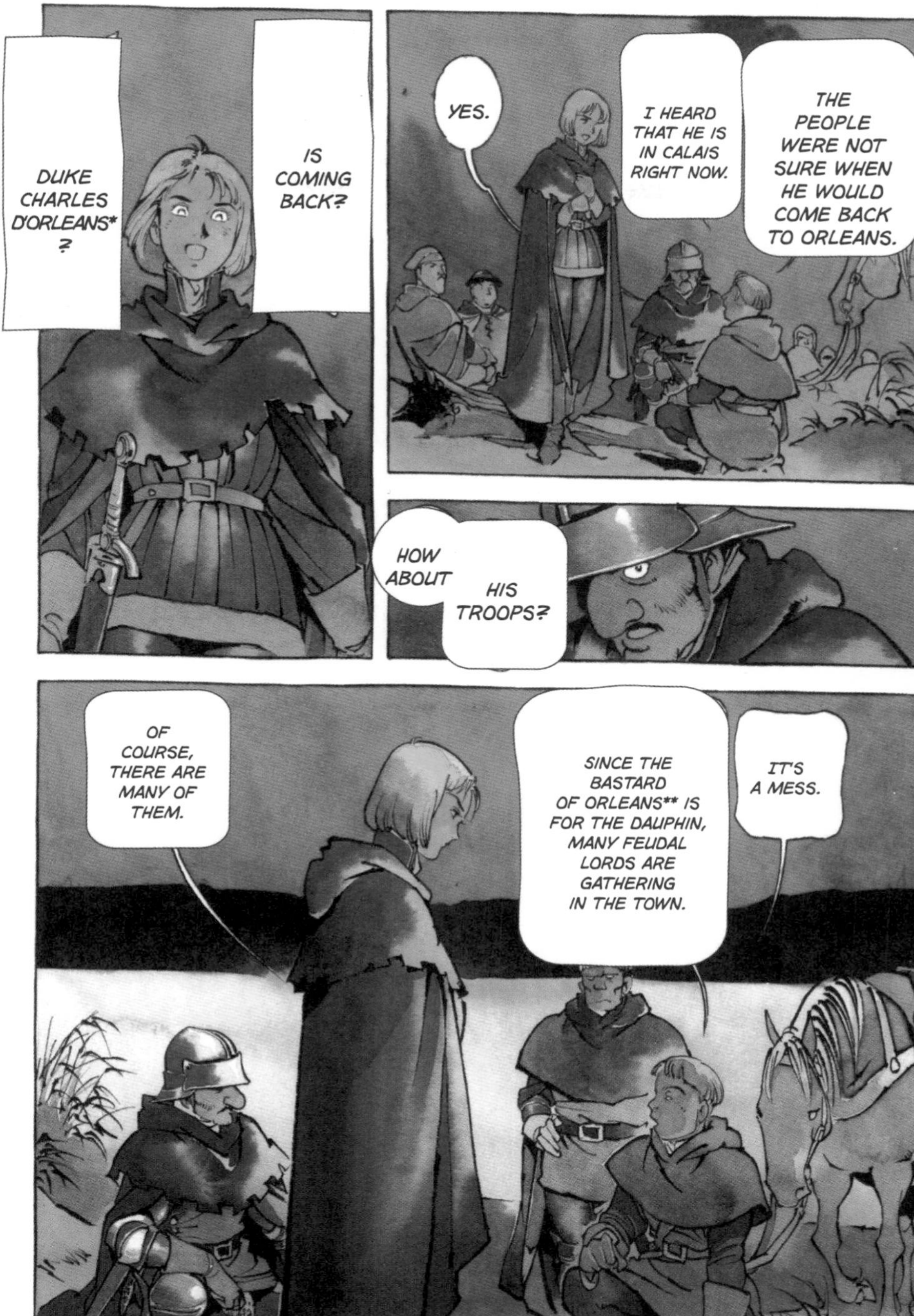
DUKE CHARLES D'ORLEANS* ?
IS COMING BACK?
YES.
I HEARD THAT HE IS IN CALAIS RIGHT NOW.
THE PEOPLE WERE NOT SURE WHEN HE WOULD COME BACK TO ORLEANS.
HOW ABOUT
HIS TROOPS?
OF COURSE, THERE ARE MANY OF THEM.
SINCE THE BASTARD OF ORLEANS** IS FOR THE DAUPHIN, MANY FEUDAL LORDS ARE GATHERING IN THE TOWN.
IT'S A MESS.

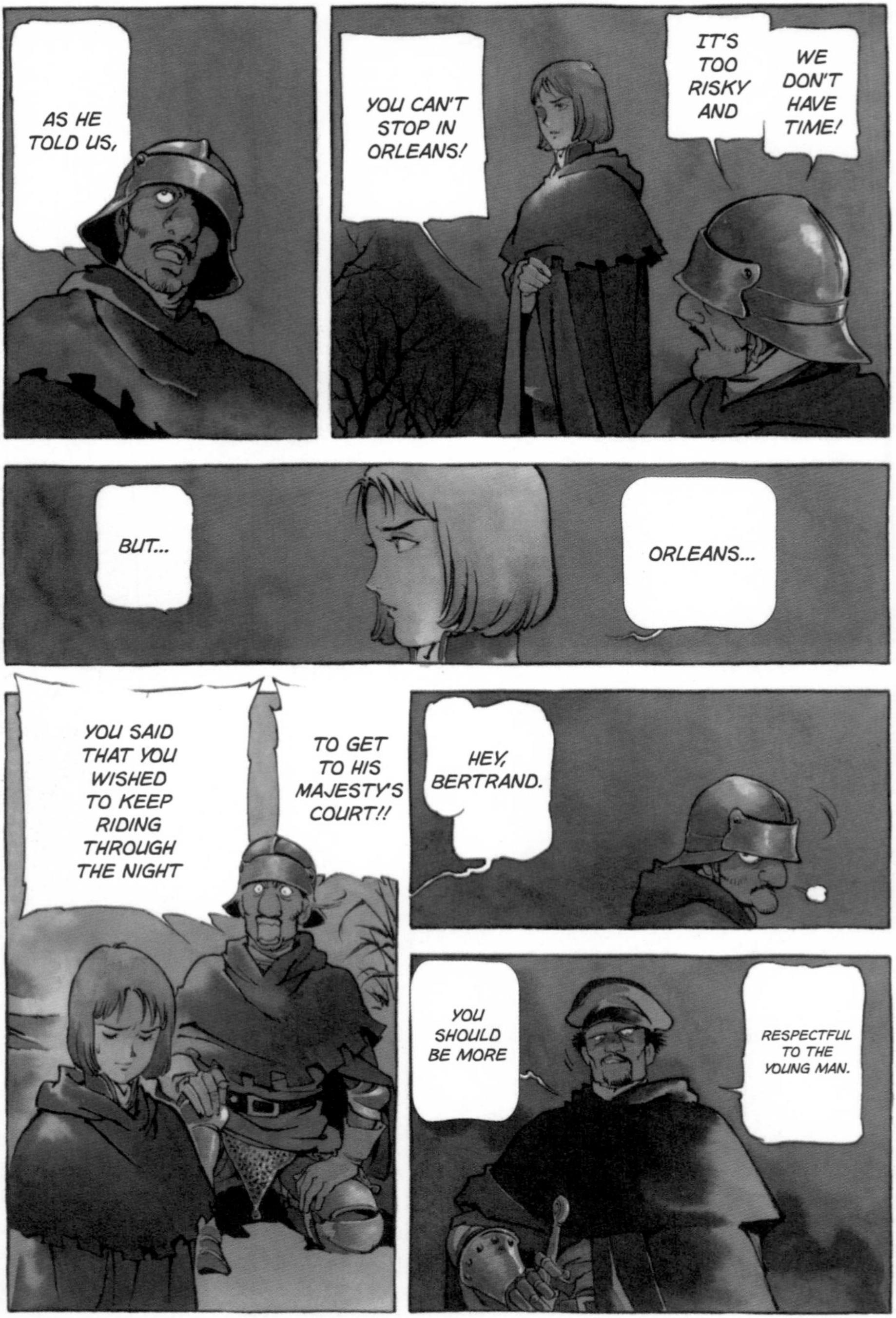
AS HE TOLD US,
YOU CAN'T STOP IN ORLEANS!
IT'S TOO RISKY AND
WE DON'T HAVE TIME!
BUT...
ORLEANS...
YOU SAID THAT YOU WISHED TO KEEP RIDING THROUGH THE NIGHT
TO GET TO HIS MAJESTY'S COURT!!
HEY, BERTRAND.
YOU SHOULD BE MORE
RESPECTFUL TO THE YOUNG MAN.

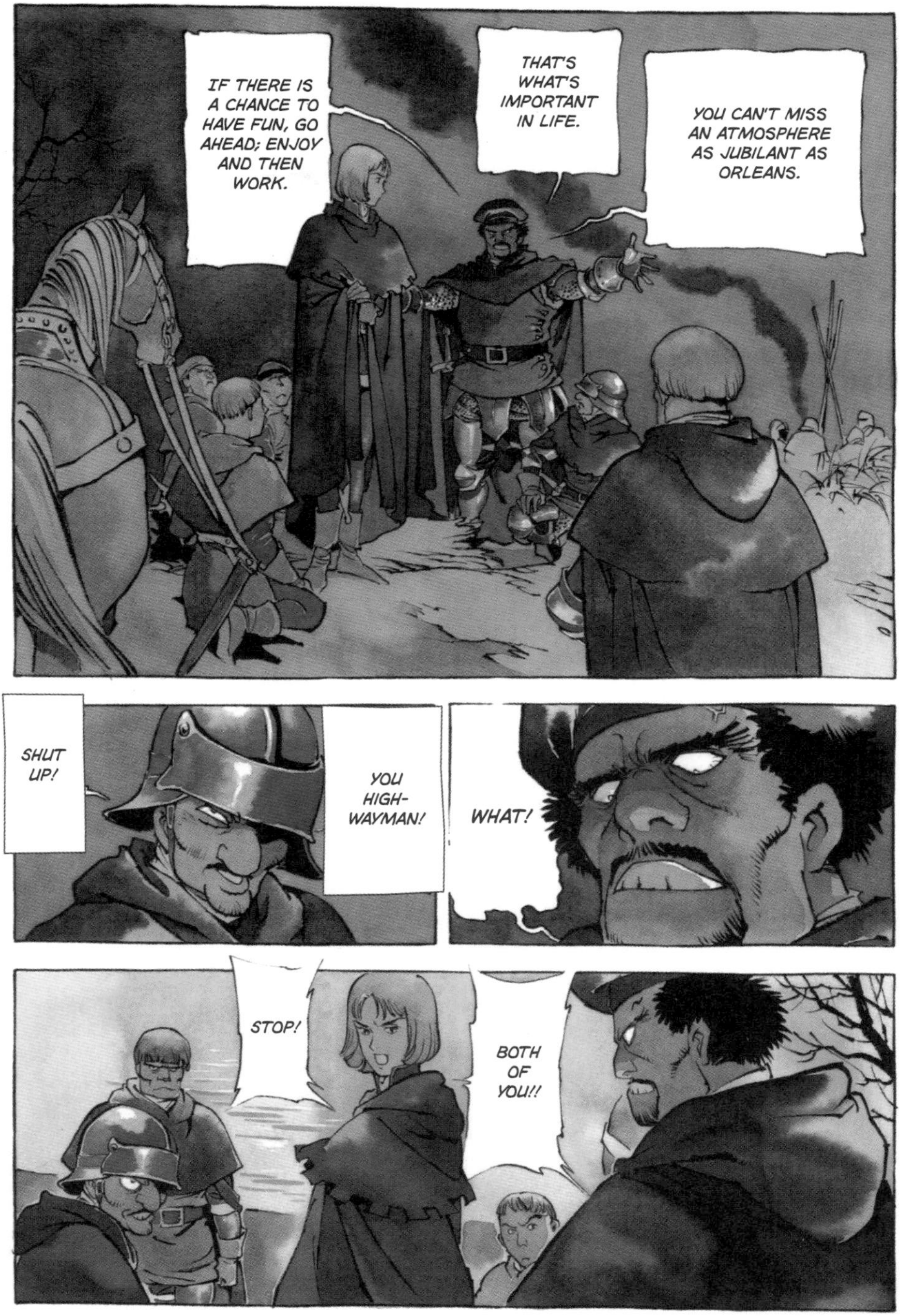
IF THERE IS A CHANCE TO HAVE FUN, GO AHEAD; ENJOY AND THEN WORK.
THAT'S WHAT'S IMPORTANT IN LIFE.
YOU CAN'T MISS AN ATMOSPHERE AS JUBILANT AS ORLEANS.
SHUT UP!
YOU HIGH-WAYMAN!
WHAT!
STOP!
BOTH OF YOU!!

IT'S GETTING DARK.

WE'VE BEEN WALKING ALL DAY LONG, EVERYONE MUST BE EXHAUSTED.

NOW THAT WE'RE HERE, CAMPING OUT OR SLEEPING IN A LODGE IN ORLEANS WILL BE THE SAME, ANYWAY.

LET'S GO TO THE TOWN.

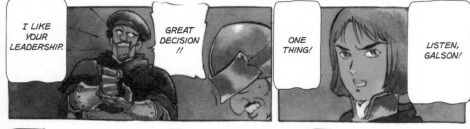

I LIKE YOUR LEADERSHIP.

GREAT DECISION !!

ONE THING!

LISTEN, GALSON!

BEHAVE YOURSELF IN THE TOWN!

IF EVEN ONE OF YOUR MEN CAUSES TROUBLE,

I'LL CUT YOUR THROAT!!

YES.

HE, HE, HE ...

I KNOW.

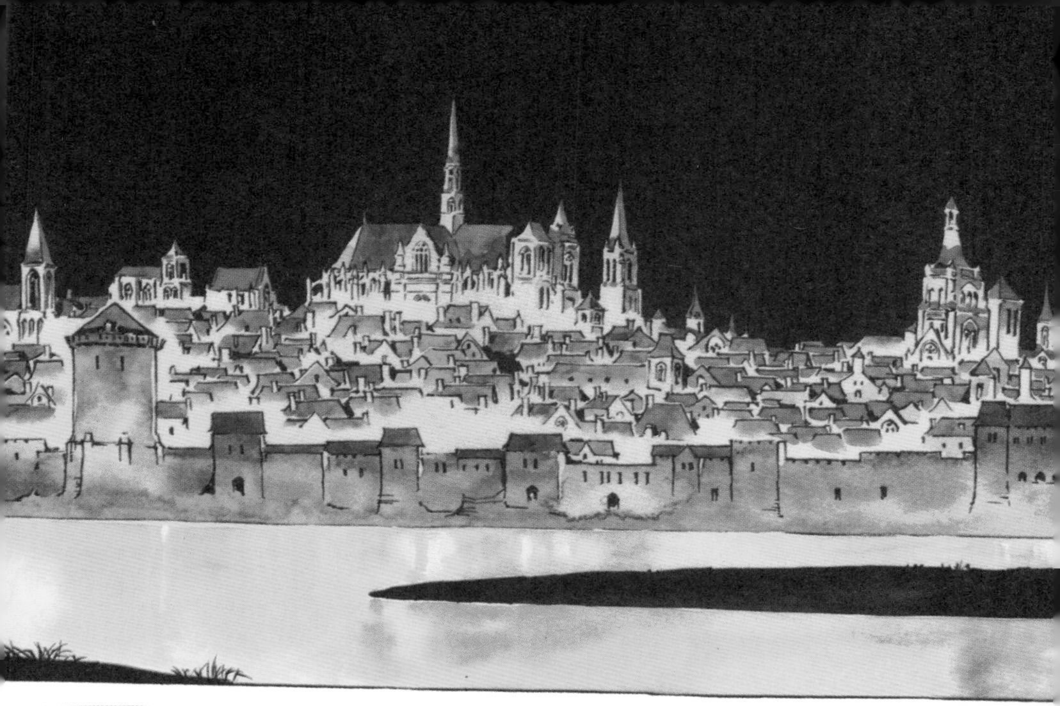

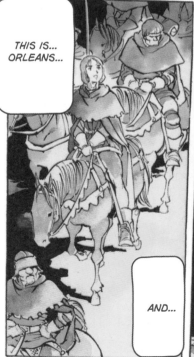

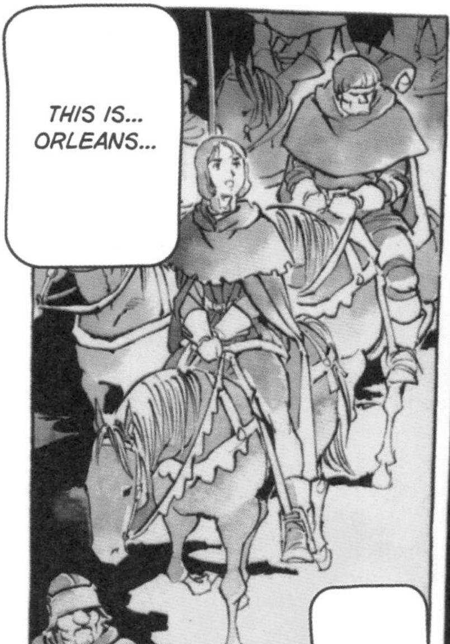
THIS IS... ORLEANS...
AND...

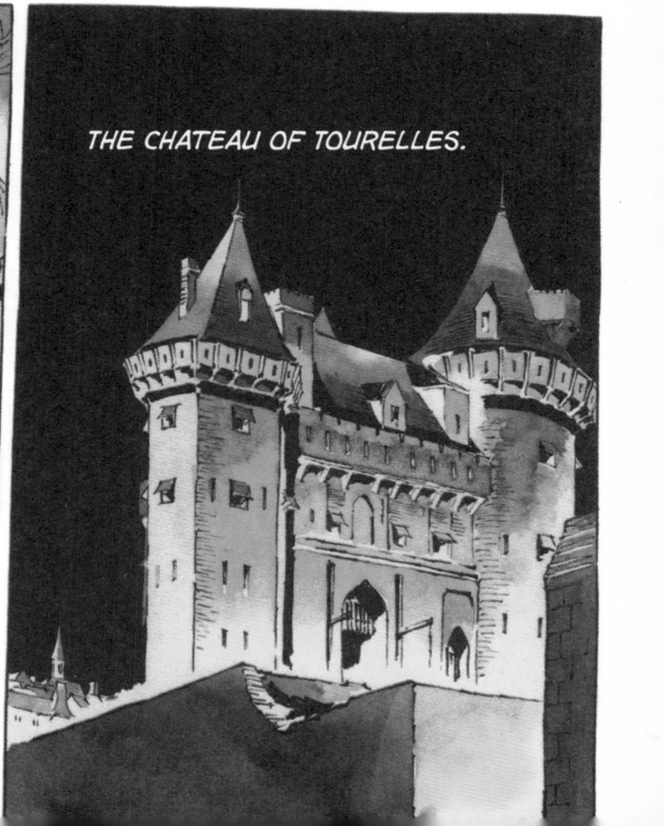
THE CHATEAU OF TOURELLES.

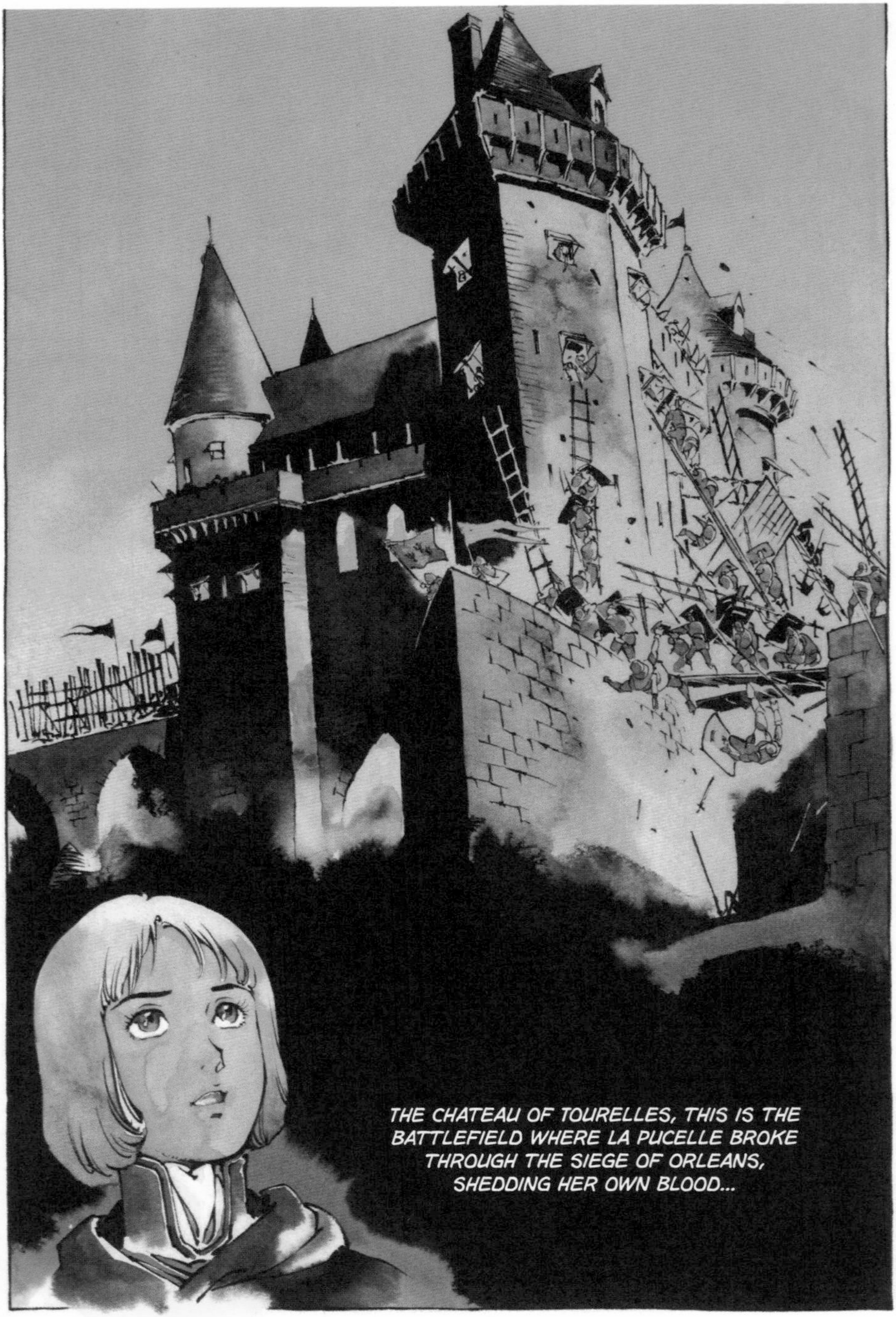
THE CHATEAU OF TOURELLES, THIS IS THE BATTLEFIELD WHERE LA PUCELLE BROKE THROUGH THE SIEGE OF ORLEANS, SHEDDING HER OWN BLOOD...

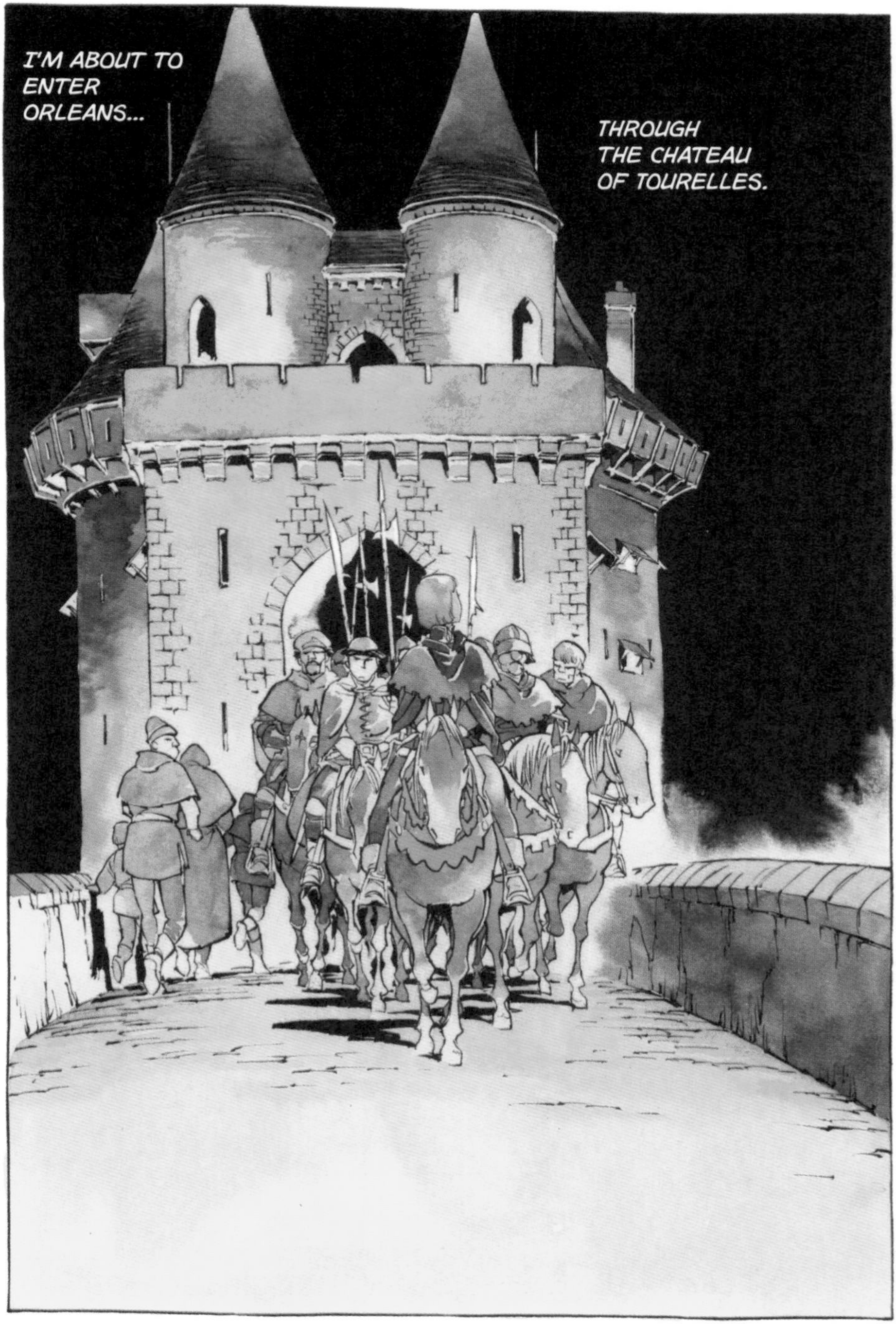
I'M ABOUT TO ENTER ORLEANS...
THROUGH THE CHATEAU OF TOURELLES.

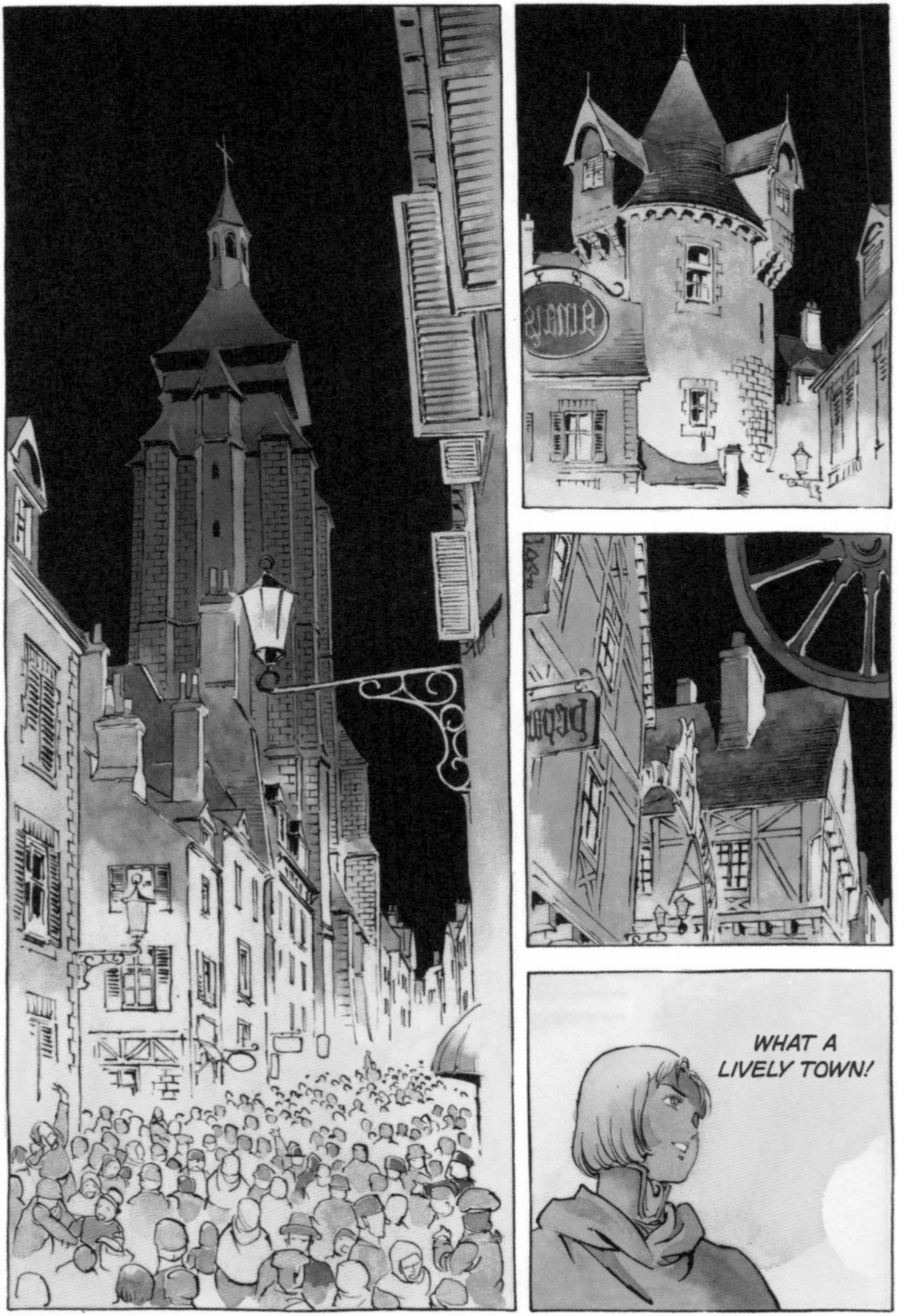
WHAT A LIVELY TOWN!

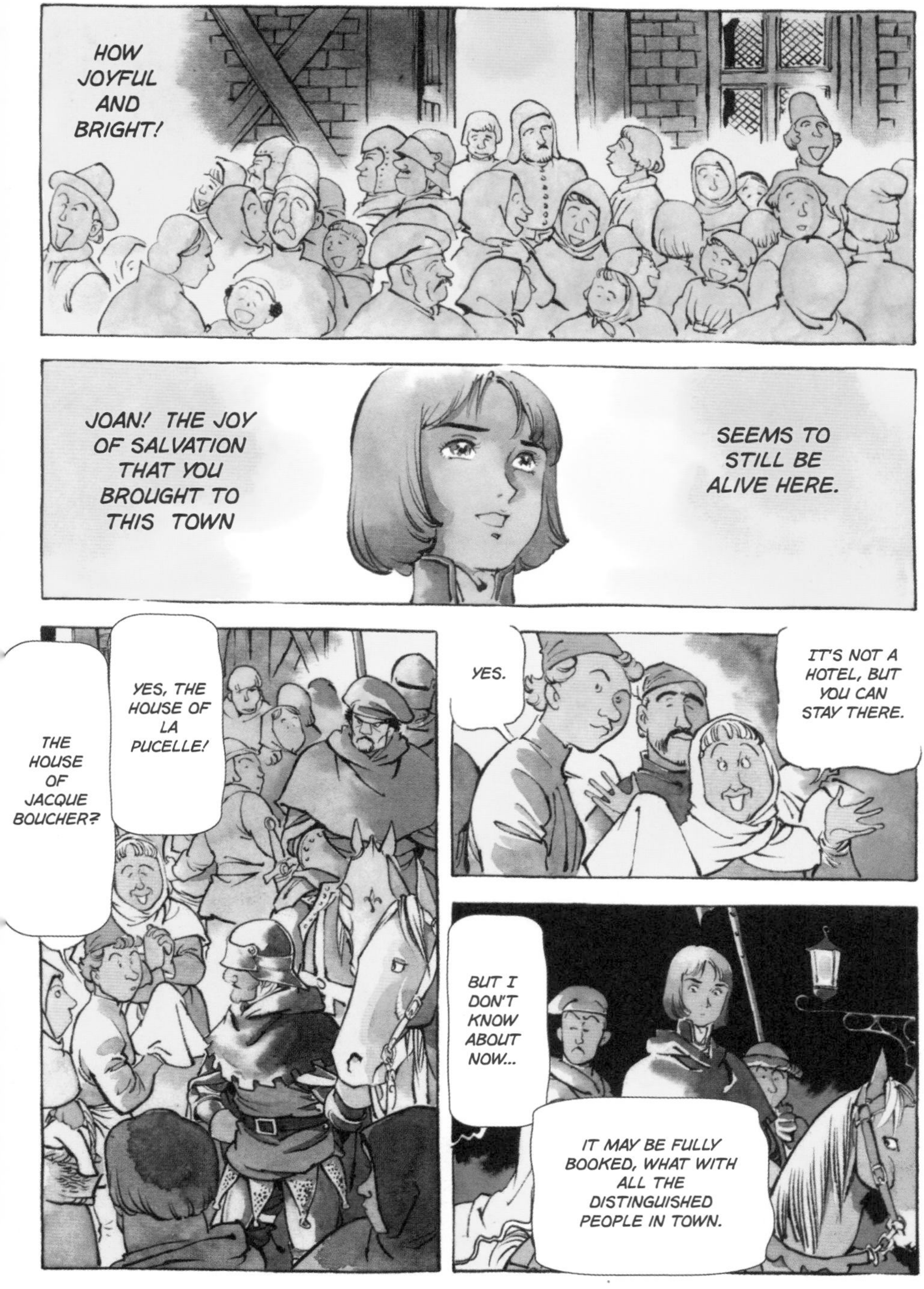
HOW JOYFUL AND BRIGHT!
JOAN! THE JOY OF SALVATION THAT YOU BROUGHT TO THIS TOWN
SEEMS TO STILL BE ALIVE HERE.
THE HOUSE OF JACQUE BOUCHER?
YES, THE HOUSE OF LA PUCELLE!
YES.
IT'S NOT A HOTEL, BUT YOU CAN STAY THERE.
BUT I DON'T KNOW ABOUT NOW...
IT MAY BE FULLY BOOKED, WHAT WITH ALL THE DISTINGUISHED PEOPLE IN TOWN.

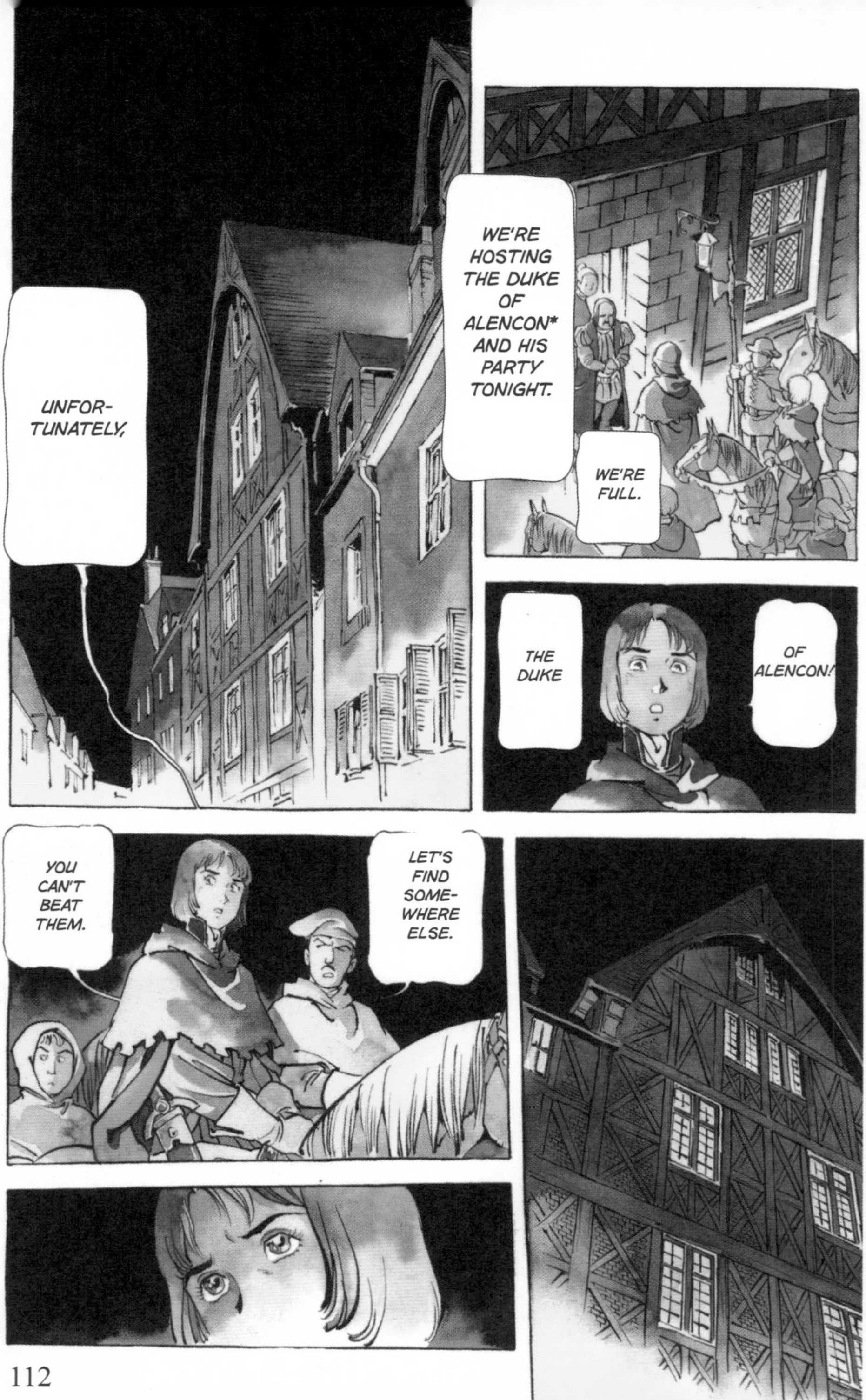
WE'RE HOSTING THE DUKE OF ALENCON* AND HIS PARTY TONIGHT.
WE'RE FULL.
UNFOR-TUNATELY,
THE DUKE
OF ALENCON!
YOU CAN'T BEAT THEM.
LET'S FIND SOME-WHERE ELSE.

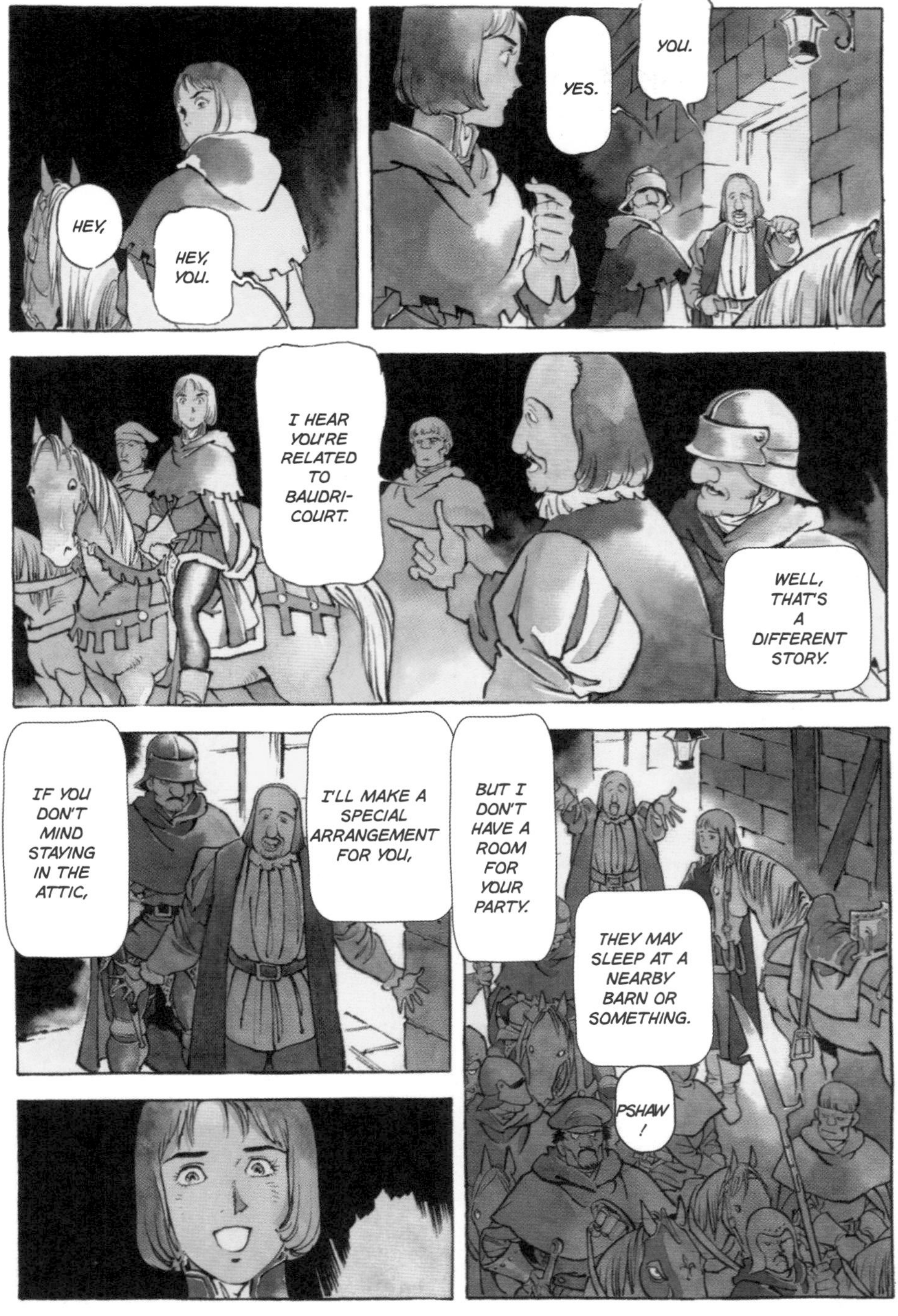
HEY,
HEY, YOU.
YES.
YOU.
I HEAR YOU'RE RELATED TO BAUDRI-COURT.
WELL, THAT'S A DIFFERENT STORY.
IF YOU DON'T MIND STAYING IN THE ATTIC,
I'LL MAKE A SPECIAL ARRANGEMENT FOR YOU,
BUT I DON'T HAVE A ROOM FOR YOUR PARTY.
THEY MAY SLEEP AT A NEARBY BARN OR SOMETHING.
PSHAW!

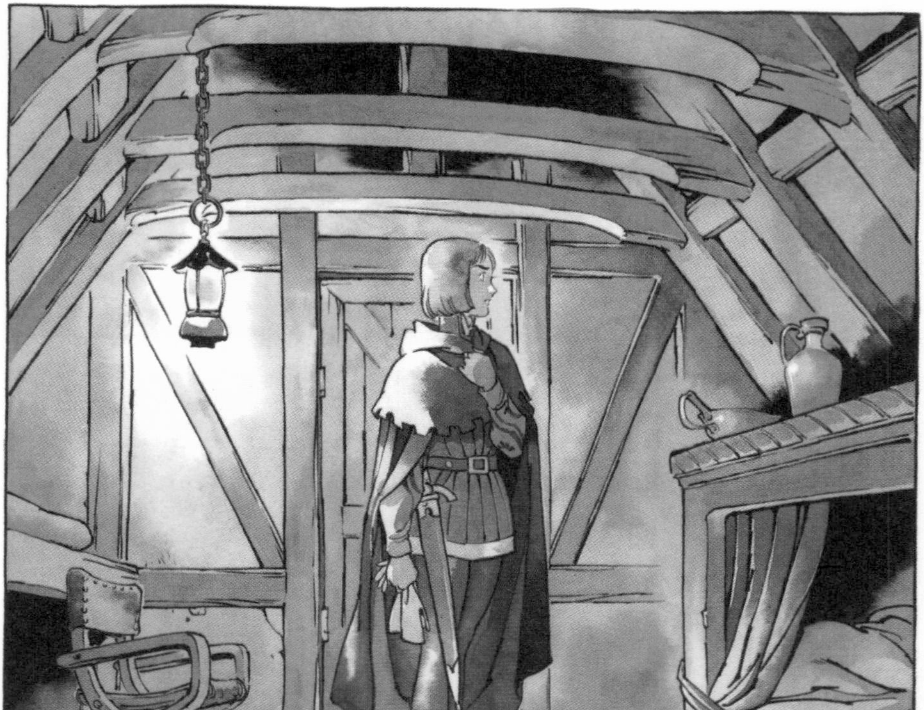

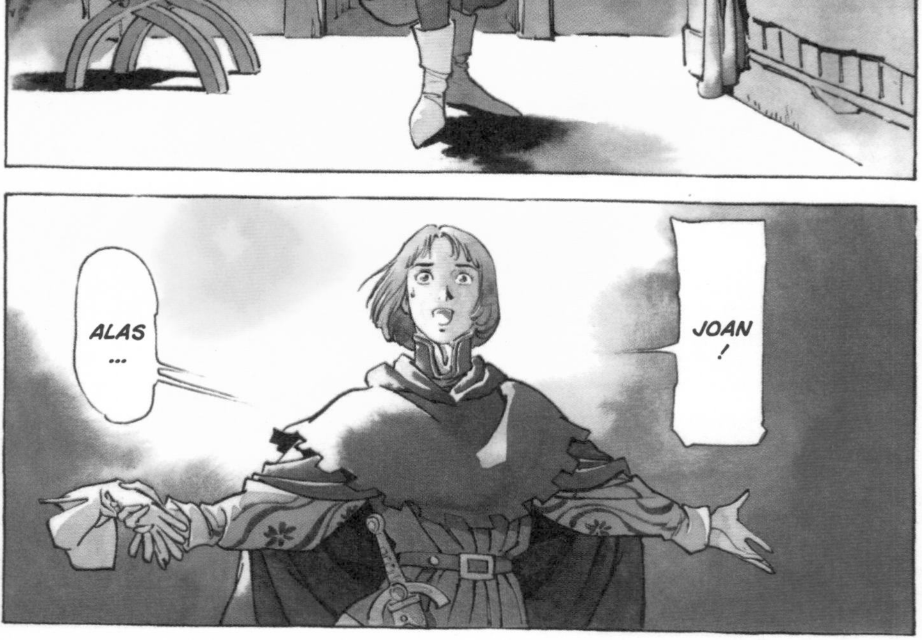
ALAS ...
JOAN !

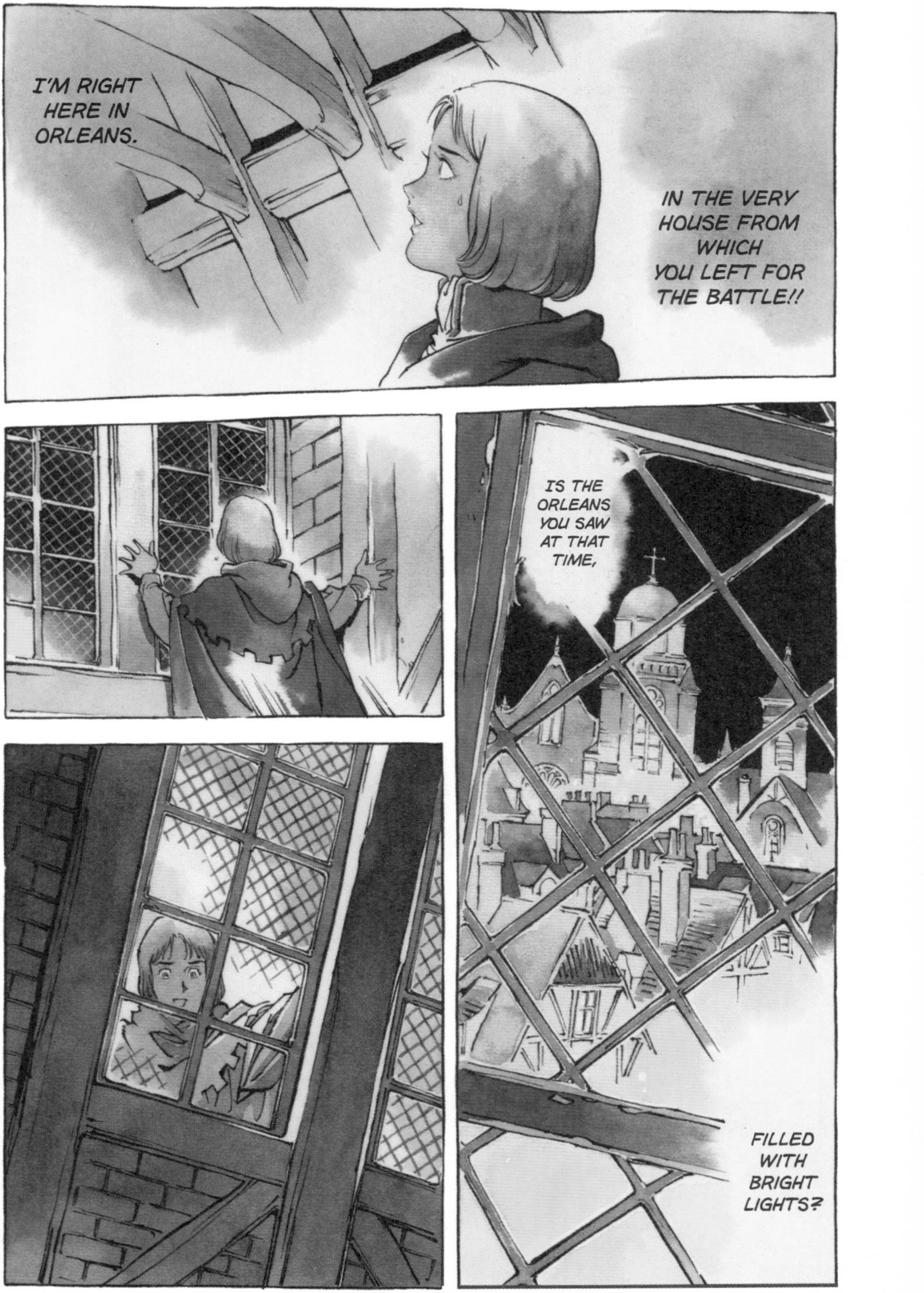
I'M RIGHT HERE IN ORLEANS.
IN THE VERY HOUSE FROM WHICH YOU LEFT FOR THE BATTLE!!
IS THE ORLEANS YOU SAW AT THAT TIME,
FILLED WITH BRIGHT LIGHTS?

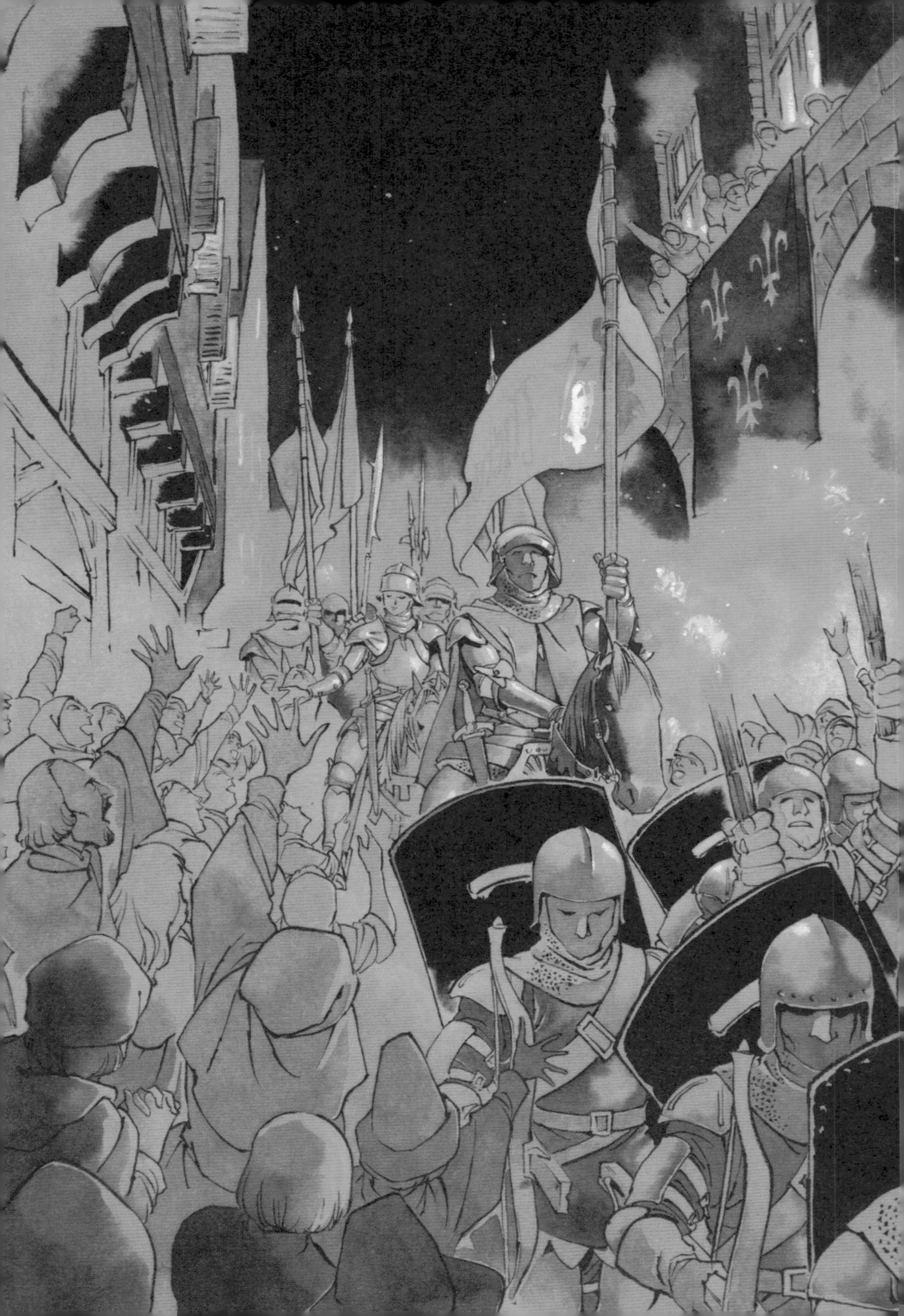

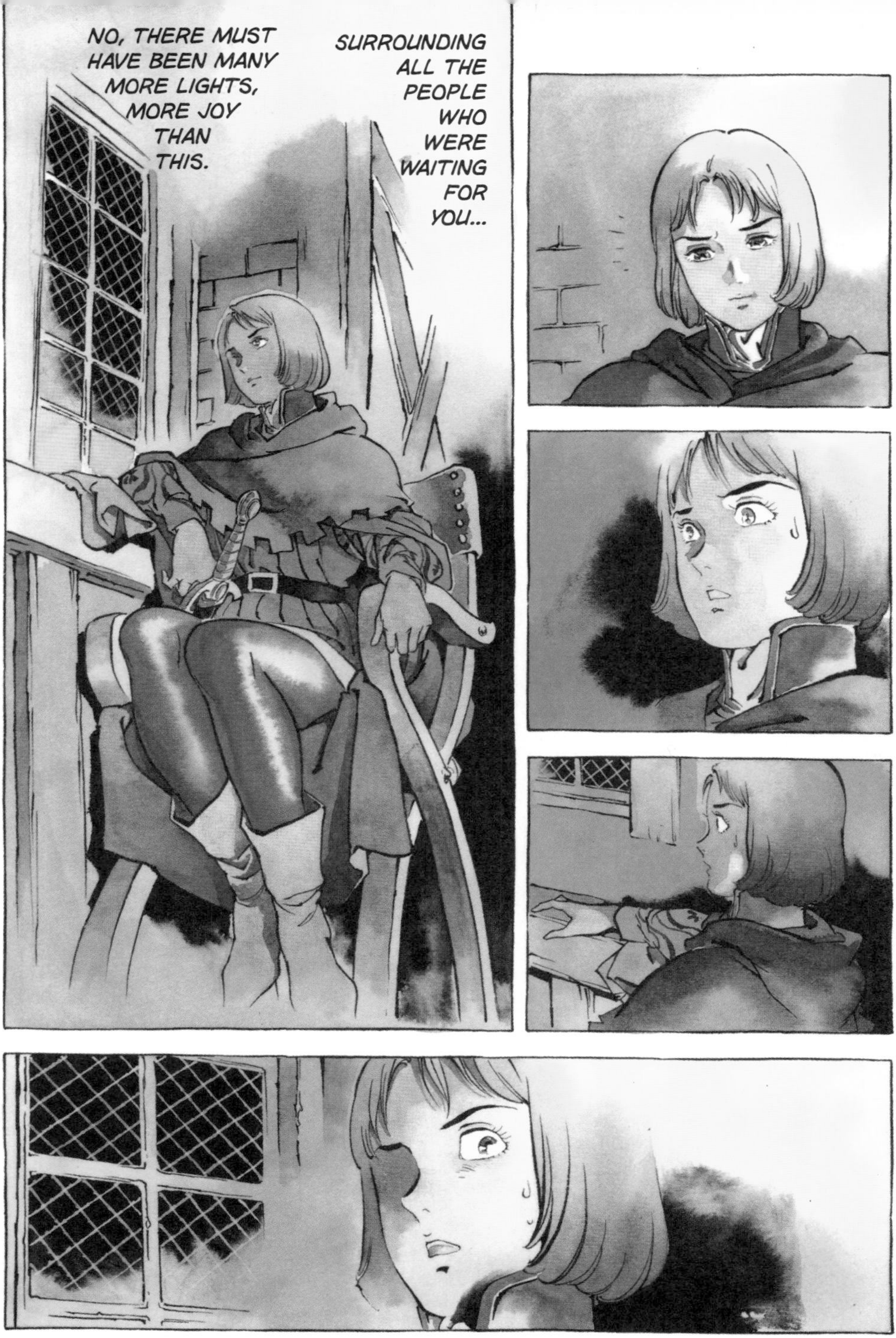
NO, THERE MUST HAVE BEEN MANY MORE LIGHTS, MORE JOY THAN THIS.
SURROUNDING ALL THE PEOPLE WHO WERE WAITING FOR YOU...

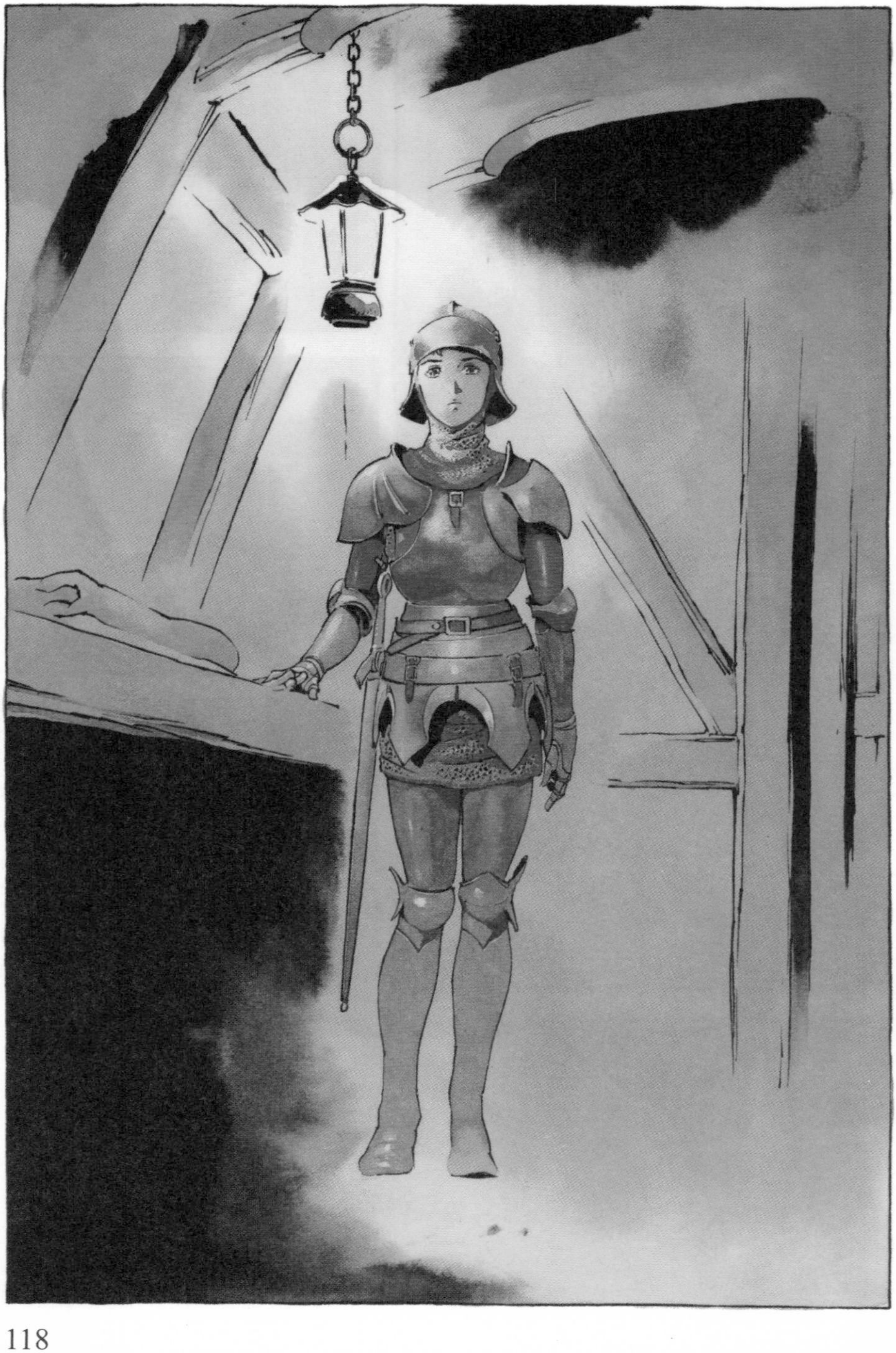

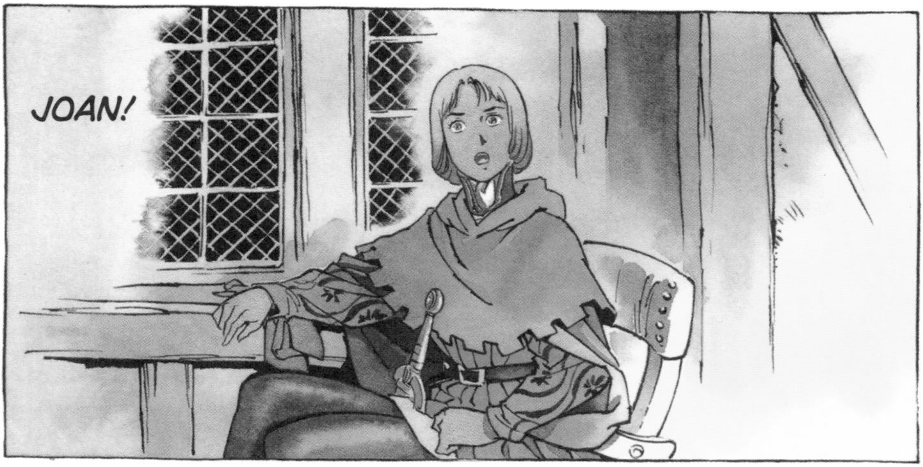
JOAN!

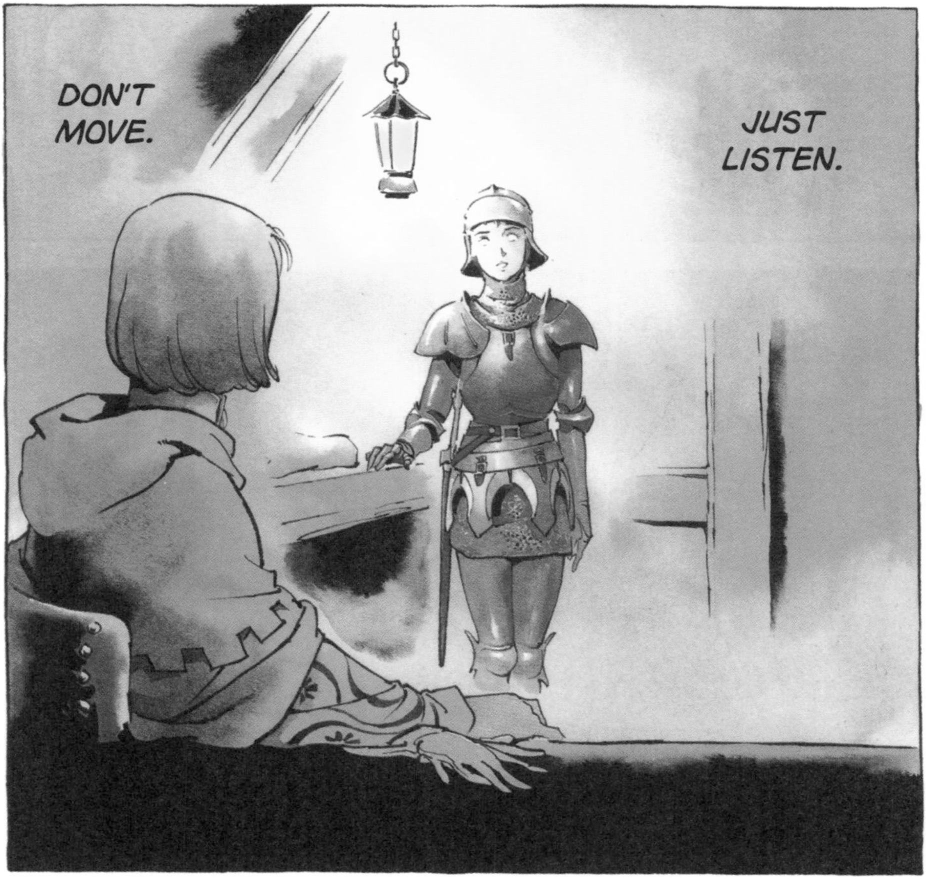
DON'T MOVE.
JUST LISTEN.

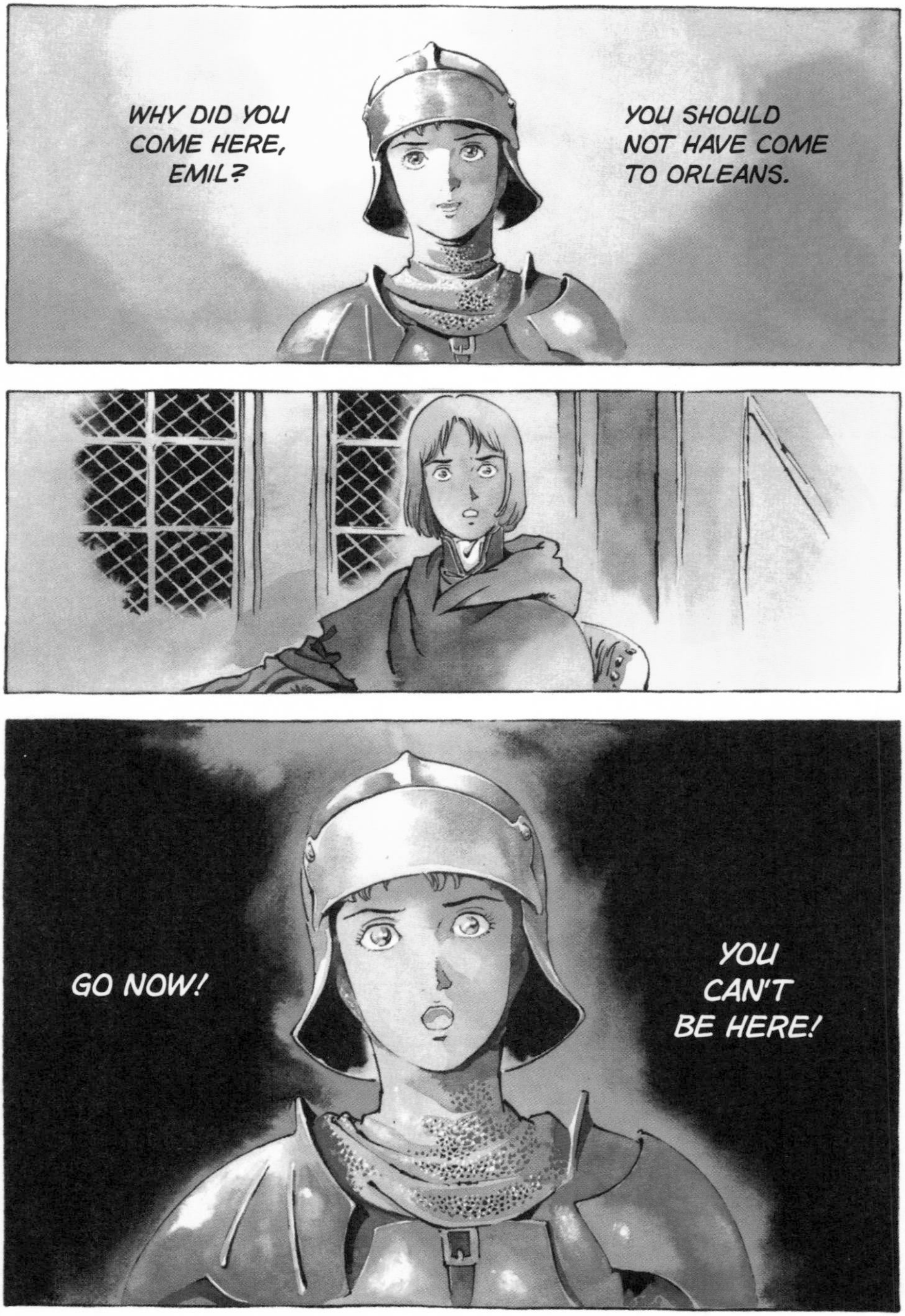
WHY DID YOU COME HERE, EMIL?
YOU SHOULD NOT HAVE COME TO ORLEANS.
GO NOW!
YOU CAN'T BE HERE!

# Chapter 3

# LOUIS

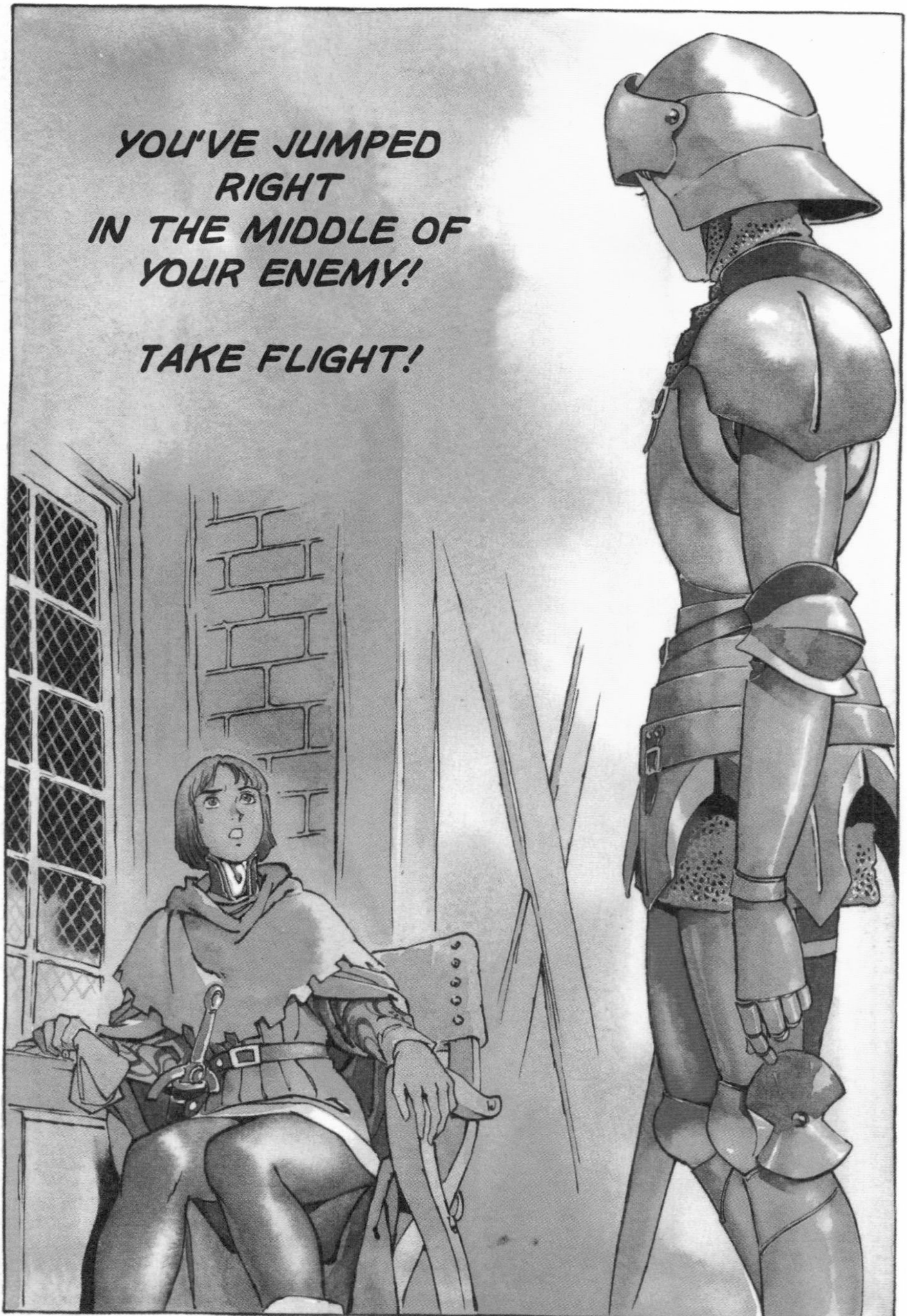
YOU'VE JUMPED RIGHT IN THE MIDDLE OF YOUR ENEMY!
TAKE FLIGHT!

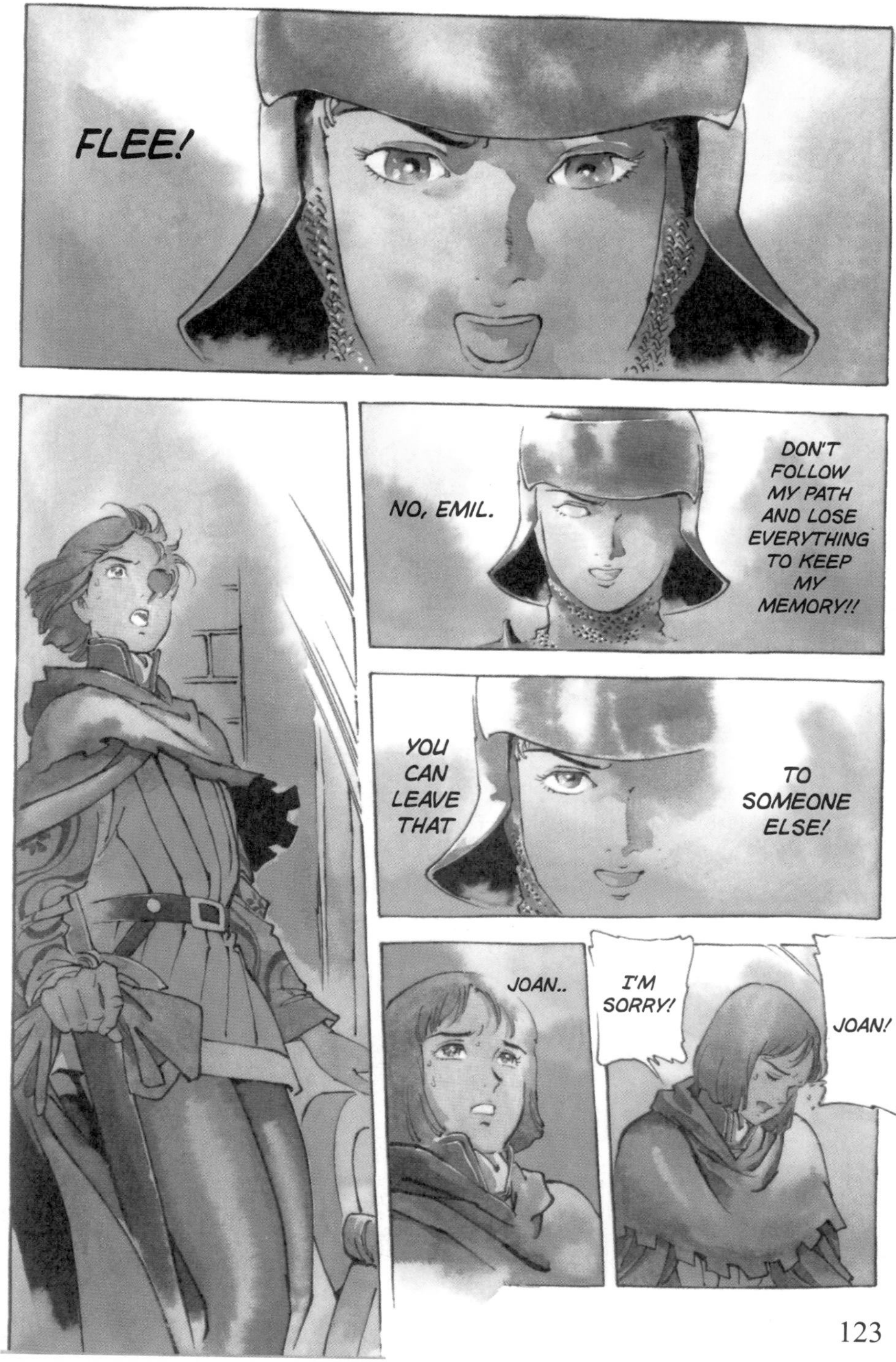

FLEE!
NO, EMIL.
DON'T FOLLOW MY PATH AND LOSE EVERYTHING TO KEEP MY MEMORY!!
YOU CAN LEAVE THAT
TO SOMEONE ELSE!
JOAN..
I'M SORRY!
JOAN!

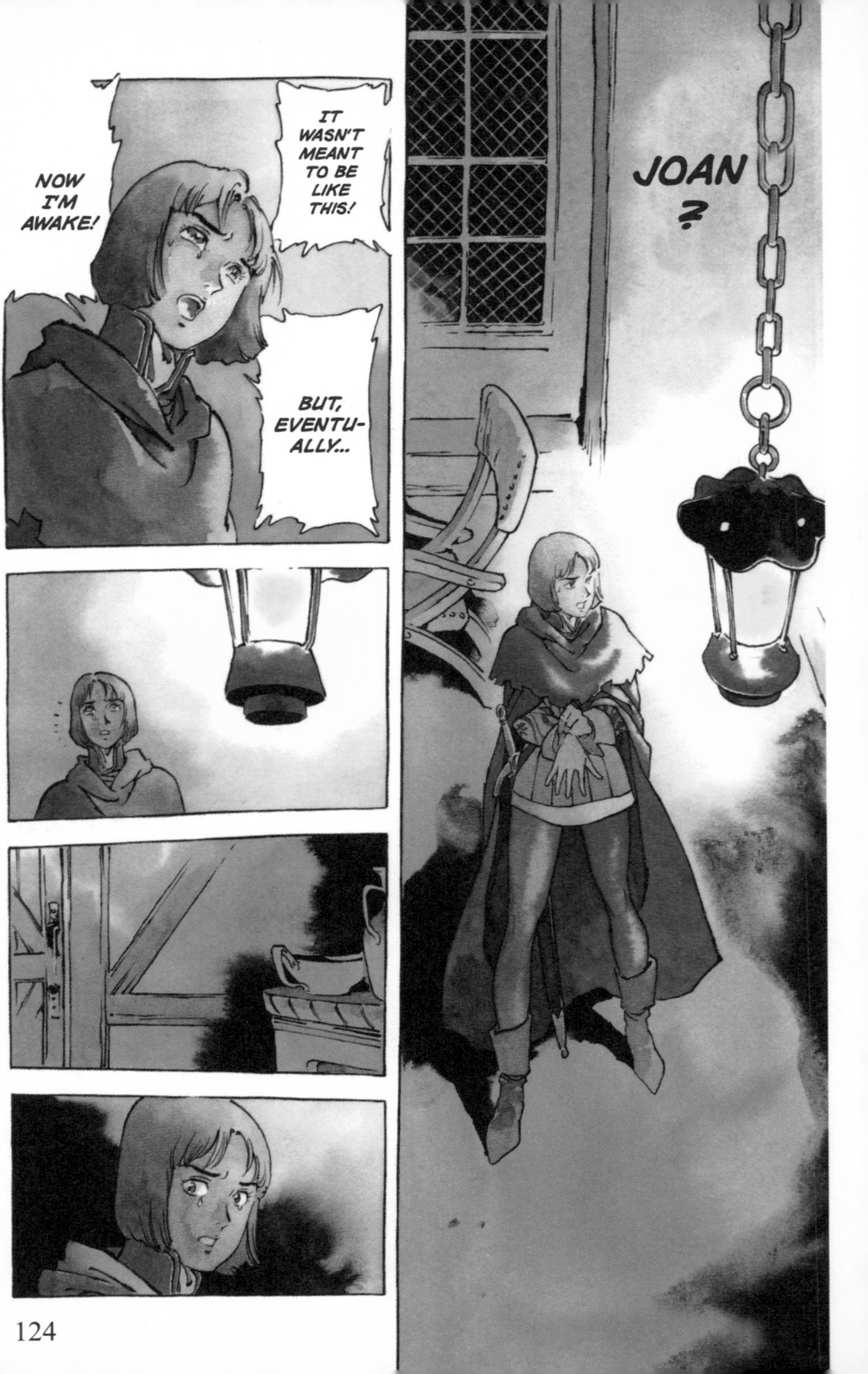
JOAN ?
IT WASN'T MEANT TO BE LIKE THIS!
NOW I'M AWAKE!
BUT, EVENTU-ALLY...

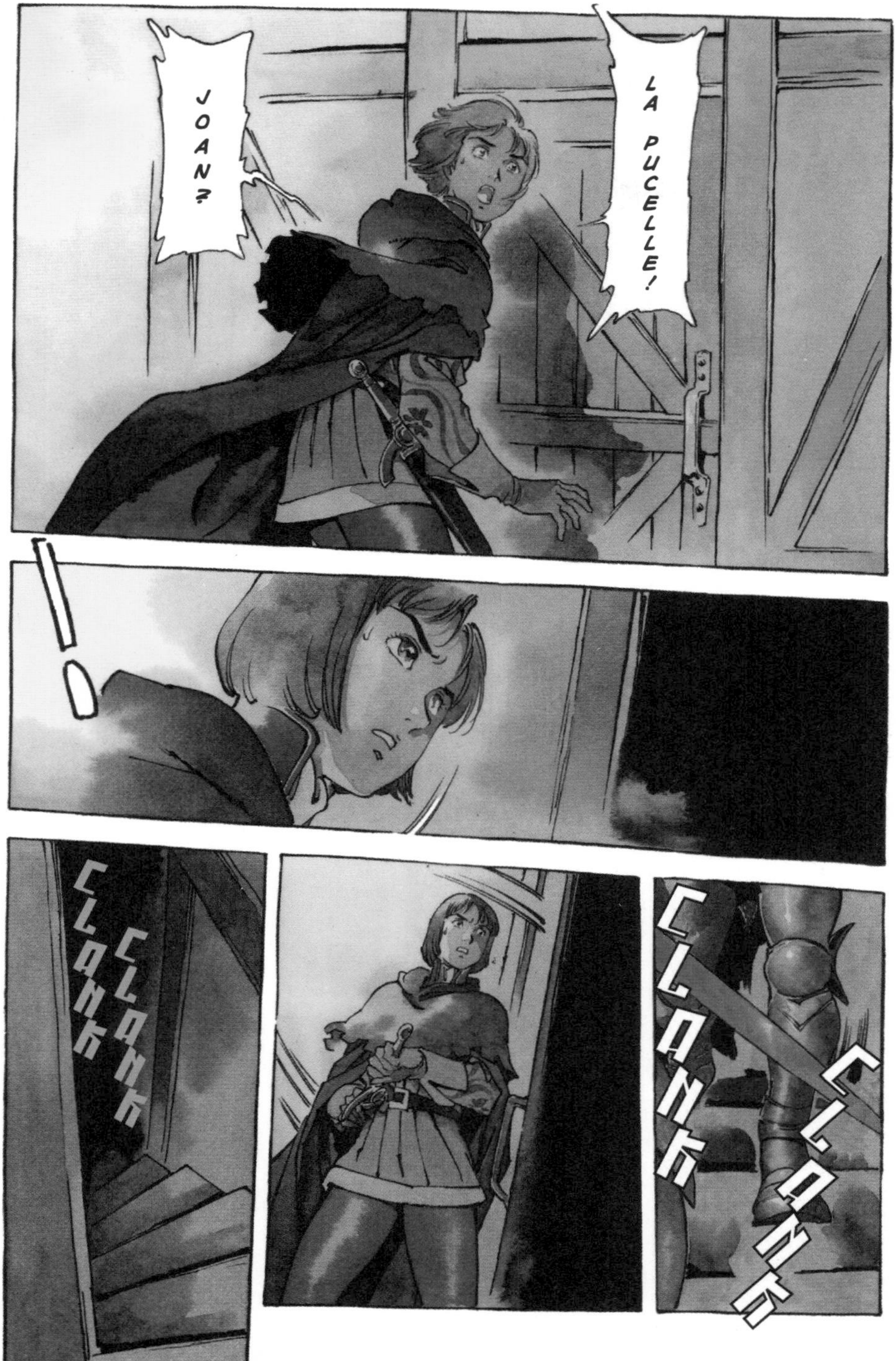
LA PUCELLE!
JOAN?
CLANK CLANK
CLANK CLANK

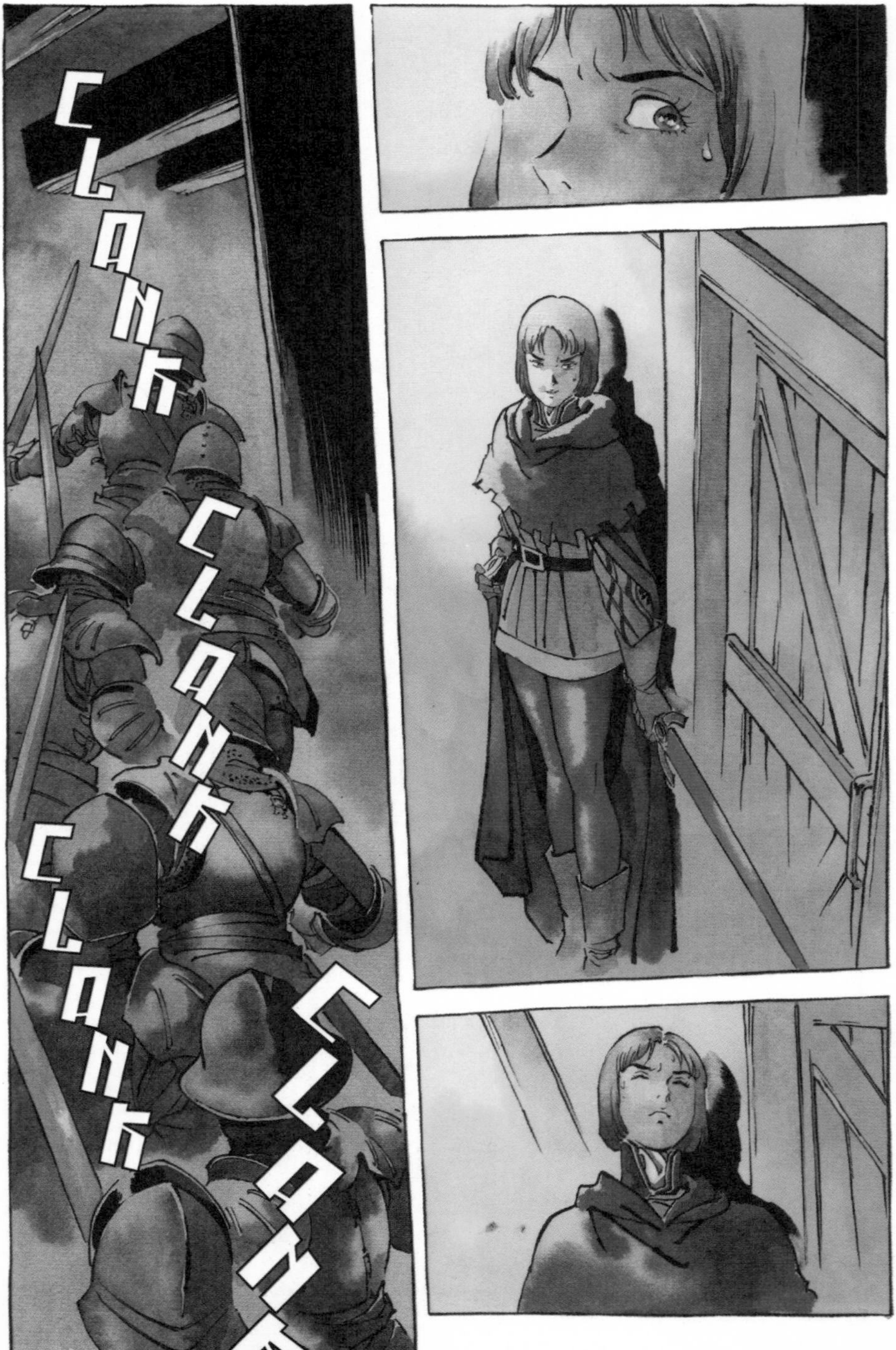
CLANK
CLANK
CLANK
CLANK
CLANK

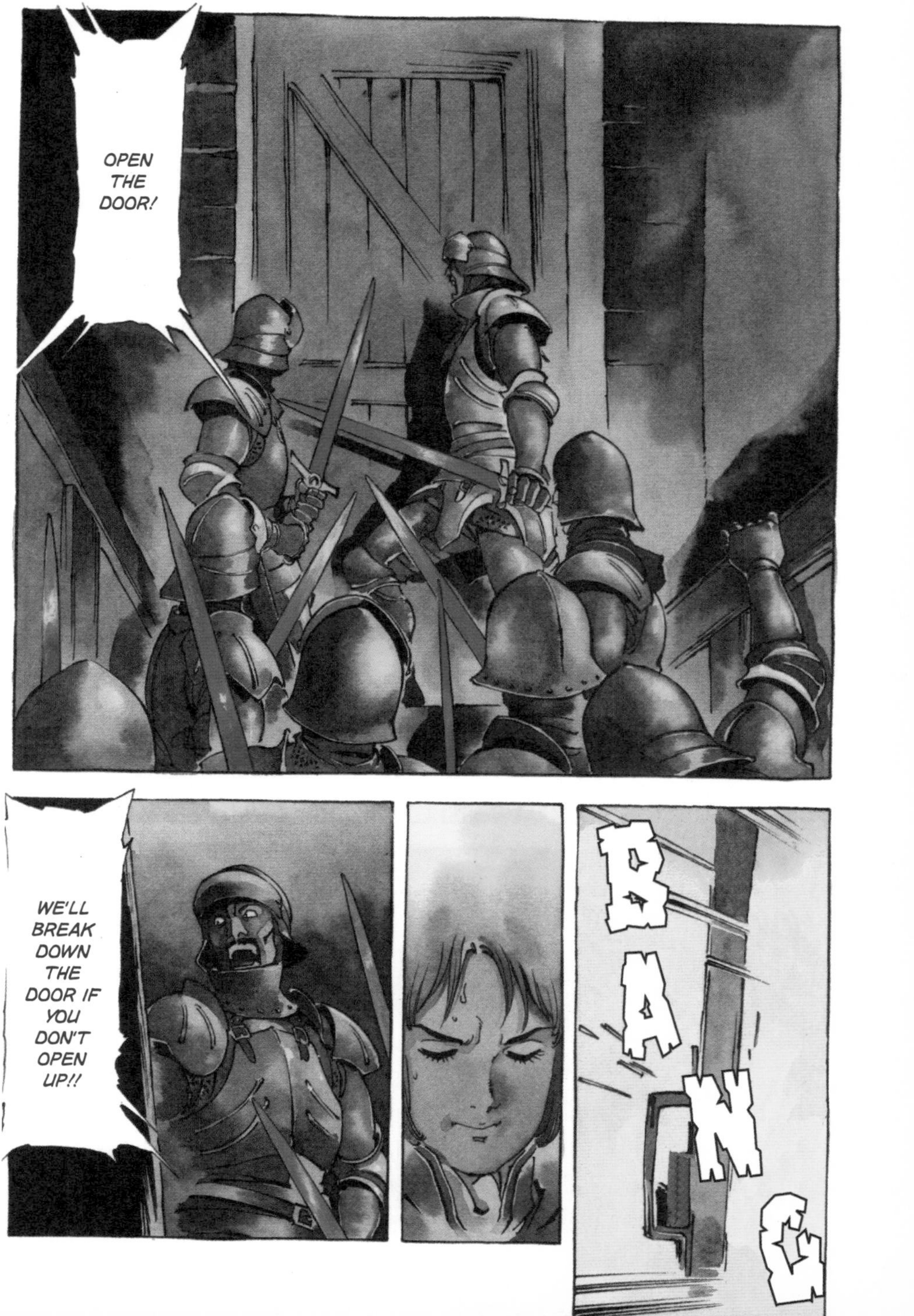
OPEN THE DOOR!
WE'LL BREAK DOWN THE DOOR IF YOU DON'T OPEN UP!!
BANG

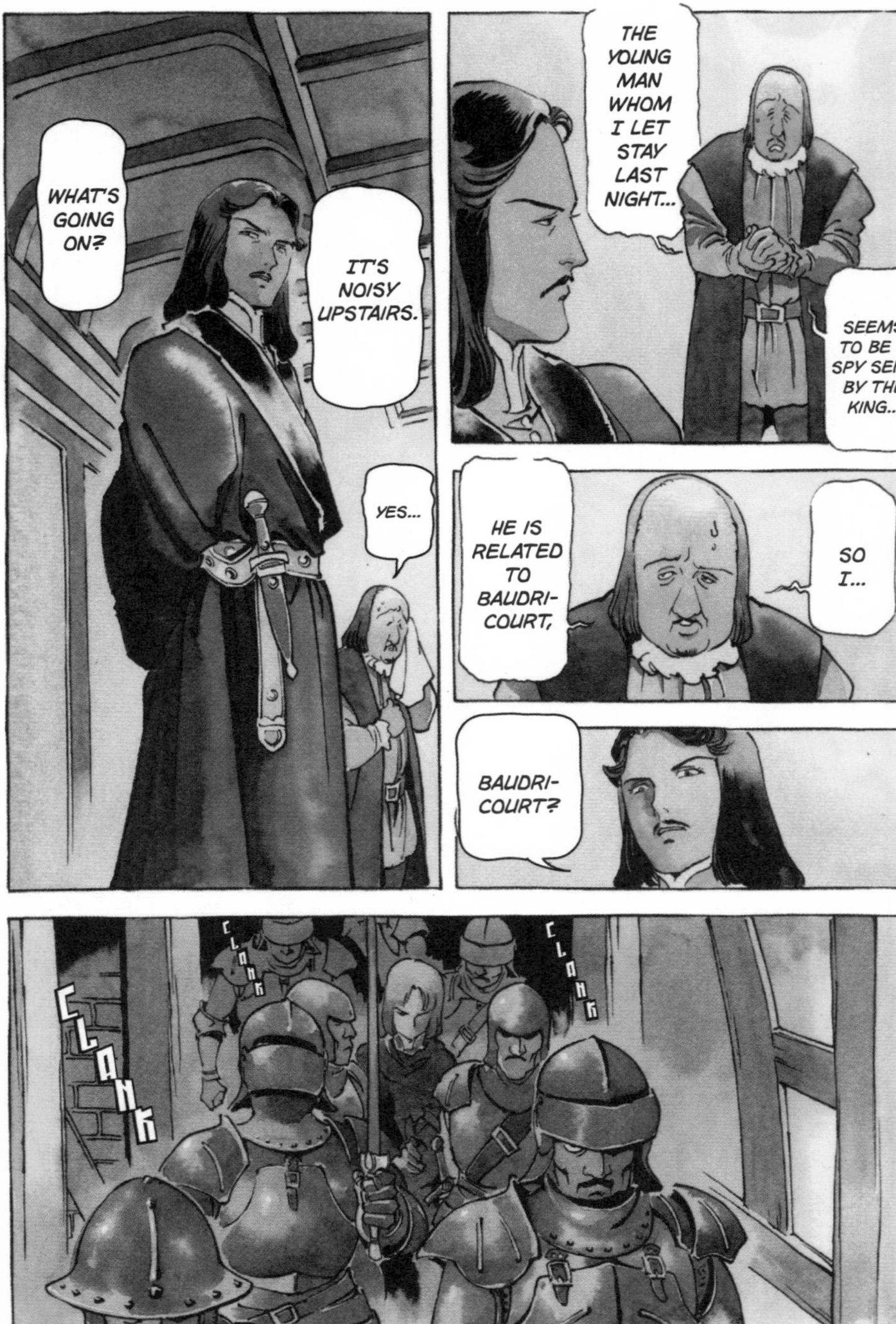
WHAT'S GOING ON?
IT'S NOISY UPSTAIRS.
YES...
THE YOUNG MAN WHOM I LET STAY LAST NIGHT...
SEEMS TO BE A SPY SENT BY THE KING...
HE IS RELATED TO BAUDRI-COURT,
SO I...
BAUDRI-COURT?
CLANK
CLANK
CLANK

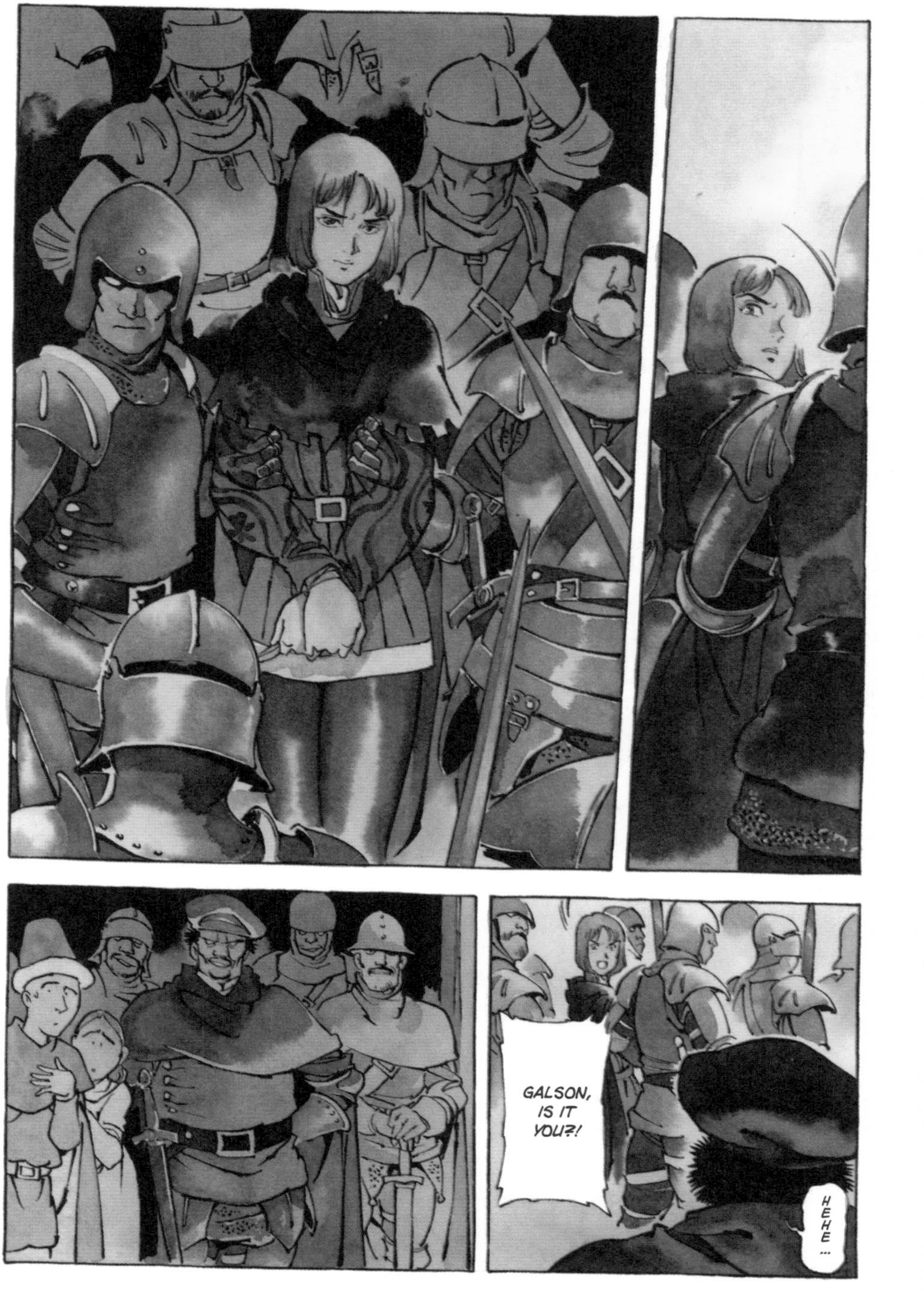
GALSON, IS IT YOU?!
HEHE ...

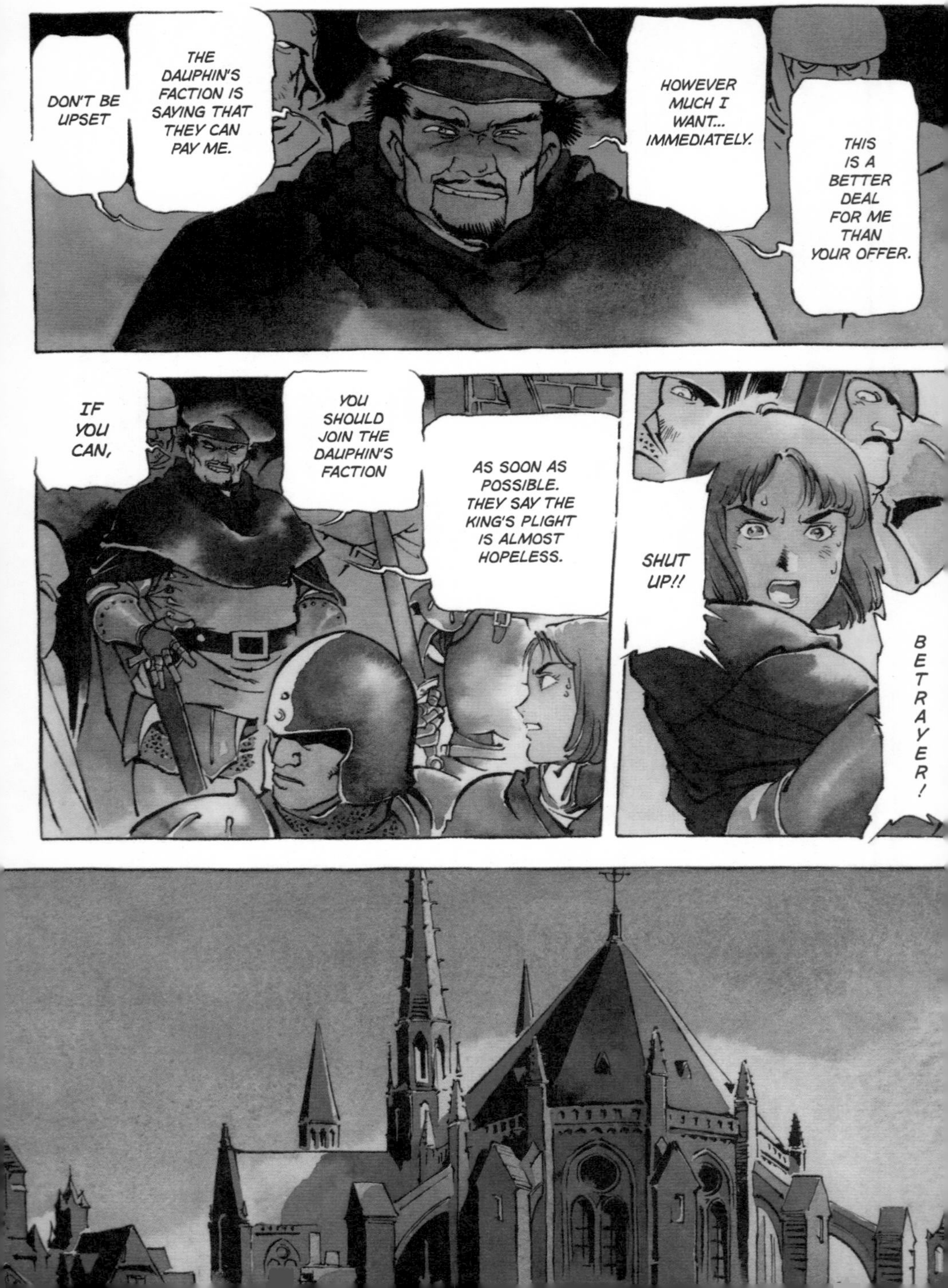

DON'T BE UPSET
THE DAUPHIN'S FACTION IS SAYING THAT THEY CAN PAY ME.
HOWEVER MUCH I WANT... IMMEDIATELY.
THIS IS A BETTER DEAL FOR ME THAN YOUR OFFER.
IF YOU CAN,
YOU SHOULD JOIN THE DAUPHIN'S FACTION
AS SOON AS POSSIBLE. THEY SAY THE KING'S PLIGHT IS ALMOST HOPELESS.
SHUT UP!!
BETRAYER!

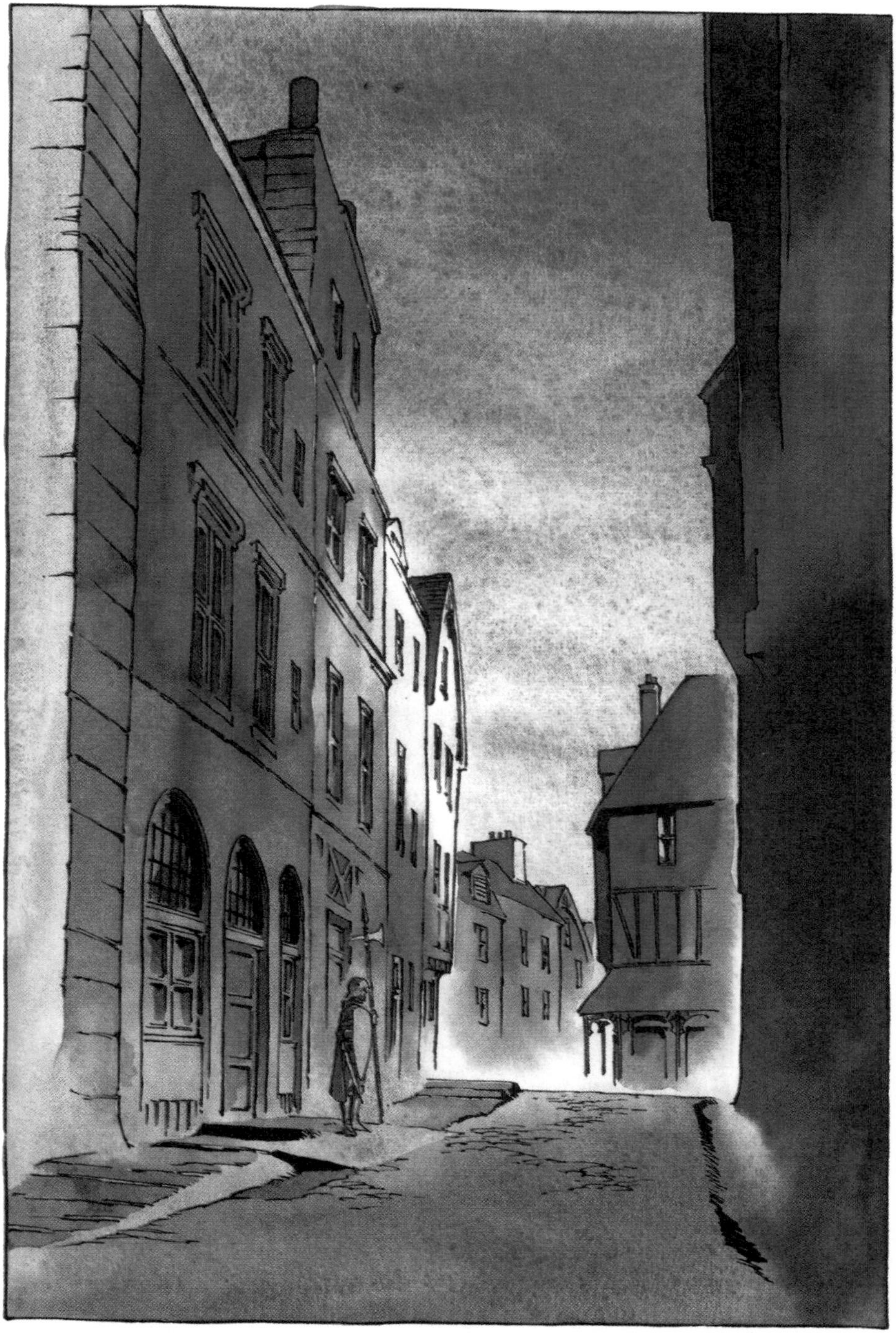

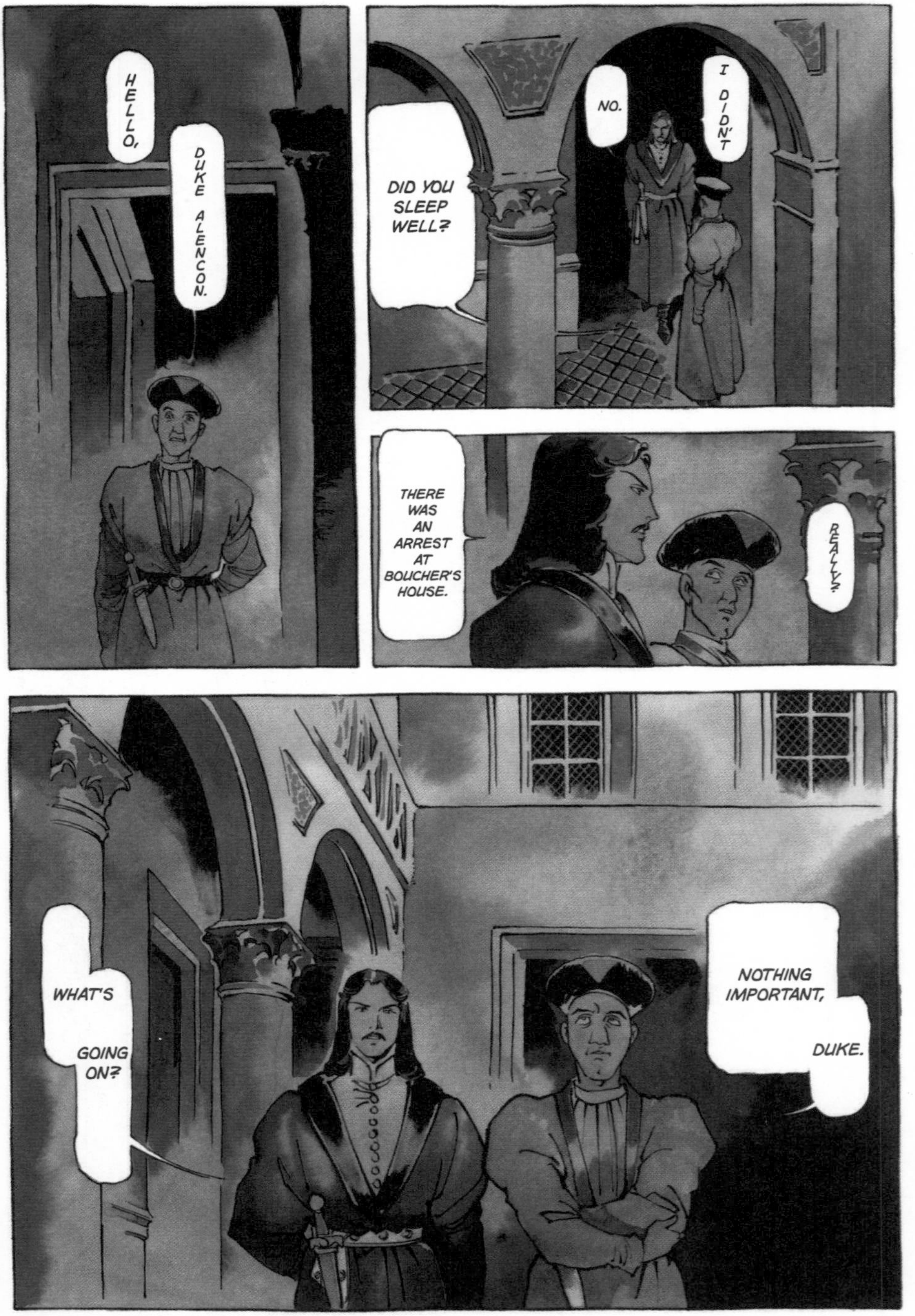
HELLO,
DUKE ALENCON.
DID YOU SLEEP WELL?
NO.
I DIDN'T
THERE WAS AN ARREST AT BOUCHER'S HOUSE.
REALLY?
WHAT'S GOING ON?
NOTHING IMPORTANT,
DUKE.

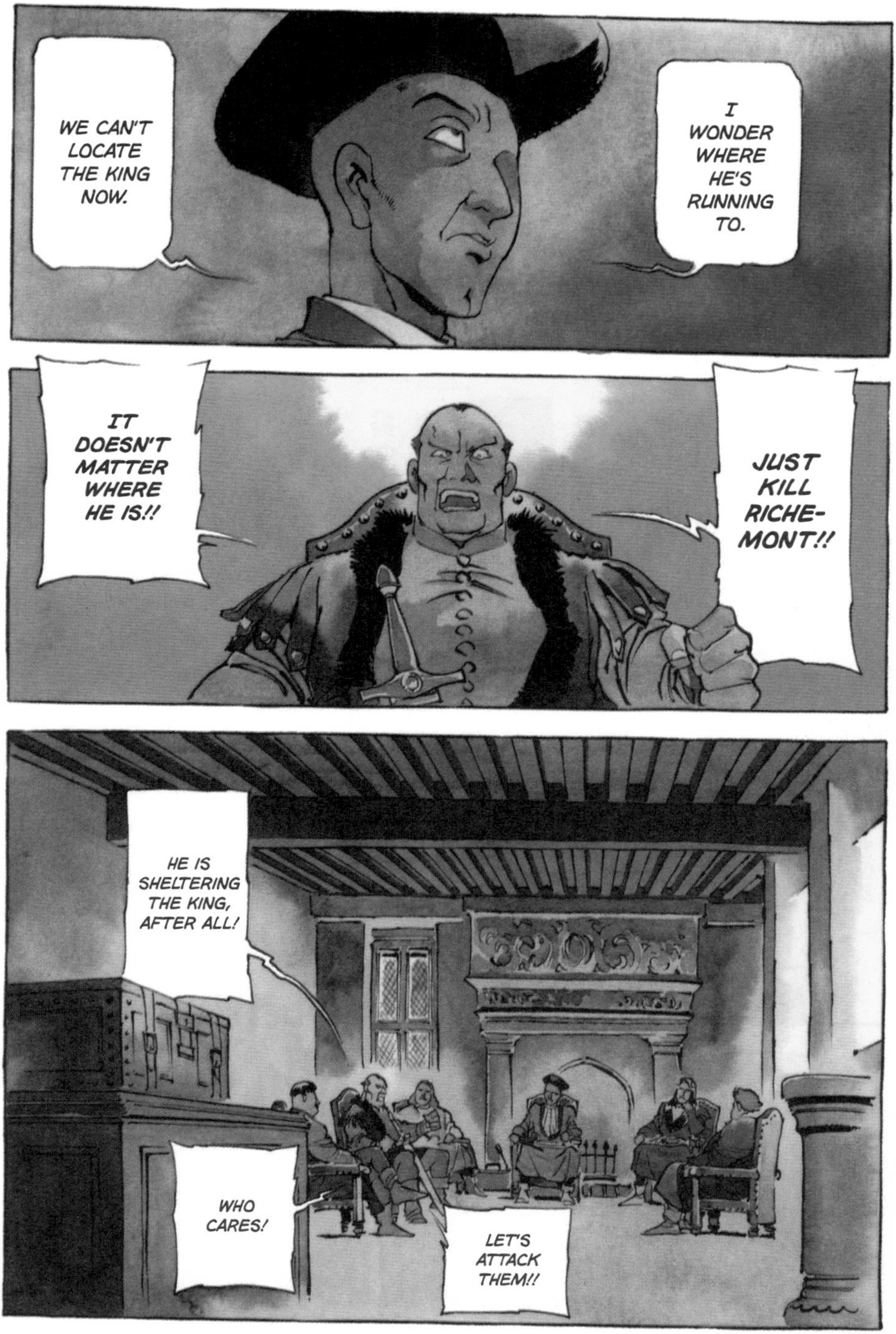
WE CAN'T LOCATE THE KING NOW.
I WONDER WHERE HE'S RUNNING TO.
IT DOESN'T MATTER WHERE HE IS!!
JUST KILL RICHE-MONT!!
HE IS SHELTERING THE KING, AFTER ALL!
WHO CARES!
LET'S ATTACK THEM!!

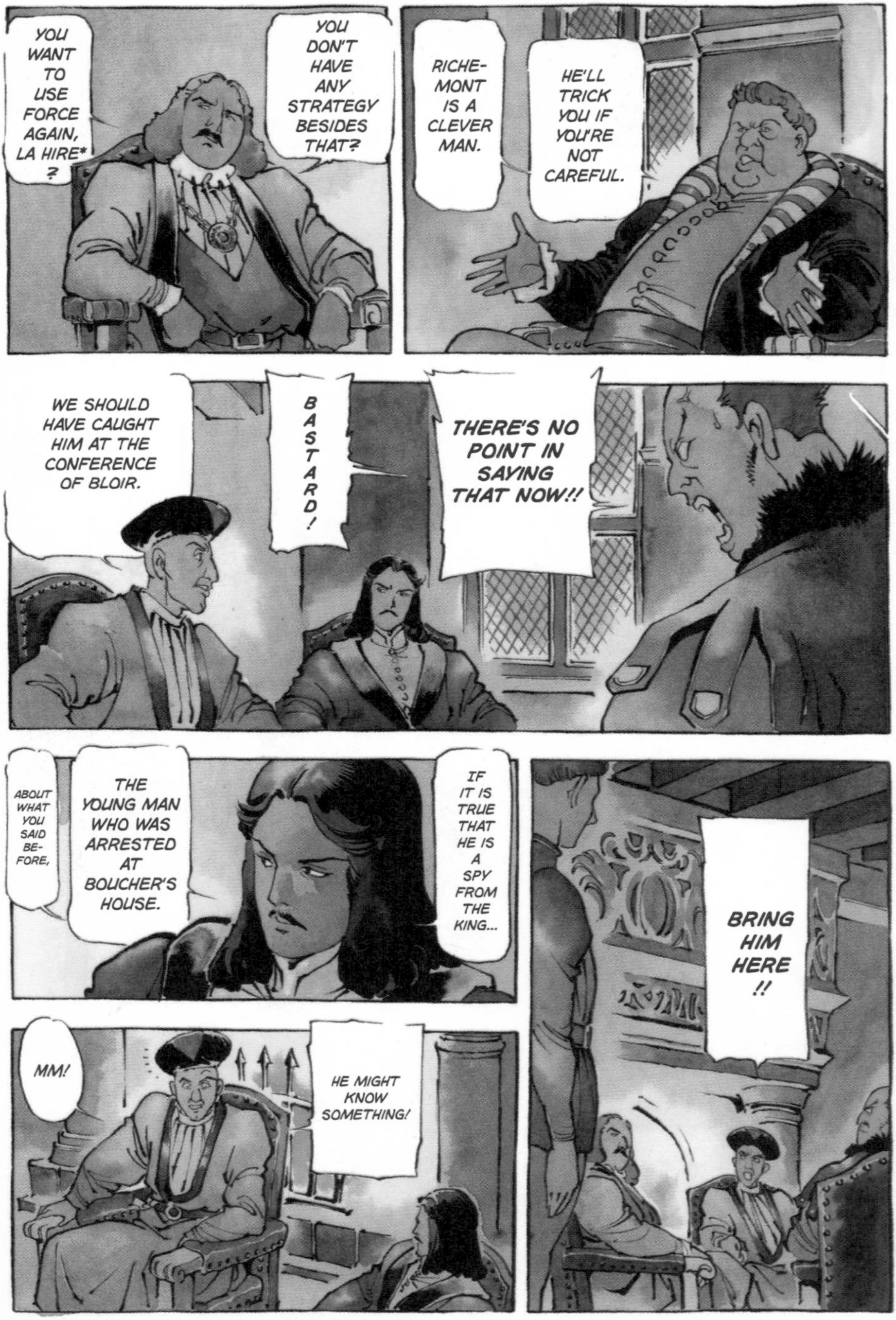
YOU WANT TO USE FORCE AGAIN, LA HIRE*?
YOU DON'T HAVE ANY STRATEGY BESIDES THAT?
RICHE-MONT IS A CLEVER MAN.
HE'LL TRICK YOU IF YOU'RE NOT CAREFUL.
WE SHOULD HAVE CAUGHT HIM AT THE CONFERENCE OF BLOIR.
BASTARD!
THERE'S NO POINT IN SAYING THAT NOW!!
ABOUT WHAT YOU SAID BE-FORE,
THE YOUNG MAN WHO WAS ARRESTED AT BOUCHER'S HOUSE.
IF IT IS TRUE THAT HE IS A SPY FROM THE KING...
MM!
HE MIGHT KNOW SOMETHING!
BRING HIM HERE!!

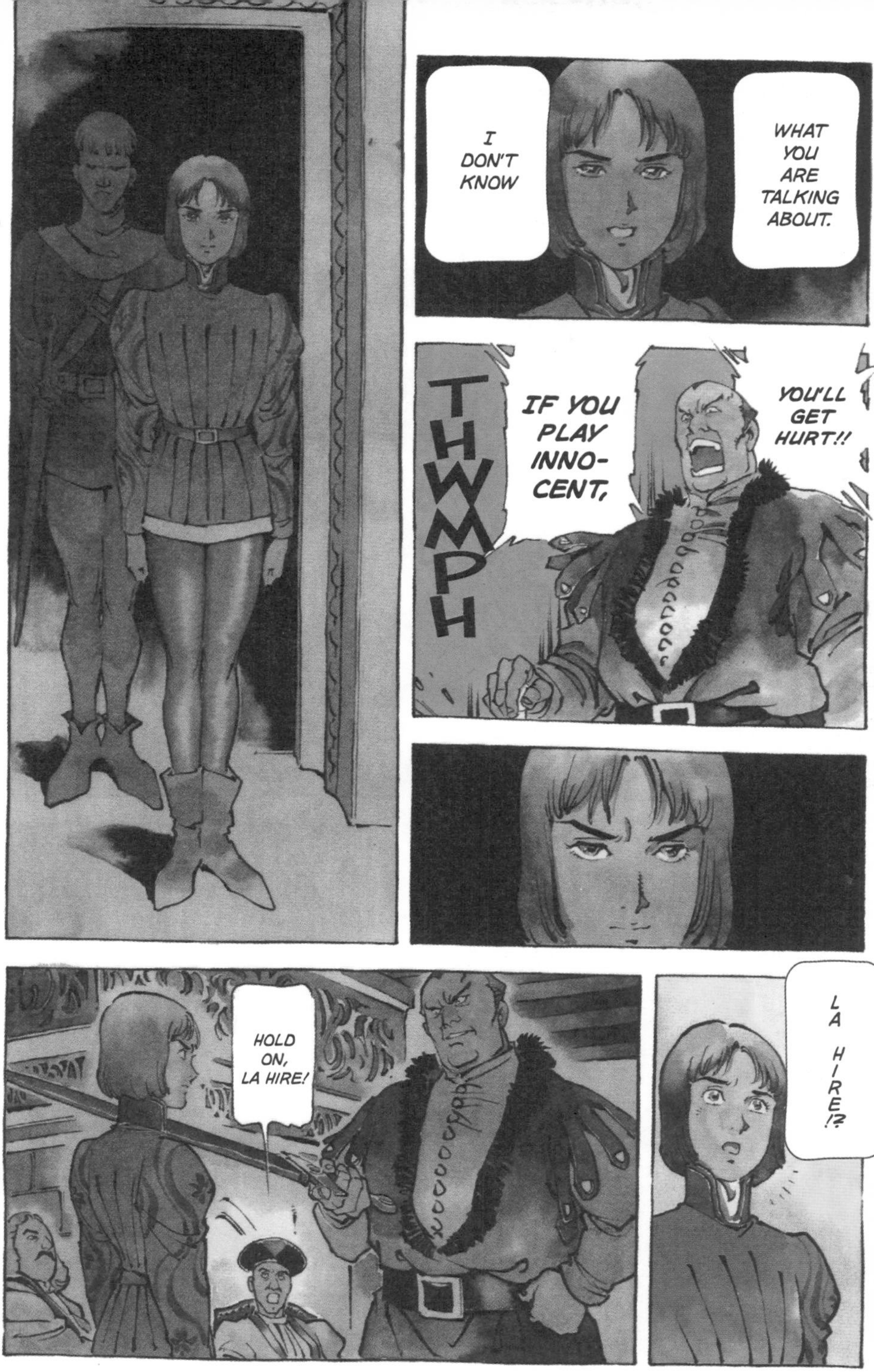
I DON'T KNOW
WHAT YOU ARE TALKING ABOUT.
THWMPH
IF YOU PLAY INNO-CENT,
YOU'LL GET HURT!!
HOLD ON, LA HIRE!
LA HIRE!?

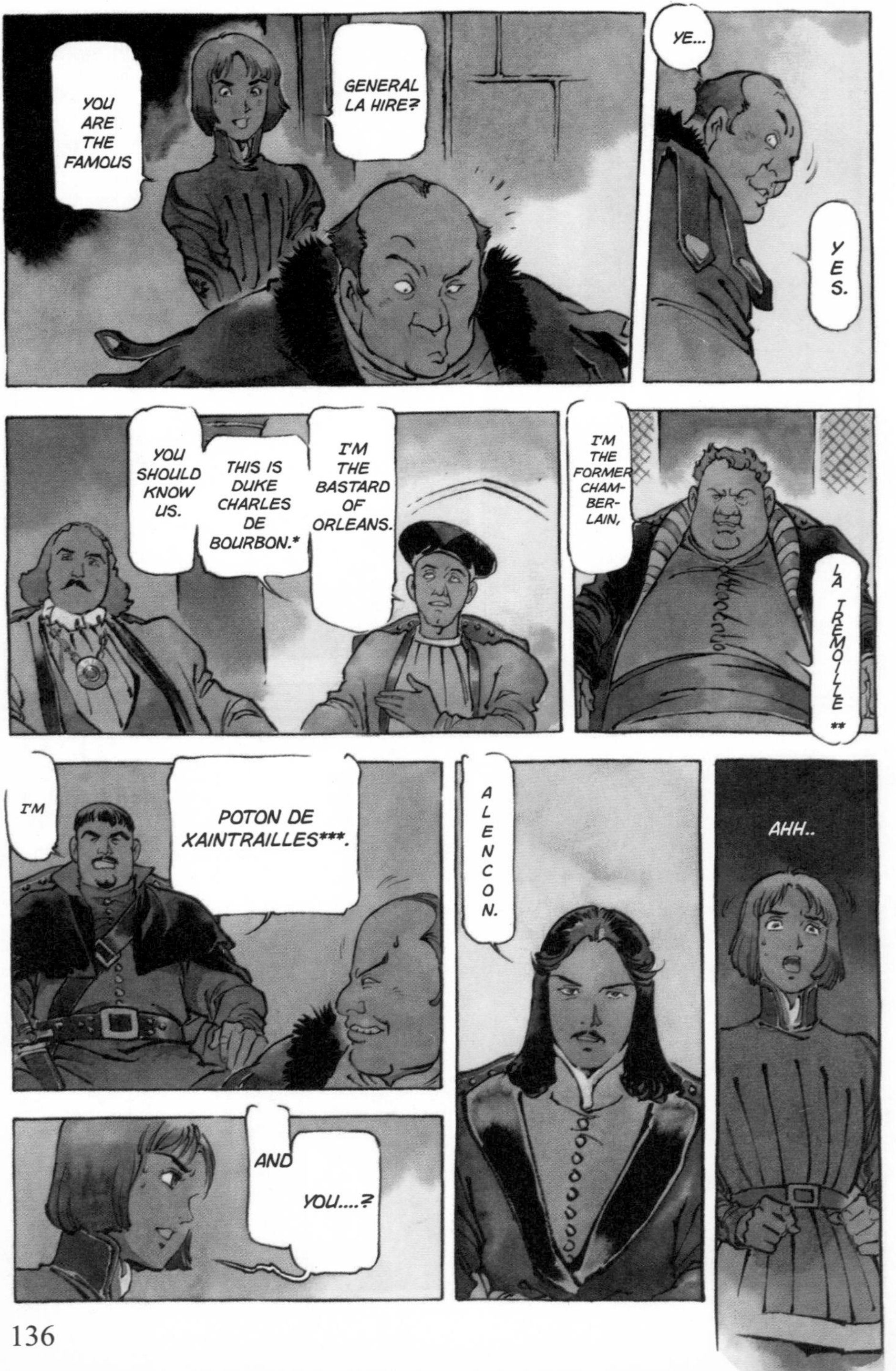
YOU ARE THE FAMOUS
GENERAL LA HIRE?
YE...
YES.
YOU SHOULD KNOW US.
THIS IS DUKE CHARLES DE BOURBON.*
I'M THE BASTARD OF ORLEANS.
I'M THE FORMER CHAMBER-LAIN,
LA TREMOILLE **
I'M
POTON DE XAINTRAILLES***.
ALENCON.
AHH..
AND
YOU....?

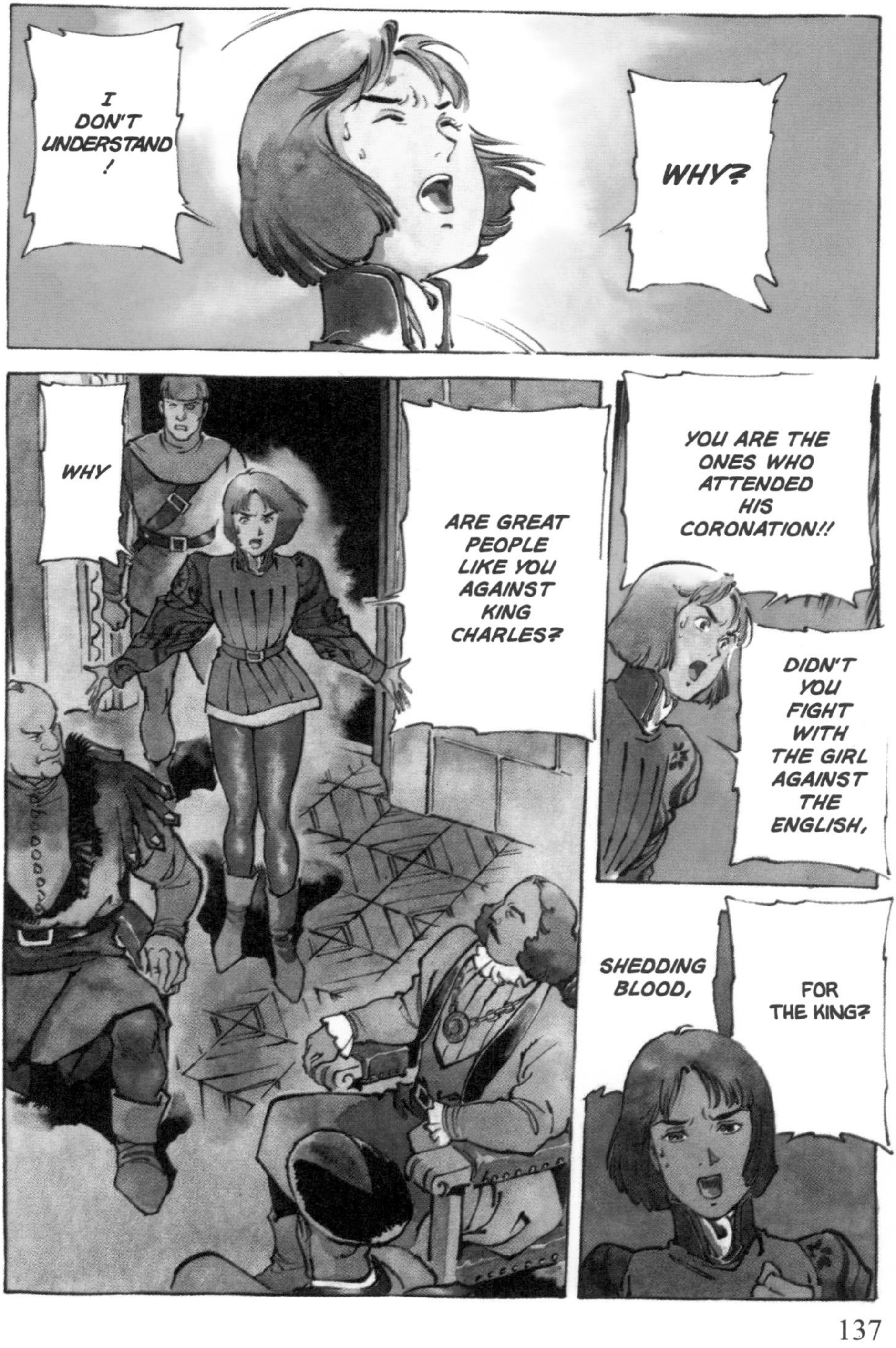
I DON'T UNDERSTAND!
WHY?
WHY
ARE GREAT PEOPLE LIKE YOU AGAINST KING CHARLES?
YOU ARE THE ONES WHO ATTENDED HIS CORONATION!!
DIDN'T YOU FIGHT WITH THE GIRL AGAINST THE ENGLISH,
SHEDDING BLOOD,
FOR THE KING?

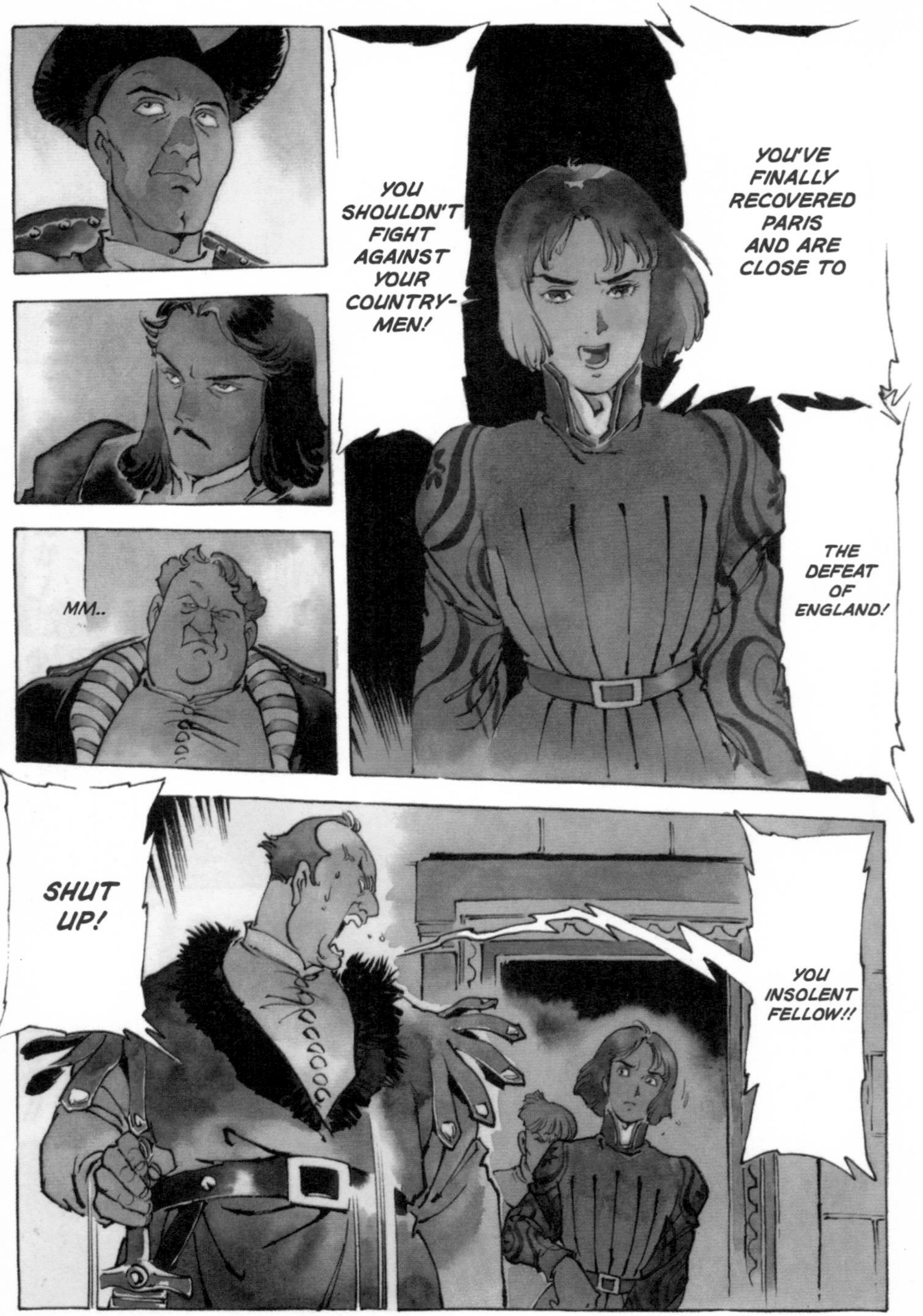
YOU'VE FINALLY RECOVERED PARIS AND ARE CLOSE TO
THE DEFEAT OF ENGLAND!
YOU SHOULDN'T FIGHT AGAINST YOUR COUNTRY-MEN!
MM..
SHUT UP!
YOU INSOLENT FELLOW!!

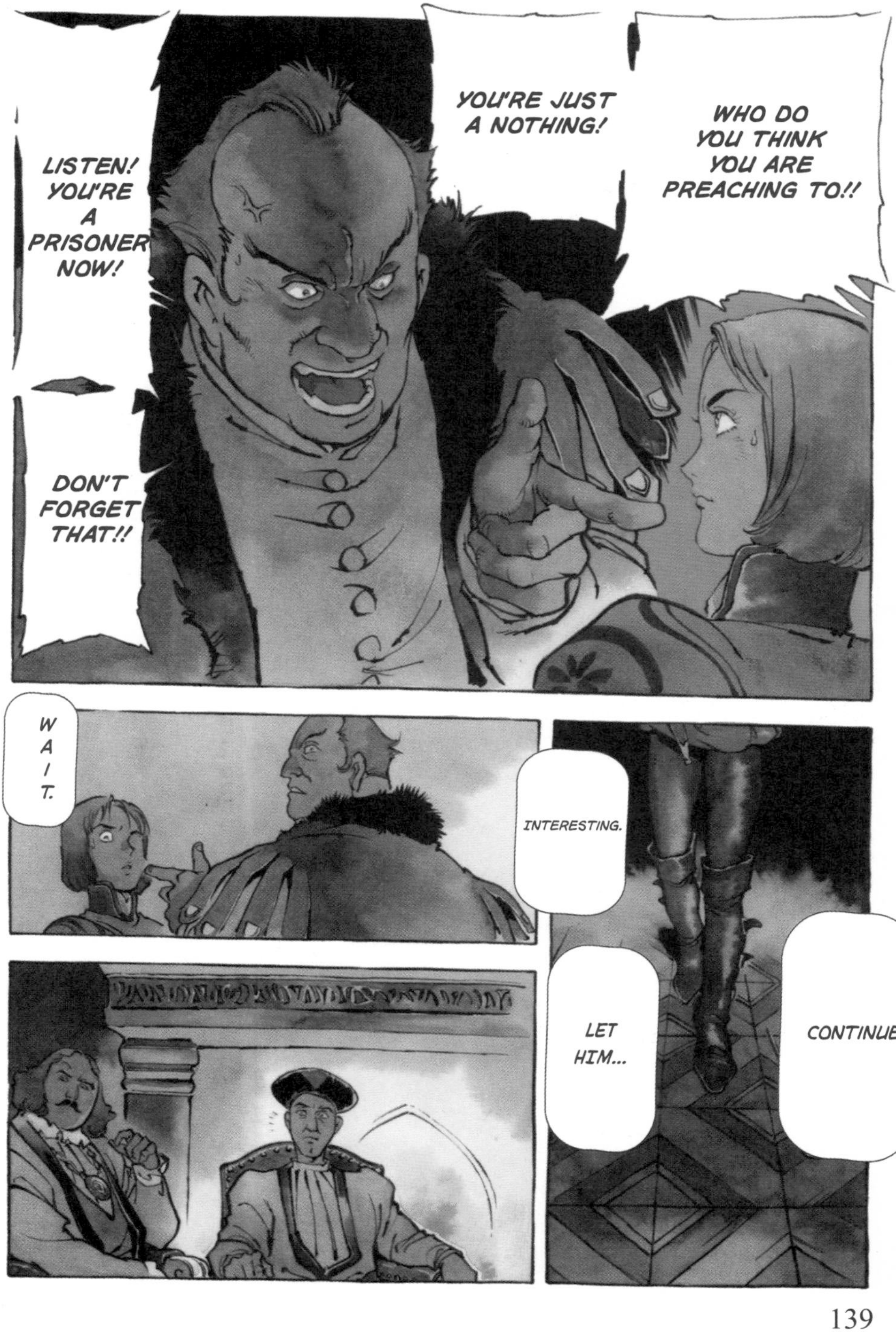
WHO DO YOU THINK YOU ARE PREACHING TO!!
YOU'RE JUST A NOTHING!
LISTEN! YOU'RE A PRISONER NOW!
DON'T FORGET THAT!!
WAIT.
INTERESTING.
LET HIM...
CONTINUE.

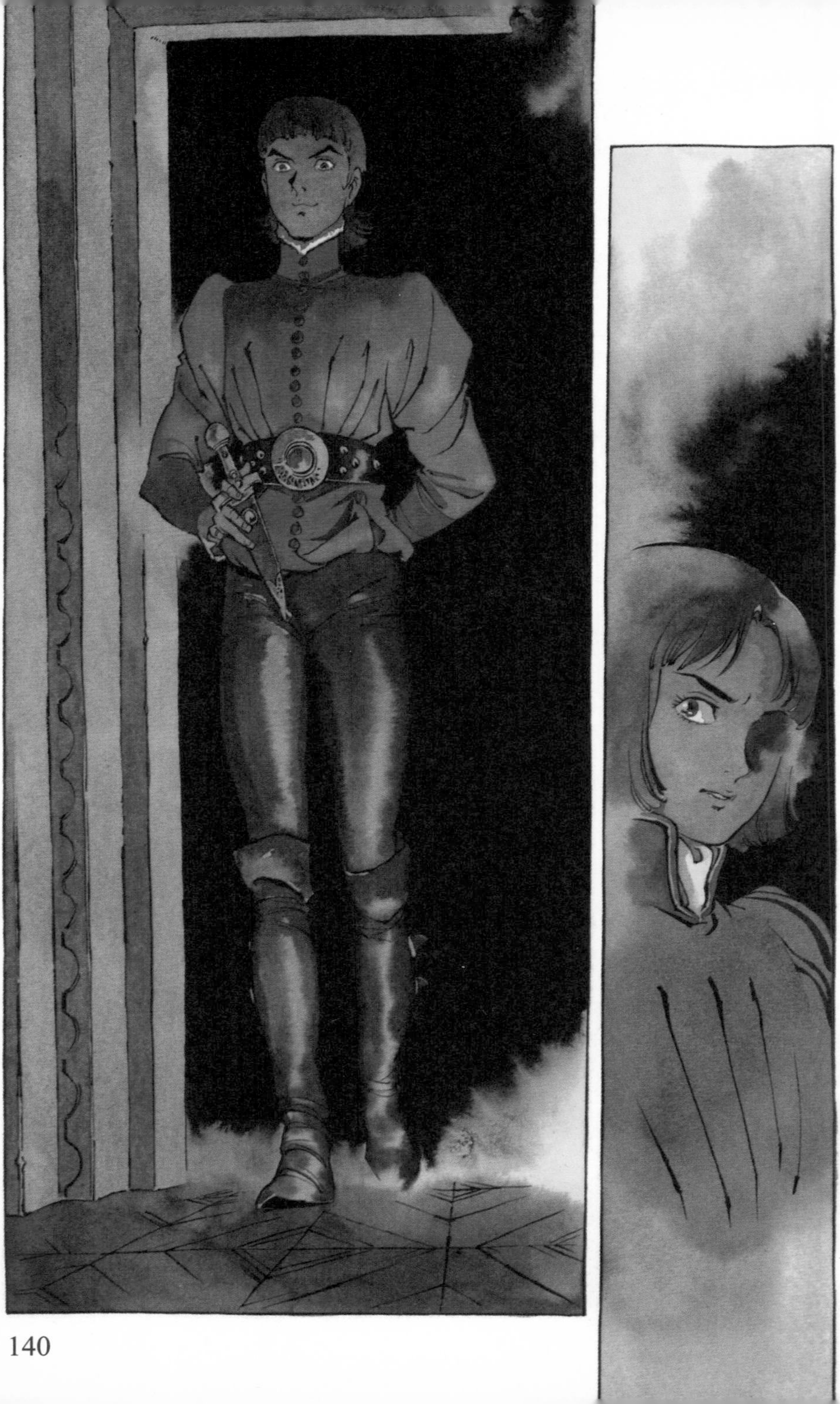

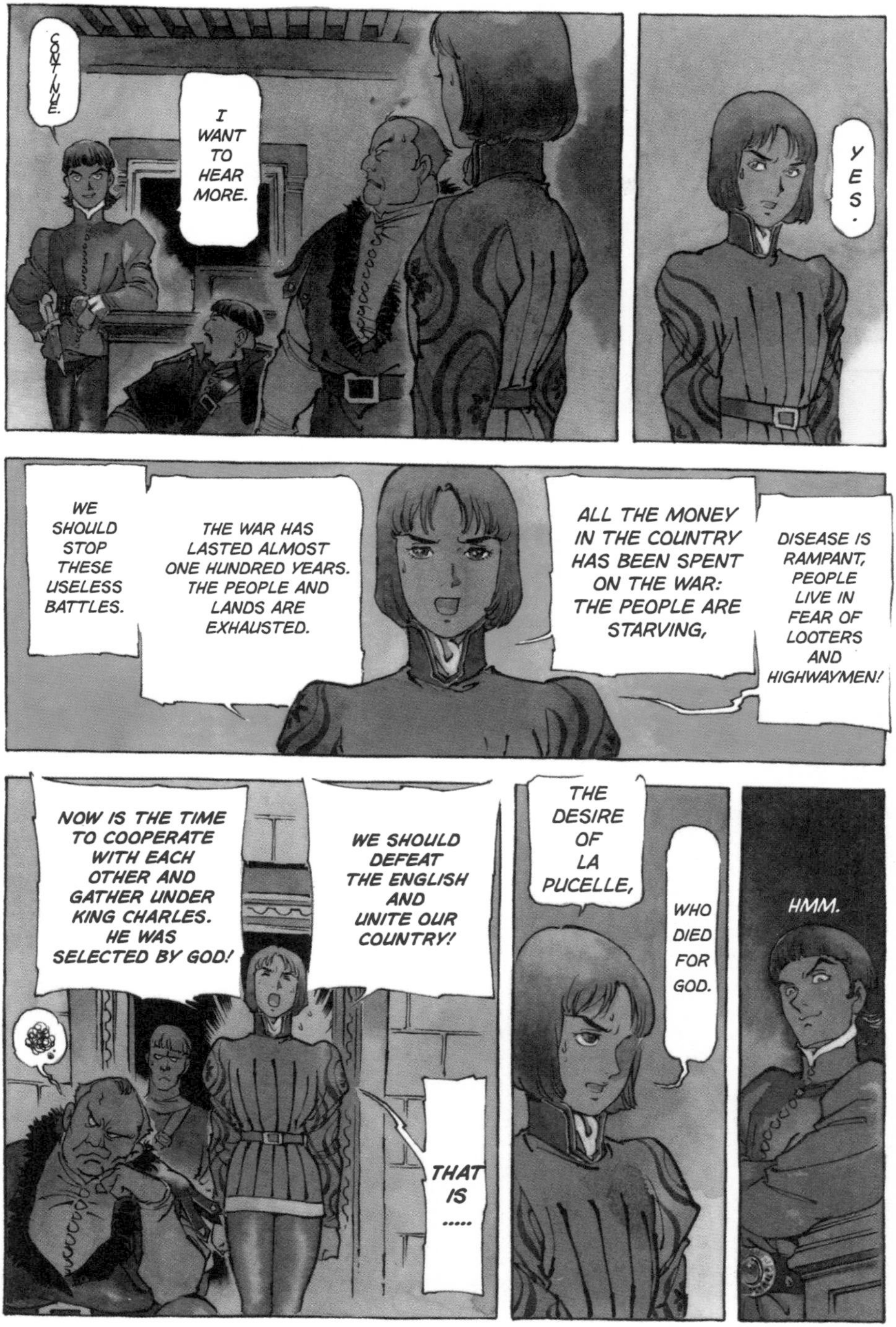
CONTINUE.
I WANT TO HEAR MORE.
YES.
WE SHOULD STOP THESE USELESS BATTLES.
THE WAR HAS LASTED ALMOST ONE HUNDRED YEARS. THE PEOPLE AND LANDS ARE EXHAUSTED.
ALL THE MONEY IN THE COUNTRY HAS BEEN SPENT ON THE WAR: THE PEOPLE ARE STARVING,
DISEASE IS RAMPANT, PEOPLE LIVE IN FEAR OF LOOTERS AND HIGHWAYMEN!
NOW IS THE TIME TO COOPERATE WITH EACH OTHER AND GATHER UNDER KING CHARLES. HE WAS SELECTED BY GOD!
WE SHOULD DEFEAT THE ENGLISH AND UNITE OUR COUNTRY!
THAT IS ......
THE DESIRE OF LA PUCELLE,
WHO DIED FOR GOD.
HMM.

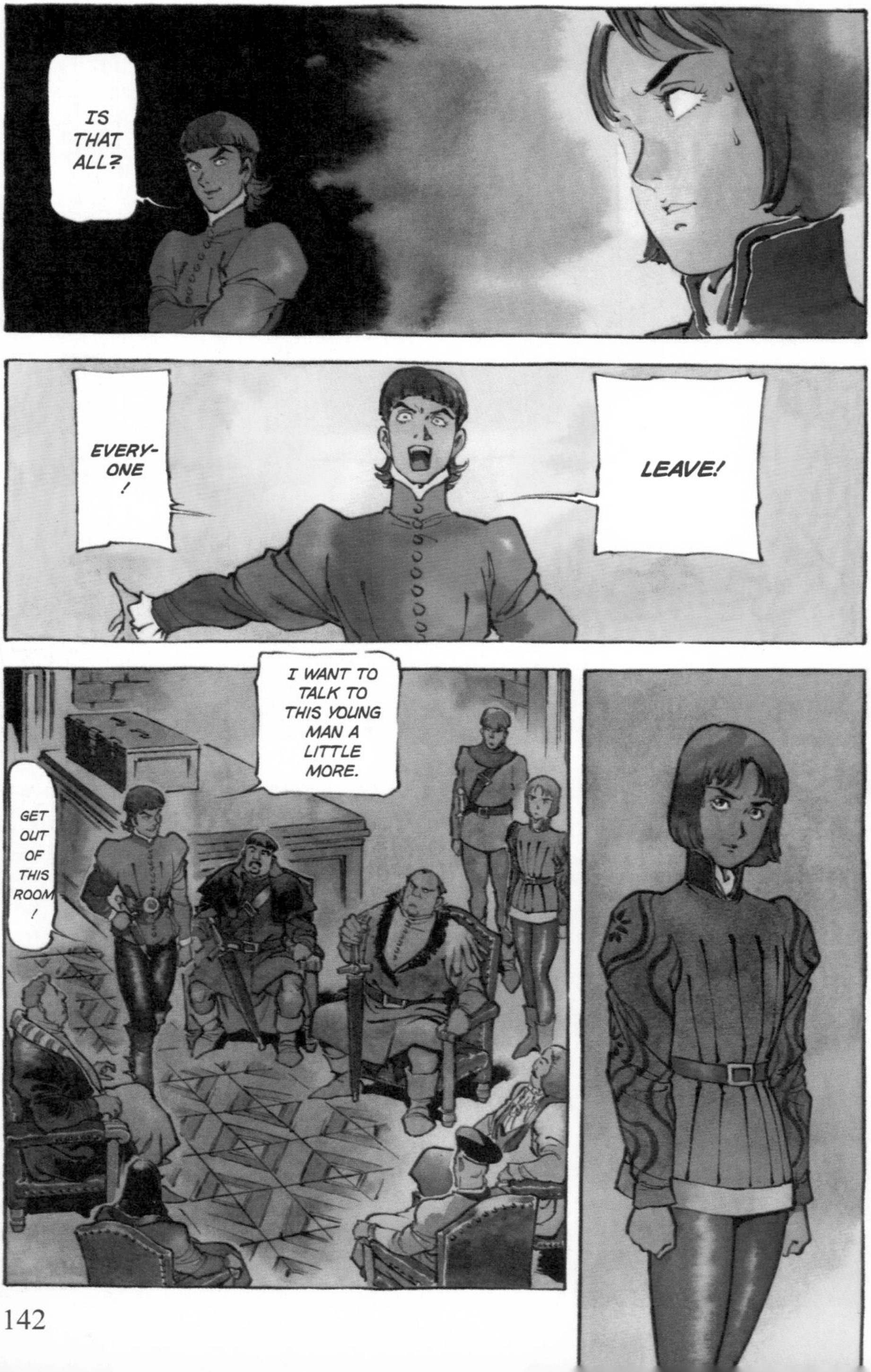
IS THAT ALL?
EVERY-ONE!
LEAVE!
I WANT TO TALK TO THIS YOUNG MAN A LITTLE MORE.
GET OUT OF THIS ROOM!

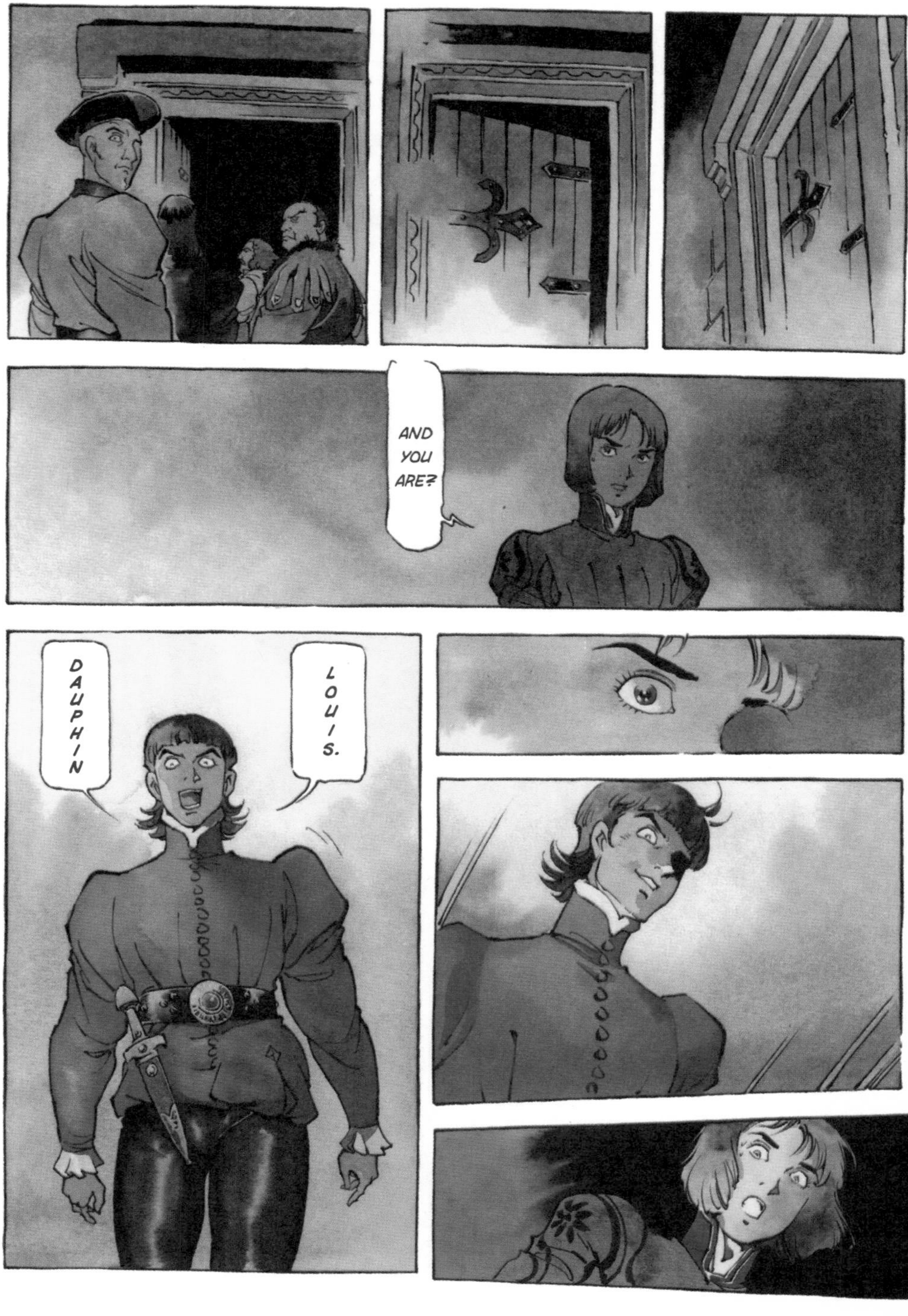
AND YOU ARE?
DAUPHIN
LOUIS.

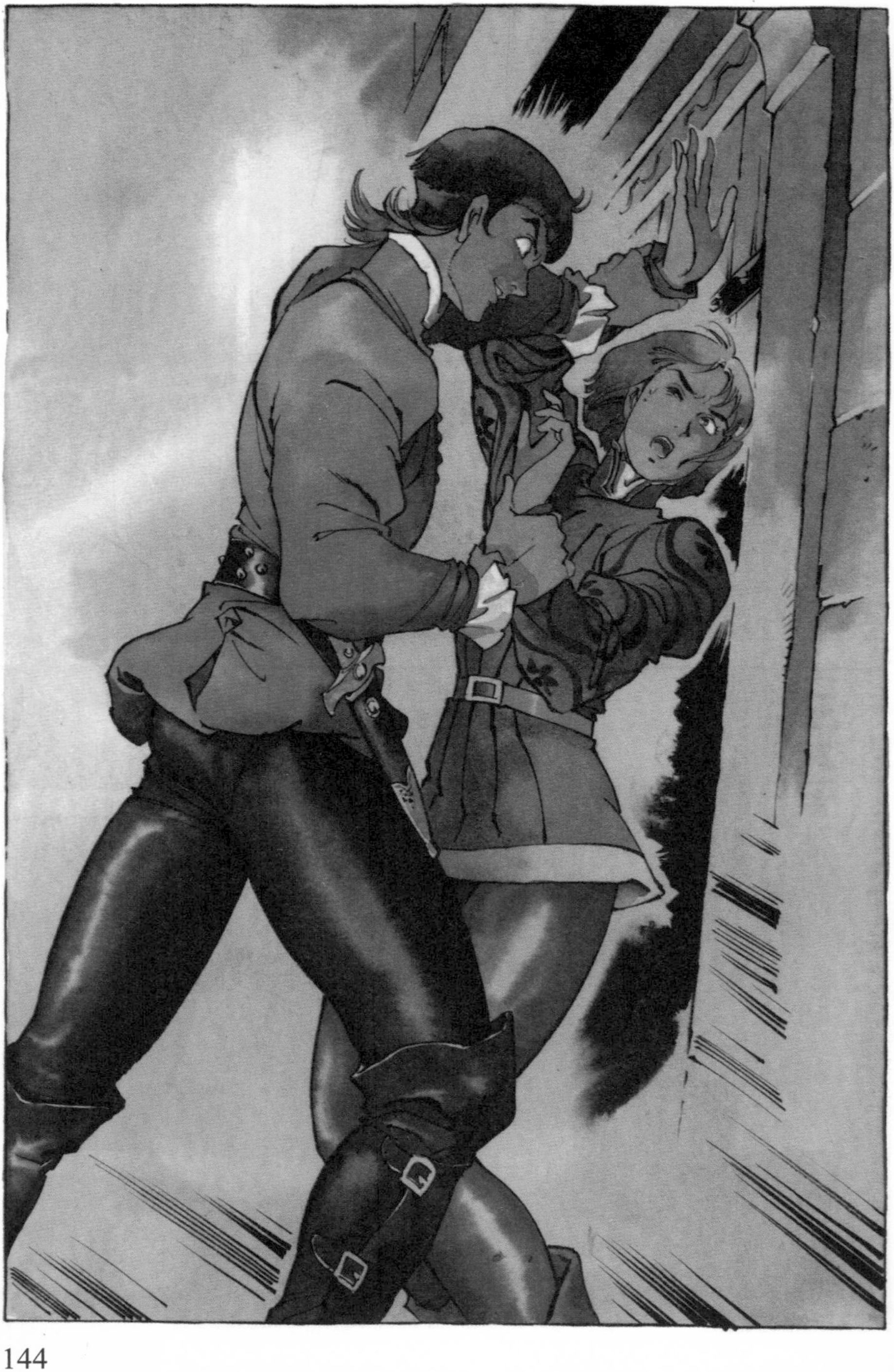

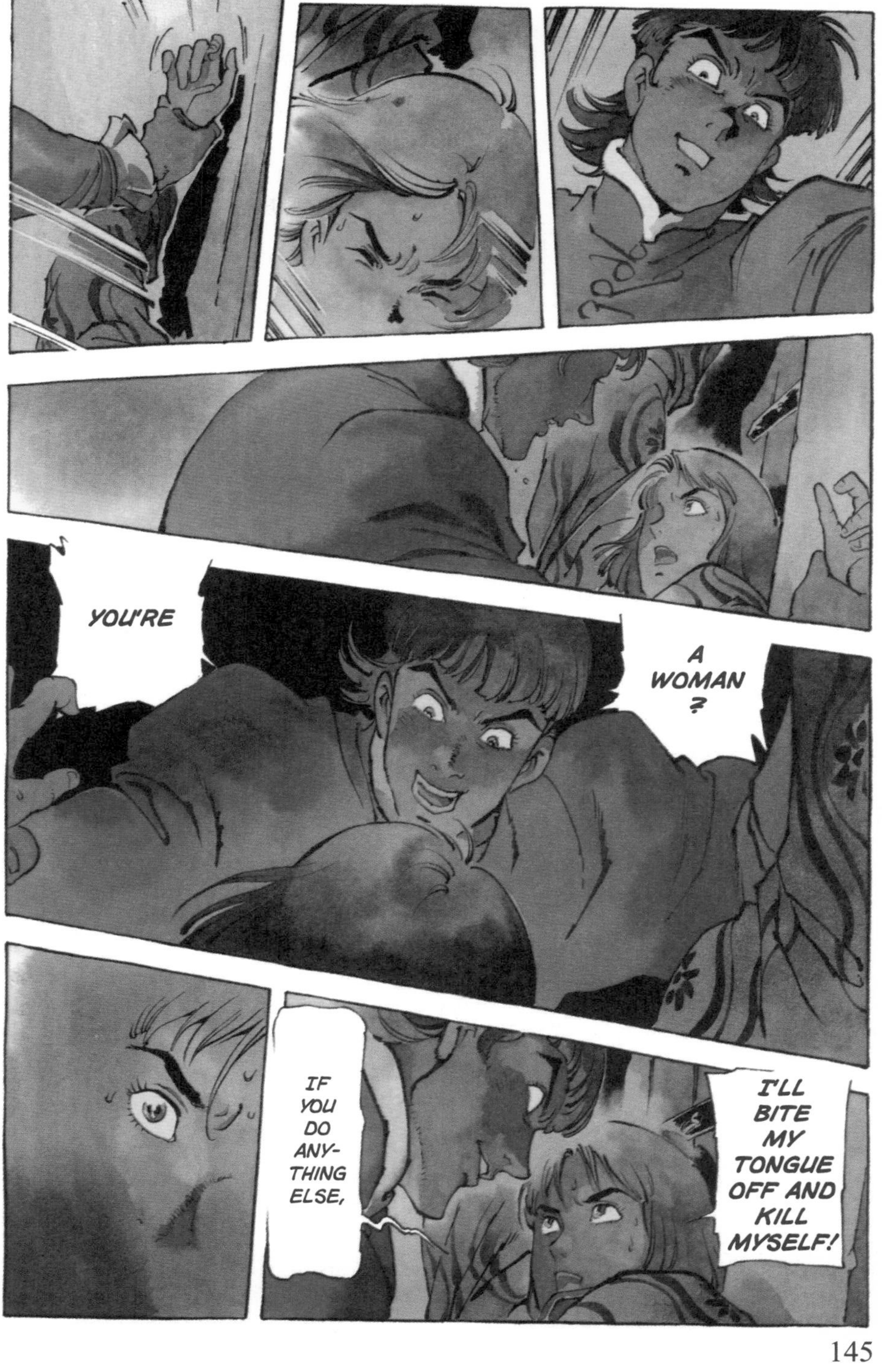
YOU'RE
A WOMAN?
IF YOU DO ANYTHING ELSE,
I'LL BITE MY TONGUE OFF AND KILL MYSELF!

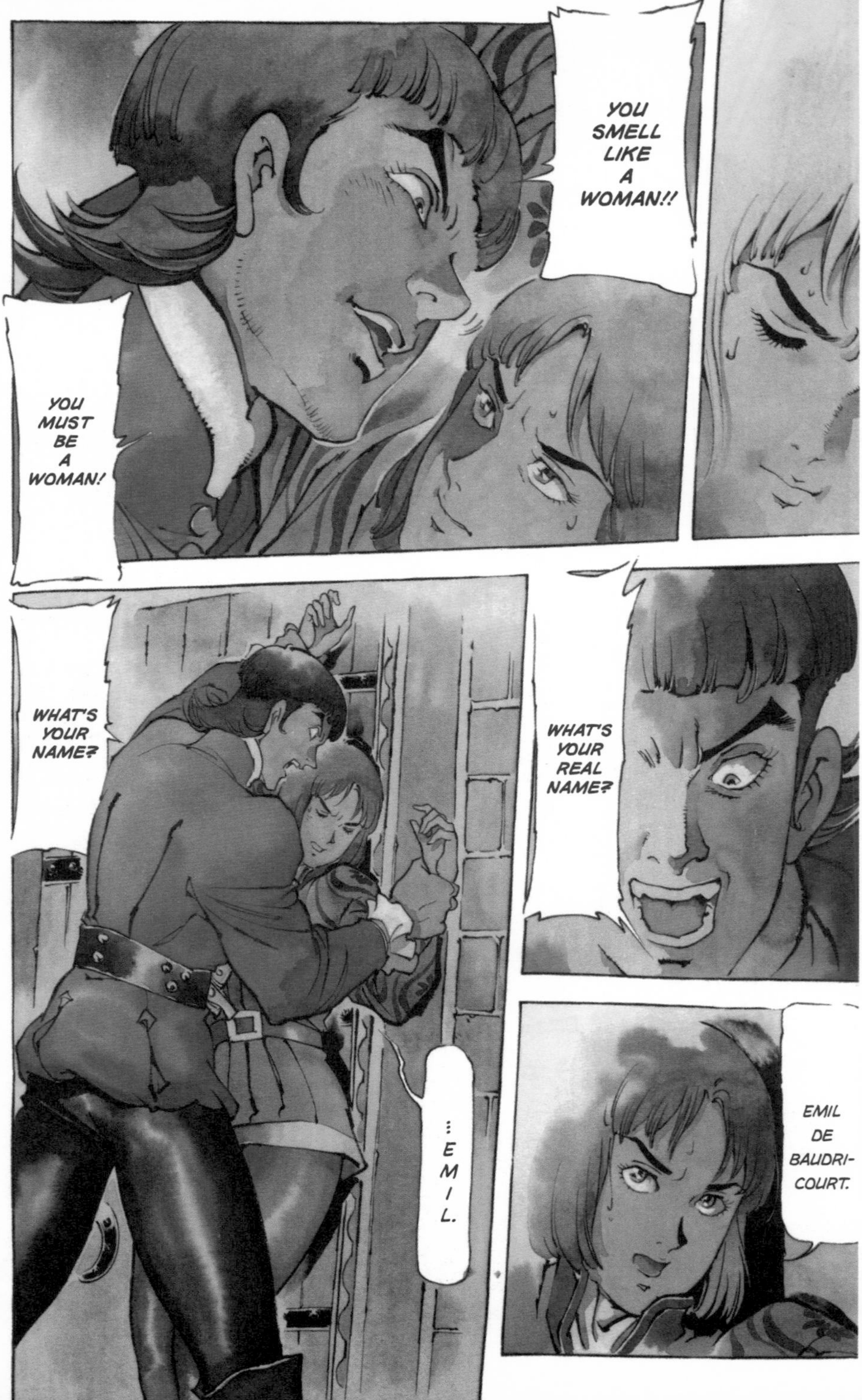
YOU SMELL LIKE A WOMAN!!
YOU MUST BE A WOMAN!
WHAT'S YOUR NAME?
WHAT'S YOUR REAL NAME?
... EMIL.
EMIL DE BAUDRI-COURT.

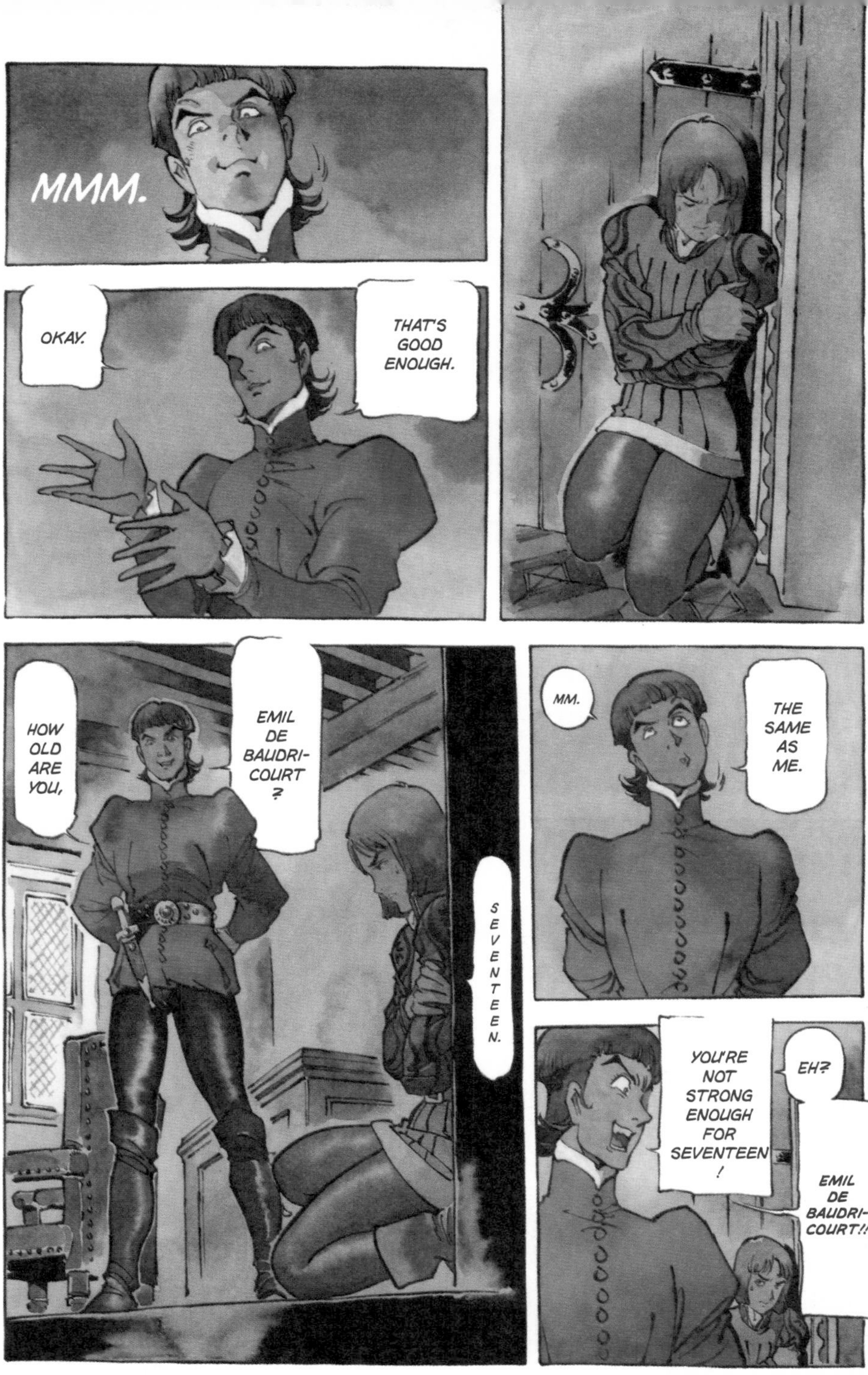
MMM.
OKAY.
THAT'S GOOD ENOUGH.
HOW OLD ARE YOU,
EMIL DE BAUDRI-COURT?
SEVENTEEN.
MM.
THE SAME AS ME.
YOU'RE NOT STRONG ENOUGH FOR SEVENTEEN!
EH?
EMIL DE BAUDRI-COURT!!

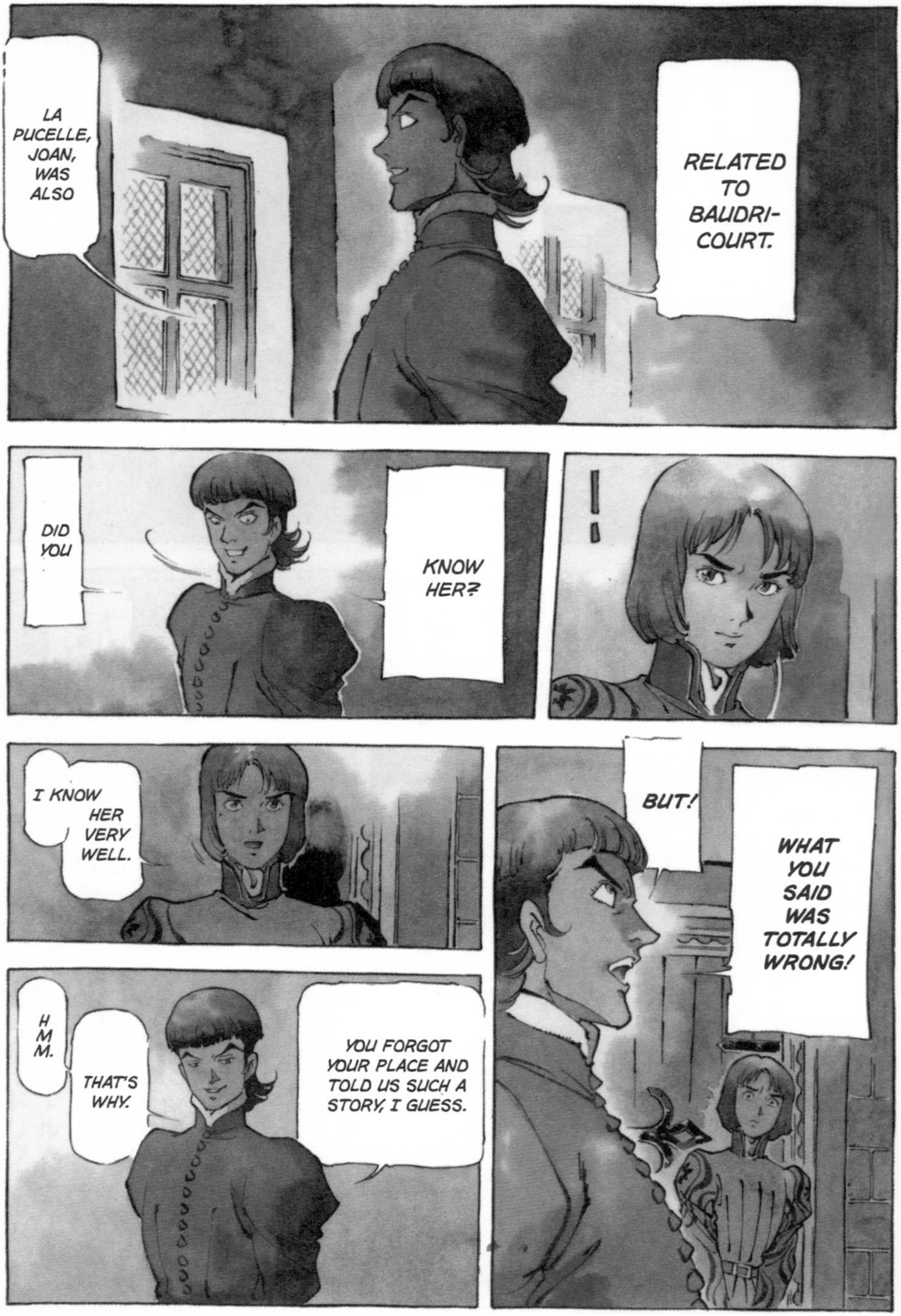
LA PUCELLE, JOAN, WAS ALSO
RELATED TO BAUDRI-COURT.
DID YOU
KNOW HER?
!
I KNOW HER VERY WELL.
BUT!
WHAT YOU SAID WAS TOTALLY WRONG!
HMM.
THAT'S WHY.
YOU FORGOT YOUR PLACE AND TOLD US SUCH A STORY, I GUESS.

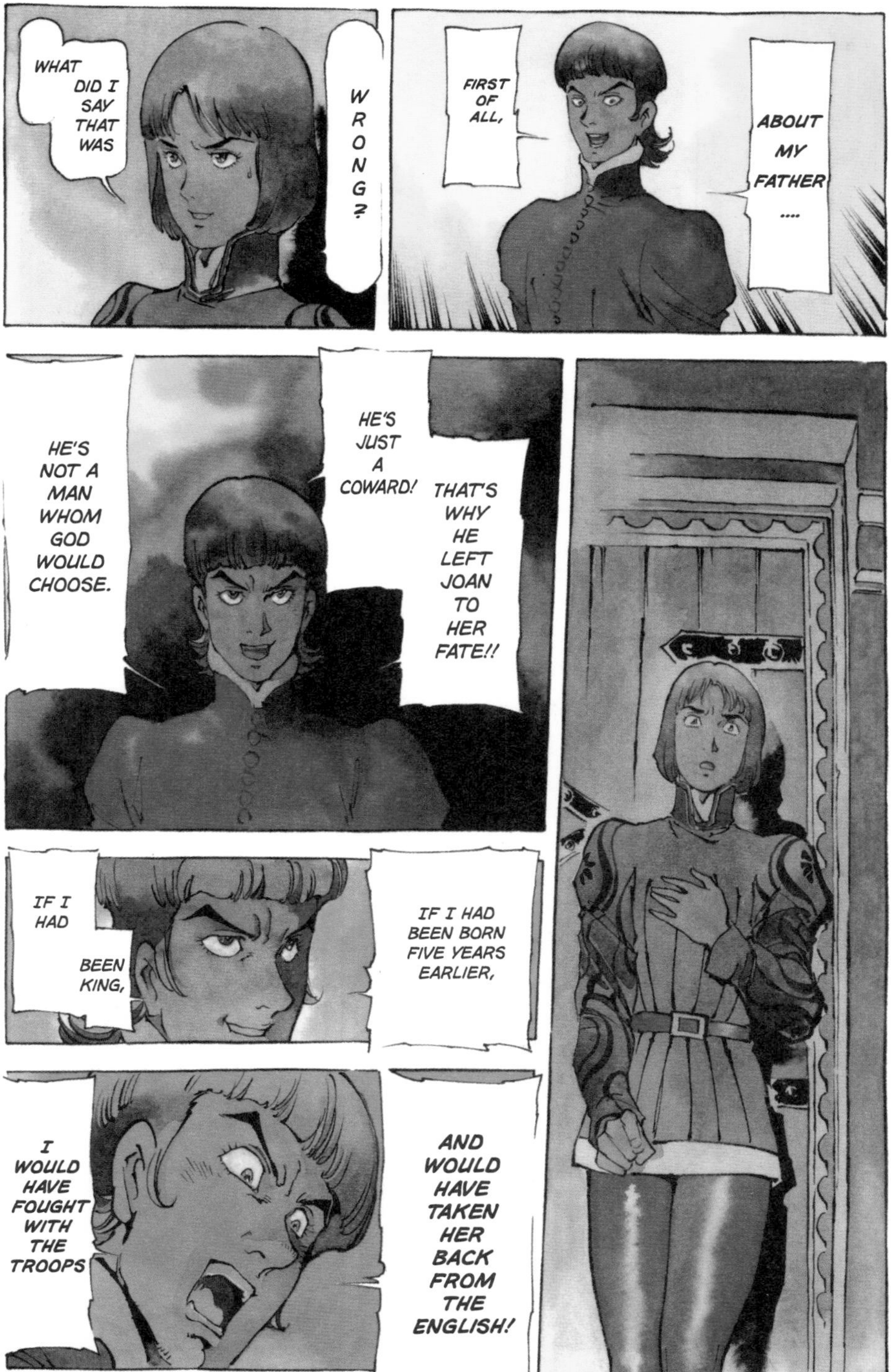
WHAT DID I SAY THAT WAS
WRONG?
FIRST OF ALL,
ABOUT MY FATHER ....
HE'S NOT A MAN WHOM GOD WOULD CHOOSE.
HE'S JUST A COWARD!
THAT'S WHY HE LEFT JOAN TO HER FATE!!
IF I HAD
BEEN KING,
IF I HAD BEEN BORN FIVE YEARS EARLIER,
I WOULD HAVE FOUGHT WITH THE TROOPS
AND WOULD HAVE TAKEN HER BACK FROM THE ENGLISH!

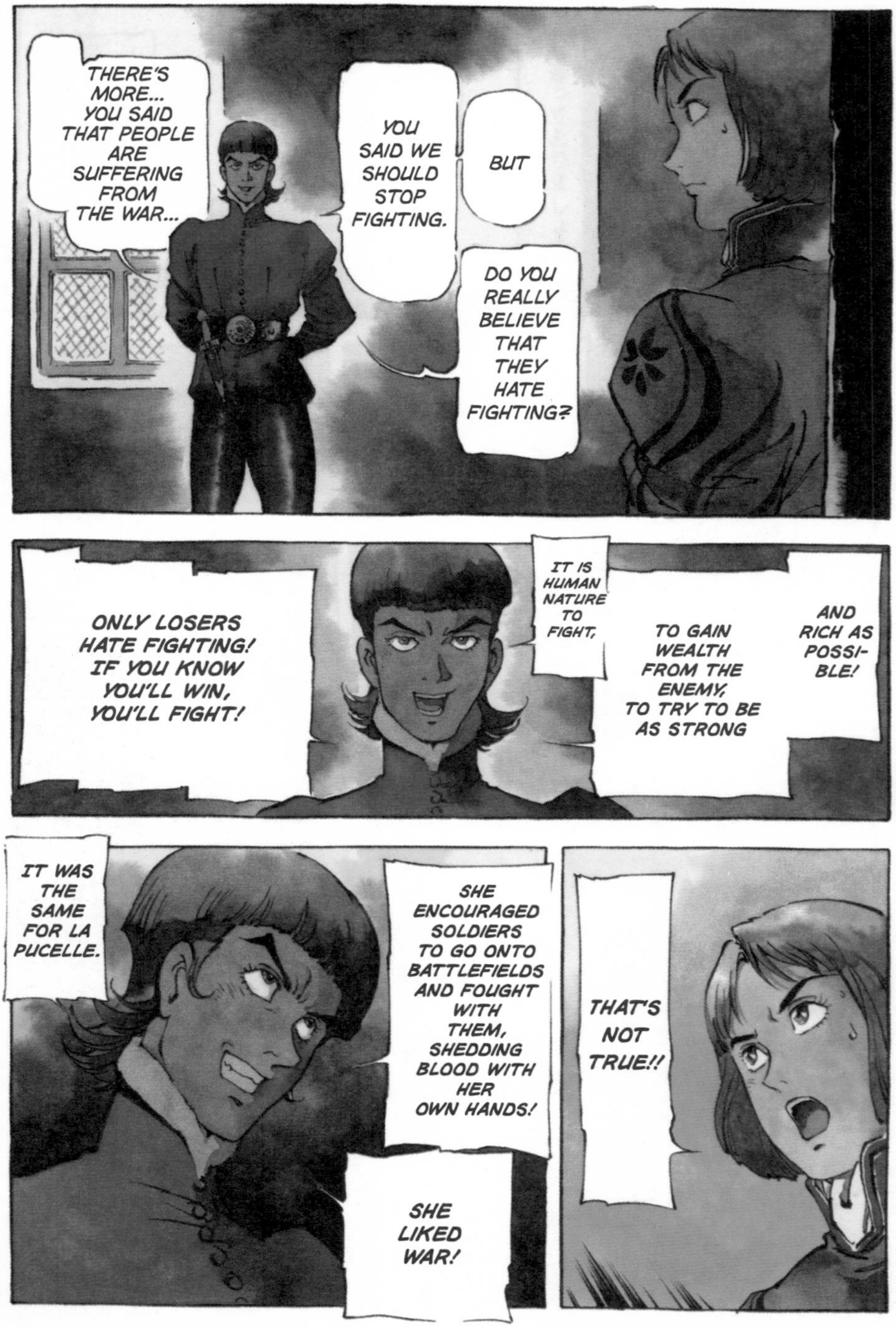

THERE'S MORE... YOU SAID THAT PEOPLE ARE SUFFERING FROM THE WAR...
YOU SAID WE SHOULD STOP FIGHTING.
BUT
DO YOU REALLY BELIEVE THAT THEY HATE FIGHTING?
ONLY LOSERS HATE FIGHTING! IF YOU KNOW YOU'LL WIN, YOU'LL FIGHT!
IT IS HUMAN NATURE TO FIGHT,
TO GAIN WEALTH FROM THE ENEMY, TO TRY TO BE AS STRONG
AND RICH AS POSSI-BLE!
IT WAS THE SAME FOR LA PUCELLE.
SHE ENCOURAGED SOLDIERS TO GO ONTO BATTLEFIELDS AND FOUGHT WITH THEM, SHEDDING BLOOD WITH HER OWN HANDS!
SHE LIKED WAR!
THAT'S NOT TRUE!!

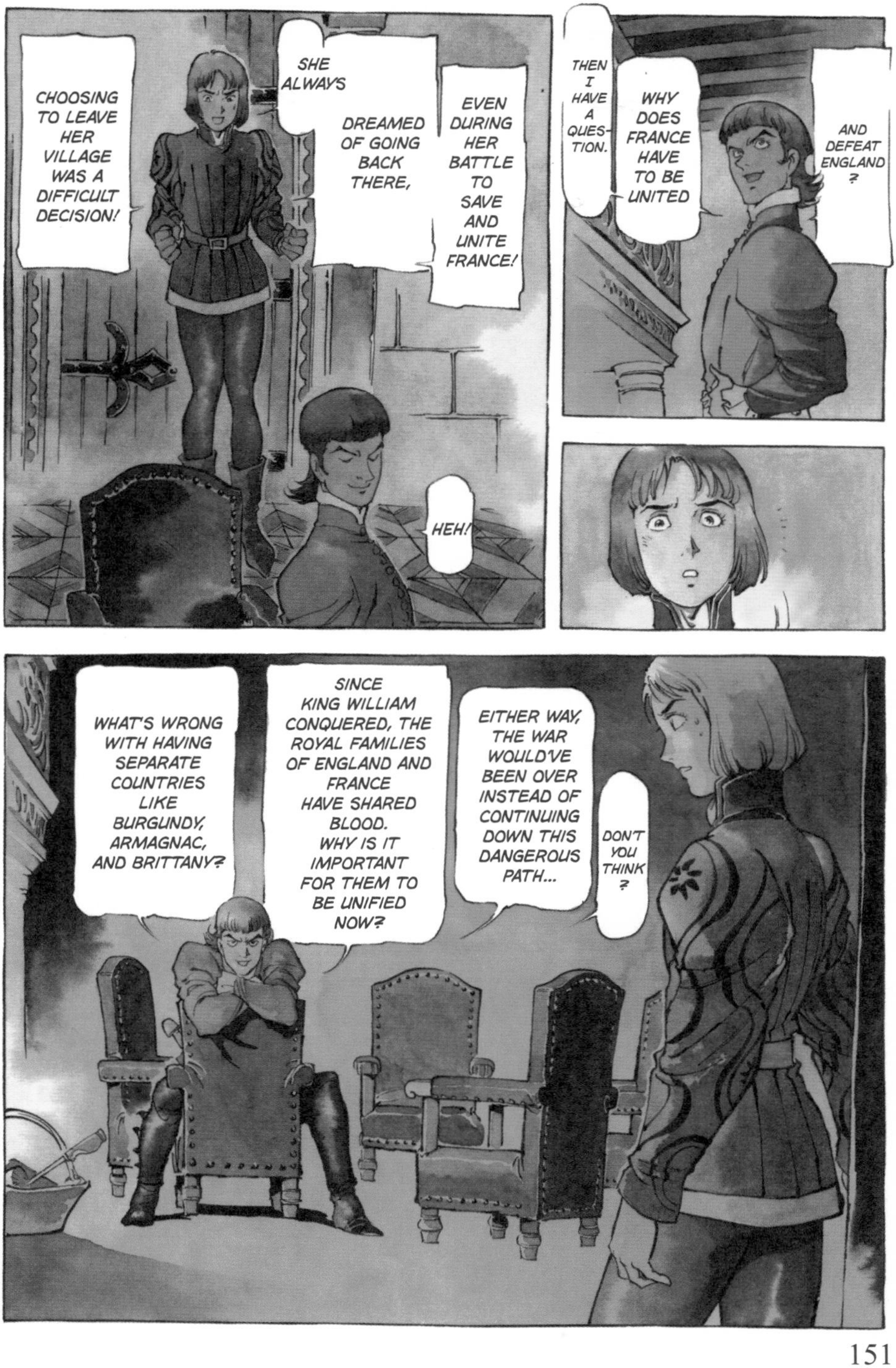
CHOOSING TO LEAVE HER VILLAGE WAS A DIFFICULT DECISION!
SHE ALWAYS
DREAMED OF GOING BACK THERE,
EVEN DURING HER BATTLE TO SAVE AND UNITE FRANCE!
HEH!
THEN I HAVE A QUESTION.
WHY DOES FRANCE HAVE TO BE UNITED
AND DEFEAT ENGLAND?
WHAT'S WRONG WITH HAVING SEPARATE COUNTRIES LIKE BURGUNDY, ARMAGNAC, AND BRITTANY?
SINCE KING WILLIAM CONQUERED, THE ROYAL FAMILIES OF ENGLAND AND FRANCE HAVE SHARED BLOOD. WHY IS IT IMPORTANT FOR THEM TO BE UNIFIED NOW?
EITHER WAY, THE WAR WOULD'VE BEEN OVER INSTEAD OF CONTINUING DOWN THIS DANGEROUS PATH...
DON'T YOU THINK?

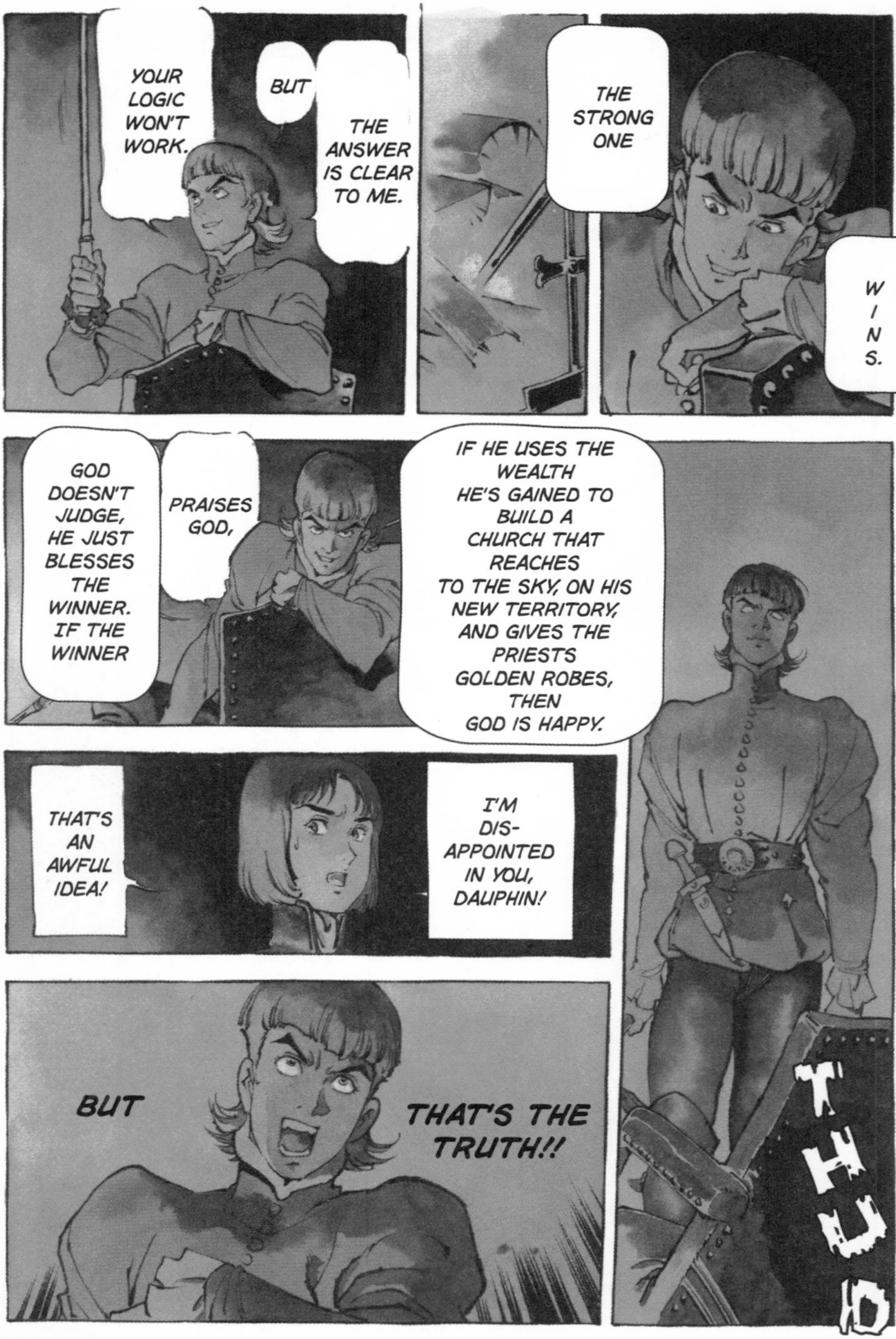
YOUR LOGIC WON'T WORK.
BUT
THE ANSWER IS CLEAR TO ME.
THE STRONG ONE
W I N S.
GOD DOESN'T JUDGE, HE JUST BLESSES THE WINNER. IF THE WINNER
PRAISES GOD,
IF HE USES THE WEALTH HE'S GAINED TO BUILD A CHURCH THAT REACHES TO THE SKY, ON HIS NEW TERRITORY, AND GIVES THE PRIESTS GOLDEN ROBES, THEN GOD IS HAPPY.
THAT'S AN AWFUL IDEA!
I'M DIS-APPOINTED IN YOU, DAUPHIN!
BUT
THAT'S THE TRUTH!!
THUD

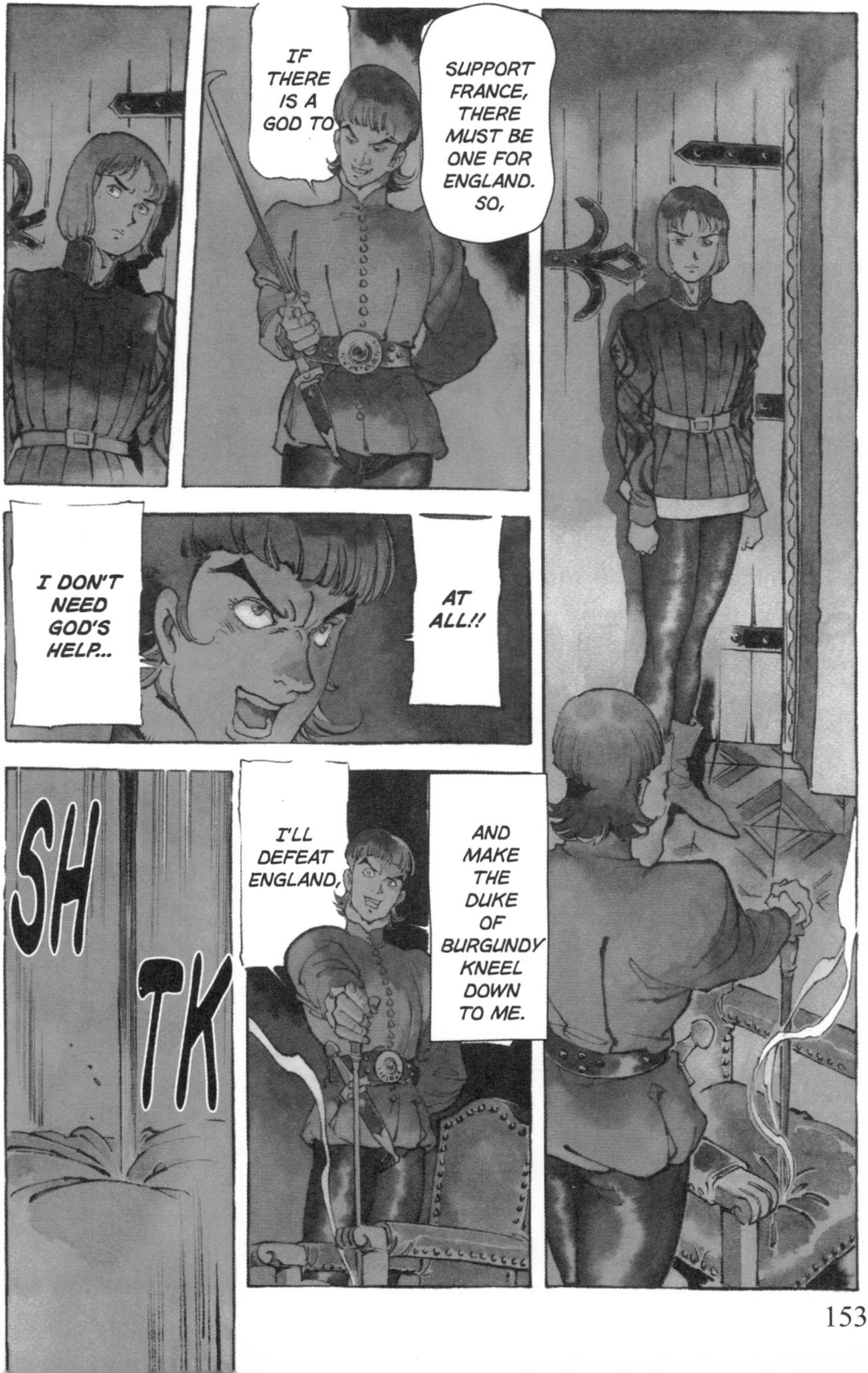
IF THERE IS A GOD TO
SUPPORT FRANCE, THERE MUST BE ONE FOR ENGLAND. SO,
I DON'T NEED GOD'S HELP...
AT ALL!!
I'LL DEFEAT ENGLAND,
AND MAKE THE DUKE OF BURGUNDY KNEEL DOWN TO ME.
SH
TK

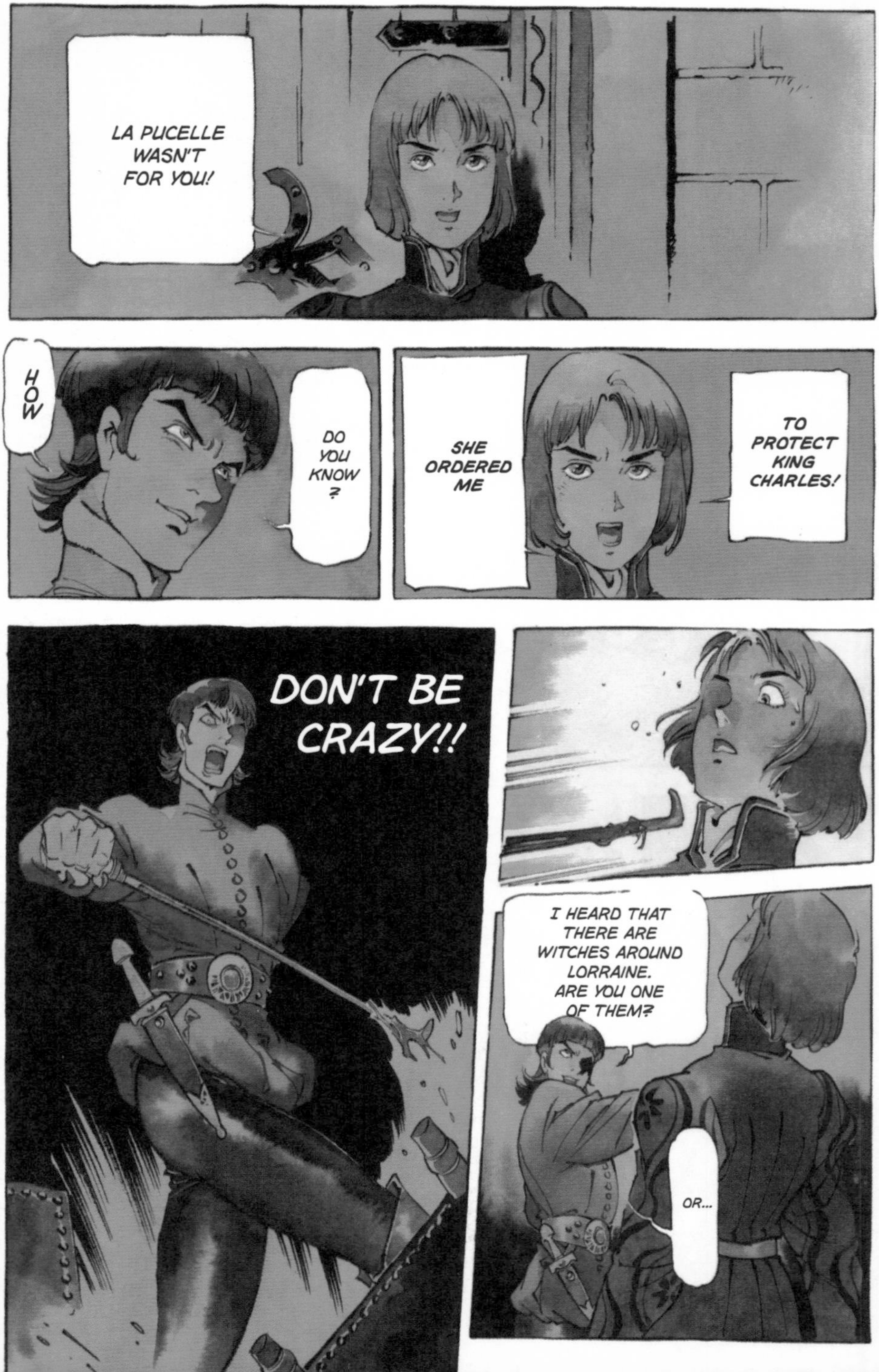
LA PUCELLE WASN'T FOR YOU!
HOW
DO YOU KNOW?
SHE ORDERED ME
TO PROTECT KING CHARLES!
DON'T BE CRAZY!!
I HEARD THAT THERE ARE WITCHES AROUND LORRAINE. ARE YOU ONE OF THEM?
OR...

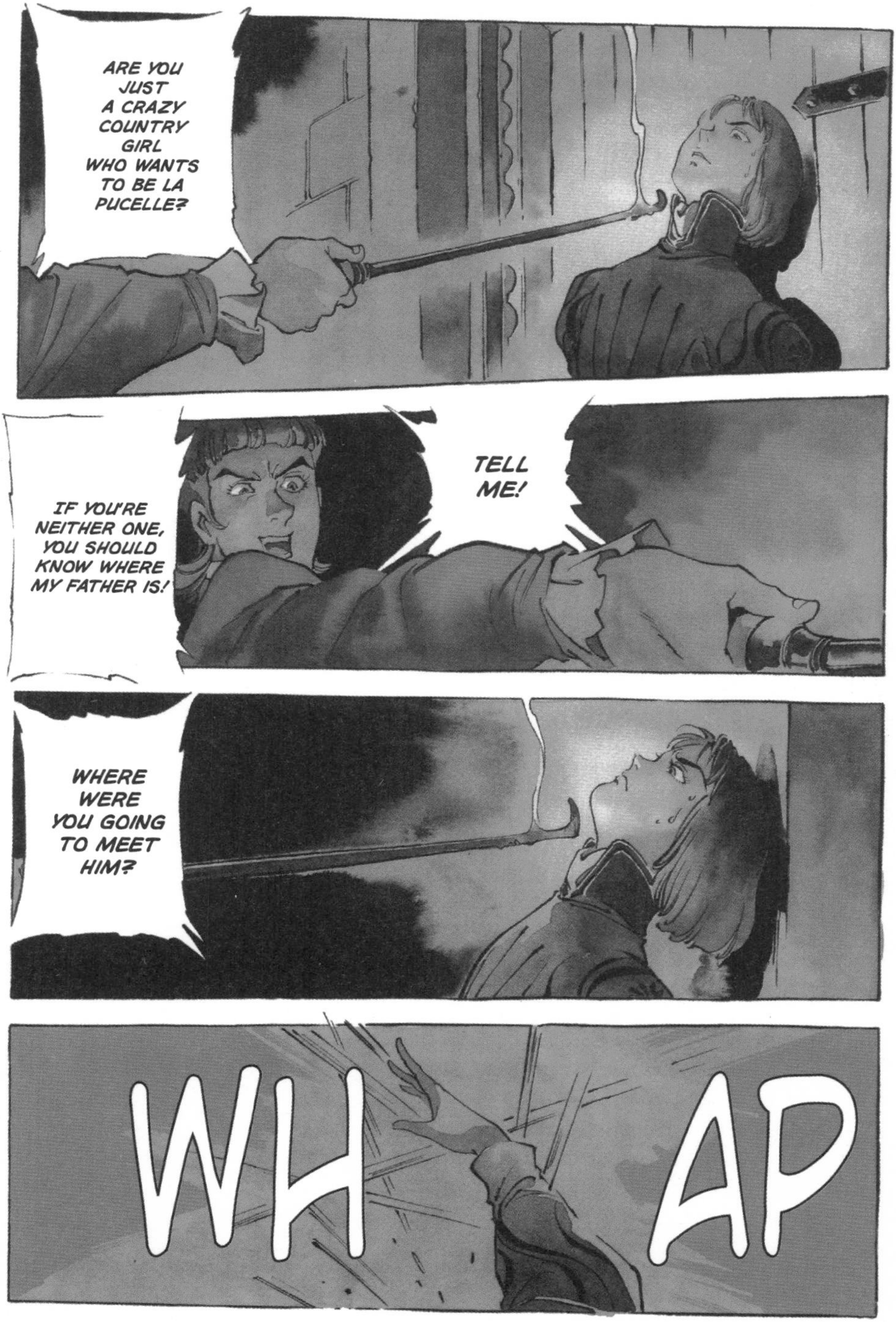
ARE YOU JUST A CRAZY COUNTRY GIRL WHO WANTS TO BE LA PUCELLE?
IF YOU'RE NEITHER ONE, YOU SHOULD KNOW WHERE MY FATHER IS!
TELL ME!
WHERE WERE YOU GOING TO MEET HIM?
WH AP

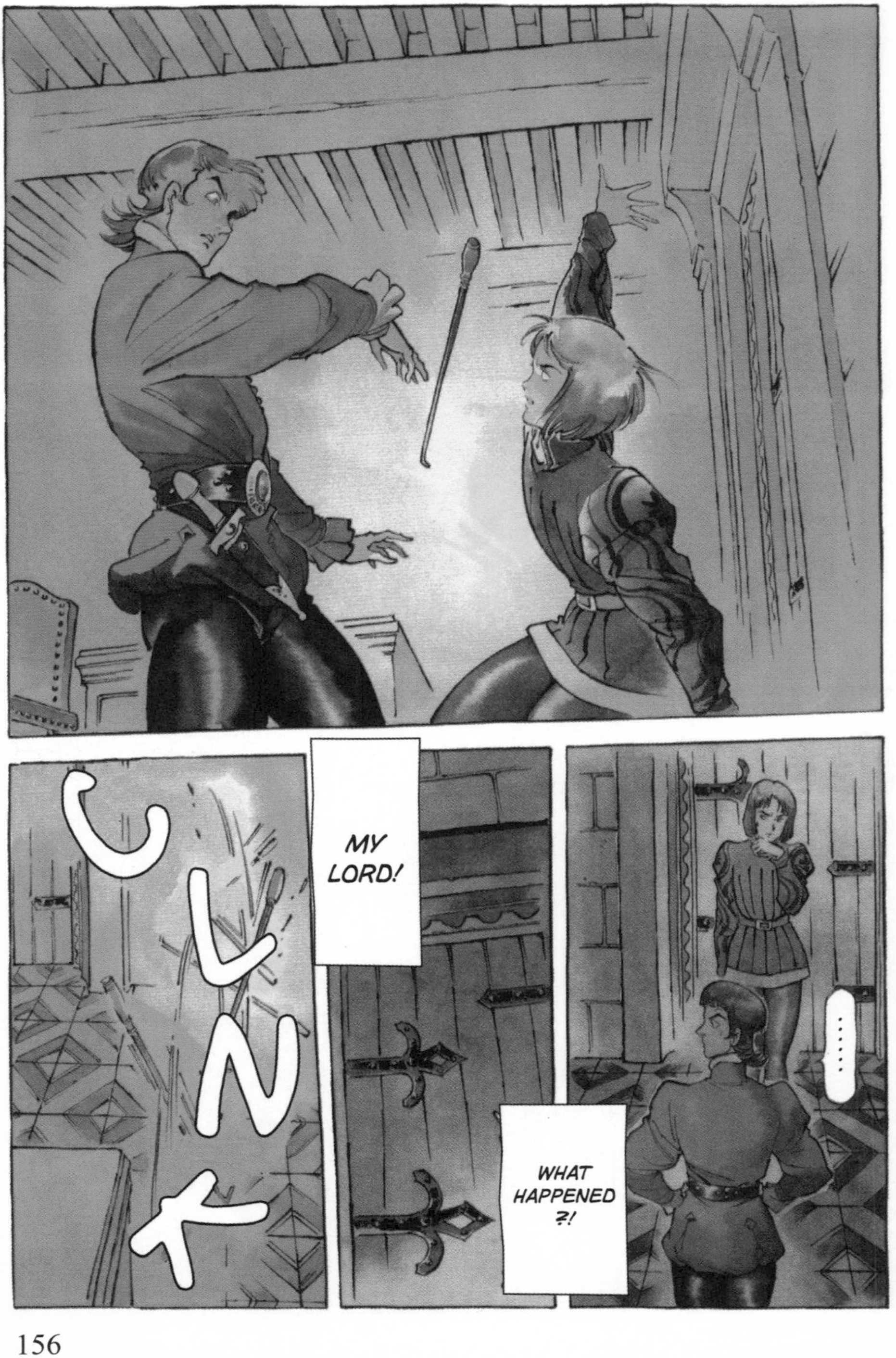
CLINK
MY LORD!
WHAT HAPPENED ?!
......

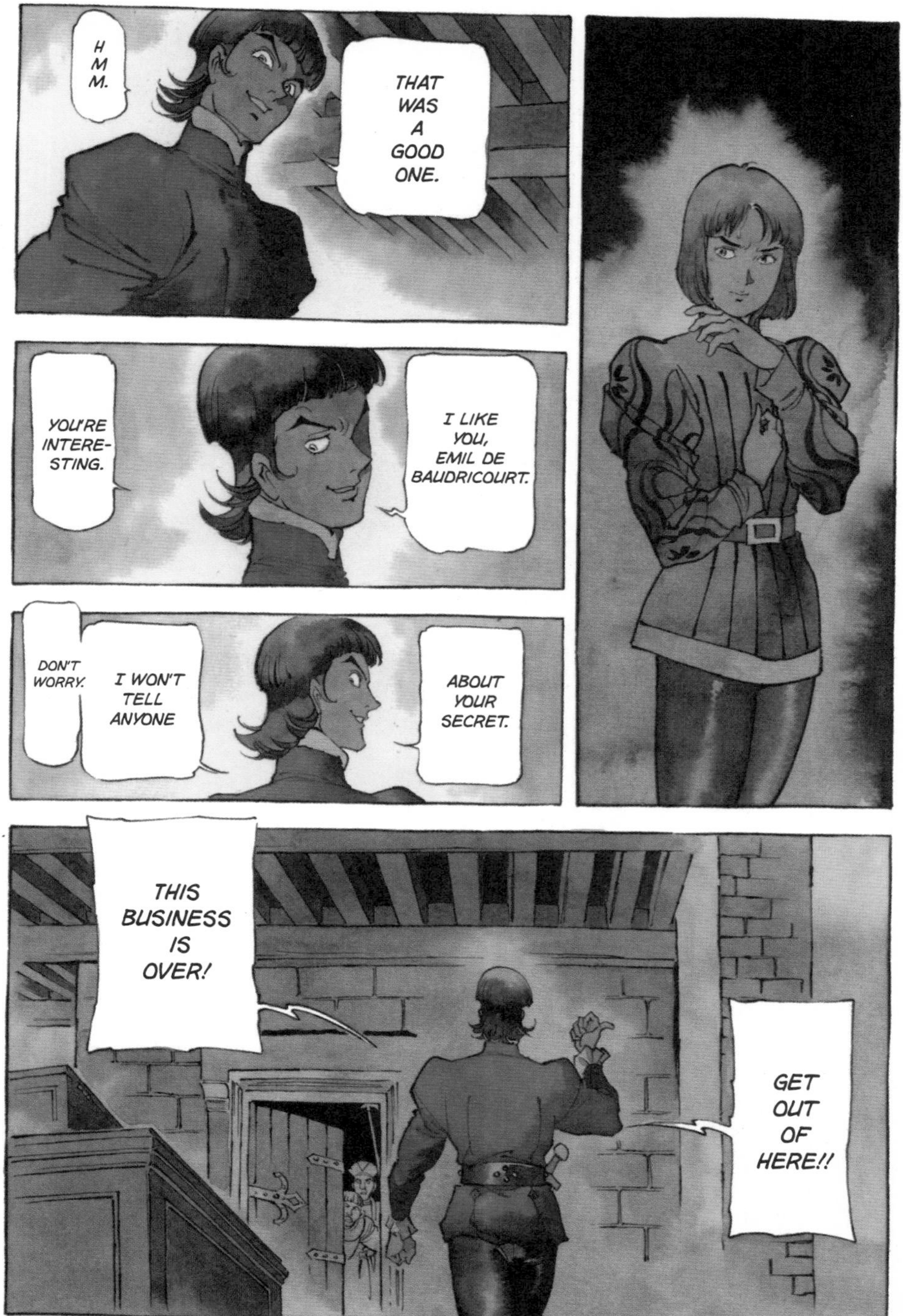
HMM.
THAT WAS A GOOD ONE.
YOU'RE INTERE-STING.
I LIKE YOU, EMIL DE BAUDRICOURT.
DON'T WORRY.
I WON'T TELL ANYONE
ABOUT YOUR SECRET.
THIS BUSINESS IS OVER!
GET OUT OF HERE!!

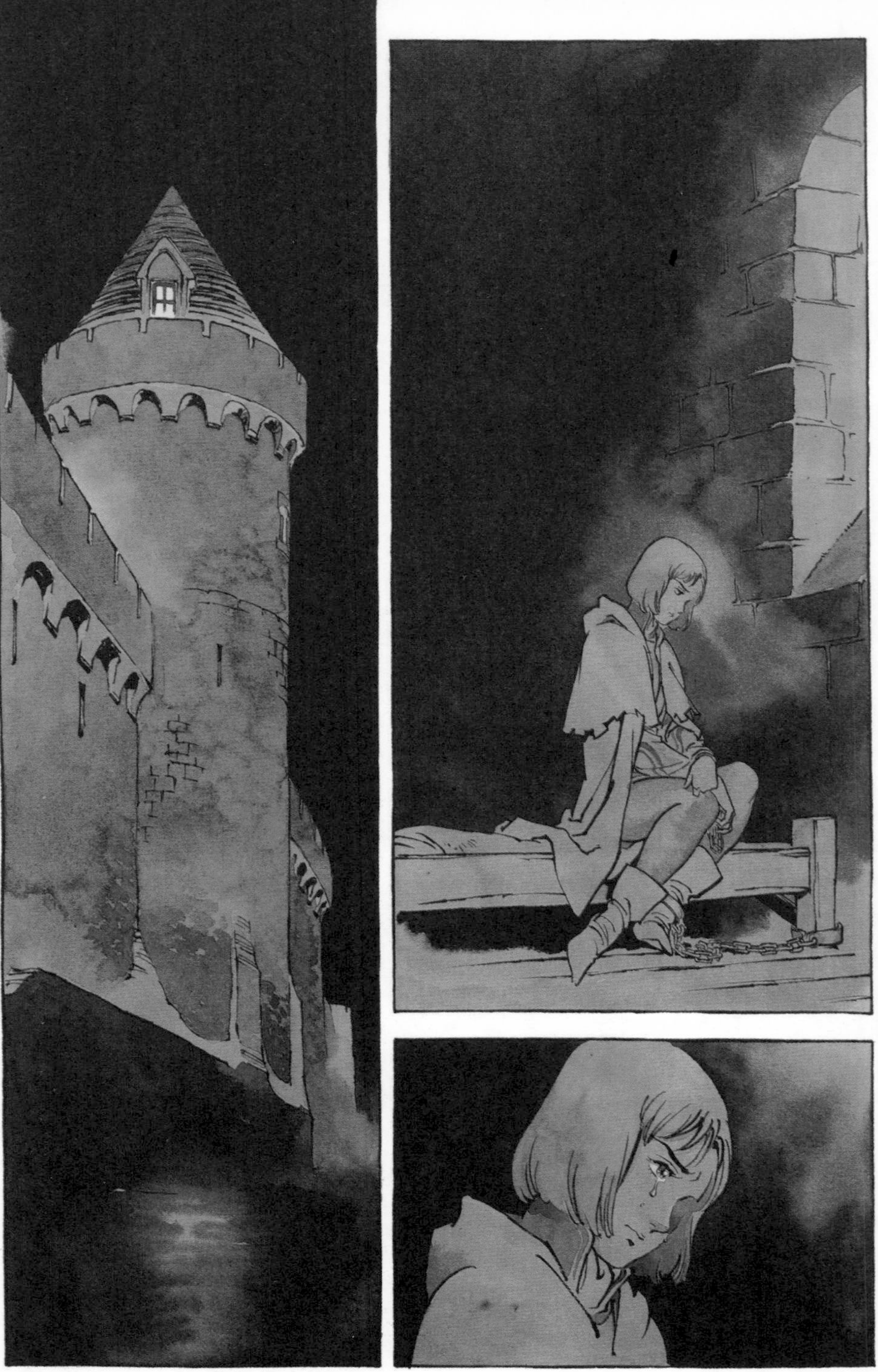

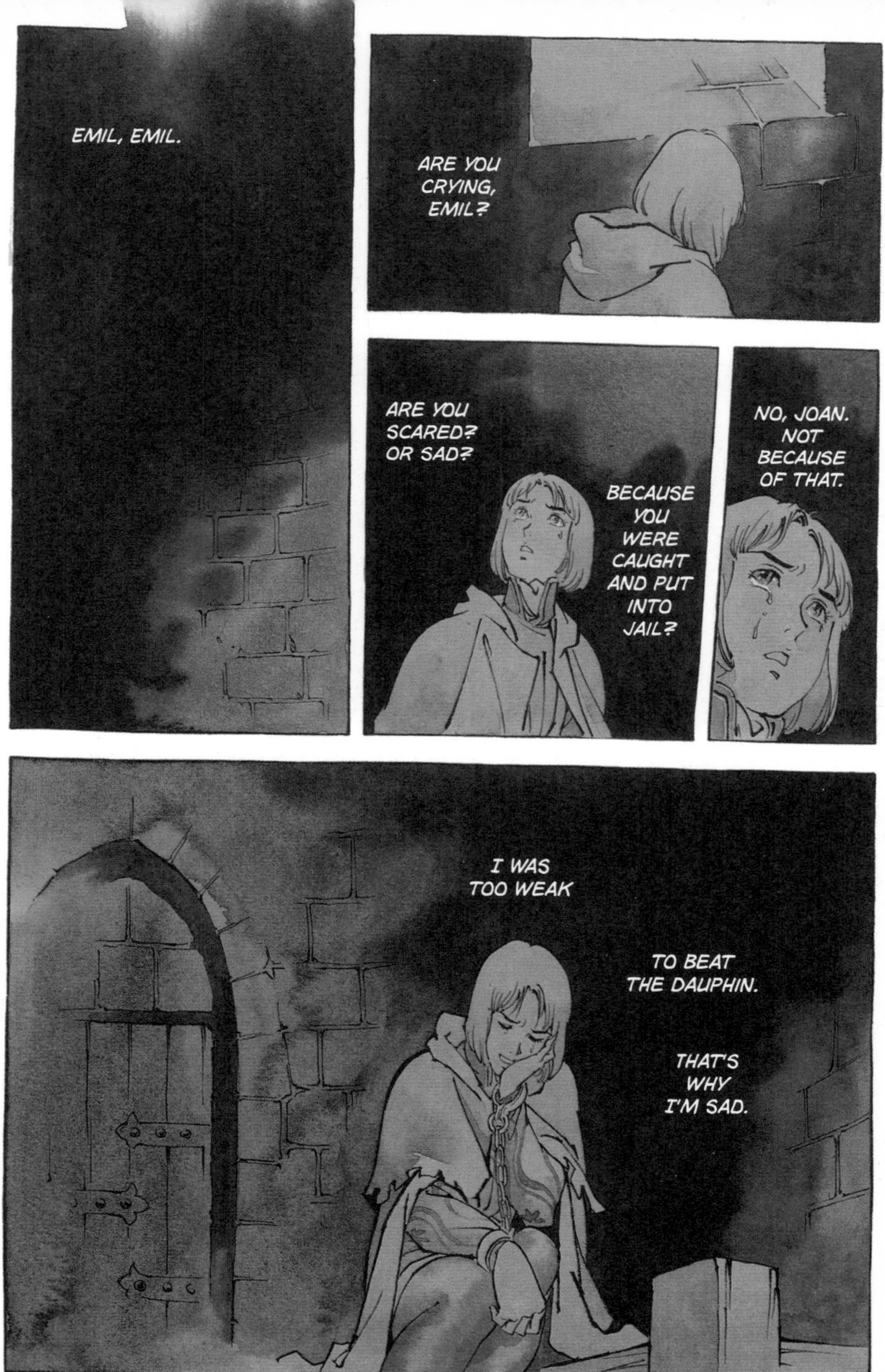
EMIL, EMIL.
ARE YOU CRYING, EMIL?
ARE YOU SCARED? OR SAD?
BECAUSE YOU WERE CAUGHT AND PUT INTO JAIL?
NO, JOAN. NOT BECAUSE OF THAT.
I WAS TOO WEAK
TO BEAT THE DAUPHIN.
THAT'S WHY I'M SAD.

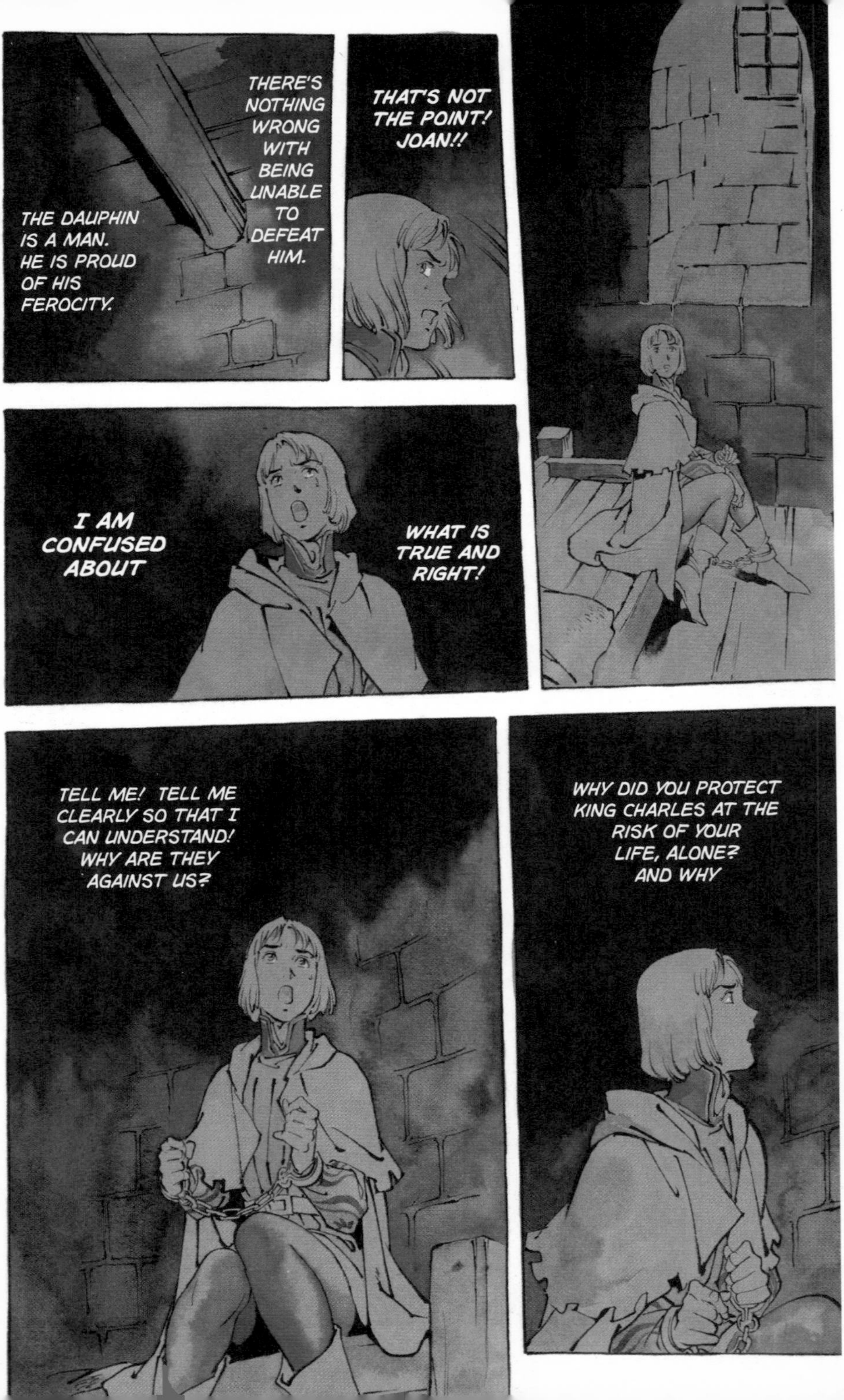
THE DAUPHIN IS A MAN. HE IS PROUD OF HIS FEROCITY.
THERE'S NOTHING WRONG WITH BEING UNABLE TO DEFEAT HIM.
THAT'S NOT THE POINT! JOAN!!
I AM CONFUSED ABOUT
WHAT IS TRUE AND RIGHT!
TELL ME! TELL ME CLEARLY SO THAT I CAN UNDERSTAND! WHY ARE THEY AGAINST US?
WHY DID YOU PROTECT KING CHARLES AT THE RISK OF YOUR LIFE, ALONE? AND WHY

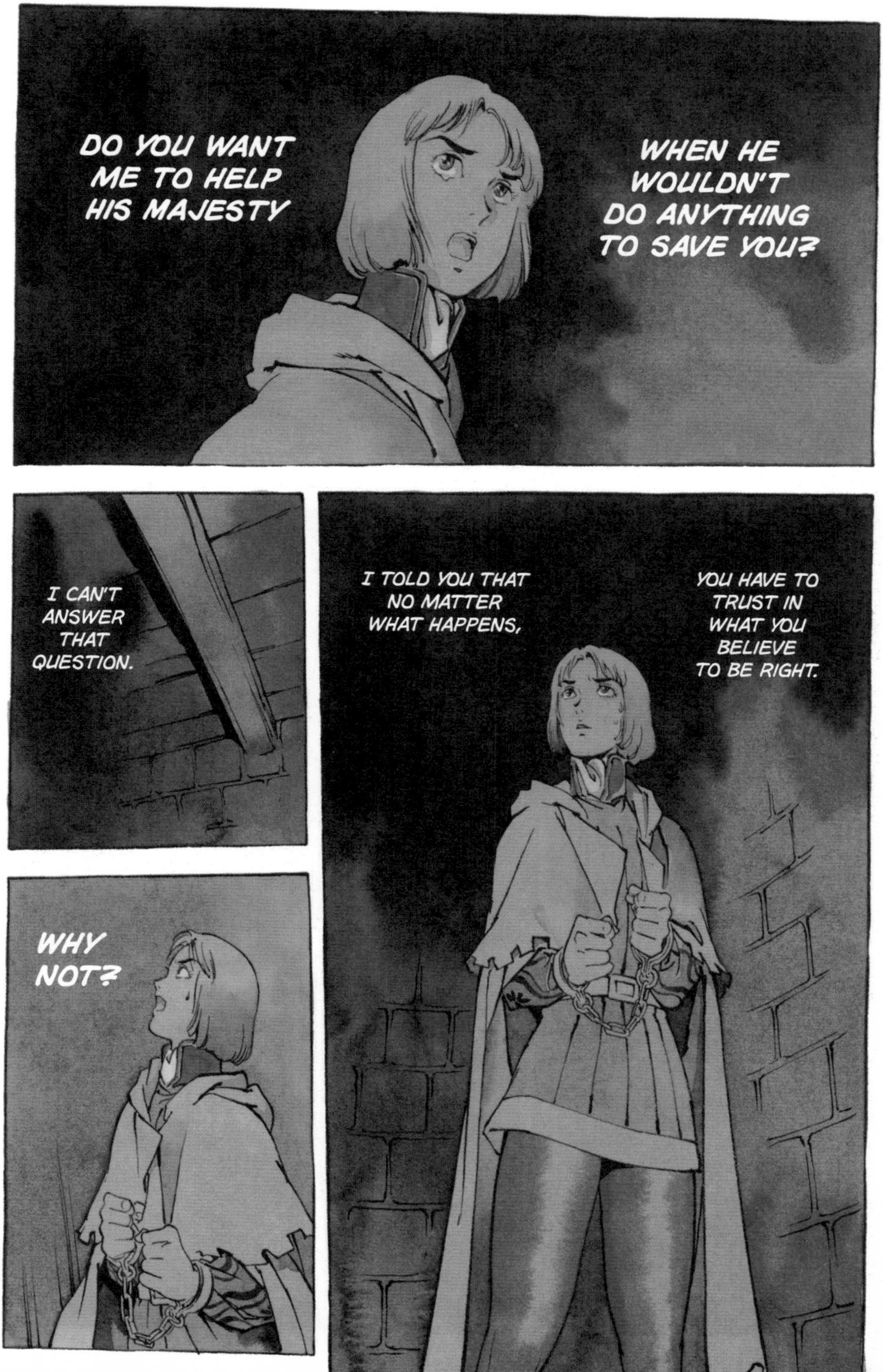
DO YOU WANT ME TO HELP HIS MAJESTY
WHEN HE WOULDN'T DO ANYTHING TO SAVE YOU?
I CAN'T ANSWER THAT QUESTION.
I TOLD YOU THAT NO MATTER WHAT HAPPENS,
YOU HAVE TO TRUST IN WHAT YOU BELIEVE TO BE RIGHT.
WHY NOT?

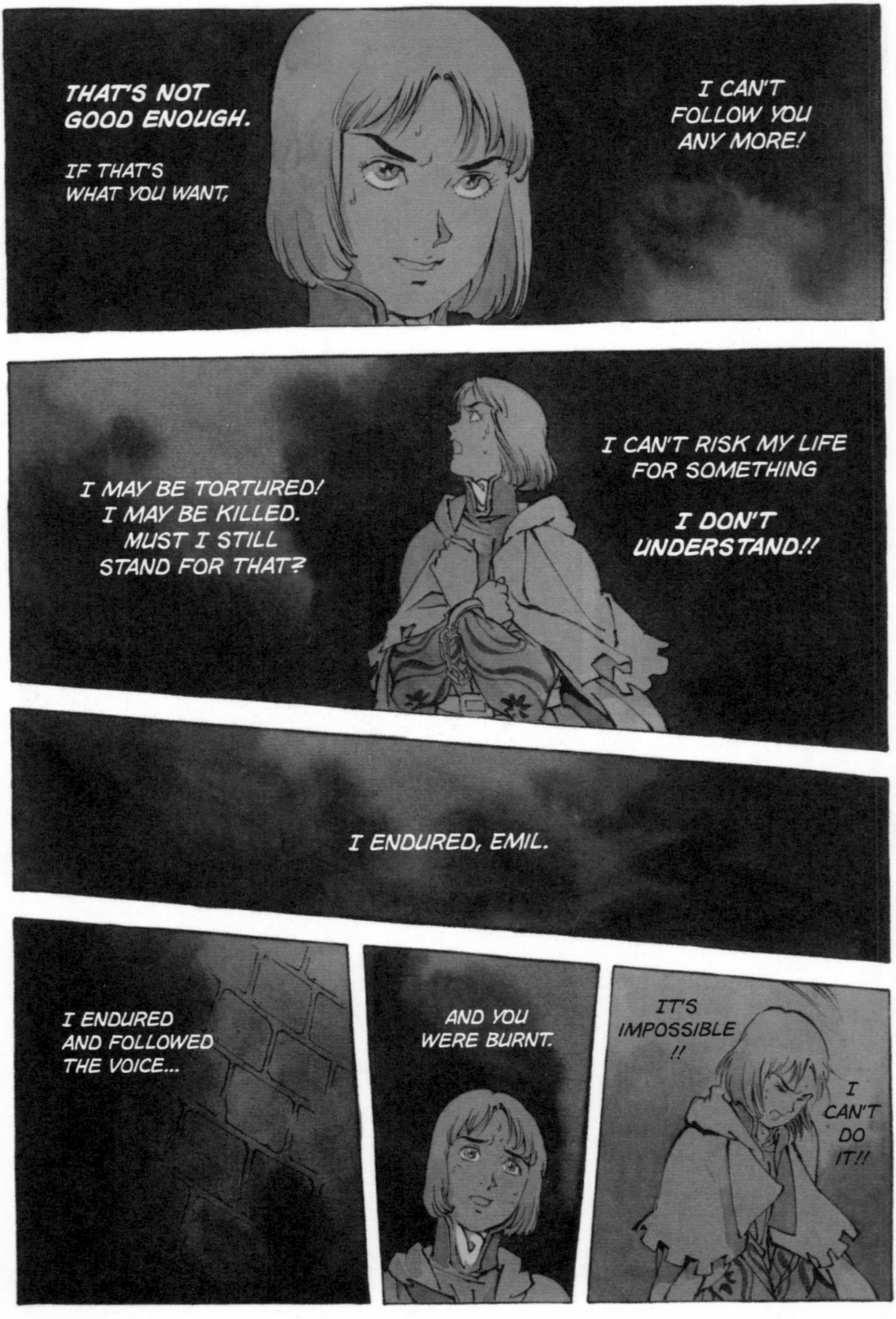
THAT'S NOT GOOD ENOUGH.
IF THAT'S WHAT YOU WANT,
I CAN'T FOLLOW YOU ANY MORE!
I MAY BE TORTURED! I MAY BE KILLED. MUST I STILL STAND FOR THAT?
I CAN'T RISK MY LIFE FOR SOMETHING
I DON'T UNDERSTAND!!
I ENDURED, EMIL.
I ENDURED AND FOLLOWED THE VOICE...
AND YOU WERE BURNT.
IT'S IMPOSSIBLE !!
I CAN'T DO IT!!

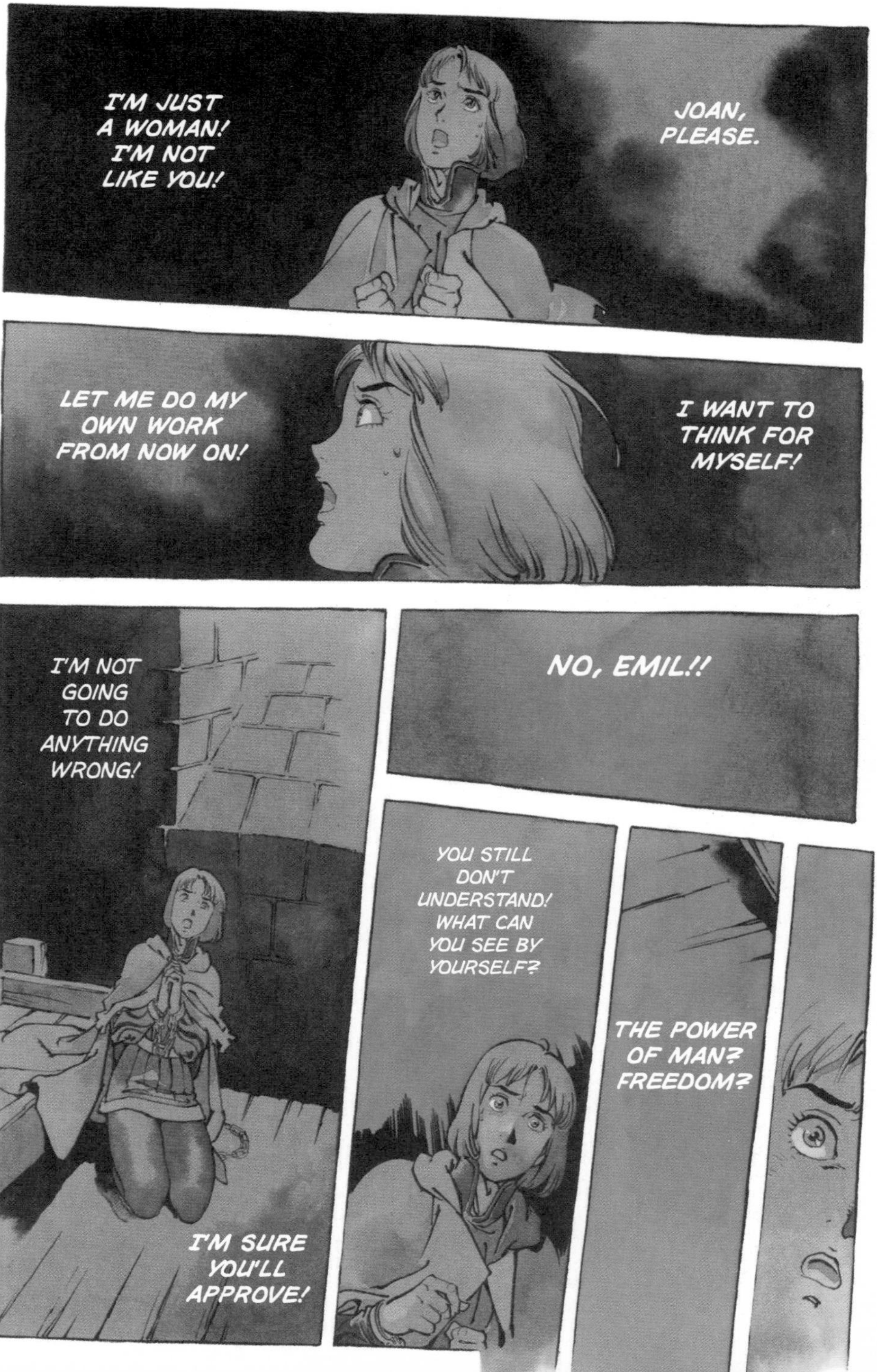
I'M JUST A WOMAN! I'M NOT LIKE YOU!
JOAN, PLEASE.
LET ME DO MY OWN WORK FROM NOW ON!
I WANT TO THINK FOR MYSELF!
I'M NOT GOING TO DO ANYTHING WRONG!
I'M SURE YOU'LL APPROVE!
NO, EMIL!!
YOU STILL DON'T UNDERSTAND! WHAT CAN YOU SEE BY YOURSELF?
THE POWER OF MAN? FREEDOM?

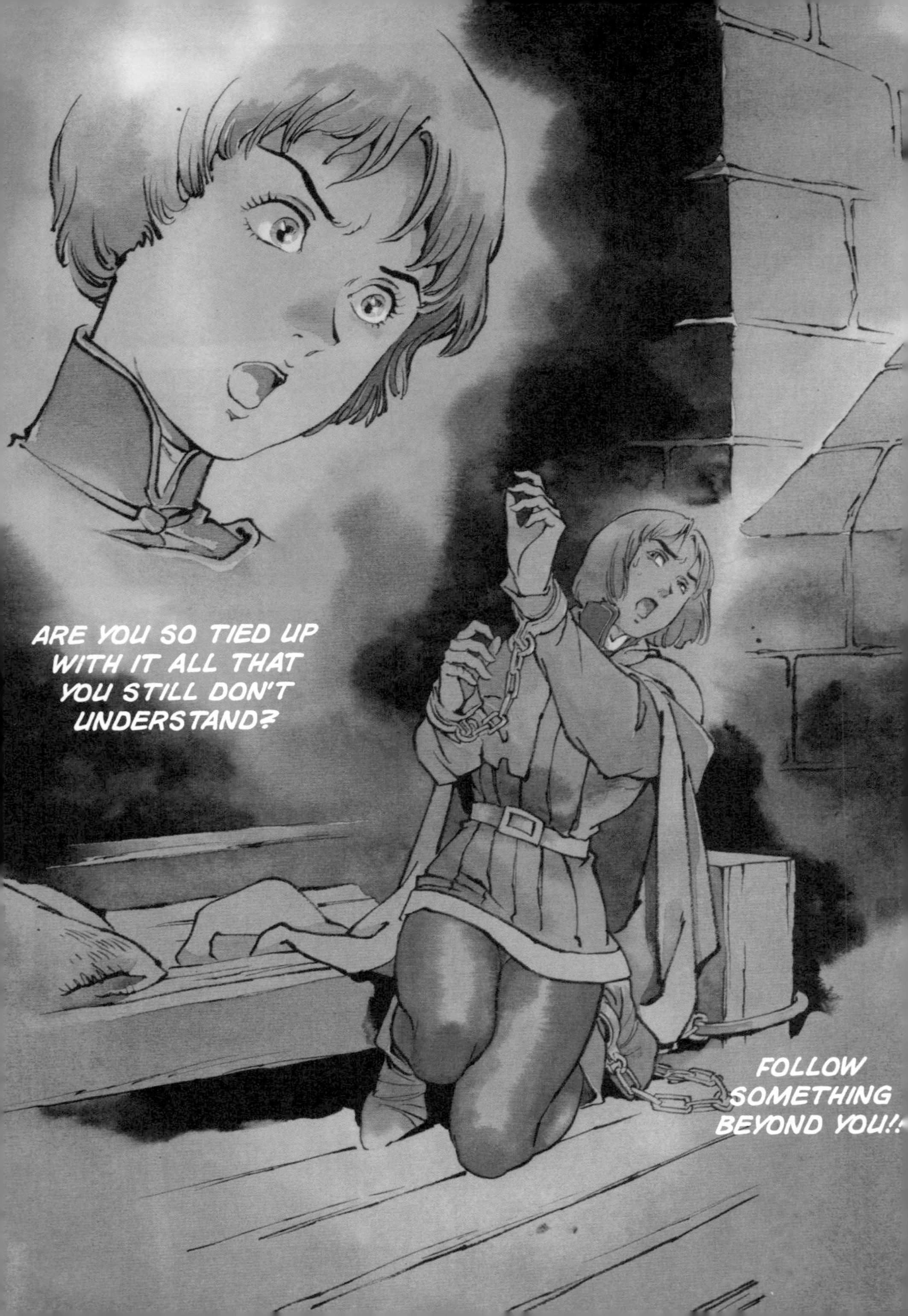
ARE YOU SO TIED UP WITH IT ALL THAT YOU STILL DON'T UNDERSTAND?
FOLLOW SOMETHING BEYOND YOU!!

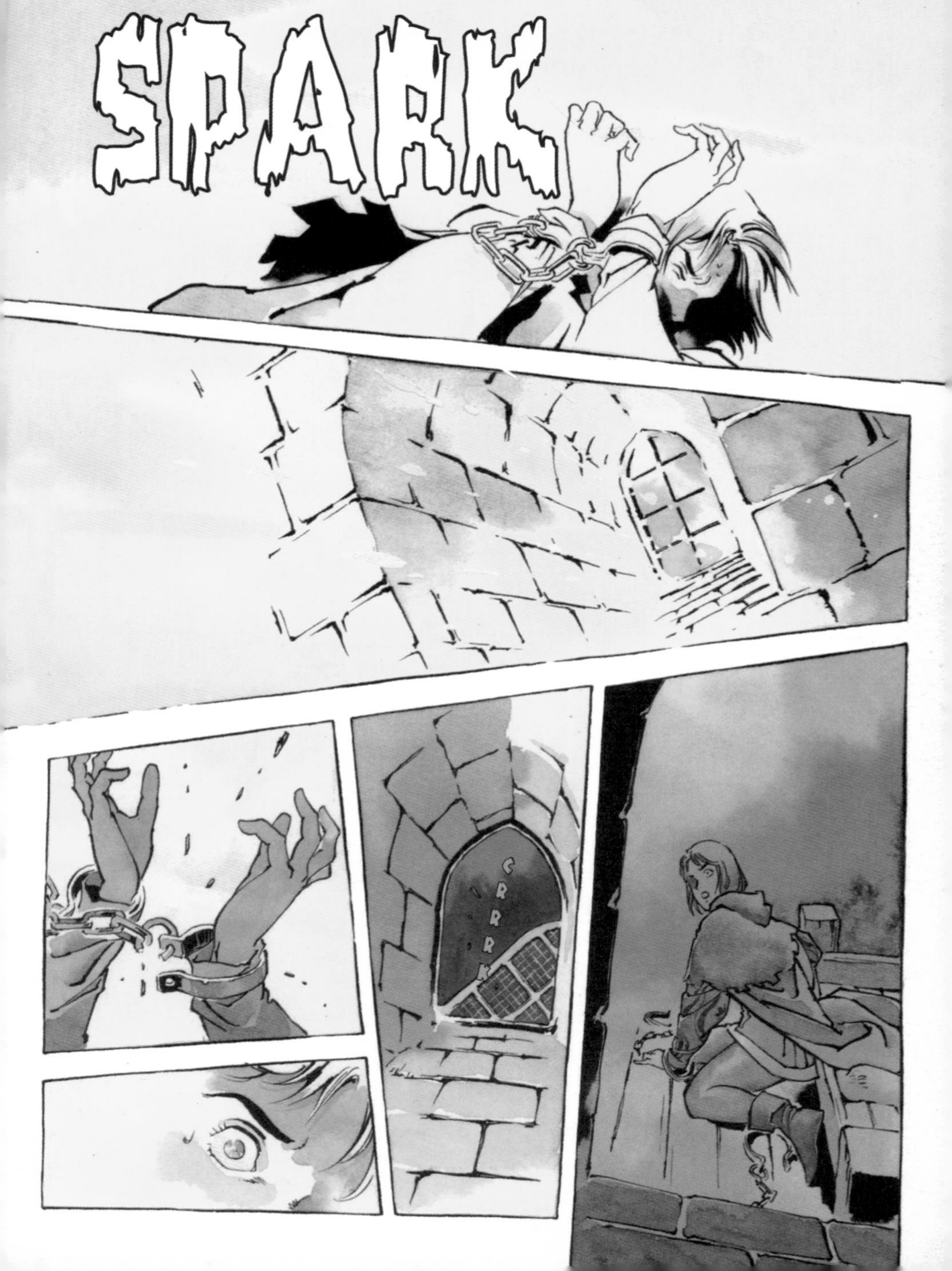
SPARK
CRRRK

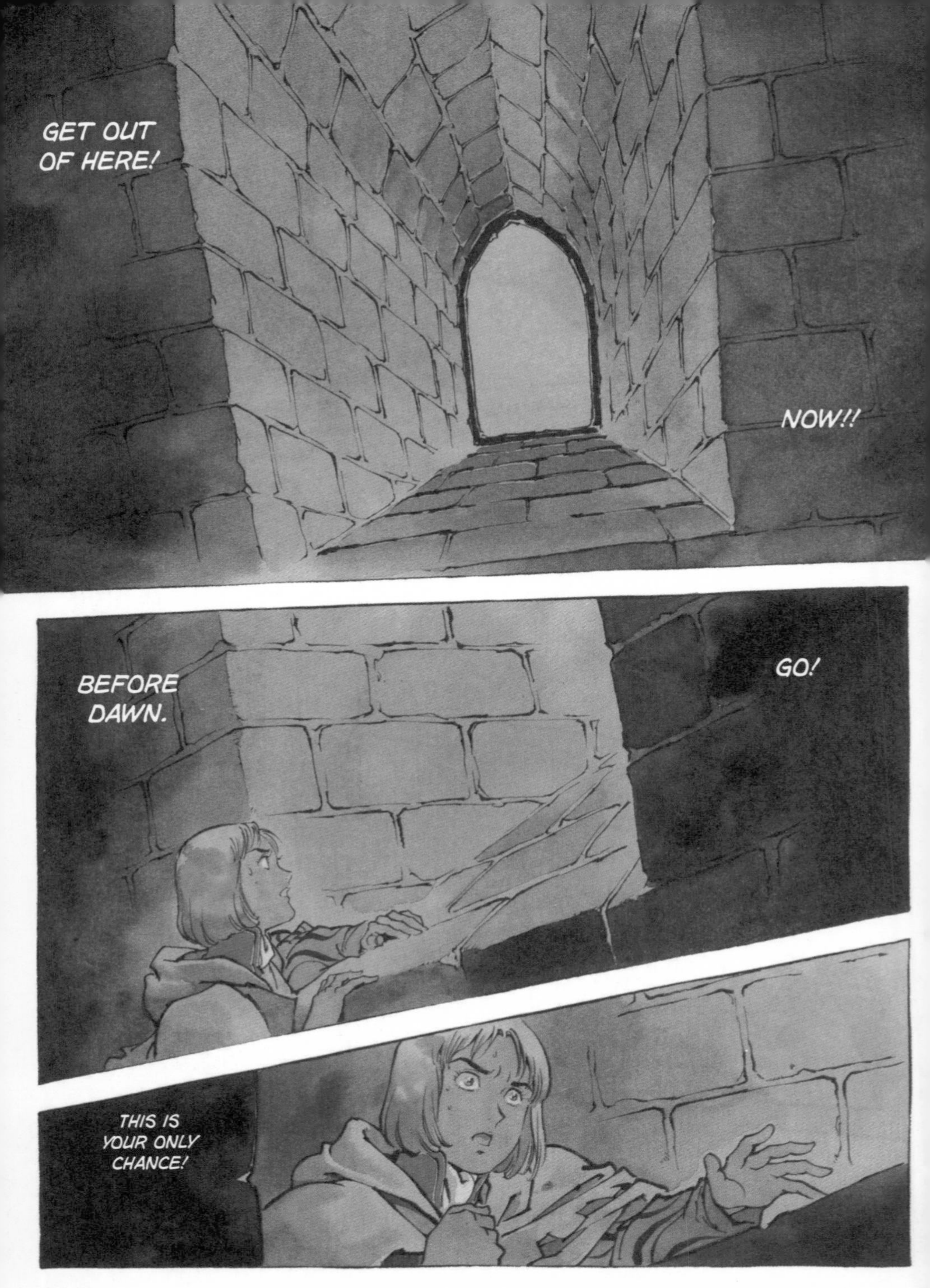
GET OUT OF HERE!
NOW!!
BEFORE DAWN.
GO!
THIS IS YOUR ONLY CHANCE!

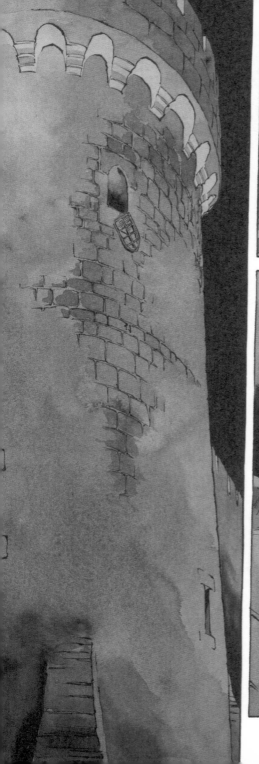

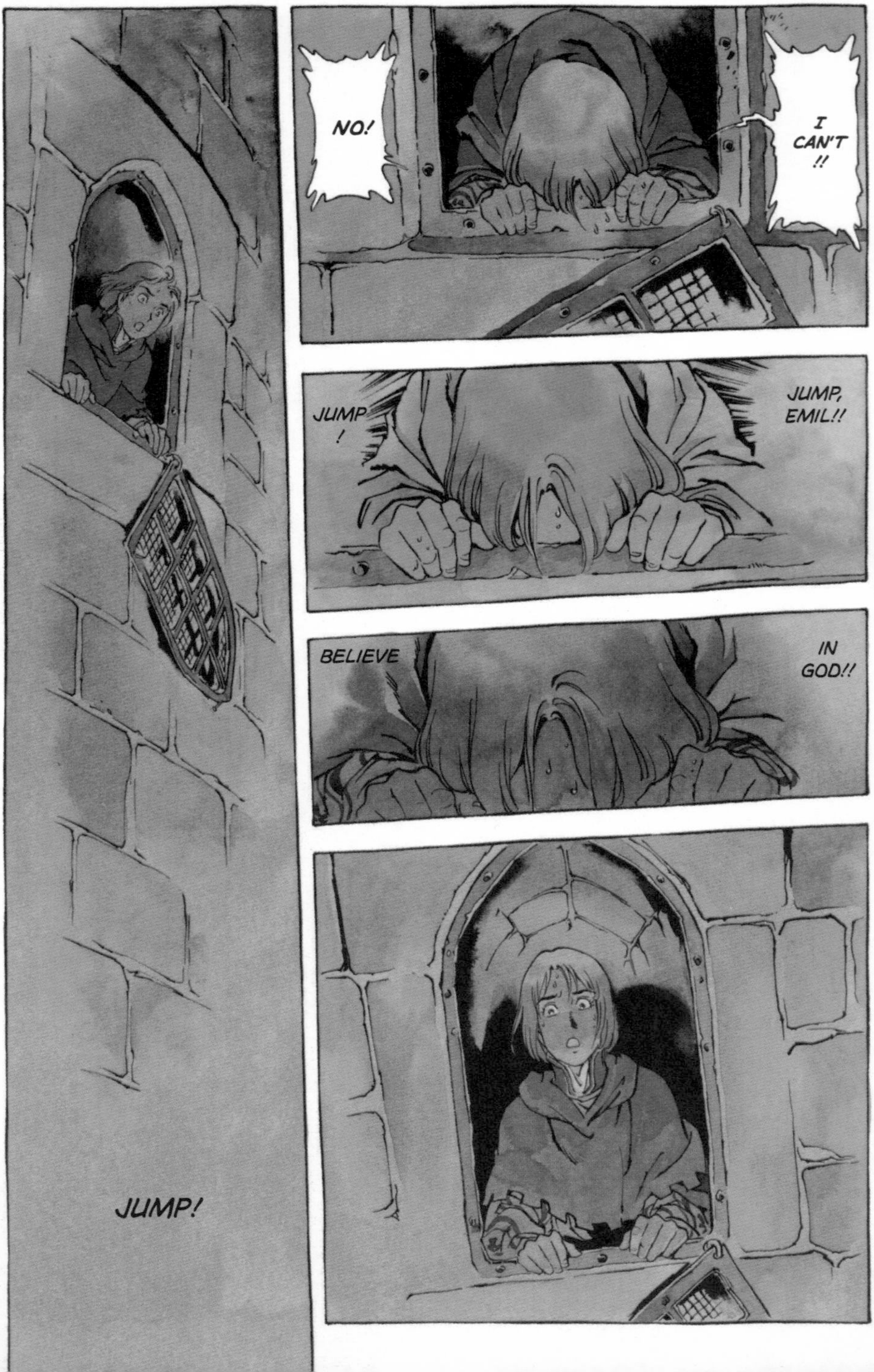

NO!
I CAN'T !!
JUMP!
JUMP, EMIL!!
BELIEVE
IN GOD!!
JUMP!

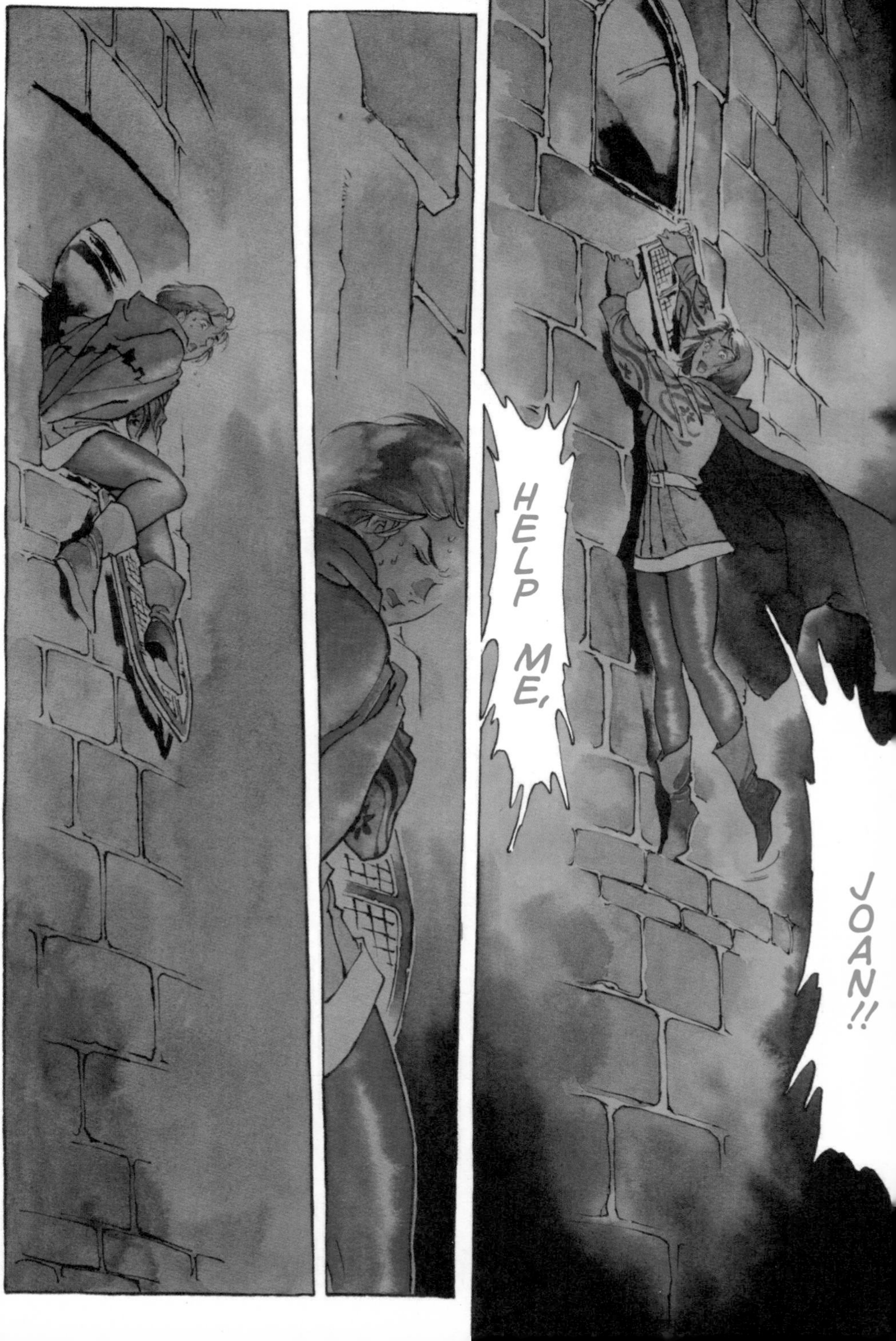
HELP ME,
JOAN!!

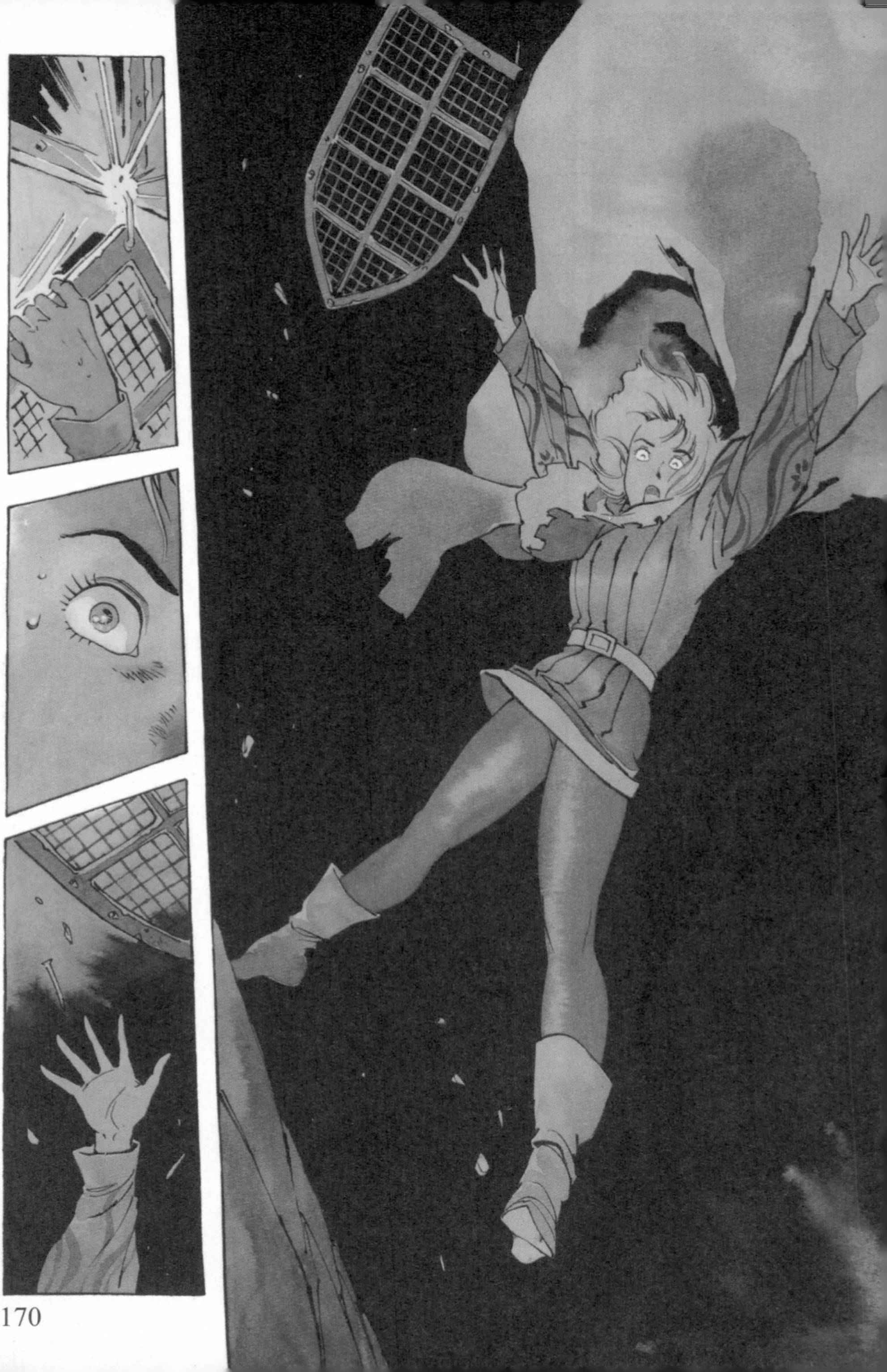

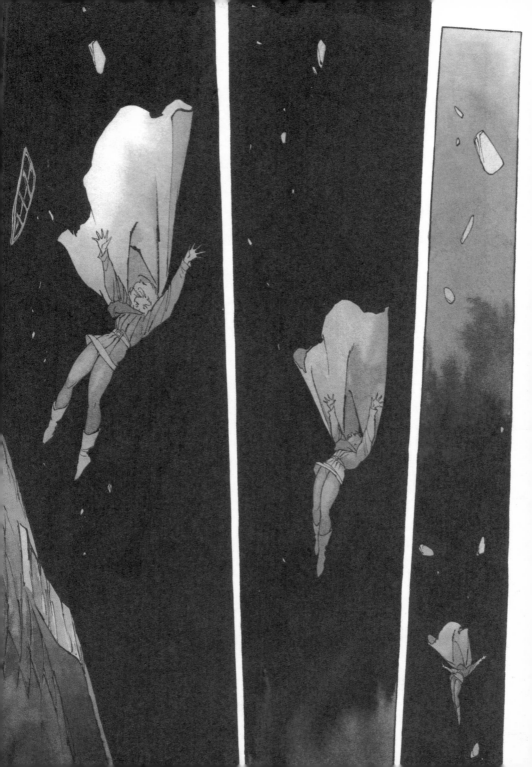

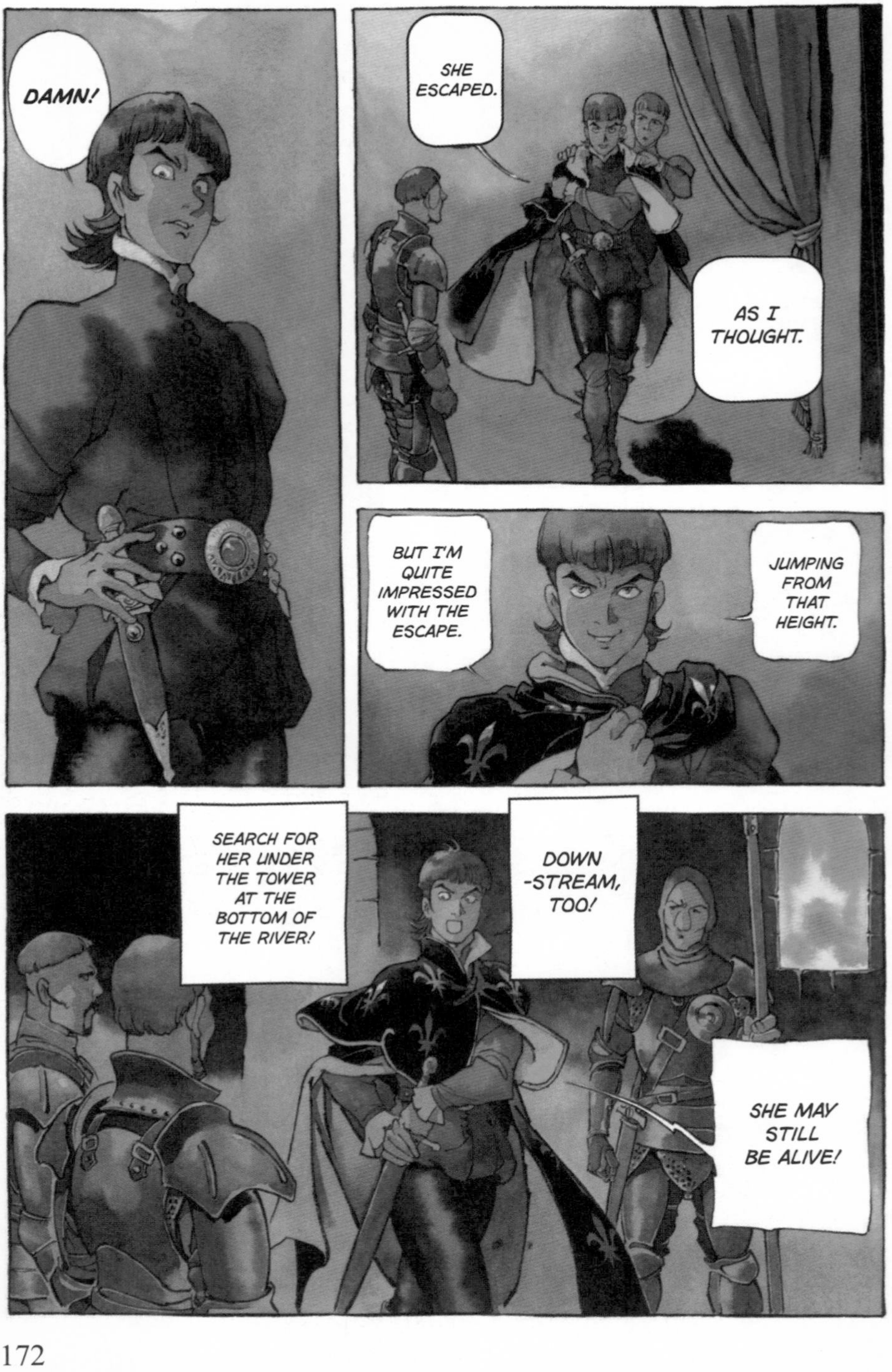
DAMN!
SHE ESCAPED.
AS I THOUGHT.
JUMPING FROM THAT HEIGHT.
BUT I'M QUITE IMPRESSED WITH THE ESCAPE.
DOWN -STREAM, TOO!
SEARCH FOR HER UNDER THE TOWER AT THE BOTTOM OF THE RIVER!
SHE MAY STILL BE ALIVE!

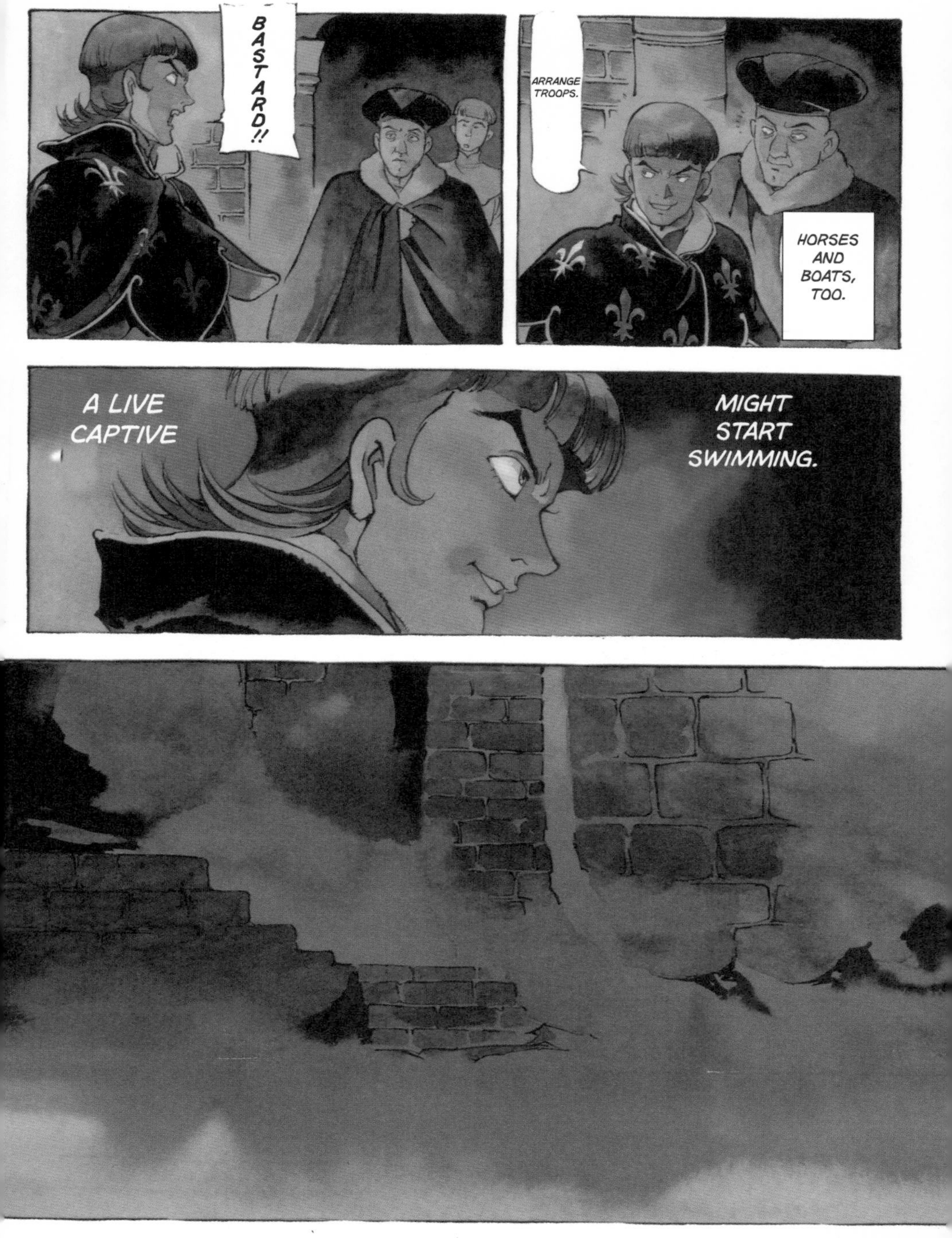
BASTARD!!
ARRANGE TROOPS.
HORSES AND BOATS, TOO.
A LIVE CAPTIVE
MIGHT START SWIMMING.

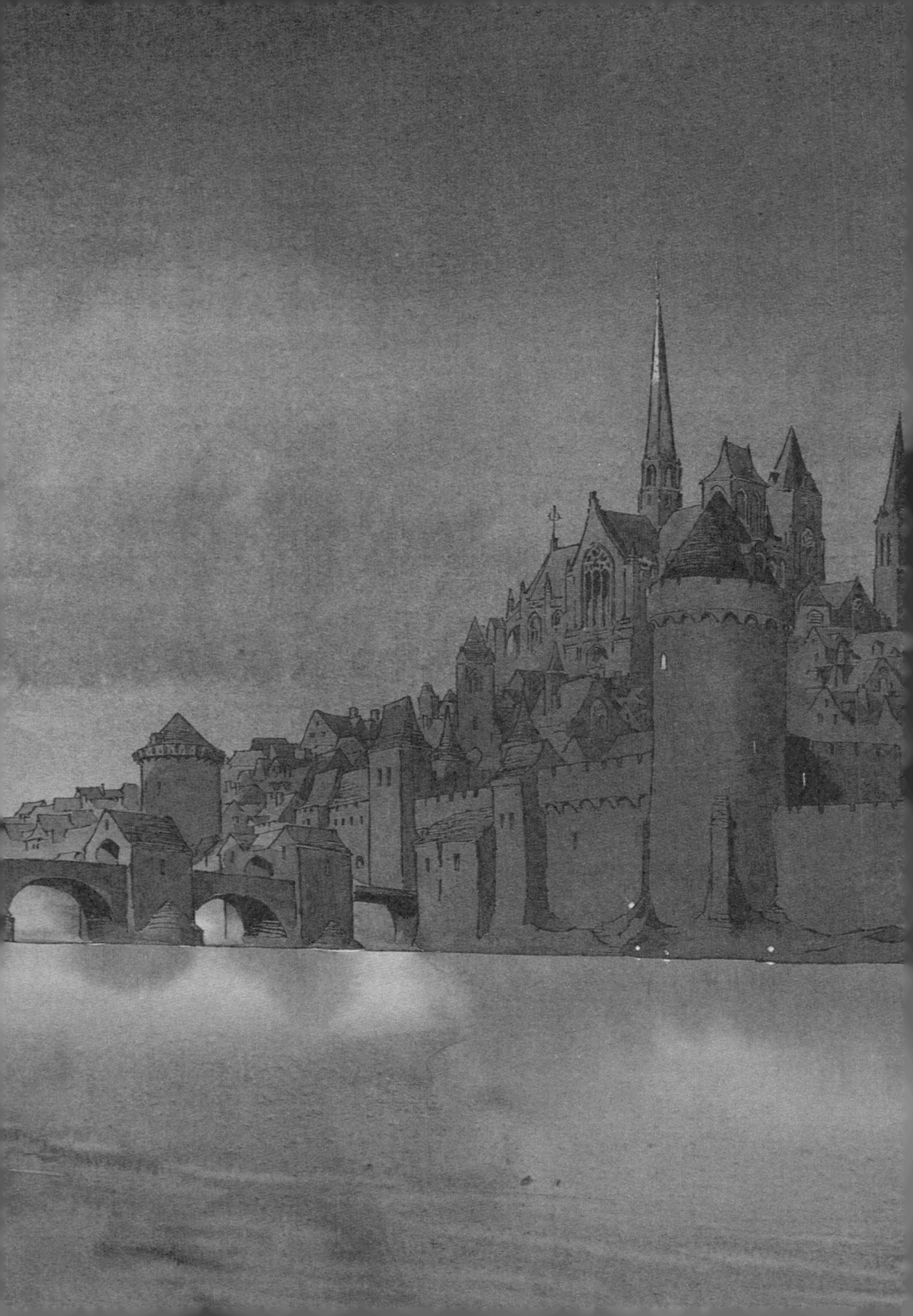

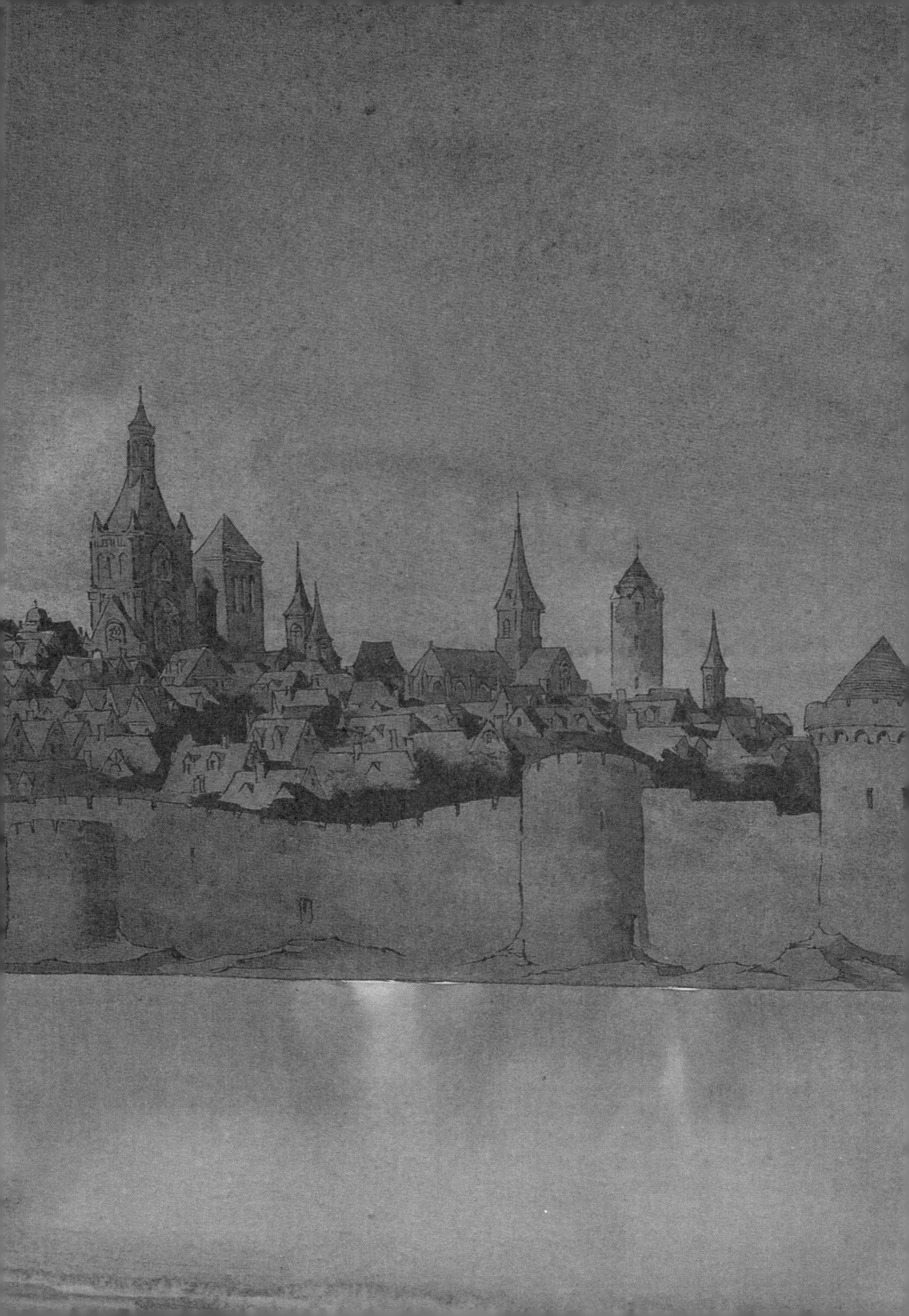

# THE AGE OF JOAN

JOAN OF ARC WAS BORN IN THE EARLY 15TH CENTURY, WHEN THE ENGLISH WERE ABOUT TO ANNEX FRANCE. AT THAT TIME, THE KING OF ENGLAND OWNED A GREAT DEAL OF LAND WITHIN FRANCE. THIS KIND OF SITUATION, ODD BY MODERN STANDARDS, HAD EXISTED SINCE THE 11TH CENTURY. IT GOES BACK TO THE TIME WHEN WILLIAM, DUKE OF NORMANDY, LAID CLAIM TO THE ENGLISH THRONE FOLLOWING HIS VICTORY AT THE BATTLE OF HASTINGS IN 1066. THE ROYAL FAMILY OF ENGLAND WERE THE DESCENDANTS OF NORMANDY, AND THROUGH THEIR MARRIAGE POLICY, THEY EXPANDED THEIR LAND WITHIN FRANCE BY INHERITING THE LANDS THROUGH BLOOD-TIES WITH FRENCH LORDS.

WHEN "THE HUNDRED YEARS WAR" BROKE OUT IN 1337, THE ENGLISH OWNERSHIP OF FRENCH LANDS WAS AT ITS FOUNDATION.

AT FIRST THE ENGLISH ARMY WAS LED BY EDWARD III AND HIS SON, PRINCE EDWARD (NICKNAMED THE BLACK PRINCE). IN 1376, HOWEVER, THE BLACK PRINCE DIED OF THE PLAGUE. HIS FATHER DIED OF A DISEASE THE FOLLOWING YEAR. THE KING OF FRANCE, CHARLES V, DID NOT MISS THIS OPPORTUNITY. HE STARTED A COUNTERATTACK IMMEDIATELY. THE FRENCH RECOVERED A GREAT DEAL OF LAND AND FRANCE WAS FREE, FOR THE MOMENT, FROM THE THREAT OF THE ENGLISH ARMY.

THE DEATH OF CHARLES V AND HIS SON'S MENTAL DISORDER CAUSED A POWER STRUGGLE AMONG THE MEMBERS OF COURT. IN 1407, JEAN, DUKE OF BURGUNDY'S ASSASSINATION OF LOUIS, DUKE D'ORLEANS, CAUSED A DRAMATIC ERUPTION IN THE ONGOING FRICTION BETWEEN THE TWO POWERFUL HOUSES. THIS RESULTED IN AN OPEN CIVIL WAR IN FRANCE BETWEEN THE SUPPORTERS OF THE DUKE OF BURGUNDY (BURGUNDIANS), AND THOSE OF CHARLES, SON OF THE DUKE OF ORLEANS, CALLED ARMAGNACS.

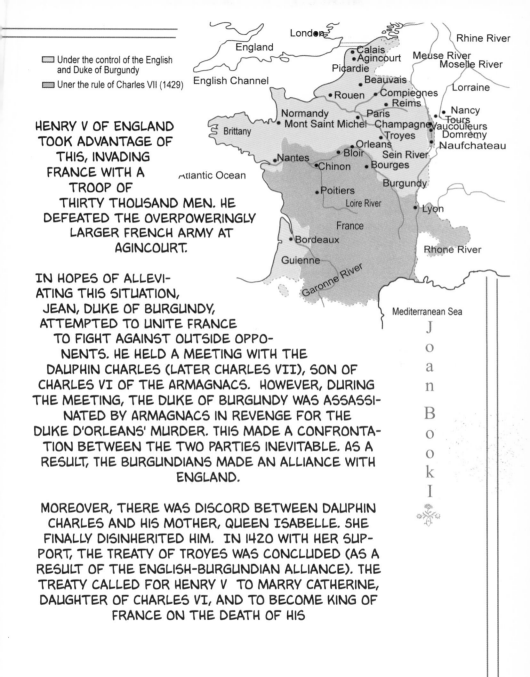

Under the control of the English and Duke of Burgundy

Uner the rule of Charles VII (1429)

London
England
English Channel
Calais
Agincourt
Picardie
Beauvais
Rouen
Compiegnes
Reims
Normandy
Paris
Mont Saint Michel
Champagne
Brittany
Troyes
Orleans
Nantes
Bloir
Sein River
Chinon
Bourges
Atlantic Ocean
Burgundy
Poitiers
Loire River
Lyon
France
Bordeaux
Guienne
Rhone River
Garonne River
Mediterranean Sea
Rhine River
Meuse River
Moselle River
Lorraine
Nancy
Tours
Vaucouleurs
Domremy
Naufchateau

HENRY V OF ENGLAND TOOK ADVANTAGE OF THIS, INVADING FRANCE WITH A TROOP OF THIRTY THOUSAND MEN. HE DEFEATED THE OVERPOWERINGLY LARGER FRENCH ARMY AT AGINCOURT.

IN HOPES OF ALLEVI- ATING THIS SITUATION, JEAN, DUKE OF BURGUNDY, ATTEMPTED TO UNITE FRANCE TO FIGHT AGAINST OUTSIDE OPPO- NENTS. HE HELD A MEETING WITH THE DAUPHIN CHARLES (LATER CHARLES VII), SON OF CHARLES VI OF THE ARMAGNACS. HOWEVER, DURING THE MEETING, THE DUKE OF BURGUNDY WAS ASSASSI- NATED BY ARMAGNACS IN REVENGE FOR THE DUKE D'ORLEANS' MURDER. THIS MADE A CONFRONTA- TION BETWEEN THE TWO PARTIES INEVITABLE. AS A RESULT, THE BURGUNDIANS MADE AN ALLIANCE WITH ENGLAND.

MOREOVER, THERE WAS DISCORD BETWEEN DAUPHIN CHARLES AND HIS MOTHER, QUEEN ISABELLE. SHE FINALLY DISINHERITED HIM. IN 1420 WITH HER SUP- PORT, THE TREATY OF TROYES WAS CONCLUDED (AS A RESULT OF THE ENGLISH-BURGUNDIAN ALLIANCE). THE TREATY CALLED FOR HENRY V TO MARRY CATHERINE, DAUGHTER OF CHARLES VI, AND TO BECOME KING OF FRANCE ON THE DEATH OF HIS

Joan Book I

# FATHER-IN-LAW.

THIS IS HOW FRANCE REACHED THAT CRITICAL MOMENT OF ANNEXATION BY THE ENGLISH. THEY TOOK ADVANTAGE OF THE INTERNAL CONFLICTS WITHIN THE FRENCH COURT. THE DAUPHIN CHARLES WAS IN BOURGES AT THAT TIME, UNDER THE PROTECTION OF SOME COURTIERS. HE APPEARED HELPLESS, EVEN PASSIVE, AS THE ENGLISH AND BURGUNDIAN MILITARY CONQUESTS CONTINUED.

JOAN OF ARC WAS BORN IN 1412 IN DOMREMY, A SMALL VILLAGE BY THE MEUSE RIVER. NEUFCHATEAU WAS LOCATED 20 KILOMETERS SOUTH, DOWN THE RIVER, AND VAUCOULEURS SEVERAL KILOMETERS TO THE NORTH. SOON AFTER SHE WAS BORN, THE NORTHERN HALF OF FRANCE WAS INVADED BY THE ENGLISH. ONLY HER BIRTH PLACE, THAT TINY AREA THAT RUNS 30 KILOMETERS BETWEEN NEUFCHATEAU AND VAUCOULEURS, BELONGED TO THE ROYAL FAMILY OF FRANCE. BAUDRICOURT, THE LORD OF THIS AREA, WAS FOR THE FRENCH.

JOAN'S FATHER WAS JACQUES D'ARC AND HER MOTHER WAS ISABELLE ROMEE. IT IS SAID THAT THEY WERE MIDDLE CLASS FARMERS. BOTH OF HER PARENTS WERE PIOUS.

ON A SUMMER DAY WHEN SHE WAS THIRTEEN, WHILE IN A GARDEN, JOAN SAW A SPARK COMING FROM THE DIRECTION OF THE CHURCH. SHE HEARD A VOICE SAYING "JOAN, SPEAK ONLY HONEST WORDS, AND DO ONLY JUST DEEDS. THOU MUST ATTEND CHURCH FREQUENTLY." AFTER THAT SHE STARTED HEARING VOICES MORE FREQUENTLY AND THE MESSAGES GOT MORE AND MORE DETAILED. "JOAN, GO TO HELP THE KING OF FRANCE AND RECOVER THE COUNTRY FOR HIM."

"GO TO SEE BAUDRICOURT, THE CAPTAIN OF VAUCOULEURS. HE WILL GUIDE YOU TO THE KING. ST. CATHERINE AND ST. MARGARET WILL PROTECT YOU."

"BREAK THROUGH THE SIEGE OF ORLEANS, TAKE THE KING TO REIMS AND CROWN HIM KING OF FRANCE."

SHE HAD TO GIVE AID TO THE DAUPHIN CHARLES AND FRANCE, WHICH MEANT THAT SHE HAD TO JUMP IN AMONGST FEROCIOUS MEN, GIVE THEM ORDERS, AND TAKE TO THE BATTLEFIELDS. IT ALSO MEANT THAT SHE HAD TO LEAVE HER FAMILY.

FIVE YEARS AFTER THE FIRST VOICE, JOAN FINALLY
LEFT FOR VAUCOULEURS. SHE PERSUADED THE
CAPTAIN, BAUDRICOURT, AND FINALLY MET WITH
THE DAUPHIN CHARLES IN CHINON. AFTER THAT, SHE
AND HER TROOPS ENDED THE SIEGE OF ORLEANS,
A FRENCH BASE SURROUNDED BY THE ENGLISH
ARMY, AND ACHIEVED HER MISSION. SHE TOOK THE
DAUPHIN TO REIMS AND WITNESSED THE CORONA-
TION OF CHARLES VII.

JOAN SUCCEEDED IN HER MISSION AND WORKED A
MIRACLE. HOWEVER, A SERIES OF TRAGEDIES WERE
WAITING FOR HER. SHE FAILED TO RECOVER PARIS
AND WAS CAPTURED IN COMPIEGNE. ACCUSED OF
BEING A WITCH BY THE ECCLESIASTICAL COURT AT
ROUEN, SHE WAS BURNED AT THE STAKE..... HERS
WAS A LIFE FILLED WITH MIRACLES AND TRAGEDY --
IT ENDED TWO YEARS AFTER SHE LEFT
VAUCOULEURS.

# SPECIAL NOTES

*PAGE 12* - *DUKE OF LORRAINE, CHARLES II, WAS THE FEUDAL LORD OF THAT REGION; LOCAT
ED BETWEEN THE KINGDOM OF FRANCE
AND THE HOLY ROMAN EMPIRE.

*PAGE 19* - *PEACE OF ARRAS: BY THIS AGREEMENT IN 1435, FRANCE, WHICH WAS DIVIDED
INTO ARMAGNAC AND BURGUNDY, FINALLY UNITED.  (REFER TO "THE AGE OF
JOAN", PAGE 176)

PAGE 20 - *RENE D'ANJOU: HE IS A SON IN-LAW OF DUKE OF LORRAINE AND ALSO A
BROTHER OF KING OF FRANCE, CHARLES VII'S WIFE, MARIE D'ANJOU. HE WAS A
SUPPORTER OF JOAN OF ARC.

PAGE 27 - *FROM THE ROYAL FAMILY OF BRITTANY: RICHEMONT'S BROTHER, JEAN, DUKE OF
BURGUNDY, ALLIED HIS COUNTRY WITH ENGLAND AND FORMER DUKE OF BURGUNDY,
PHILLIP; THEREBY ALLOWING ENGLAND TO TRY TO INVADE FRANCE.

PAGE 103 - *CHARLES D'ORLEANS:  HIS FATHER LOUIS WAS MURDERED BY JEAN, DUKE OF
BURGUNDY (REFER TO "THE AGE OF JOAN", PAGE 176).  IN 1415, HE WAS CAPTURED
AT THE BATTLE OF AGINCOURT AND HELD PRISONER FOR 25 YEARS BY THE
ENGLISH.
**THE BASTARD OF ORLEANS: A BASTARD OF LOUIS D'ORLEANS.  AFTER HIS BROTHER
CHARLES WAS CAPTURED, HEBECAME ONE OF THE MOST ACTIVE LEADERS IN THE
DEFENSE OF ORLEANS. HE PARTICIPATED IN JOAN OF ARC'S CAMPAIGN AND WAS
SIGNIFICANTLY SUCCESSFUL AS A MILITARY COMMANDER IN VARIOUS PLACES.

PAGE 112 - *DUKE ALENCON:  JEAN II, DUKE D'ALENCON. HE WAS TAKEN PRISONER AT THE
BATTLE OF VERNEUIL BY THE ENGLISH. AFTER THE RELEASE, HE JOINED
JOAN'S ARMY AND WAS DEEPLY TRUSTED BY HER.

PAGE 134 - *LA HIRE: "LA HIRE" IS A NICKNAME THAT MEANS "ANGER". HE USED TO BE A
COMMANDER OF CHARLES VII'S MILITARY. LATER HE BECAME A SINCERE FOL
LOWER OF JOAN OF ARC, AND FOUGHT IN VARIOUS BATTLEFIELDS FOR HER.

PAGE 136 - *CHARLES DE BOURBON: IN 1429 HE LOST "THE BATTLE OF HERRINGS" WHICH
LEAD TO THE DEFENSE OF ORLEANS. LATER HE PARTICIPATED IN JOAN'S MISSION.
**LA TREMOILLE: HE WAS AT THE POST OF CHAMBERLAIN AS A FAVORITE RETAINER
OF CHARLES VII, BUT ALWAYS MANEUVERED TO KEEP JOAN OF ARC AWAY FROM
THE KING.
***POTON DE XAINTRAILLES: LIKE LA HIRE, HE WAS ONE OF THE SINCERE FOLLOWERS
OF JOAN OF ARC. HE FOUGHT FOR CHARLES VII TOGETHER WITH LA HIRE.

# Additional

*comics*
## ONE
## Manga Titles

### JESUS by Yoshikazu Yasuhiko

Jesus. Teacher, healer, savior. The story of one of the most revered figures in human history is revisited in this full-length graphic novel, featuring breathtaking full-color art by Yoshikazu Yasuhiko.

*Volume 1-2 are available in ebook format.
*200-207 pages each

### KAZAN by Gaku Miyao

Kazan is a boy warrior searching for his childhood companion on a desert planet. Magic and swordplay accompany Kazan and his friends on the road to the legendary land of Goldene.

*Volume 1-3 are available in ebook and hardcopy formats.
*187-201 pages each

### MAICO 2010 by Toshimitsu Shimizu

Maico's a charming young woman who also happens to be an android--and the sexy new DJ of Japan Radio! She ends up entangled in a human love triangle, plenty of scandal and intrigue surrounding the station, and a mysterious military organization that wants her dead!

*Volume 1-4 are available in ebook and hardcopy formats.
*184-209 pages each

Visit www.ComicsOne.com to see our entire selection!

# Additional comics ONE Manga Titles

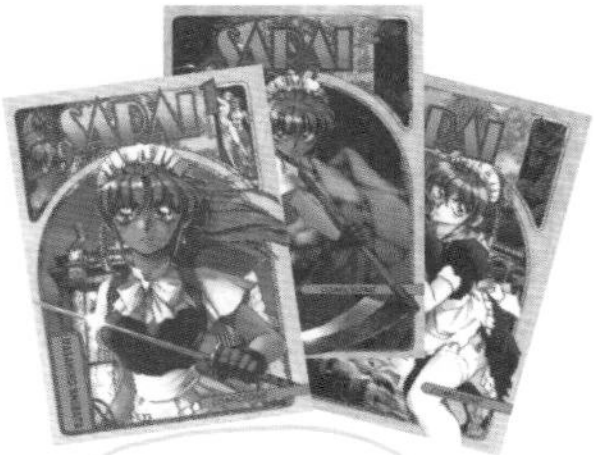
SARAI

***SARAI by Masahiro Shibata***
Genetic disorders have destroyed the future. Among humankind's remnants, teenage warrior maids like Sarai fight for honor and survival in a land where no one lives past their 17th year.

*Volume 1-3 are available in ebook and hardcopy formats.
*194-204 pages each

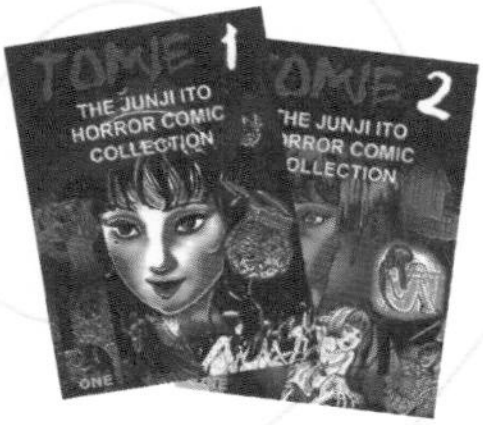
TOMIE 1
THE JUNJI ITO HORROR COMIC COLLECTION
TOMIE 2

***TOMIE by Junji Ito***
Tomie is the girl you wish you could forget. She is the one you shouldn't have touched, shouldn't have smiled at, shouldn't have made angry. She's quite lovely and you just might love her to death.

*Volume 1-2 are available in ebook and hardcopy formats.
*220-248 pages each

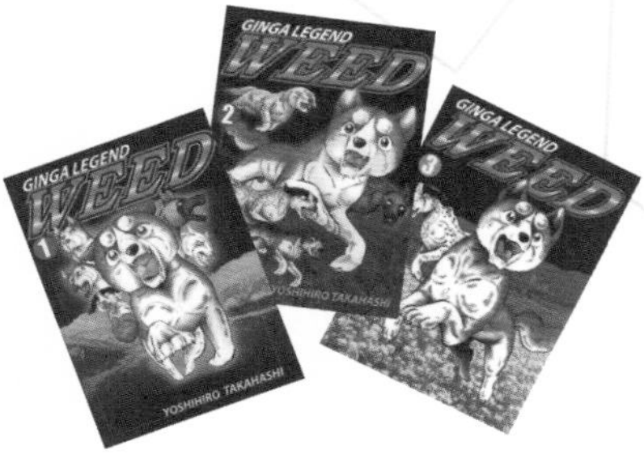
GINGA LEGEND
WEED
YOSHIHIRO TAKAHASHI

***WEED by Yoshihiro Takahashi***
Weed is a courageous little dog who believes he's the son of the legendary Boss Dog, Ginga. After his mother dies, Weed begins an adventurous journey to find his father in the Okubo Mountains.

*Volume 1-3 are available in ebook and hardcopy formats.
*238-240 pages each

Visit **www.ComicsOne.com** to see our entire selection!

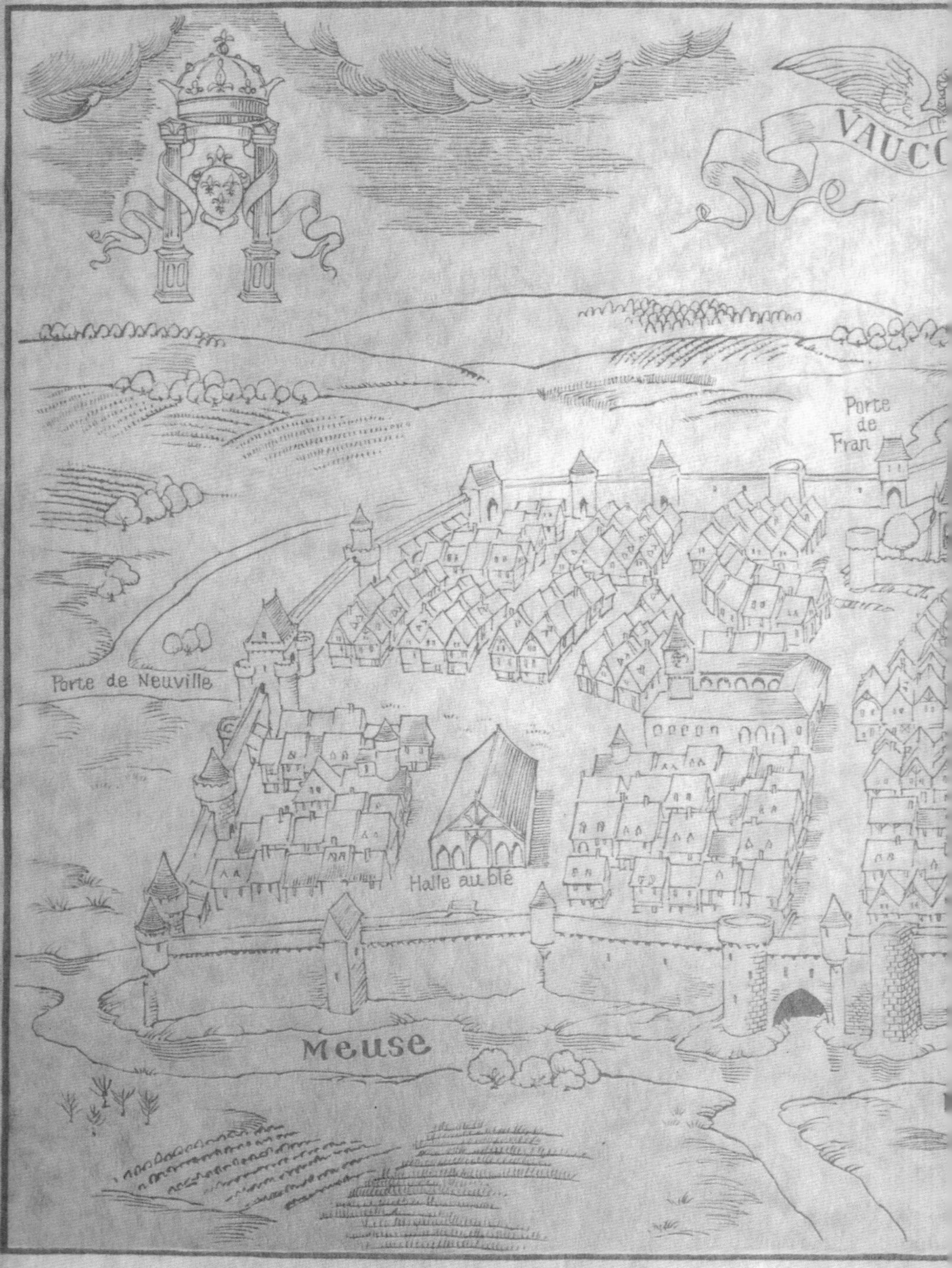

VAUCO
Porte de Fran
Porte de Neuville
Halle au blé
Meuse

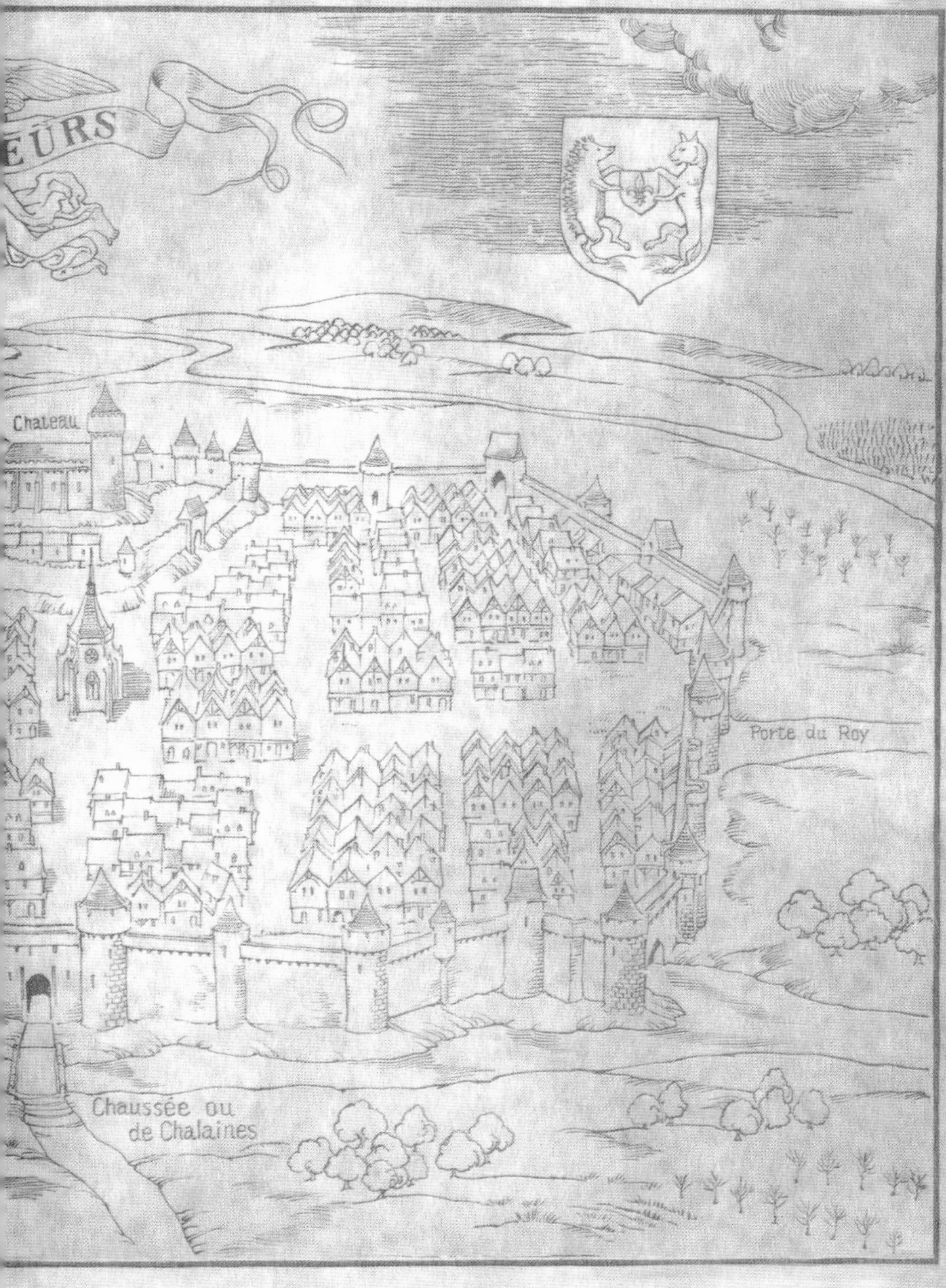
EURS
Chateau
Porte du Roy
Chaussée ou
de Chalaines